3000

D1245335

WITHDRAWN

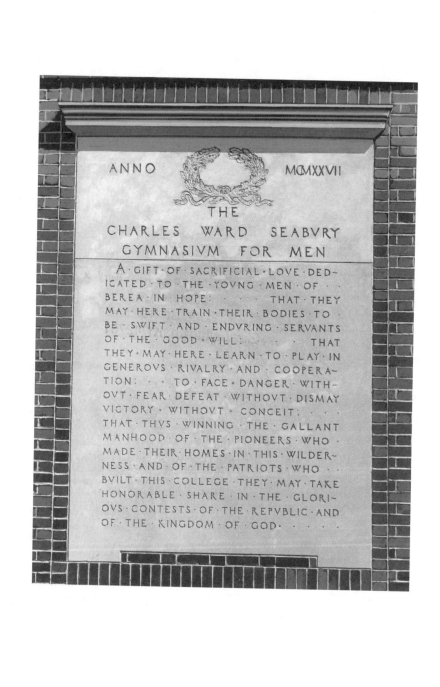

ANNO   MCMXXVII

THE
CHARLES WARD SEABVRY
GYMNASIVM FOR MEN

A · GIFT · OF · SACRIFICIAL · LOVE · DED-
ICATED · TO · THE · YOVNG · MEN · OF · ·
BEREA · IN · HOPE: · · · THAT · THEY
MAY · HERE · TRAIN · THEIR · BODIES · TO ·
BE · SWIFT · AND · ENDVRING · SERVANTS
OF · THE · GOOD · WILL: · · · THAT
THEY · MAY · HERE · LEARN · TO · PLAY · IN
GENEROVS · RIVALRY · AND · COOPERA-
TION: · · TO · FACE · DANGER · WITH-
OVT · FEAR · DEFEAT · WITHOVT · DISMAY
VICTORY · WITHOVT · CONCEIT: · · ·
THAT · THVS · WINNING · THE · GALLANT
MANHOOD · OF · THE · PIONEERS · WHO ·
MADE · THEIR · HOMES · IN · THIS · WILDER-
NESS · AND · OF · THE · PATRIOTS · WHO · ·
BVILT · THIS · COLLEGE · THEY · MAY · TAKE
HONORABLE · SHARE · IN · THE · GLORI-
OVS · CONTESTS · OF · THE · REPVBLIC · AND
OF · THE · KINGDOM · OF · GOD · · · · ·

B for Berea

The Amazing Story of Berea College Basketball
in the Words of the Men Who Played it

Volume 2:
Back to the Mountaintop
1970-2000

by Tom Chase

Foreword by John Cook

The Overmountain Press

JOHNSON CITY, TENNESSEE

TABLE OF CONTENTS

FOREWORD by John Cook

Books about sports and sports figures are as numerous as kids wearing Air Jordans. However, a book about a sport at a college that approaches athletics in a much different manner than does any other in the country is a rarity. At many colleges and universities today the emphasis is definitely on the "athlete" in student-athlete. Berea is among those who have maintained a healthy balance of the two.

When Tom Chase first shared with me his idea of a book about men's basketball at Berea College, I was intrigued and, I must admit, a little skeptical. As statistician for the men's basketball program since 1970, I admit to bleeding "Berea blue." I wouldn't trade the experiences I've had with the program over these twenty-nine years for anything, and I wouldn't want to see a book written that didn't portray its specialness accurately. How would he be able to capture the essence of a program that started as one confined to intramural competition, became a solid member of a strong conference that initially included several major state universities, and has continued to field competitive teams while eschewing athletic grants-in-aid?

As Director of Admissions at Berea from 1975 to 1997, I observed first-hand the difficulty Berea coaches have in recruiting. They must, of course, compete against schools that offer athletic grants, but there are other obstacles as well. For example, to be eligible for admission to Berea College a student must not only meet rigorous academic standards, but must also qualify on the basis of financial need. There is a complicated formula which takes into account family income, family size, and number of children in college, but basically if a family's resources are such that they can be expected to pay more than the cost of room, board, and books, the student isn't eligible for admission.

Over the years, as part of the admissions process, I personally talked with many young men who wanted to come to Berea and play basketball. Often an outstanding prospect met the academic requirements but had to be denied admission because his parents' financial

John Cook sings the national anthem before the final game in Old Seabury, February 18, 1995.

resources were slightly above the maximum for eligibility. Because the College makes exceptions to its need policy only for graduates of Berea Community High School, these young men enrolled at other area colleges, and we had to face them on the court for four years. At least half a dozen became all-conference and all-American selections.

In addition to its financial need and academic guidelines for admission, the College enrolls eighty percent of its students from 339 counties in southern Appalachia and the state of Kentucky. Since active recruiting is confined to this area, rarely does the College find a basketball player from outside the "Berea territory."

Chase's approach to his project was unique. He conducted personal interviews with more than 100 men who earned Berea College degrees while competing for the Mountaineers from the late 1920s to the present. These interviews depict a basketball program that has played a significant role in preparing student-athletes for life. Tom Chase has more than adequately captured the essence of the Berea men's basketball program, and I am pleased to recommend this book as a must-read for anyone who is interested in Berea College and for others who love the game of basketball.

November 16, 1999

Preface

On the evening of February 26 in the Berea College centennial year of 1955, its men's basketball team defeated their counterparts from Georgetown College 74-66 at Berea's Seabury Gymnasium to win that season's Kentucky Intercollegiate Athletic Conference tournament. Minutes later, the winning team's starting five — Irvine Shanks, Don Ruggles, Darrell Crase, Bill Masters, and Joe Lake — posed with the championship trophy for a cameraman employed by the *Lexington Herald*. The resulting photograph, displayed prominently in the February 28 edition of the state's second-most-circulated newspaper, offered convincing proof to an incredulous public that the event had really happened.

Berea's unexpected victory had tremendous symbolic importance. Although in 1955 the line between amateur and professional athletics at the college level had already been blurred nearly to the point of invisibility, it was well known that the Berea team was an anachronism. The five starters and their teammates were bona fide college students, not hirelings who were compensated for their services as athletes by the school they represented. College sports' governing bodies, the NCAA and NAIA, did not allow schools to pay athletes in cash, but they had established and regulated a system that permitted colleges to exchange certain goods and services (typically instruction, books, room, and board) for an athlete's allegiance.

All the KIAC schools, Berea included, were NAIA members, but Berea was alone in choosing, as a matter of principle, not to pay for play. Moreover, Berea demanded that all its students make reasonable academic progress toward a degree and work at college jobs to help defray the costs of their education. Students who fulfilled these academic and labor obligations and wished to devote their spare time to basketball or other sports did so in the knowledge that they would suffer a competitive disadvantage against quasi-professional opponents whose talents usually outshone theirs and whose lot was almost always easier.

Berea College athletes, who played only for fun and the satisfaction of testing their ability, will, and character, embodied an ideal of amateurism that was admired by some, derided by others. By 1955 the general public attached no stigma to pay-for-play contracts, oxymoronically termed "athletic scholarships," for college athletes, and certainly not every Berea player was such an ardent crusader for the cause of amateurism that he would have refused such inducements had they been offered to him elsewhere. It was true that Berea's academic standards were high, but Berea could not and did not claim to offer an education that was vastly superior to what was available at the other KIAC schools. The *Herald's* readers shook their heads in puzzled wonderment. If these players were good enough to win the KIAC tournament, why were they enrolled at Berea?

The photograph was doubly startling because Berea's championship team was racially integrated. In February 1955 no other college basketball team in Kentucky could make that claim. The state's infamous Day Law, which since 1904 had forbidden the education of black and white students under the same roof, was amended in 1950 to allow integration at the college level, and by mid-decade more than half of Kentucky's colleges and universities had enrolled African-American students. But integration in the classroom did not extend itself to the basketball court at any school but Berea, which had preached, and attempted to practice, the doctrine of equal opportunity for its entire hundred-year existence.

Throughout the basketball-mad Kentucky of 1955, white college coaches and administrators continued to insist that there were no black players sufficiently skilled to deserve athletic scholarship offers. Berea, on the other hand, held tryouts that were open to all students, after which the best players were selected to the team without regard to their race, color, or creed. The triumphant ending to Berea's 1955 season was a victory for brotherhood, fair play, and the idea that more could be achieved if black and white people were free to work together. Happily, those lessons were not ignored by the citizens of a state where the game of basketball is still exalted, where every game at every level of competition is intensely contested and even more intensely observed, where every play is endlessly discussed, dissected, and disputed, and every player lionized, scrutinized, analyzed, and criticized.

Both sportsmanship and purity of purpose characterize the Berea athletic tradition, and that tradition has continued unbroken to this day. But the players, whatever they might represent, must also be viewed as people, not symbols. What motivated these individuals to come to Berea? What did they aspire to, and what did they achieve? What was it like to be a Berea College athlete, a Berea College student, and finally a Berea College graduate? The answers are in this book.

The basketball players whose personal narratives comprise the core of this book were students of dual distinction: they had what it took to play significant varsity minutes while earning a Berea College degree. In Kentucky, as in most of America, college athletes are their institutions' most visible representatives in the community. No spectators gathered to cheer when these students, or any of their classmates, distinguished themselves in their schoolwork, labor, and community service. While it is sometimes said that our society overvalues the accomplishments of athletes, let it be remembered that the individuals who speak to us in these pages exemplified the ideals of a noble and unique institution. B For Berea is a book about sports, but it is also a book about Berea College.

The Berea College Story

What is Berea College most famous for? Right: its students work. All of them. Berea's student body consists primarily, although not solely, of students from southern Appalachia. Young people applying for admission to Berea must display academic promise and financial need. If they are admitted they pay no tuition, but they must spend at least ten hours of every week working at a college job. While labor is a student's obligation to the college, it is valued for its own sake, for it fosters responsibility and provides practical experience.

What else is important to know about the College? Berea is a four-year, residential, liberal arts college that enrolls 1500 students. The city of Berea has a population of about 11,000. It is located in Madison County on the southeastern edge of the Bluegrass region of Kentucky, just a few miles from the foothills of the Cumberland Mountains, a southwestern offshoot of the Appalachian range. Richmond, the Madison County seat, is the site of the somewhat misnamed Eastern Kentucky University, a public institution ten times the size of Berea College.

Berea College's heritage and character are strongly Christian, but it was not founded by, nor has it ever allied itself with, a particular Christian sect. This further sets Berea apart from its college neighbors that were established before 1900: Georgetown (Scott County, Baptist); Transylvania (Fayette County, Disciples of Christ); Centre (Boyle County, Presbyterian); Union (Knox County, Methodist); and Cumberland (Whitley County, Baptist).

The College has never permitted secret societies. When the Greek-lettered literary societies it originally encouraged began to resemble social fraternities and sororities, the College abolished them.

Madison County is what is known as a "moist" county. It is legal to sell alcoholic beverages in Richmond, but not in Berea. ("No saloons!" the College proclaimed in its early advertisements.) Despite its name, Boone Tavern, the elegant hotel and restaurant the College operates, does not serve liquor, but the College is anything but somber. It presents a friendly face to the visitor, and many non-Bereans, intrigued by the idea of the College, travel to Berea to learn more about it. Berea may be the only college in America that is simultaneously a tourist attraction. That some students fulfill their labor requirement producing high-quality crafts that are marketed by the College enhances Berea's appeal to the public.

It also enhances a regrettable image problem. Students who produce crafts are not Santa's elves, and students who come from the mountains are not shoeless rustics. They are simply students, which is how they would like to be regarded. While college officials point with pride to the school's uniqueness, students sometimes feel uncomfortably stereotyped. Former President Willis Weatherford understood this. "The quickest way to make our kids mad is to call them poor," he remarked. "Our students don't feel poor. They don't have the look of poverty. They don't feel underprivileged."

After Earl Hamner, the creator of "The Waltons," a popular network television series inspired by his youth in rural Virginia, attempted to compliment the students of Berea by comparing them to the fictional Waltons, he was probably surprised to learn that many students were offended, not flattered. Student Joe Lamb probably spoke for many when he lamented in the *Pinnacle*, the student newspaper, "It is a rather nauseating feeling to have Berea broadcast across the nation as a 'Hill College' where students are rewarded for being able to milk a cow or drive a nail the fastest. Why doesn't the college occasionally boast of its fine academic programs instead of its needlecrafts, woodcrafts, or labor programs?" Lamb's point was well taken.

Near the Kentucky River in northern Madison County stands a monument to the Transylvania Company, whose agents, including the celebrated Daniel Boone, built a fort on the site in 1775. The Company's aim was to establish a colony of white settlers in a region inhabited almost solely by Indians. The monument was erected in 1935 by the National Society of Colonial Dames of America. Its inscription praises the company's partners as "men of courage, faith, and vision: investors in a glorious dream of winning the wilderness for the white man."

That was indeed the dream of the Transylvania Company and those it beckoned to the dark and bloody ground of eighteenth century Kentucky. What ensued after the building of Fort Boonesborough was a war of conquest, but it was more than that. It was race war, which meant total war. Neither side was interested in finding practical ways to share the land. Both sides, Indian and European, killed men, women, and children wherever they could find them and destroyed their food and shelter. Victory was defined as extermination, not surrender, and the better-armed and supplied whites would win this war of attrition. After just a few short decades there were no Indians left in Kentucky. All had been slain or driven out.

Having wrested possession of Kentucky from one race of people, the white newcomers (or more accurately, many of the wealthier among them) began almost immediately to undertake the exploitation of another. To reduce labor costs and increase their prosperity, they became participants in a system which kidnapped and enslaved African men, women, and children. In Kentucky, it seemed, one race could not coexist with another; one must either annihilate or subjugate the other.

As the nineteenth century progressed, however, many thoughtful people in Kentucky began to dream a different dream: of putting an end to the state's sad legacy of hatred, cruelty, and violence. If it were true that "God...hath made of one blood all nations of men," as the Bible said in the seventeenth chapter of Acts, how could the ill use of one race by another be justified?

Enter the Reverend John Gregg Fee.

Berea College was founded by a genuine American hero. The model of a Christian activist, John Fee was convinced that involuntary servitude was un-Christian and preached against the practice at a time when many established churches embraced it. Ordained a Presbyterian in Cincinnati, Fee was dismissed from the Synod for his views. Thereafter he delivered his eloquent sermons at a succession of rural churches in northeast Kentucky, solidifying his reputation as a staunch antislavery advocate. Eventually an emancipationist book Fee wrote found its way into the hands of Cassius Marcellus Clay, a well-to-do Madison County landowner.

Despite his residence in the region of Kentucky where proslavery sentiment was strongest, Clay believed as Fee did. In 1854 Clay offered Fee a ten-acre parcel of land in the southern portion of the county if the reverend would move there and establish a church. Fee accepted the offer, built a home for himself and a church for the families who lived nearby, and named the settlement Berea, after the Greek town whose devout citizens welcomed Paul and Silas in Acts 17. In 1855 Fee opened a school in Berea.

Berea's proximity to the slaveholding communities of the Bluegrass provoked hostility from the start. This became open harassment later in the decade after the powerful Clay withdrew his support after deciding that Fee had become too zealous for his liking. Uncompromising and inflexible in his opposition to what he regarded as an unmitigated evil, Fee would not keep silent. Quite the contrary: heartened by the success of the school he had started, Fee made plans to expand it to a college "opposed to sectarianism, slaveholding, caste, and every other wrong institution or practice."

This was too much. In December 1859 a band of sixty-two armed irregulars, their passions aroused by Fee's enterprise and the shocking news of abolitionist John Brown's capture of the U.S. arsenal at Harpers Ferry, Virginia, rode into Berea. Fee and his followers were ordered to leave the state within ten days. The Bereans, who had broken no laws, appealed to Governor Beriah Magoffin for protection, which that craven functionary withheld. Brute force had won the day once again, and the banned men and their families departed.

But Fee foresaw a more enlightened time. He spent the war years in exile in Ohio, burning to return to Kentucky to finish what he had started. Had the doughty preacher chosen to remain in Berea in 1859 he would certainly have been murdered, his light snuffed out forever. Fee was courageous, but unlike John Brown, he was not foolhardy. His quest for brotherhood needed a leader, not a martyr.

Fee was not a violent man, and he would not arm himself even for defensive purposes. What was it about him that was so threatening to the powers that were? It was simply this: Fee was winning people over. He had something important to say about equality and human dignity, and many who listened to him were being swayed by both the vigor of his faith and the cool logic of his arguments. As radical as Fee's ideas seemed to the slaveholders and their allies, they could not ignore him as one did a mere windmill-tilter or bayer at the moon. Too many people were listening to Fee and being persuaded by his message.

After the fighting ended in central Kentucky, Fee returned to practice the principles of equality he had never stopped preaching. The revived

Berea College began admitting students in 1866. Its mission was to educate, but also to erase social divisions and unify people in order "to further the cause of Christ." To this end it was conceived as nonsectarian, coeducational, and racially integrated. Under the administration of President Edward Henry Fairchild, a professional educator whose services the Berea trustees secured from Oberlin College, the new institution set about promoting these three radical ideas, despite threats and occasional physical attacks by the Ku Klux Klan and its sympathizers. The Klan wished to restore the day when inequality was enforced by violence. Its views did not prevail, thanks in part to the steadfast influence of the institution John Fee founded.

Fee was eighty-two years old and still living in the community in 1898 when Berea College student Marion Harold Fredericks composed a tribute that was published in the *Berea College Reporter:*

When the poor slave was crouching low
Beneath oppression's cruel hand,
And clanking chains and groans of woe
Were heard across our mighty land,
One man stood firm through storm and hate,
To free our land; beneath the rod
Of mobs he stood, in meekness great,
For right, for liberty, and God!

To Berea Ridge came John G. Fee,
Still firm and true in slavery's night,
And kindled what has proved to be
A holy spark of truth and light.
The victim of the foulest wrong,
He never faltered in his way,
And with a radiance clear and strong
The light he kindled shines today.

The school he founded now has grown
To be an honor to our land.
From Freedom's cradle no more the moan
Of anguish comes; today we stand
Americans all, unfettered, free.
O, great and noble deeds were done
By Berea's founder, John G. Fee.
God speed the work that he begun!

Berea College grew into a collective entity that was more than a college in the sense that we understand the term today. For many years its trustees operated not just a College, which provided postsecondary education in the liberal arts, but also an elementary school (Knapp Hall); an Academy, or high school; a Normal School for the certification of teachers; a Vocational School offering instruction in such trades as agriculture, carpentry, printing, nursing, and stenography; and a Foundation School for pupils who needed improvement in the basic "3 R's." In 1925 an "Opportunity School" for adult learners was added. Based on the Danish folk school model, the Berea Opportunity School had no entrance requirements and gave no examinations, grades, or diplomas. Its purpose was to furnish adult learners with intellectual and social stimulation. By the mid-twentieth century, however, the Normal School, Vocational School, Foundation School, and Opportunity School had closed. After World War Two the Academy, much to the confusion of future historians, took the name of the Foundation School. Its flag would continue to fly until the late 1960s, when it and the Knapp Hall elementary school were eliminated.

Labor was an important part of the Berea College story from its outset, although the requirement that all students work was not instituted until the administration of President William Goodell Frost (1892-1920). While it was not (and is not) easy to run any large enterprise on part-time, unskilled labor, Frost believed that all of the needy students Berea sought should have the opportunity to earn money to defray their expenses. Students were already working at custodial, agricultural, clerical, and construction jobs. Under Frost the College set up such industries as broomcraft, brickmaking, and woodworking.

During the nineteenth century the College educated blacks and whites, and men and women, in roughly equal numbers. The institution's biracial character was disturbing to some white observers who had favored the abolition of slavery on humanitarian grounds but were not ready to accept black citizens as social equals. For many years the majority of the white students were Northerners. Fee and Fairchild wanted Berea to serve the historically isolated southern mountains, where racial animus was less pronounced than anywhere else in the South. Frost proposed that the College recruit its student body almost exclusively from this region. If Berea was not actually in the mountains, it was not far away, and in Frost's judgment the institution could do the greatest good by providing educational opportunities to the able but moneyless young people of southern Appalachia.

Integration at Berea was not without its occasional tensions, but blacks and whites lived and learned together there for decades. What had begun as a Utopian experiment became a vibrant and stable community of scholars whose successes were well known and closely observed. In the spring of 1904, however, the Kentucky legislature dealt the College a severe blow when it passed a law forcing segregation, which it had already mandated in the state's public schools, upon every educational institution in the state, public or private.

Berea College fought the Day Law (named for its sponsor, Democrat Carl Day) all the way to the United States Supreme Court. In November 1908 that body affirmed the validity of Day's brainchild, ruling that states had the absolute right to "alter, amend, or repeal" the charter of any corporation operating within its borders. The Berea College its founders had intended was out of business. Perhaps luckily for John Fee, who died in 1901, he did not live to see a government of scoundrels repudiate all he had worked for. Blacks and whites would not attend the same schools anywhere in Kentucky until the 1950s.

Although Berea's trustees briefly considered moving the entire institution to another state, the College stayed where it was and disenrolled its African-American students as it was compelled to. Then Berea officials and alumni set about raising money to endow a school for the students it was no longer permitted to educate. Lincoln Institute, located in Shelby County, some eighty miles from Berea, was incorporated in 1910. Once established, Lincoln Institute operated thereafter with its own trustees and administrators, and the monies it raised for itself. It existed until the Day Law's repeal rendered it obsolete.

With the makeup of its student body radically transformed, the College decided to focus all of its attention on the southern mountain region. Since 1915 the College has admitted only small numbers of non-mountain students from outside Kentucky. It enrolled African-American students again in 1950, at the first opportunity it was permitted.

Berea College has always been different, and because it is unusual it has always had to sell itself vigorously to both prospective benefactors and prospective students. Perhaps its most important selling point has been its high ideals. All of its leaders have been unapologetic idealists.

Consider a typical incident in the presidency of William G. Frost. On a Sunday in 1912 Reverend Frost led chapel services at the College. Instead of preaching a sermon, Frost read from a book about the efforts of a judge, Ben Lindsey, to establish a children's court in Colorado. Frost identified strongly with Lindsey's struggles to overcome the venality and self-interest of the Denver politicians with whom he had to deal. Finally Frost, inflamed in equal measure by Christian zeal and social conscience, asked his students to join hands with him and recite this Good Citizenship Pledge:

> We hereby pledge ourselves to use all the political power and influence we possess for the public welfare. We will treat the interests of the community as a sacred trust. We will not sell our vote, influence, or official favor for any money, influence, or other reward. We will do our utmost to persuade others to adopt these principles and to punish those who violate them.

Berea students expected to be inspired as well as educated. In a "Special Student's Edition" of the Citizen, Berea's weekly newspaper, dated January 1, 1907, an unnamed teacher wrote:

> If the new year is to be better for you than the old one has been, three things you must do – and you can do them:
> First, you must believe in yourself. You can do more than you think you can, and more than you ever have

before. You were meant to be greater and better than you are. You can do some things that no one else in the world can do. You have a splendid year before you.

Secondly, you must believe in those about you. They are a good deal worse than you think, but they are also a good deal better than you think. They are more ready to help you and more ready to do what is fair and right than you think. If you believe in them they will help you and you can help them.

Thirdly, you must believe in God. Believe that he loves you and will do everything that is good for you if you are obedient to Him. He knows what you need much better than you do, and He has much finer, grander plans for you next year than you have for yourself. Believe in Him and let Him make you what He wants you to be, and you will be sure to have a Happy New Year.

Berea's blue and white-clad athletes have been competing since the administration of President Fairchild. Here is another area of college life which Berea conducts with high ideals. Berea's coaches work hard to produce the best teams possible, but not one of them has ever been notified that he must win games in order to keep his job.

Darrell Crase, a Berea College basketball star of the 1950s who would later earn a doctorate in physical education and devote his life to teaching the subject at the university level, has observed that "any student admitted to Berea, whether he possesses an interest in athletics or science or music, must meet the same admission standards. As a student at Berea, the athlete does not receive any special favors or inducements. He is required to shoulder a similar academic load as other students and participate in the student labor program, working at least ten hours per week. He does not receive any special attention or favors in regard to housing on campus or eating in the college cafeteria. Participating in athletics under these conditions requires of the athlete many sacrifices."

The situation Crase described has not changed since he wrote those words in 1964. An anonymous former varsity athlete, queried by Crase, expressed the Berea athletic credo perfectly. "Pay is not the proper incentive for an athlete. An athlete should participate in sports solely because he enjoys the contest, so much that he is willing to make extra sacrifices in order to participate."

The Great Commitments of Berea College (1993)

Berea College, founded by ardent abolitionist and radical reformers, continues today as an educational institution still firmly rooted in its historic purpose "to promote the cause of Christ." Adherence to the College's scriptural foundation, "God has made of one blood all peoples of the earth," shapes the College's culture and programs so that students and staff alike can work toward both personal goals and a vision of a world shaped by Christian values, such as the power of love over hate, human dignity and equality, and peace with justice. This environment frees persons to be active learners, workers, and servers as members of the academic community and as citizens of the world. The Berea experience nurtures intellectual, physical, aesthetic, emotional, and spiritual potentials and with those the power to make meaningful commitments and translate them into action.

To achieve this purpose, Berea College commits itself

> To provide an education opportunity primarily for students from Appalachia, black and white, who have great promise and limited economic resources.

> To provide an education of high quality with a liberal arts foundation and outlook.

> To stimulate understanding of the Christian faith and its many expressions and to emphasize the Christian ethic and the motive of service to others.

> Th provide for all students though the labor program experiences for learning and serving in community, and to demonstrate that labor, mental and manual, has dignity as well as utility.

> To assert the kinship of all people and to provide interracial education with a particular emphasis on understanding and equality between blacks and whites.

> To create a democratic community dedicated to education and equality for women and men.

> To maintain a residential campus and to encourage in all members of the community a way of life characterized by plain living, pride in labor well done, zest for learning, high personal standards, and concern for the welfare of others.

To serve the Appalachian region primarily through education but also by other appropriate services.

The Seventies

In the summer of 1969 Berea College basketball coach Clarence H. "Monarchy" Wyatt was promoted to the post of Director of Athletics, and a new coach, Wilson C. Sergeant, was appointed to guide the team. Wyatt had coached basketball at Berea for twenty-four seasons. Although the Mountaineers' record in 1968-69 was a modest 10-14, Wyatt's final team was the school's best in a decade. He had won at Berea in the late forties and early fifties, but thereafter the increasing professionalism of Berea's rivals frustrated the veteran coach's best efforts to attract talented athletes to Berea. Now a younger man would try to win games at a school which had never granted athletic scholarships and had no intention of changing this policy. The basketball team would continue to do the best it could with student-athletes who came to Berea to work, study, and play the game for the love of it.

If adherence to the amateur ideal meant losing records in intercollegiate competition year after year, well, that was simply the way it would be, and years of disappointment at Berea had convinced many observers that the concepts of victory and purely amateur athletics had ceased to be compatible in the increasingly competitive world of college basketball. Neither the athletes nor the coaches were ever satisfied to lose. On the court as in the classroom (and in life), effort was valuable but never to be regarded as an adequate substitute for success. The Athletic Department's goal was never merely to preserve Berea's high ideals; it was to find a way to win consistently without relinquishing those ideals.

A native Kentuckian, W.C. Sergeant knew a lot about the Kentucky Intercollegiate Athletic Conference, in which Berea competed. He had played his college ball at Berea's old rival Union College. The final game of his college career was Union's 77-65 defeat by the fabled 1954-55 Mountaineers in the opening round of the 1955 KIAC tournament. After graduation Sergeant played and coached in the U.S. Army and then, mirroring the experience of C.H. Wyatt, became a successful high school and junior college coach in the Bluegrass State. His high school teams in Corbin and Louisville won seventy percent of their games over a ten-year period. In March 1969 he directed Sullivan Junior College in Louisville to the National Little College Athletic Association championship.

A man with ideas, Sergeant instituted an uptempo style that changed the face of Berea basketball. His 1969-70 team won only six of the twenty-one games it played, but in one of their victories the Mountaineers scored 134 points against Oakland City College, a school record that still stands. That this game was played at home and avenged an earlier loss to the Oakland City crew intensified the team's aura. The Sergeant-led teams were exciting, and Berea fans flocked to Seabury Gym to watch them.

In 1970-71 Sergeant produced what many had thought to be unattainable at Berea, a winning basketball season. He topped even that accomplishment by engineering the Mountaineers' 119-100 triumph over Georgetown at the following year's Homecoming game, Berea's most decisive defeat of the hated Tigers in decades. But success had its price. Sergeant's methods were different than those of C.H. Wyatt, which the school had had a long time to get used to. Consequently, the new coach's fit at Berea was not entirely smooth. Not everyone supported Sergeant behind the scenes.

On February 6, 1971, the program received the kind of publicity it did not want when tempers boiled over in Berea's game with Pikeville College at Seabury Gym, causing the officials to terminate the contest with nine minutes left to play. The Mountaineers led the Bears 76-72 when a bench-clearing, fist-swinging melee erupted, an ugly "basketbrawl," as it was termed by the *Louisville Courier-Journal*. After the referees submitted their report to the KIAC offices, commissioner Jack Thompson ruled that both teams were equally to blame for the incident. He declared the game "no contest" and ordered that it be replayed. When Pikeville refused to travel to Berea again that year, the event went into the books as a forfeit win for the Mountaineers, surely the most embarrassing "victory" in the school's history.

In the ultracompetitive and physical game of basketball it is never easy for a coach to hold the tempers of each of his players in check at all times. Occasional lapses in sportsmanship had occurred on Wyatt's watch, most memorably in another game with Pikeville on December 11, 1965, but no Berea College game had ever degenerated into such violence that it had to be stopped, and none ever would again. Sergeant was a decent man who in no way excused his team's deportment in the Pikeville game, but fairly or not, the episode bruised his reputation.

Whether Berea administrators failed to communicate what they wanted of Sergeant or Sergeant failed to heed their message, the College and its coach became increasingly uncomfortable with each other and parted company after just three seasons. In the early 1970s, however, the College had to concern itself with matters far more serious than its basketball team.

The decade began tragically. On a wet night in March 1970, Dean of Labor Douglas L. Massey was killed when his car skidded into a telephone pole on Scaffold Cane Road, a short distance from the campus. Only thirty-seven, Massey left a wife and two school-age daughters.

Doug Massey was a native of Somerset, Kentucky, who enrolled as a Berea College student in 1950 and graduated four years later with a degree in geology. Like Wilson Evans, his predecessor as Dean of Labor, Massey had an athletic background. He was a four-sport letterman in both high school and college and served as a valuable reserve guard on C.H. Wyatt's excellent 1952-53 and 1953-54 basketball teams. Enlisting in the U.S. Navy after graduation, Massey was a member of all-Navy teams in basketball and baseball.

After his Navy tour of duty Massey returned to Berea as an instructor in

President Willis Weatherford

physical education. While teaching at Berea and earning his master's degree at Eastern Kentucky University, Massey coached the Foundation School basketball team and college cross-country and track teams, winning a KIAC championship in track in 1958. In 1961 he was appointed Director of Alumni Affairs. He became Dean of Labor in 1968. An able teacher and administrator and a dynamic, well-spoken, and outgoing personality, Massey was a popular Berean on campus and off. His death in his prime hit the community hard.

Massey's diplomatic skills might have helped ease the racial conflicts that were beginning to plague the institution. After a number of hostile incidents occurred in the fall of 1971, conflict reached its zenith in December when the College's announcement that a black counselor's contract would not be renewed provoked a sit-in by a group of black students on the second floor of Lincoln Hall, where much of the College's important administrative business was conducted. To cool the situation President Willis Weatherford, a man of stature and wisdom, chose resolute action over dithering. Although fall classes had not ended nor final examinations been given, Weatherford ordered the College closed. This bold decision, controversial at the time, was the right one. The students went home. When they returned in January, as scheduled, tensions had relaxed sufficiently to allow dialogue to take place without intimidation and threats.

Weatherford's critics believed that he had sown the wind and reaped the whirlwind. One of his goals upon taking office in 1967 had been to increase the enrollment of black students at Berea. As a result there were more African-Americans at Berea by percentage in 1971-72 than at any four-year school in the state except for historically black Kentucky State University. After Weatherford's crisis management restored equanimity on the Berea campus in January 1972, he had this to say about the situation:

> Some people both inside and outside the College have told me that they thought Berea was the last place where such racial tension could possibly develop. They were shocked and surprised that "it happened here." My answer has been that it is precisely because Berea has placed a greater emphasis on brotherhood and interracial education that it has developed some racial tensions.

It is simply a sociological fact that a larger minority develops a greater sense of pride and identity than do isolated individuals, and this is a factor of life that our colleges as well as the society at large must learn to live with creatively.

Other persons have pointed out that Berea faces an extremely difficult task in that, while the institution is committed to brotherhood, a significant number of students both black and white neither believe in it nor wish to practice it. Not being able to control attitudes, the College is caught between its own ideals and the attitudes of significant numbers of community members.

The only bond which I can see as equal to the challenge of uniting us is a fellowship of love in Christ. A firm belief in our common humanity can go at least part way toward common understanding, and this may be all that some members of our community can fall back upon. But for those who understand all men to be children of a common Father, living in love and fellowship is not only natural but is also God's will for us. Attaining this outlook and conviction is what we should strive for in the Berea community.

The face of Berea College was changing in other ways. One by one the College closed its dairy, creamery, lumber mill, candy kitchen, bakery, and poultry farm. After the bakery's demise in 1974 a college spokesperson explained in the *Pinnacle* that "each of the industries was begun to provide for the college's needs at the least cost, and to employ students in a meaningful educational situation. As mass production made it possible to buy for less, the trustees decided the financial loss was worth more than the education they provided students, that the money might be better used in the total education program." After some soul-searching on the matter, however, the College chose to retain most of its craft industries and to continue to operate Boone Tavern, the still first-rate dining and lodging establishment adjoining the campus.

Oscar Gunkler and C.H. Wyatt retired from their administrative posts in the Athletic Department. The basketball team continued to struggle under Roland R. Wierwille, the coach the College hired to replace W.C. Sergeant in 1972. The hard-charging Wierwille was a product of robust programs at Eastern Kentucky, where he played, and Berea's KIAC rival Transylvania, where he had assisted two of the nation's brightest young coaches, C.M. Newton and Lee Rose. While Wierwille possessed an unquenchable thirst to excel, he was quick to demonstrate that he understood, accepted, and endorsed the Berea way of doing things. There would be no cutting corners under Wierwille: he expected his players to go to class and perform their labor assignments as Berea athletes always had. But could Wierwille, or any coach, find a way to win consistently under these conditions?

Each of Wierwille's first three teams, while always competitive and capable of upsetting any opponent when they played their very best, lost more games than they won. This had been the norm at Berea for the past decade. Under Wierwille the Mountaineers played a running, aggressive brand of ball that pleased its fans, while prevailing in more than a few contests on the strength of superior conditioning and attention to fundamentals. Wierwille was getting the most from the talent he had, but the fact remained that the better talent was still being lured by Berea's gelt-flashing rivals.

Wierwille stuck it out, and in 1975 he got lucky. That fall four freshmen enrolled at Berea whose exploits would restore the program to respectability and beyond. The Berea teams that featured the "Big Four" –- Ed Flynn, Craig Jefferson, Bill Nichols, and Arno Norwell — would win seventy-nine games and lose only thirty-three, and unlike the storied "Fab Five" of the University of Michigan a generation later, each of the "Big Four" would stay at Berea four years and earn his degree. That was the Berea way, and the Wierwille way.

This talented and hardworking quartet made a difference right away. With freshmen Flynn, Jefferson, Nichols, and Norwell in their lineup the Mountaineers won seventeen of twenty-four regular-season contests before knocking off Campbellsville and Georgetown in the early rounds of the 1976 KIAC tournament to qualify for the finals. On the morning of the tournament's final game, columnist Dave Kindred of the *Louisville Courier-Journal* marveled:

Coach Wierwille with his 1977-78 starters: Ed Flynn, Craig Jefferson, Arno Norwell, Bill Nichols, and Cluster Howard

It's Pikeville against Berea. In terms of money spent on basketball, that's like the Celtics against the downtown YMCA ... Pikeville gives scholarships to its players. To pay their way through school, the Pikeville fellows shoot jump shots. At Berea, the starting five includes a janitor, a horticulturist, a dormitory monitor, an equipment manager, and an intramural director. To pay their way through school, they work.

Wierwille told Kindred, "Berea wanted a good athletic program to go along with its good academics. I knew that even without scholarships we could get the overlooked players and make a winner, and we've done it."

Although Berea lost by six points to Pikeville and then to Kentucky State in the NAIA District 32 playoff game that, had they won, would have earned them a trip to the national tournament in Kansas City, the 1975-76 season was a great success, and it bred success. None of the four "Big Four" teams ever had an off year. Probably the best of them was the 1977-78 squad that dominated the KIAC, leading the conference in winning percentage, rebounding, and free throw shooting. Flynn, Jefferson, Nichols and Norwell were named to the all-conference team. Bill Nichols was named Player of the Year and Roland Wierwille Coach of the Year.

Although none of Berea's great 1970s teams made it to the national NAIA tournament, no one disagreed with Roland Wierwille when he said, "We accomplished more than anyone ever thought could be accomplished at Berea. There is not another school in the country with the type of program that we have."

"A good athletic program in proper perspective can help the whole attitude on campus," Wierwille observed. "Athletics can create a common cause and spirit that's otherwise hard to obtain."

Dennis Grant   1967-71

I'm very proud of my Berea College degree. When I hear about famous people in the state or in the nation who are graduates of Berea College, it pleases me to think that I also graduated from Berea.

My dad worked at the post office in Canton, North Carolina. We lived on a kind of mountainous farm with my grandfather and grandmother, who tended the place. I grew up working with them. We had a tobacco base for some years, but my dad believed that people shouldn't smoke. So he gave up his allotment, and we didn't raise tobacco any longer. We raised commercial tomatoes instead.

A man named Jack Duckworth lived in Canton, and he had run track for Berea College and graduated from there. He paid the bus fare for me and a friend of mine to visit Berea and look the place over. I was a country boy

Dennis Grant

who hadn't been away from home much, so that was a different experience for me. Coach Wyatt met us at the bus stop. We played some pickup basketball in the gym that night. I liked Berea and knew its reputation, because some of my teachers had gone there. Financially I qualified, so I decided that Berea was the place for me. My friend, however, enrolled at Western Carolina University.

When I started at Berea the basketball team had had a long stretch without a winning season. Wins were hard to come by, especially in the conference, but the program was improving with players like Doug Layne, Bob Conley, Dave Olinger, Dave Maynard, and Tommy Reynolds. The two years I played for Coach Wyatt were not winning seasons, but we won some games. We managed to beat Cumberland, Campbellsville, Transylvania, and Pikeville, and those were quality wins.

In my second year we were playing in Wilmington, Ohio, and getting beat pretty badly. I believe I started that game. Coach Wyatt got angry at us, and I don't blame him. He jerked out the entire starting team and put in five more. When the starters came out of the game we sat down at the end of the front row of bleachers. The second five didn't have much luck either, so Coach Wyatt continued to substitute individuals. Every player who came out went down to the end of the row. Gradually the distance between Coach Wyatt and the team increased, and finally he had to get up and walk down the row to make substitutions. At that point somebody in the stands yelled out, "Put in the bus driver!" That's a funny story about a frustrating evening.

I was fairly close friends with all the players, although I didn't run with them particularly. My closest friend among the players was probably Lanny Huff. Lanny and I came in at the same time. He didn't get to play much, but he was hard-nosed and determined to stay on the team. He would always battle, and I liked that in him.

I got along well with Coach Wyatt and liked him very much. Some people thought the game might have passed him by. A few of the things he did seemed a bit archaic. In practice we warmed up to some of the folk dancing tunes that were used in the PE classes. We didn't mind doing it particularly, but it didn't seem quite appropriate for a basketball team. There are many different ways for basketball teams to practice, and perhaps Coach Wyatt was ahead of his time.

When I heard the news that Coach Wyatt would no longer be coaching the team, my reaction was mixed. I was saddened that his basketball coaching career had ended, because it had been such a large part of his life for so many years. But I was hopeful that the new coach, W.C. Sergeant, would revitalize things a bit, especially the offense.

Under Coach Sergeant our offense was more uptempo. We did more pressing and tried to score off the press. Our practices were well-organized, and they were hard, though not unbearable. Coach Sergeant had a businesslike manner. He could get angry at a player or at the team, but it was not his nature to go berserk. I do remember playing Wilmington at home in my junior year, and although in that game I scored the most points I ever scored in college, we lost by a wide margin. Coach Sergeant was very displeased, so he made us stay after the game and practice.

I started regularly in Coach Sergeant's first year, my junior year. The next year he brought in a lot of new players, and I didn't start all the games as a senior. I averaged more points in my junior year than in my senior year. I was always listed at six-four, but I was maybe a little less than that. I played forward. I was a good

Dennis Grant: "I wish I could have played with him for four years"

— 17 —

Jimmy Hairston: "A person you could count on"

rebounder, but never the primary scorer, although I averaged double figures in both my junior and senior years. I got most of my baskets on fast breaks or rebounds and stickbacks.

When I was a senior Berea College had its first winning season since the 1950s. Coach Sergeant brought in some talented newcomers, and the veterans had matured some. The best of the Sergeant-recruited players that year were probably Charlie Bacigalupi, a strong, hard-nosed battler and rebounder; Jimmy Hairston, a good scorer; Bill Fox, a little guard who got a lot of assists; and Roy Smith, with whom I competed for playing time. I liked Roy even though I competed with him.

One time a six-eight or six-nine player from South Carolina came to Berea for a visit. He got into a fight at the dorm, and Coach Sergeant came to me and gave me his car keys and some money and said, "Take him as far south as you can and put him on a bus back home." I rounded up one of our managers and Darlene Devere, a cheerleader who was my girlfriend. The three of us took the guy to Asheville, North Carolina, and put him on a bus. Then we drove to my parents' place, which wasn't far away, and spent the night. Coach Sergeant trusted me with things like that.

My senior season was marred by what the newspapers called the "basket brawl" with Pikeville College. There were two incidents in the game, and I was on the floor for both of them. I'm not sure which one happened first. I remember Ron Newkirk of Berea grabbing a Pikeville guy and their team retaliating. Ron was an effective player but he was a bit awkward, not real mobile, and I'm sure his actions were unintentional.

The other incident involved me directly. We were on the free throw line. The free throw wasn't made, and when we went up for the rebound I was sandwiched between two Pikeville players. They knocked me down. I didn't normally have a quick temper, but when I was getting up I saw a boy coming at me, and I caught him in a head lock and started punching him in the face. Later he had to have some stitches near his eye. After the game somebody told me that the two boys who elbowed me were Golden Gloves boxers.

Tensions ran so high that they finally erupted. Both benches emptied and spectators came out of the stands onto the floor. The game was stopped, and the officials grabbed the books and ran. It was an ugly scene. Pikeville had a little guard who really got worked over.

At one point I got buried under a pile of Pikeville players, and Jimmy Hairston went crazy and threw them off me. When I went back to the dressing room I had the dusty prints of athletic shoes on my legs and back. After the game I regretted everything that had happened, and I hoped there would be no adverse ramifications for either Berea College or Pikeville College. We weren't scheduled to play Pikeville again before I graduated, but I wondered what would happen the following year. Evidently, however, there were no futher problems between the two teams.

Jimmy Hairston was a person you could count on. He gave everything he had in every game, and in a fight he was the kind of guy you wanted on your side. Jimmy was black, and when the campus was shut down briefly that year due to racial problems, he and I discussed what was going on. Jimmy had a mind of his own, and he wouldn't let himself be pressured into doing anything he didn't think was right. He was a fair-minded person, and I appreciated and respected him for it.

Studying, working, and basketball took up a lot of time, so I had to discipline myself. Every evening after practice I ate, went to the dorm, got my books, and went to the library. I couldn't study in the dorm because it was too noisy. I studied in the library until it closed, and then I went to bed.

When I came to Berea I didn't know what I was going to major in. Eventually I chose math because I liked the subject and liked Dr Steve Boyce's classes. He was an excellent teacher. He was thorough in his explanations. He broke it all down for us, step by step, and led us through it. Dr Boyce was always prepared, always organized, and he related to students very, very well. After I graduated and was studying for my master's degree at Eastern Kentucky University, I had some classes that were supposed to be at a higher level than my undergraduate classes at Berea. With my Berea background I found them rather easy.

My labor assignment was in the Admissions Office, figuring grade-point averages of the students who were applying to come to Berea. In the summer after my sophomore year I worked in a paper mill in North Carolina, but that job wasn't available the following summer, so I stayed in Berea and worked on the college farm. I put up hay and worked in the dairy. The College sold the dairy that summer. They sold the milking machines before they sold the cattle, so we had to do the milking by hand. Darlene and I got married that summer. Then in my senior year my labor assignment was

Steve Boyce: "Always prepared, always organized"

to teach a basic math class.

After I graduated I went into the Army reserves. I was on active duty for about four months. Then I returned to Berea College and did my student teaching. By that time Roland Wierwille had been hired to coach basketball, and my labor assignment was to work with him.

Coach Wierwille inherited a team that wasn't tremendously talented. In December we went down to Cumberland and were beaten by forty points. On the bus ride back he said to me, "Tonight there was nothing we could do about it, but I cannot let the players think that."

Before the next practice he had me put time on the score clock, maybe five minutes. He told the players that five minutes was the amount of time they'd spend running figure eights that day, but that I would add a minute every time they made a bad pass or missed a layup or something of that nature. Well, finally I had to cheat to give the team some relief. But later in that same season we played Cumberland at home and beat them. That's the kind of person Coach Wierwille was. He believed that discipline led to success.

I did a graduate assistantship at Eastern for a semester. Then in 1973 I started teaching math at the Berea Community School. I did that for fifteen years before moving into the central office. I've been there ever since. Now I'm the director of pupil personnel, which means I'm responsible for student enrollment, attendance, and health.

After leaving school I played on a couple of industrial league basketball teams and probably played some church league ball too. I still play a little bit of pickup. Oddly enough, I developed a better shot after graduating from college. But I enjoyed the college game and scored what I scored.

Wilson Evans was Darlene's labor supervisor at Berea, and he used to give her used tennis balls. She played some tennis in PE and instructed a little bit, and then I picked it up. I've been playing tennis ever since I got out of college. I love competitive sports, and now tennis has taken basketball's place for me.

July 23, 1998

W.C. Sergeant   Coach 1969-72

I loved the people at Berea, from the administration on down to the faculty, the staff, the students, and the people in the town. They were super. You could not ask anywhere for better people than those individuals who came to our games. They would come to cheer for us and support us. I loved talking with them after games or the next day on the street or in the classroom. They really enjoyed the type of basketball that we played, and they would always take time to comment about the game and compliment what we were doing. A coach appreciates that type of support.

I coached basketball and taught a normal load. I lived in Talcott Hall with my wife Shirley and three young children. One of them attended elementary school, another was in preschool just across campus, and the youngest was at home. We had a babysitter come in and take care of her. Shirley was the counselor of ninety-plus freshman girls at Talcott Hall.

Those girls were tremendous, and she thoroughly enjoyed that experience.

Our teams at Berea College lacked height and physical strength, so in order to be competitive we had to use a pressing technique, a transition game, taking advantage of mistakes. The first year I was there we inherited two fellows who were six-six, but after that the tallest players we had were about six-four. We were playing against six-seven and six-eight people and big guards at the Georgetowns and Cumberlands and Unions, so we had to learn what things we could take advantage of, weaknesses on the other team, things they couldn't do.

I believe in the press. I say that because you always have some individuals who are not quicker than others. But those individuals might be good scorers, for example, who help the team play better in a team concept. You have to compensate for those individuals. When we were pressing, if we had people in who were slower afoot or didn't have the quick hands or quick reaction or anticipation, we could always put them in a position where we could hide them on the press. If the ball penetrated, they

Coach W.C. Sergeant: "Our press helped us pull off some real upsets"

were taught how to react to it and overcome their lack of quickness and speed. That's the way we approached it.

On the other hand, we sometimes had an individual on the bench who was a better player than some of the players who started, but we were not the best team with that individual playing. I learned at the beginning of my career to work with such an individual and say, "You are the best, but in order for you to play, you have to conform to the team concept." That makes the team stronger.

We worked on quickness every day. We had quickness drills, quickness reacting to different situations. If the ball goes one place, anticipate where it will go next and be ready defensively. We worked on making the ball go to the opposing player who wasn't a good shooter or a good ballhandler.

We worked on footwork, which is often overlooked today. When you're playing defense you adjust to the individual you're guarding. If he's quicker than you, you don't play as tight on him as you would if you're quicker than him. If he's righthanded you maybe play him to the right a quarter of a man or even as much as half of a man, depending on his quickness. If he's lefthanded, the same thing in reverse. If he can go either way well, you have to play him straight up. If he gets around you, your teammates must anticipate. We taught a rotation designed to prevent good shots.

Our game was transition, so we tried to mesh our offense with our defensive scheme. We ran with the ball whenever we had the opportunity. With our lack of size, we didn't get the opportunity to run every time. But when we'd come down the floor, the way a pass was thrown would indicate a specific play. I was not a person who sat on the sideline and held up a sign or yelled out, number one, number two, number three play. The pass itself, the cut itself, the movement of the ball and the movement of a person or two people determined the offensive pattern that we ran. That was difficult for other teams to scout and difficult to plan against, and that's some of the reason we were successful. The players learned to react to situations. If the opponent was playing one way, we could go another way, and they would not anticipate it. So we could take advantage of the opponent's weaknesses and the opportunities they gave us.

I have a teaching background. You always want to have a lesson plan when you go into class, and you have to have a lesson plan in coaching too. We had a lesson plan every time we went out on the floor. That was our practice schedule. It was divided into minutes and seconds. If we were going through a drill and were not through that drill when the time came to end it, we stopped that drill. I've always felt that repetition on a long-term basis is more conducive to learning than teaching something by trying to cram it in.

If you're teaching a math fundamental and the students don't get it today, you have to teach it tomorrow. So we'd come back the next day and make our lesson plan, just like in teaching. We'd adjust our practice schedules to meet specific needs, so that people would learn their responsibilities and increase their skills over a period of time.

We had so many tough opponents. Campbellsville is a good example. Lou Cunningham was an excellent coach, and he could go out and get talent with scholarships. We had to make up for that with our style of play and our desire to be successful. Our games with Campbellsville were always close, and we finally beat them in 1971.

I remember a comment I heard one of the years I was at Berea. Camp Henderson, a senior citizen who had been one of the outstanding officials in the state of Kentucky, was being interviewed by WHAS radio. The announcer asked him who were the best coaches he had seen in Kentucky, and he said, "I can't recall his name, but the gentleman coaching at Berea College does one of the most outstanding jobs I've ever seen. He has a press that I've never seen used before in any area of the state. I think he's one of the best." Now, that was a compliment! He didn't know me, and I didn't know him.

Our press helped us pull off some real upsets. Oakland City College in 1969-70 had a team that played somewhat similar to what we did, but they were more wide-open. They gave scholarships, and they had some excellent athletes. They had scorers. They had one person who averaged close to thirty-three points a game, something very high. They had a guard who did the same thing. They just had basketball talent. They beat us at Oakland City, but the game was exciting all the way. They ended up winning by four points. It was a very, very close game, and we had a chance to win it right at the end.

But when Oakland City came to Berea, we were ready for them. They were going to shoot the ball, so the game was very high-scoring. But with our pressing style of play, we got the ball for a lot of layups. In beating Oakland City that night we scored 134 points and broke the school record. That was an outstanding game. The players, from that, realized that if they put forth the effort and dedication it takes, they could win. Our fans, the townspeople and Berea College people, were very proud of us. When they're proud of something, that makes you feel good and your players feel good.

Another upset that stands out in my mind was against Wright State University, a program everyone is familiar with. They were our first opponent in 1970-71. Wright State played at Cumberland the night before, and I went down there to scout them. When I walked in the gym and saw them warming up, I wondered why in the world we scheduled a team like that for Homecoming. They were big. They were talented. Our tallest starter was about six-four, and their shortest starter was a six-four guard. Their other guard was six-six, and under the basket they were in the six-seven, six-eight, six-nine vicinity. Everybody who came in off the bench had size too. They beat Cumberland pretty handily, and Cumberland always has an outstanding basketball team. So all the way home that night I wondered what we were going to do.

We decided not to change our style of play too much. Our quick transition game had been successful the year before. Sure enough, we jumped out very quickly on them. With our press we were able to take the ball, to intercept, to stop their offensive scheme. We won by twenty-odd points. That to me was an outstanding win, to beat Wright State, and it was to the people in the stands too. Later on we also beat Cumberland, who were seldom ever beaten.

A lot of alumni remember the next year's Homecoming game against Georgetown. Berea had had a huge rivalry with Georgetown College, but for some reason the schools broke off the relationship. Berea and Georgetown had not played each other for several years.

Many alumni who came in for that game wanted to know, "W.C., why did you schedule Georgetown College?" My philosophy had always been to play the best schools you can play. If you play well against the best, if you play hard and represent the school well, it's no disgrace to lose. And if you play those schools and don't play well, that shows you the things you've got to work on. I accepted the Georgetown game as a challenge.

By the time the game started, there was no way anyone could get into the gymnasium. They were standing outside begging to get in. Inside they were standing under the basket, standing on the floor. I think our fellows felt a little intimidated because of who we were playing and the history of the series and the crowd that was there, because they weren't used to playing in front of crowds like that. After about six or seven minutes we substituted the second five for the first five, and for some reason this group just took the challenge. We went from an eight or nine-point deficit to tied or leading at the half. In the second half we started the first five back, and we won going away.

We played at Pikeville in the KIAC tournament that year. Pikeville had beaten us twice. Before that game a rainstorm came, and we got flooded. Very few people could get there. The true fans braved the weather. In cars they had to cross a swinging bridge to get over the river to where we were playing. That night our players played right to the game plan that we had planned for them, and they won. They played with heart, and that's all you can say.

We'd had a tough game with Pikeville at Berea the previous year. That game was very rough and aggressive, because Pikeville played that way. With just a few minutes to go a Pikeville player started swinging, and our players retaliated. We were ahead at that time, and maybe it was humiliating for Pikeville to be behind Berea College. Several of our students, reacting emotionally, rushed onto the floor. But the officials did a very good job of stopping it.

When I talked to the team after the game, I started out as always with something positive. I praised their hustle, the effort they were putting forth, and their desire to do well in that game. But I said that sometimes in the heat of battle we get too carried away. In this particular game, one individual got carried away, and that got everybody involved. I said, "We've got to be above that. If anything like that happens, understand it and walk away from it. Don't let it fester and turn into something like this did. We have to control ourselves, control our emotions, so that nothing like this will ever happen again."

It never did. Sometimes these things happen when teams are playing hard. It shouldn't happen, but once in a while it does. We always taught, "You're a team." When our player got involved and a couple of Pikeville players got involved, our whole team got involved too. We used to say all for one and one for all, and that day our players carried that philosophy a little bit too far! But our two schools had known each other for a long time, so the next year we played Pikeville again. There was no animosity. Nothing was said, nothing was done. Their coaches and I had always been friends, and we remained friends.

Basketball has been one of the most important things in my life. As a kid in Barbourville, Kentucky, I went to the local high school games, and I idolized some people there. They were excellent individuals who went to our church, and I tried to duplicate the things they did.

I did not get an opportunity to play until I was a junior in high school. Herb Tye, the coach, thought I was too small, but once I got the opportunity I made the most of it, and he became a real supporter and encouraged me. I played just one year there because at the end of my junior year my mother died. I went to Springfield, Illinois, to finish high school.

I came back to Barbourville to visit, and I happened to go see Coach Tye. He said, "W.C., I sure would love to see you go to Union." I said I would be interested. I had several college offers in Illinois, but to come back to my old home town and play would be a dream becoming true. So he called the coach at Union. They had me do a tryout, and then they offered me a scholarship.

Bill Boyard was the Union College basketball coach at that time. He was an excellent coach although he had not played college basketball or even high school basketball. He had played college football. He was a rough man, but a man of strong integrity and loyalty. He brought me to Union, and I had tremendous respect for him.

The third game of my freshman season was against Berea. I came in off the bench and had an excellent game. I started the fourth game, and I ended up having a good career at Union. At five-eight and a half I played point guard, but I could shoot the ball and score when necessary.

In college I recognized that I wanted to be a basketball coach. I wanted to emulate some of the coaches I had known. Maybe I could help other people the same way that I had been helped.

I became a student of the game. I read every book on coaching that I could get my hands on. After college I played and coached in the Army and ended up winning what they called the national championship of the Army against some very good competition, including some people who had played professional basketball.

You learn from both positive and negative situations. I certainly learned a lot of things not to do, but I tried to take the positive things and learn from those. I'd go to coaching clinics whenever I could. Sometimes they were good clinics and sometimes they were bad clinics, but I'd always learn something I could take back with me and implement into my philosophy.

I became a high school coach. We had some excellent players who were recruited by major colleges. A lot of times those college coaches would spend the night, and we'd stay up all night discussing and debating teaching techniques and coaching philosophies. From those discussions I learned ways to coach, ways to get a point over, what to do and what not to do in certain situations, the relationships you've got to have with individuals.

I did graduate work in school administration at the University of Kentucky because when I got through coaching, I wanted to be a school administrator. In the summer months Coach Adolph Rupp taught a class in the theories and techniques of coaching. He had some high school coaches in there and a few college coaches too. I asked him if I could audit his class, and he said, "Sure." Well, after three or four days the entire semester's conversation was between the two of us! That was to my advantage. I learned a lot about transition, because he was a transition coach. Rupp's assistant, Harry Lancaster, an outstanding coach and an outstanding individual, had a lot of insight too. Those experiences helped me develop my ability to teach.

I came to Berea from Sullivan Junior College in Louisville. We had just won the national junior college championship. I had recruited the whole team myself, mostly local players. Some had just got out of high school and wanted to stay in Louisville. Others had gone to a four-year college and didn't like it or got homesick. It was a talented group of players that jelled into a team that played together very well. We were the underdog in every game we played in the tournament. In the final game Albany Junior College of Albany, New York, was favored to beat us by fifteen or twenty points. We beat them by twenty or twenty-five points to win the national championship.

That accomplishment led to more and more recognition throughout the state. I had the opportunity to talk to several four-year colleges. The Berea College job was sought by maybe forty coaches, many of them outstanding men. The job was offered to me. Shirley and I always enjoyed a small community, so we went to Berea.

The best basketball anywhere is played in the state of Kentucky. There can be no better college basketball played anywhere. The KIAC was always an underrated conference. Coaching in the KIAC was a real challenge, something I wanted to do in a conference I was familiar with. At the time Berea hired me I knew a lot of the KIAC coaches. The coach at Union, for instance, was a very good friend of mine. He'd stay in our house when he'd come to Louisville to recruit.

Coaching at Berea offered some unique challenges. One of the primary ways that people learn about an institution and its philosophy is through that institution's athletic programs. Sometimes it appeared that Berea College did not fully realize what athletics can do for an institution. Perhaps the Admissions Office at that time regarded athletes as persons who did not have the academic ability to succeed in college. For some reason there were a lot of people in academia who thought that any athlete was just a dumb athlete who couldn't do anything else. I guess I accepted that as a personal challenge, because that's the farthest thing from truth. There were many athletes who were brilliant people like Bill Bradley or Jerry Lucas. Many, many professional athletes were, and are, college graduates.

Of course, Berea College did not give scholarships. When we were out recruiting students, we could not use the word "scholarship". Even so, there were some misunderstandings about this. For example, there was a coach in Louisville who had several very good players on his team. I invited him to bring his players to Berea. I explained to him that we couldn't pay any of his expenses, but as prospective students the players could eat in the dining room, and that's the only thing they got. But when the coach got ready to leave, he asked me for gas money.

I said, "I explained that to you. We cannot do that. We cannot give your players scholarships or any other incentives to come here. We cannot even give you gas money." He went back to Louisville and called several times requesting money. Finally he tried to intimidate me by saying, "I will go above your head."

This man went to the President and told him that we promised him all these things. The President talked to me, and I said, "There was no such thing." That ended it, but that's how stories get around sometimes. No, Berea College gave no scholarships, although about every team we played offered full scholarships.

I wanted to get quality student-athletes to come to Berea. I say student-athletes because people who come to college must come as students. In our particular situation we needed good athletes who we could get without giving aid. When you're teaching English, you should get the very best English students you can. When you're teaching drama, you should get the very best drama students you can. When you're teaching music, you should get the very best musicians you can. I felt the same way about the Athletic Department.

We spent a lot of time and research in finding individuals who were not recruited or who were overlooked or left over. We spent a lot of time on the phone getting recommendations and contacting the recommended people to suggest that they come to Berea for a visit. A lot of alumni helped us do that.

I had confidence in my ability to teach and coach. I had learned so much from other people by observing them and reading their books and discussing their techniques and philosophies of coaching, and the position I played in college helped me gain insight into the game. A point guard has to get everybody involved, all the players. The other positions, it's not so much that way. All the things I had learned helped us win the national championship at Sullivan Junior College.

It was this success that we brought to Berea: getting people to believe in themselves, to believe that if they played to the best of their abilities good things would happen. As I've said, if people play to the best of their abilities and they lose to a better team, there's nothing wrong with that. But if they don't give their best and they lose, they're not learning anything. You should always do the best you can, in English class or in drama class or in music class or on the basketball court.

To me the purpose of coaching amateur athletics is not to win at any cost but to promote the good of everyone you're coaching. I loved working with young people at a time in their lives when they were forming their own philosophies and their own ideas about how the community should be and how the world should be. As a teacher or coach you work with them every day, and one of the most important things any coach can teach is that no one is better than anyone else. I guess I'm idealistic, and I kind of look for a utopia or something. The real aim of teaching and coaching, I think, is to make a better community, a better world. I still have that philosophy.

After leaving Berea College I started a business working in investments and insurance. We did a lot of retirement planning and estate planning, that type of thing. Later I moved back to Louisville and became an assistant to the President at Spalding College, now Spalding University.

Spalding had been an all-women's school and had only three or four percent men when I came. We tried to attract students. Spalding had been recruiting in only one area of Louisville, so we started doing a lot of public relations work with other local high schools. Because I knew the principals and counselors of these schools, I introduced them to the Spalding administrators. Today Spalding has increased its enrollment by about 300 students, with a tremendous increase in male enrollment. They are recruiting in schools they never looked at before. Spalding has gone from a non-sports program to basketball, soccer, volleyball, and softball for women and basketball, soccer, and golf for men.

A few years ago I went back to work with Berea College as an assistant to the President. I traveled the northeast states, from northeast Virginia to Washington D.C., Philadelphia, Buffalo, Rochester, Syracuse, and into New England, meeting many, many Berea alumni. I got them involved in fund-raising-type things they had never been involved in before. I called on the chairman of the board of trustees, Roland Goode, who lived in Philadelphia. Roland and I became the best of friends, and I can't say enough about him.

I learned so many things from people who had the firsthand experience of attending Berea. Their dedication to and support for the College gave me an even broader respect for its accomplishments. Through these associations I've truly learned what Berea's about, what its purpose is. To give students from the Appalachian area an opportunity to attend an institution where they can get a fine education is really a fantastic goal, a fantastic thing to strive for.

Shirley and I have many excellent friends in Berea, and we hope the small part that we have played there has helped Berea College. If we can do anything to promote Berea College, we're willing to do it.

June 24, 1998

Roy Smith   1969-72

At Bishop David High School in Louisville I was a good basketball player, but not a great basketball player. I knew I wouldn't be able to excel at a big college, but I enjoyed the sport and wanted to continue playing it. After I graduated, W.C. Sergeant, who had been coaching junior college ball in Louisville, was hired to coach at Berea College. He came to talk to me and several other Louisville-area players. We went over to visit Berea, and I liked what I saw and enrolled there.

I'm six-four. In high school I played center. At Berea I played three positions: center, power forward, and, as an experiment, shooting guard . Berea had both a freshman and a varsity team, and I got to play on both levels right away.

I liked Coach Sergeant's open game. I had a shooting touch from the outside, but I was big enough to play underneath. Coach Sergeant gave me the freedom to go in or out. I had some jumping ability, so

Roy Smith: "We beat a lot of good teams"

when I played guard, which I really liked, I could post up underneath on the inside. When I played forward or center, opponents found it difficult to guard me on the outside. So I could use my ability to drive, or I could shoot the outside jump shot, drawing the big men away from the basket.

I spent my whole career getting banged around by people bigger than me. In high school and in college I was going up against six-eight people and getting killed. Coach Sergeant thought I'd make a good off guard, so we worked diligently on my ballhandling. I welcomed the opportunity to be an off guard and get away from the action around the basket, to be the abuser instead of the abused.

Coach Sergeant believed in letting us exploit our individual talents. One of our guards, Ken Maynard, was extremely quick, so we would often clear out and let him drive to the basket. A lefthanded guard named Jimmy Hairston had the ability to go one-on-one with people. We had a fairly tall team and we were mobile, which surprised a lot of our opponents. We played mainly a zone defense, and I was either on the wing or in the middle. With my quickness and ability to read where the offensive player was going to throw the ball, I got a lot of steals.

When I joined the team, the veteran leaders were Dennis Grant and David Maynard, who were holdovers from the Coach Wyatt era. Dennis was tall and lean. He didn't have that much natural ability, but he had the heart of a lion. Dennis had a strong desire to win, and he tried to instill that in the younger players like me. He inspired us to give it that extra effort.

Dave Maynard was Ken Maynard's older brother. He was six-five and had a lot of raw talent. Dave was hard-nosed, and he gave it his all. He'd run into a brick wall.

Our first practices under Coach Sergeant were intense. The team was a mixture of the old and the new, and we were all out to prove ourselves. We banged and hit each other and used a little extra elbow. It took a while for cohesion to develop, but once it did, we had a good blend.

The newcomer who showed the most leadership was Bill Broome, a little red-headed guy from Corbin, Kentucky. Bill was a hustling ballplayer who was always urging us to do better. I was closest to Charlie Bacigalupi, who roomed with me my first two years. We were both from Louisville, and that helped us bond. Charlie had grown up at Boy's Haven and played basketball at Trinity High School.

Charlie was a very intelligent and warm human being. He had a mus-

Charles Bacigalupi: "He was so big and muscular"

tache and long hair, and he was so big and muscular that he came across as kind of rough when you first met him. But Charlie would do anything in the world for you. For some reason Charlie was the brunt of many of our jokes. I remember lacing his jock strap with analgesic balm. He tore out of the gym squalling like a dog. He was big enough to kill us all, but he didn't. He had a heart of gold.

The guys on the team got along well. We went everywhere together. There was some racial friction on campus, but it never affected the basketball team. Jimmy Hairston and the other black players fit right in. I don't remember a single moment when the white players wouldn't accept the black players, or they wouldn't accept us. We all blended together. Coach Sergeant recruited that kind of player.

I never heard a discouraging word among ourselves or directed at us. We just went about our business.

Compared to a lot of the teams in the KIAC, we didn't have a wealth of talent. We won games on sheer determination. We got after people. We pressed people. We tried to take them out of their game. We weren't the best team out there, but we beat a lot of good teams, and we played strong competition. We even played Eastern and Morehead. Our freshmen played the University of Louisville freshmen. Coach wanted to send a message: "Berea can compete with these people. We're a small school, but that doesn't mean we're any less than anybody else."

We had a tough rivalry with Pikeville College. I'll never forget the "basket brawl" that occurred my sophomore year. That was one of the games I played guard. There was a lot of shoving underneath the basket, back and forth. The referees let it get out of control.

Suddenly all hell broke loose underneath the basket, and people started jumping out of the stands. In an instant it was pure chaos. I was guarding one of Pikeville's star players, and he and I just looked at each other as if to say, "What in the world is going on?" The coaches came onto the floor to help the officials try to separate people. Finally the referees took off their whistles, threw them on the scoring table, and left. Then, just as quickly as it started, it stopped. The whole thing was totally senseless. It was something I had never seen before in my entire life as a basketball player.

Coach Sergeant was disappointed that we didn't conduct ourselves with more poise. There's a lot of stuff that goes on during a game, a lot of trash talking, but you've got to step above that. You elbow people, but you don't intentionally foul them. I'd never do that. Pikeville was a rough team, but all the teams we played were rough, and we should have handled ourselves better.

The following year Pikeville defeated us home and away. After the regular season ended we had to travel to Pikeville to meet them in the KIAC tournament. Their fans taunted us, saying we didn't have a chance. It was a close game back and forth, but we beat them. Some of the Berea fans went down to watch the game, and they were quite happy about the way we played. It was a moment to be treasured. Normally we came right back to Berea on the bus after a road game, but on that occasion we spent the night. That was quite a thrill for us.

Our next opponent was Cumberland. Once again the game was close. Cumberland had a defender on me to guard me the entire game, which was unusual. We lost in overtime, but I thought we should have won it. We had our chances, but we made some mistakes at the end. I was very disappointed.

That was a rough season for me. In a game shortly after Thanksgiving I stole the ball and went in for a layup. The referee blew his whistle for some reason. I turned in midair to see what the call was and blew out my left knee. I felt like I'd been shot. The pain was so intense that I don't remember anything that happened in the next several minutes. When I came to my senses I was sitting on the bench, and I heard the trainer say, "We've got to get him downstairs." With help I hobbled down the stairs.

I didn't want my career to end there. I was determined to play again, no matter what. I went to several doctors in Berea and Lexington, and I worked my rear end off. As I drove back home for Christmas vacation the knee was still stiff. I was driving with one leg. But by late January or early February I was able to come back to the team.

Coach Sergeant told me I was coming back too soon, but I wouldn't listen to him. A doctor warned me that if I came back too soon, by the age of forty I'd be incapable of playing anything more strenuous than golf. That prophecy seems to be coming true. A year ago I quit playing basketball. I'd been playing with a group of about fifteen guys. We've known each other since grade school, but now that we're getting older, our numbers are dwindling.

Coach Sergeant and I hit it off real well from the beginning. I thought the world of him and his wife and his children. He treated us like family. We went to his house, and one time we even baby-sat his kids. I remember him bringing his little boy to practice.

Coach Sergeant was easygoing, but when he wanted to make a point his voice level would change, and we knew then that he meant business. I had tremendous respect for him. Coach Sergeant wanted to take Berea College basketball to another level, and I don't know if the College was ready for that type of change. When he told us he was no longer going to be the coach, I was devastated.

I didn't play basketball my senior year. I was unhappy about Coach Sergeant leaving, my knee wasn't in the best of shape, and I'd cut my hand while working construction in August. It was just a mixture of things. I decided to call it quits.

My first labor assignment was cleaning the English building: sweeping the floor, arranging the desks, wiping the boards down, putting everything in order. I had to work between six and nine. I went from there to cleaning and vacuuming the library. I liked that a lot better. I could choose my own hours. I could either do it in the morning or the afternoon, whenever I had free time. That was very convenient.

I took my studies seriously. If you didn't maintain your grades, extracurricular activities like basketball didn't mean anything. A road game didn't exempt you from your early class the next day. The professor would say, "You did that on your own choice. I'm here to teach you." You couldn't lay in bed and say you'd make it up. That was totally unacceptable. You knew you had to take care of your academic and labor obligations. That helped me. I knew what was expected, and I just did it.

I started off as an education major, but in my first week of student teaching I knew I couldn't be a teacher. So I switched to business administration. When I decided that education was not going to be my major, Bill Stolte, who was a counselor there, guided and directed me in working out a class schedule that would allow me to graduate in four years. That was very important to me, and I appreciated his help very much.

After graduation I moved back to Louisville, where I still live. I'm working as a team leader at General Electric. As people leave the company we haven't been replacing them, so we're trying to find new ways to get the work done with the number of people we have. We're trying to pull people together to work as teams. That's the biggest thing we're working on right now. It's a challenge, but I enjoy it. I'm out dealing one-on-one with people, not hitting keyboards in an office.

My Berea College degree has opened a lot of doors for me simply because of Berea's reputation. When I tell people that I graduated from Berea College, they often say, "You really earned your degree if you went to Berea College." People know you worked hard, that you weren't a slouch. That means a lot. My experience at Berea was very beneficial, and I thoroughly enjoyed it. I'd do it over again in a heartbeat.

June 24, 1998

Larry Bruner   1970-74

I was the ninth of eleven kids in our family. My dad worked in a hospital where he washed clothes. My mom was a housewife. I was the only one of the eleven children to go to college and graduate.

Hazel Green High School no longer exists, but I'm proud to say that I was one of the old Hazel Green Bullfrogs. In my senior year our team went thirty and two. In our first game in the Kentucky state tournament we played Paris, who had a player named Pete Moore who later played with me at Berea. We lost in the quarterfinals, but each one of the eight seniors on our team was offered a college scholarship somewhere.

I was recruited to Berea by Coach W.C. Sergeant. He was a very personable man, and I enjoyed playing for him. I had the opportunity to play quite a bit as a freshman. I'd go through a two-hour JV practice and a two-hour varsity practice in the same day. One night we played Eastern. I and my roommate, Mike Jones, played the entire JV game, then turned around and played half the varsity game, and I think the two of us were the leading scorers in both games. The next night we went to Morehead, and the same thing happened. As you might guess, I was in the best condition of my life.

The freshmen were not treated as freshmen by the upperclassmen. They didn't try to separate themselves from us. Dennis Grant, for instance, was a good leader who always made us feel a part of the team. I wish I could have played with Dennis for four years.

I'm six feet tall. I played several positions. As a freshman I played point guard, but I also played center. That's hard to believe, I know, but the best part of my game was inside. In one game against Pikeville, who had a seven-footer named Danny Moses, I got fifteen rebounds. Although I wasn't a shooter, I could score. I had some great moves around the basket, probably because as a kid I played a lot of games of me-against-two-people. I was a good defensive player, too. I think I led the team in steals. I played a lot of minutes and would probably have played more if I'd been a better shooter from outside.

We were trying to build up the program at Berea, which wasn't easy because our opponents gave out scholarships and we didn't. Coach Sergeant brought some good players to Berea, but he tried to keep everybody happy, and that hurt him. We had some internal problems. Bill Pearson, who came to Berea from Chicago, was an experiment that didn't work out too well. Bill had some talent, especially as a rebounder, but he had a bad temper. While Bill was visiting the campus in February 1971 we played a game against Pikeville, and a fight broke out. Bill wasn't even in school, but he came out of the stands and kicked a guy's teeth in. That fall he enrolled at Berea. One night Bill got upset in the dressing room and yelled at Coach Sergeant, but Coach kept him on the team.

I think Coach Sergeant believed that the people he recruited were talented enough to win on talent alone. We played a run-and-gun style, not undisciplined by any means, but free-lance. We scored a lot of points, but we lost a lot of games because we didn't have much defense. No matter what the situation, however, Coach Sergeant always believed he was going to win. One night we were down by twenty points to Union College with about a minute and a half to go. Coach Sergeant called a timeout. In the huddle he looked at us and said, "Guys, if we get two or three quick baskets, just like that we'll be right back in it!" There was no three-point shot in those days, either.

When Coach Sergeant left, I was the only player named to the committee to choose his replacement. I enjoyed interviewing the candidates and showing them around. I knew that the next coach would have to be very strict, because success is not possible without discipline. Two of the candidates, Roland Wierwille and Don Meyer, impressed me as excellent coaches. They were both strict and demanding men. Coach Wierwille was hired, and he was the right choice for Berea. Coach Meyer went on to have a successful career at David Lipscomb University.

We always knew where we stood with Coach Wierwille. The first day he came in, he had a team meeting and went over his rules. A lot of us had long hair. He told us that if we could pull our hair over our eyes, it was too long. He wouldn't allow cursing. That impressed me, because I came from a very Christian family. Coach Wierwille had played for Paul McBrayer, whose every other word was a curse word, and he said to us, "If you think you can tell me a curse word I haven't heard, let me know."

Coach Wierwille's practices were organized. Each day we knew what we were going to do, because the schedule was posted in the locker room. We worked a lot on fundamentals, and for conditioning we ran eights. That meant starting at one end of the floor and running baseline to baseline,

The 1970-71 freshman team. Front: Mike Jones, Larry Bruner, James Long. Back: Coach Doug Layne, Roger Marcum, Ovie Hollon, Joe Rosselot.

down and back, down and back, down and back, and down. That's actually seven trips, but Coach Wierwille called them eights. We'd have to run eight of those. On Monday he might have us run the eights in forty-four seconds, followed by a one-minute rest. He believed in quick rests because in a timeout or on the free throw line we'd have just a minute to rest and recover. On Wednesday we'd run the eights in forty-three seconds, then on Friday we'd shave a second off that. Running eights got us in shape.

I adjusted to Coach Wierwille easily because I had played for demanding coaches in high school. I was used to hearing, "Never quit. Never roll over and quit." In Coach Wierwille's first year we were stretching one day at the beginning of practice, and he was walking around on the balcony. We had lost three or four games in a row, and we knew he was mad and upset. In a loud voice he asked us, "What's the best thing we can do?"

I misunderstood what he said. I thought he said, "What's the worst thing we can do?" So I yelled out, "Just roll over and quit!" The rest of the players laughed so hard they couldn't get off the floor. But that relieved the tension, and we had a pretty good practice.

I believe that only one of the players who had played for Coach Sergeant in his final year and were still in school when Coach Wierwille arrived did not come back to the team. That was Roy Smith, a good shooter from Louisville. We tried to get Roy to come out and play, but he was very loyal to Coach Sergeant and wouldn't do it. On the other hand, Mike Faulkner and Joe Rosselot and my cousin Roger Marcum, who didn't play in 1971-72, came back to the team when Coach Wierwille was hired. As for me, all I wanted to do was play, and because both coaches played me I was happy.

The guys on the team got along pretty well once things settled down. We were all sort of hippies, but Joe Rosselot more than anybody else. Nothing seemed to bother Joe. He was a good person. Charles Bacigalupi was another individualist. Charles always had a dictionary with him, and on the bus or wherever he was, he'd sit there exploring new words. Speaking of new words, some people had trouble learning our names. I knew those two teammates of mine as Joe Ross-a-loe and Charles Batch-ia-lupi. Once we were playing at Cumberland College and happened to see a tape of our team that had been filmed for scouting purposes. Whoever was announcing the play-by-play was saying things like, "Here's Back-a-loopy, over to Roos-a-lott, back to Burner, back to Back-a-loopy." He didn't pronounce any of our names correctly.

My closest friend was probably Mike Robinson. He and I roomed together. He was a great passer. I was also close to Phil Perry, a good shooter who was probably the best player on our team. In my senior year the NAIA started a Kentucky-Tennessee all-star game, and Phil and Joe and I were named to the Kentucky team. I scored the first two points in that game.

I had some serious back problems between my junior and senior years. During a workout that summer a disc slipped out. It was the fourth one up, and I had to have surgery in Lexington to remove it. After the operation I had to lie flat for four weeks. I couldn't sit up or go to the bathroom. For four months after that I had to wear a brace. I missed some school because of it.

I took a swimming class that semester, and as part of the class I had to bring up a ten-pound brick from the bottom of the pool. That was unbelievably painful. When I reported for basketball practice before the season started, my legs were gone. I ran the eights, but afterwards they had to carry me off the floor.

I had to learn to walk all over again, let alone run. I didn't think I was going to be able to play basketball, and I talked things over with Phil and Mike. Both of them said they weren't going to play that season, either. We decided we'd break the news to Coach Wierwille the next day.

I went into Coach's office and told him I wasn't going to play because of my back and this and that. He looked at me and said, "We're going to do conditioning today at three-thirty. If you're there, that's fine. If you're not, don't come in tomorrow." He told Phil and Mike the same thing.

About two-thirty Phil looked at me and asked, "What are you going to do?"

"I don't know. What are you going to do?"

"I'll play if you play."

I said, "Well, I'll play if you play."

We decided we were going to play. I doubt if we ever had any real intention not to play. So we found Mike and told him. Mike said, "Oh no, not me. I'm not going to play."

Phil and I got dressed and went out on the floor and stretched, looking at the clock. About five minutes before the start of practice, Mike finally came strolling up the stairs. So all three of us played. If we hadn't showed up, we would have been off the team. That's the way Coach was, and that's the way he is today. He tells people exactly where they stand with him.

The back injury cost me some playing time. I'd been a starter since I was a sophomore, but I didn't play as much as a senior. Late in the year we were playing at Transylvania, and I dove after a loose ball. My face hit a guy's knee and one of my front teeth broke right in half. I was lying on the floor, and Coach came out and asked, "Are you hurt?" I hadn't played many minutes in that game, so I looked up at him and said, "Just my feelings." But Coach had to help me off the floor, and Pete Moore replaced me. I had to go to the hospital. Later the Transylvania coach, Lee Rose, came to see me there.

I was a physical education major. For some reason I could never get an A in Coach Monarchy Wyatt's classes. I'd be there every day and do all the work, but he would always give me a B. I don't know what his rule was, but Coach Wyatt was a super individual. He'd won the state championship at my high school, Hazel Green, in 1940. He liked music, and when we'd go over to his house we'd sing while he played the guitar.

Athletes at Berea were not allowed to miss classes. Sometimes we'd drive to a road game and not get back until three in the morning, but we'd get up in time for an eight o'clock class. I never considered that a burden. The happiest years of my life were my college years.

I worked in the gym the whole time. For a while I was a supervisor in intramurals, where I learned a lot about organizing. In my senior year I couldn't move around too well after my back surgery, so I was given the not-too-tough job of sitting and counting how many girls used the swimming pool.

After I graduated I got a job teaching physical education at a junior high school in London, Kentucky. I started coaching basketball in my second year. We weren't very successful that year, winning only four or five ballgames. The next year we improved, and the year after that we went undefeated and won the county championship. When several grade schools and a junior high school consolidated, I got the job there. I went twenty and one that year and twenty-four and two the next. After that I was hired as an assistant coach at Laurel County High School, where I had a chance to coach a lot of the players I'd had when they were younger.

In my first year at the high school, 1981, we were good enough to go to the state tournament. The next year we won the state championship when Paul Andrews hit a shot from halfcourt to beat North Hardin. But I wanted to be a head coach, and I was hired to do that at Middlesboro High School. We went to the state tournament in my first year. I spent ten years at Middlesboro and had some nice ballclubs, with three teams ranked in the Top Twenty-Five. Then I was at Harlan for couple of years, where I worked with boys and girls. I took the boys to the state tournament one year.

Now I'm trying to build a program at Louisville Fairdale. It's going well, and I enjoy it. Coaching in Louisville is different than coaching out in the state. There are twenty-two high schools in Louisville, and kids can go to any school they want to. It has been difficult to get good athletes to come to Fairdale, but we're improving our image. We've got a great faculty, and Fairdale is being recognized more and more as one of the best schools at helping kids who other schools might not want. We're keeping those kids and doing our best to help them.

Early in my coaching career my teams played the way we did at Berea under Coach Sergeant: five-man fast breaks, fill the lanes and go. From Coach Wierwille I learned a lot about coaching fundamentals. Under him it was fundmentals every day, over and over and over.

Coach Wierwille started using the offense called the double-low in my senior year at Berea. A lot of people have been using it since then. We used it at Laurel County High School when we won the state championship in 1982. Quite a few high school coaches have won with it, and I'm one of them. Coach Wierwille still runs it, although he's added a few things to it. He's got more movement now. It's a good offense.

Unlike many coaches today, I believe that everybody on the team should be able to handle the ball, even the big guys. I want all my players doing the same drills in practice. I don't want all the guards on one end working on guard moves and the big men at the other end working on post moves. Even though I played guard, I learned post moves. I have all my players doing the same drills because I believe it makes everyone better.

I'm thankful that W.C. Sergeant recruited me to go to Berea College. Everything worked out great for me. Both Coach Sergeant and Coach Wierwille influenced me. They were a big part of my life.

August 5, 1998

Joe Rosselot   1972-74

I grew up in a small town in southern Ohio called Owensville, which is in Clermont County near Cincinnati. My father was a mechanic. He ran his own business, but he later sold that business and went to work for a larger company. My mother was a secretary. She was the assistant to the principal of the grade school I attended.

In my senior year in high school I was the leading scorer and rebounder in the conference in Clermont County and wanted to play college basketball. I was recruited by a few small colleges in Ohio and visited some of the schools. I also visited Transylvania College in Lexington. The coach at one of our rival high schools was a Berea College alumnus. He and my high school coach had been discussing where I might be going to college, and he suggested that I consider Berea. After learning about the school and finding out about the program, I visited Berea and got excited about going there. I was swayed by the friendliness of the people in the community and around the campus. There was a warmth and sincerity that I hadn't seen in some of the northern towns I'd been to. My family was in the income range that made me eligible for Berea, so it was an easy decision for me.

During my visit I was very impressed with Coach W.C. Sergeant and his plans for the Berea program. He introduced me to some of the players, and I scrimmaged with them. I liked the style of basketball that Berea played. In high school I had been in a system which was very defense-oriented, playing the game at a slower pace than many of the high schools and col-

leges in Kentucky played. Berea under Coach Sergeant was very much a fast-breaking kind of team. It was an exciting style of basketball for the fans, and it was very appealing to me.

I was part of what was touted as one of the best group of freshman basketball players ever to enroll at Berea. Several of my teammates had been on good high school teams and had very successful high school careers. Mike Faulkner and Mike Jones both averaged over thirty points a game their senior seasons and had been recruited by some major college teams. Roger Marcum and Larry Bruner had lost very few games in high school and played in the Kentucky Sweet Sixteen tounament the year before.

Joe Rosselot: "My commitment to Berea was strong"

There were definitely high expectations for us as a group.

All I really knew about Berea was that it was a high-quality small college. I knew very little about the specifics of the school and who it served. Not having lived in the traditional region for the school, I wasn't aware. The system Berea had and the way its tuition system worked were never explained to me. Coach Sergeant gave us the impression that we would have everything taken care of financially when we came to school, that there would be no expense for us as far as going to school. That turned out not to be the case.

We were surprised when we received our first semester bills just like all the other students. We asked Coach Sergeant what we should we do with those bills. He told us not to worry, that everything would be taken care of. We waited patiently, following up every few days, and finally he told us to pay the term bills, and he'd try to get us reimbursed for those costs. We did it, but eventually we realized that he wasn't going to be able to follow through.

I went to the Cashier's Office and said to the woman at the window, "My understanding is that my term bill is supposed to be taken care of, but I'm not sure what the procedure is." I told her that I was on a basketball scholarship. She started laughing and said, "There are no basketball scholarships at Berea College." She explained how the Berea system worked.

Once I got past my frustration with Coach Sergeant, I came to respect the way Berea serves its students, and it didn't bother me to be paying my share, as small as it was relative to that at other private colleges. But I had enrolled under a different set of assumptions, and I was not financially prepared to pay the nominal fees that were required of every student. It threw us all for a loop, those of us who had come to Berea under the same assumptions.

All of us who had been recruited went ahead and played on the freshman team that first year, but it was certainly a challenging season. We started off with a win but then lost several games in a row. Two teammates who were also my closest friends, Mike Faulkner and Roger Marcum, didn't make it through that season. Mike tore ligaments in his ankle during practice, requiring surgery which ended his season and limited him for the rest of his basketball career. Frustrated, Roger decided to leave the team at Christmas break. I was also frustrated but decided to finish out the rest of the season.

In the second half of the season the freshman team competed with only seven players, which led to a humorous ending to a double-overtime game at home against the Pikeville freshmen. Players kept fouling out on both sides until Berea was down to three players and Pikeville four by the time the game ended. During our last timeout I asked Doug Layne, the freshman coach, who was going to throw the ball inbounds if it came down to one-on-one. The fans got a big laugh out of that game.

After that season several of us decided not to play for Coach Sergeant the following year. Although I admired Coach Sergeant's style of play, I questioned his integrity as a coach. Larry Bruner was the only player from our freshman team to play as a sophomore. Mike Jones transferred, and the rest of us played intramural. Several junior college transfers enrolled the next year to help fill the void. At times I regretted not playing with some of the players on that team. Berea was one of the highest scoring teams in the country that year and was exciting to watch.

I never considered transferring. My commitment to Berea was strong once I was working and studying there. So I chose to play intramurals and get my education at Berea rather than transfer simply to play varsity basketball somewhere else. I've always loved the game of basketball, but it was only one aspect of my life. I didn't place all my emphasis on playing basketball.

When Coach Sergeant left Berea after my sophomore year, I found out that Roland Wierwille was one of the candidates to replace him. I had met Coach Wierwille before, when he was an assistant coach at Transylvania when I visited their campus as a senior in high school. Bob Wiesenhahn, my high school coach, was one of the co-captains of the University of Cincinnati Bearcats team that had won the national championship in 1961. He knew Coach Wierwille, who had originally enrolled at UC before transferring to Eastern Kentucky University. When I went to visit Transy I formed a very good impression of their entire program. Lee Rose was their coach. He and Coach Wierwille treated me very professionally, but at that time they didn't have a scholarship available for a player of my size and style, so there wasn't a place there for me.

Coach Wierwille came to Berea to interview for the head coaching position, and while he was on campus he and I had a lengthy conversation. I gave him my perspective on the problems that the program had been having, and I told him that there were several of us who hadn't been playing for Coach Sergeant who would return to the program if he were hired. I felt very positive about him as a person and a coach.

Everybody reacted positively to Coach Wierwille when he was chosen as the new coach. He was stricter than what some guys were used to or preferred, but some of us were used to playing for coaches who were that strict. We knew that he'd been part of a successful program at Transy, and we looked forward to the same thing happening at Berea. Coach Wierwille was very similar to my high school coach in his approach to coaching, so I had no trouble getting accustomed to his style.

Coach Wierwille was a very structured practice coach and very big on conditioning. When school started he warned us to begin conditioning before official practices began, because we would be running a lot on the first day. Most of the guys did some jogging but only halfheartedly prepared. The day of the first official practice was hot and humid, and by the time we were finished running a series of wind sprints known as eighths (for eighth of a mile), everyone on the team either vomited or was nauseous and hovering over a garbage can. It was pretty obvious that he was serious about conditioning. He demanded a lot of hard work out of everybody.

Sometimes in game situations Coach Wierwille would get too excited and lose his composure, but overall he was a very positive influence on the people who played for him. He tried to instill in his players a sense of integrity about themselves and about the game. His deep love for the game was very obvious.

He stressed playing good, strong defense. His inclination was to be a man-to-man coach, but with the particular personnel we had and the way we matched up with other teams, we had to rely on zone defenses more than he probably preferred. He wanted us to play the double-low post offense while maintaining a controlled tempo. Take advantage of mistakes, push the ball up the court when it's there, and if it's not there, try to read defenses and stay under control. Good fundamental basketball.

That first season under Coach Wierwille, Phil Perry and either Larry Bruner or Mike Robinson started at guard. Ted Cash came off the bench at guard. Since Larry was also effective around the basket, he sometimes played forward also. There was quite a bit of juggling of the lineup, but Ron Owens and I often started at forward along with Chuck Bacigalupi, who had played three years for Coach Sergeant, at center. Roger Marcum and Mike Faulkner rotated with Ron and me at forward, and Ovie Hollon and J.R. Feagan rotated with Chuck at center.

The following year Phil Perry, Mike Robinson, Ted Cash, Gary Ferguson, and Tony Jones all rotated quite a bit at guard. At forward it was usually Larry Bruner, Pete Moore, Jerry Harris, or me starting, with Glen Tate coming off the bench. Lamar Crenshaw started at center with J.R. Feagan as his backup. Coach Wierwille substituted a lot and juggled the lineup frequently, looking for successful combinations. I'm sure it was a challenge for Coach Wierwille in those first couple of years because we didn't quite have the personnel to match up to some of our competition, but we always played hard.

I was an average player who was more inclined to work for a jump shot than to drive to the basket. During games I tried to keep an eye on what was going on all over the floor and be a steadying influence on my teammates. I wasn't a big scorer, but I had a few good scoring nights, which were always fun. Because I was a low post player in high school, I had to learn to face the basket as a forward. On defense I had to learn how to guard players farther away from the basket. The weakest part of my game was strength. I'm six-six, but I was thin and lacked the strength to battle effectively with a lot of the guys I needed to compete with inside.

Seabury was a fun floor to play on. We used to take advantage of the overhanging track to try to pin opposing players in the corner and make them shoot from near the end line where it was difficult to get a shot off. Because of the size of the gym and our fan support, it was an exciting place to play. The gym was always packed. It was like having an extra player on the floor.

Cumberland was our greatest rival. They were always at the top of the league, and every game with them was a big game. As we struggled through Coach Wierwille's first campaign, they beat us very handily at their place early in the year. Later we played them at Berea in front of the home crowd. Cumberland had an excellent player in Maurice Byrd, probably the best player in the league. But we put together a really good game, played them close, and were finally able to pull away at the end to beat them. That was a very big win.

A month later we played Wright State at home. We were behind by thirteen points at halftime, and in the locker room Coach Wierwille was livid about the way the game had gone. He had one of those portable chalkboards set up in the room, and as he talked about his frustration he kept hitting it with his fist. With every syllable he would pound the board. Finally the chalkboard broke into pieces. We went back out for the second half, rallied back from that big deficit, and won the game by six points. That was a another memorable night.

Many of Georgetown's players often had an arrogant attitude toward Berea's players, and whenever we played them, some of their players taunted us. That always brought out a little extra effort in me. I wanted to beat Georgetown more than anybody else. In my final year we beat them at Georgetown. I had a really good game that night, which was very satisfying.

Dan Armstrong was a sociology teacher whom Berea had shifted to humanities and composition courses. I got a lot out of a class I took with him as a freshman. The College had started a course called Issues and Values to amalgamate English composition with exposure to current topics. I found it to be very inspiring. Dan brought issues before the class that made us think about what was going on in the world outside the little communities we came from. That class was important in my evolution as a person.

I carried quite a few hours in the labor program, and it was a challenge for me to keep up academically. I ended up working two different jobs while playing varsity basketball, and that didn't leave a lot of free time. Students who played basketball at other colleges were often pampered, but at Berea there were teachers who went out of their way to make it a little tougher on the players. They wanted to avoid the appearance that anyone was getting preferential treatment. It could be tough to complete an assignment if we had a road trip. I remember times when teachers shrugged their shoulders and said, "That's your problem." The athletes who tried to succeed in their studies had a bit tougher road to travel than some of the other students did.

During my last two years in school I was a teacher's assistant to Dr Robert Menefee in the Business and Economics Department at the same time that I was monitor in Draper. I unlocked the building every morning at six or six-thirty, supervised the student janitors who cleaned it, and locked it up each night at eleven. During the daytime hours I worked for Dr Menefee.

I respected Dr Menefee very much. He and I had many enjoyable discussions. I was an economics major, and we talked mostly about the economic issues of the day. Dr Menefee had a warm personality and a dry sense of humor. He was quick to laugh and kept people at ease. Some of the students who attended the Principles class he taught were required to take it in order to meet a requirement. They weren't all that interested in

Robert Menefee: "A warm personality and a dry sense of humor"

the topic and gave him the nickname "Boring Bob." In economics that's not unusual moniker for a teacher to have, because of the subject matter.

Ideally a college education helps you grow up and realize what the world's all about, and it gives you a better perspective on anything you do. My education at Berea did that for me. I was very satisfied with it. It taught me what it was like to work, and Berea's commitment to service gave me a sense of duty, inspiring me to try to do something to help others. Most of the work I've done has been to provide some service to people. I value that very much.

I ended up doing different kinds of work, not following a traditional career path. I lived in the Berea area for quite a few years. I worked as a carpenter, tried organic farming, and worked in agricultural marketing and community development with the Save the Children Federation. An interest in energy use in agriculture led me to Vermont to study renewable energy and energy-efficient building design. Later I managed a two-year solar demonstration project for the Kentucky River Foothills Development Council. With a friend who was an architecture school graduate I started an energy-efficient design/build business in Berea in the early eighties.

The high interest rates of those years made it tough to succeed building custom energy-efficient homes. After a few years I moved on. I became coordinator for the State of Kentucky Energy Cabinet's Alternate Energy Office, where I was able to provide technical assistance and programs on renewable energy and energy-efficient design and construction around the state. I enjoyed the work, but by the mid to late eighties interest in renewables and energy efficiency had dwindled due to lower oil prices.

I left Kentucky when my wife had a career opportunity in Florida. After working in the construction business for a while, for the last several years I have been co-managing a branch office for the Palm Beach County Planning, Zoning, and Building Department. It's interesting work. Because of the hurricane threat along the Atlantic coast, there are many concerns and considerations about the way buildings are designed and built.

I'm looking forward to moving on at some point to the next step in my career, possibly in a different field. I have tended to stay in most of my jobs five years, and then I start yearning to do something different. Right now I'm looking around for the next thing I want to do. I have a strong interest in health and nutrition. For several years I've toyed with the idea of going back to school so I can get into the health field. I haven't felt like starting Biology 101 and going back that far through the educational process again, but it's still a possibility. I also enjoy cooking, so I've thought about going to cooking school, just to do something totally different.

August 11, 1998

Roland R. Wierwille (1)   Coach, 1972-

I had always respected Berea College before I arrived in 1972, for its athletic and academic accomplishments. I felt it an honor to continue that reputation and tradition.

I was thirty-two years old when the job opened up at Berea. I'd had great experience at Transylvania under C.M. Newton and Lee Rose, and I wanted to be a head coach. I thought I was ready.

There were 125 applicants for the Berea job. They interviewed three. One candidate had just finished his doctorate at Indiana University. The other man was an assistant somewhere. They interviewed the three of us, and they offered the job to the man with the doctorate from Indiana. Howard Holman was his name.

I got beat, and I was disappointed. A week later I was up in Cincinnati, where I'm from, cutting the grass for my mom. She came out and said, "Roland, you have a call from Berea College."

The head of the Physical Education Department, Bob Pearson, was on the line. He said, "That fellow we hired has turned us down. He got a job in Florida. Would you consider coming to Berea?"

I was still a little peeved at not getting it the first time, so I said, "I've got to think about it. I'm going to stay up here for a couple of days, and then I'll come back and talk with you." So I went back and talked some more with him, and I talked with the president, Dr Willis Weatherford. They encouraged me to do it.

I talked it over with Cecilia, my wife, and our three daughters. I took my two oldest girls out on our boat and said, "Girls, your dad's been offered another job. We'd live in Berea. What do you think?" I can still hear my oldest daughter, who was in the third grade, saying, "Dad, whatever you think is right, we'll go." So I took the job.

I grew up in Madeira, Ohio, about fifteen miles northeast of Cincinnati. My mom and dad came over here from Germany in the early twenties. They met in Cincinnati, got married, and had three boys and two girls.

Laura, my oldest sister, made up her mind that she was going to go to college. She wanted to teach. My mom and dad were very hard workers, but at that time they really didn't understand college. If it hadn't been for Laura wanting to go to college and showing the way for her brothers and sisters, I don't know if the rest of us would have gone. George, my oldest brother, became a medical doctor, and my next brother, Walter, got a Ph.D in engineering. Carolyn, my younger sister, went to college and graduated and also became a teacher.

I played basketball and football and golf at Madeira High School. After I graduated I went to the University of Cincinnati for one semester. I was a walk-on basketball player. They had one of the great college teams of that time, with Oscar Robertson in the class ahead of me. I knew that I would not play there. My high school coach was an Eastern Kentucky University graduate, and he called them about me. I went down there on a full basketball scholarship.

That was the greatest thing I ever did. I got a chance, and I made the most of that opportunity. I went to Eastern and played three years of varsity basketball and three years of varsity golf. I graduated in three and a half years, with a summer school session.

My brother George brought me down to Eastern on old Route 25. That was before the interstate was built. Jim Baechtold, the assistant basketball coach, was the first person I met on campus. He was waiting for us and showed me around. He had graduated from Eastern in 1952, then went to the NBA and played five years for the Baltimore Bullets and New York Knicks.

Jim Baechtold taught me a lot. He was a much more talented basketball player than I was, but he worked with me because he liked my aggressiveness. I was aggressive, but he showed me how to be more aggressive. Although I was never a good shooter, he worked with my shot, and he showed me good fundamentals that he had learned from the best players. He helped me improve my basketball abilities, and he taught me to grow up a little bit, too.

I'm six-five and a half and played at 215 pounds. I was not a finesse player, and I knew that. I made up for it by playing very, very hard. I took a lot of pride in that. I didn't back up from anyone. Sometimes I should have, but I didn't! I never thought that I didn't fulfill my responsibilities to my coach. I had limited ability, but I gave it everything I had, and that's why I could play for a Division I school.

In 1959 we won our conference and went to the NCAA tournament. Louisville beat us in Lexington, and in their next game they beat Kentucky. The next year we were second place in the conference, and the third year we were co-champions. We had a playoff with Morehead in the old Alumni Coliseum in Lexington, and Morehead beat us. So in three years we were champions, we were second place, and then we were co-champions. I think we were very respectable! At one time we were ranked twentieth in the nation in Division I. I feel very good about being a part of Eastern and their basketball program in the late fifties and early sixties.

I didn't think about coaching until about my junior year. I had a lot of respect for EKU head basketball coach Paul McBrayer. He was a very intense coach and very dedicated to his players who were loyal to him. I was so loyal to him that we had a very good relationship that continues to this day.

He ran me out of practice once, on a day when I wanted to fight everybody. I wasn't having a good practice and got mad at myself. The intensity in my personality bubbled over, and I started swinging. Coach McBrayer said, "Wierwille, get out of here before you hurt somebody."

I got in my car and took a ride by myself down to the Kentucky River, the old Boonesborough Park. I thought hard about leaving school. I was embarrassed for being run out of practice. But it wasn't for not hustling; I just went goofy for a couple of minutes. So I sat there and thought, "I've got to go back, because if I don't go back, I can never go home. I would let too many people down."

I went back to the house where the basketball players stayed and went to bed. The next day I got up and went to class, and then I showed up for practice. Coach McBrayer never asked me to come and talk to him, never said anything else to me. I think he was glad I came back.

Coach McBrayer was so dedicated to the game, he wanted us to play as hard as we could for him. And we won some great games against some awfully good teams. We beat Western when they were in the Top Twenty in the nation. We went down to North Carolina State when they were

Young Coach Roland Wierwille: "I thought I knew everything, but I didn't"

in the Top Ten in the nation and beat them on their home floor. We beat Louisville when they were twelve and zero. The key was organization and discipline. We were never late to practice, and when the team traveled, we were always on time or we were early. Coach McBrayer didn't take any crap. We did it his way.

I had two majors at Eastern, business education and physical education and health. When I did my student teaching in my last semester, I decided that I wanted to coach. So after graduation I went back to Madeira High School as assistant basketball coach under my high school coach, and assistant football coach and golf coach. I also taught business education, typing, everything in that field.

The next year I became the head coach at Madeira in basketball and golf, while still serving as assistant in football. But I realized that going back to my high school was a mistake. I had just turned twenty-two years old, and I was too young. The teachers didn't look at me as a colleague. So when people ask me about going back to teach or coach at their own high schools, I say, "Don't do it right away. If you do it, you can't go right back."

After two years at Madeira I coached a year at Berea High School, and then I decided to go back to Eastern and get my master's degree. I had married Cecilia in the meantime, and we had a couple of kids pretty quick. I was going to school full time, I was substitute teaching, and I was the graduate assistant coach at EKU in basketball, so I was very busy.

After I finished my master's, the assistant coach's job opened up at Transylvania. Coach C.M. Newton had taken a sabbatical leave to go back to Alabama to work on his doctorate. Lee Rose, his assistant, took the team to the national tournament. When C.M. Newton came back, Lee Rose left to take the assistant's job at the University of Cincinnati.

Transylvania was the first job as a college assistant that I had applied for, and I was very nervous. There were a couple others who were interviewed, both Transylvania graduates. One was a very successful high school coach in Lexington, Al Prewitt from Henry Clay High School. Later I learned that they were really after him when I interviewed, but he turned it down because he didn't want to be an assistant after being a head coach at the high school level. The other guy turned it down also. So I got a call saying that if I wanted to accept the job, it was mine. I didn't have to think about it. I said, "I'll be there." I was twenty-five years old.

I knew that if C.M. Newton were to leave, Lee Rose would be the head coach if he had the opportunity to come back. That's the way it happened. I was under C.M. Newton for three years and Lee Rose for four years. C.M. Newton is now the athletic director at the University of Kentucky, and Lee Rose is an assistant with the NBA Charlotte Hornets. He is also well known for taking two Division I schools to the Final Four, North Carolina-Charlotte and Purdue.

Both C.M. Newton and Lee Rose helped me a lot. Coach Newton was organized, and he had a great knowledge of the game. He was a completely different personality than Coach McBrayer, my college coach. I don't know if I ever heard him yell at a player, where Coach McBrayer would do that. Lee Rose was in between. He was another well-organized coach with a great knowledge of the game. I was under three coaches who really knew the game and who knew how to organize. Practices, meetings, travel, they were organized. It's so important that you have that in your coaching philosophy.

When I came to Berea the program was not in good shape. There were problems, and at the time I interviewed I really didn't get what was going on. If I had known, I might not have come. C.H. Wyatt, who had been the coach for twenty-four years, was the athletic director. He answered to Bob Pearson, the head of the department. Bob Pearson was a very professional person. He said, "I'll help you in any way I can." If it hadn't been for him and knowing that he was going to be behind me, and Coach Wyatt, I probably would have left after that first year.

When I came on campus for my first interview a person came up to me and told me, "You've got to keep an eye on C.H. Wyatt." Well, I did keep an eye on him, because he became a very, very good friend of mine! He was as much like a father to me as my own father was. He tried to help me whenever I went to him. If I didn't know what to do, being a young coach, or if I had a problem with the budget, he always was right there. I had so much trust in him that I could go to him when I had a personal problem or anything.

C.H. Wyatt was Berea College all the way. He didn't have the win-loss records that would indicate a good coach. That's what's wrong with our profession: to some people wins and losses dictate if you're a good coach or not. Not to me. C.H. Wyatt was an excellent coach. He was short on talent most of the time because he had to work under stricter guidelines than I did when I came.

Coach Wyatt worked in the fifties and sixties before federal grants started to pour into education. At that time students with families who had a limited income could go to Berea College much, much cheaper than they could go to Eastern or Morehead. Under those conditions Berea could really handpick its students, fill each freshman class with top students. Admissions closed in April, and in April a lot of high school players didn't know what they were going to do yet. So that was a handicap for recruitment of student athletes.

I was not able to recruit for my first team at Berea College, but three or four players who had quit the team and played intramural basketball the year before decided they wanted to come back. I got those people, we started working, and ended up pulling some big upsets. We beat Cumberland that first year, which nobody expected.

John Cook was named Director of Admissions, and I found I could count on his cooperation. He would help if I got a name of a student-athlete who qualified for Berea College. He would call and talk to the parents about the educational requirements and how much it would cost. But those students had to be eligible to come to Berea College, because John wasn't going to break the rules. We never did.

Willis Weatherford was the President when I came. He was a good Christian man who was completely dedicated to Berea College. He came to my house several times and we talked. I considered him a very good friend, but not a personal friend, for I had to respect his position as President. He was always very respectful to me, and I was always very respectful to him. He was godfather to my son, which tells you how much I respected him.

Willis Weatherford wanted a good, clean program that the school could be proud of, and that's what we had. He would come to a few games a year. He wasn't really an athletic-minded person, but he wanted us to be a competitive team.

When I came to Berea the facility was run down. Little by little, going through Bob Pearson and Coach Wyatt, I worked to get approval for repairs and improvements. We put in a drop ceiling and a new floor, got nice locker rooms. Each summer we had students painting and cleaning, and I worked myself, even though I didn't get paid for it.

When I became a head coach I thought I had all the answers. I thought I knew everything, but I didn't. At thirty-two I was still on the young side. I had worked under good people at Transylvania, but as an assistant I was always told what to work on. But as a head coach you are in charge, and you have to determine what you'll work on. When I started at Berea we didn't even have an offense against full-court pressure. I made a lot of mistakes early, but I learned through experience. Even today after thirty-seven years as a coach I learn from my mistakes.

In those days my emotions hurt me some on the bench and in practice. Instead of thinking things through, I got too excited, too high-strung. I had an assistant, Charles McIntyre, who coached the JV team, and he did a nice job, but I was in charge of all the varsity. I didn't have a person who was an assistant-assistant on the bench.

One day I ran a player out of the gym. I can't remember why. He didn't bad-mouth me or talk back, I've never had a kid who did that, but I ran him out. I said, "Get out of here. Get on downstairs."

Coach Roland Wierwille: "When he told us what we were going to do, we did it"

The minute I said it, I wished I hadn't. He left, and we talked the next day. He really thought he was going to quit.

I said, "If I had to do it over, I would never do it. It was just emotional. I want you to come back, but if you don't I can understand why, because I don't know if I would." We talked more, and he decided to stay on the team. He became one of the finest players who ever played at Berea.

I never ran another player out. That was one of the few times in all these years that I embarrassed a kid. Some coaches embarrass kids on the floor, but I don't like to do that because I never wanted to be embarrassed. I embarrassed that kid, and he had a lot of pride. Even today, if I'm going to get on a kid, I'll do it in my office or I'll get him off to the side. But I'm not going to yell at him in front of his teammates. I feel strongly about that.

I learned a lot about handling players from C.M. Newton and Lee Rose. Coach Newton was slap-them-on-the-back, hey, it's okay. Lee Rose would get right in their faces. I'm both. You have to know your players' personalities. Some kids, if you raise your voice, they're going to go hide. Another kid, you raise your voice and he'll go the other way. You need to know how you're going to handle each individual, and you have to figure that out in their freshman year, that's part of coaching.

Our men's basketball team had a lot to do with improving race relations on campus and improving the relationship between the town and Berea College as a whole. The College had had some racial problems the year before I came. When I arrived in 1972 we did not have an African-American on our team. I worked very hard to correct that. Our first recruit was an African-American, Tony Jones from Hazard High School. We recruited student athletes who were both black and white, and when people saw them coming together and having success, that helped the whole attitude on campus. People saw these young men working together, hugging each other, slapping each other on the rear end, and that had such a positive effect on our campus. And at a time when the town of Berea and the College were a little divided, our basketball team brought a lot of people to Seabury Gym who would never have come on campus otherwise. That really helped the relationship between the townspeople and the College. I went out and sold season tickets to get people to come. Before that not many people would come, but little by little we had them coming to games.

The turnaround at Berea College began in 1975 when we came across four high school players, the Big Four. I'd like to take a little credit, but those players could play naturally. To get four players like that in one year and have all of them stay in your program for four years, that doesn't happen very often, especially at this level.

They were players who were overlooked. Arno Norwell had played on an inner-city team. Craig Jefferson was going to go to Lees Junior College. Nobody wanted Bill Nichols, and he became our leading scorer, a great player for us. Ed Flynn wanted to be an agriculture major, so that's how we got him.

Because all four of those players could play, I didn't want one of them sitting on the bench. So I played all four of them with one guard. Then I didn't have to worry about who was going to start, who was going to play. The Big Four were going to play, and the ones who were sitting on the bench knew it. They were head and shoulders above everyone else, and they proved it. That team could probably have competed against an Eastern at that time.

Those four student-athletes changed everything. People started looking at us and saying, "Berea College, not too bad!" That laid the groundwork for attracting better players to Berea, and that led, eventually, to a new facility.

We needed a new facility because we weren't allowed to play the NAIA District 32 playoff games at Berea when we earned the home court advantage. Our floor wasn't big enough, so we had to play on somebody else's floor. If we had had a regulation floor, we would probably have made it to the national tournament in both 1978 and 1979. Playing at home would have helped us win two very close final games.

In the 1978 finals we lost to Cumberland by one point in the last second when a foul was called when we were one point up, and their player went up and hit both free throws. I can still see it. Then the next year we had a lead against Kentucky State, and I got excited because we'd never been to the nationals and we were so close again. I got so emotional that I forgot how to place our players to attack and beat their press. We lost that one too, and those are the two low points of my career, losing those two finals when we could have been to the national tournament both years. If I was coaching those two games today, with my experience, I think we would have a lot better chance to win. But I was younger then, and I wanted it so bad that I didn't do a good job of coaching.

Eventually, of course, we got a new gym, and one of the arguments for it was the fact that we couldn't play basketball playoff games at home. I even heard the President say it.

Sometime in the late seventies I got a call from the chairman of the board of trustees of a college that we played. He told me that the school was looking for a coach, and the board wanted to know if I was interested. I said, "Let me think about it." After I talked it over with Cecilia, I decided I was better off at Berea.

Gary Ferguson   1973-75

I grew up in Hazard, Kentucky. When I was in elementary school my dad worked in coal mining, which was about the only thing that was there. Later he got on with the gas company and finally retired from that organization. Mom worked in the school system as a teacher's aide, then worked for Sears Roebuck.

I played basketball at Dilce Combs High School and then at Alice Lloyd Junior College. After two years at Alice Lloyd I wanted to continue my education. I had heard a lot about Berea, and my coach, Jim Rose, set up an interview for me. Roland Wierwille was looking for a guard, and he told me he wanted me to come to Berea. So I enrolled there.

We had a good team at Alice Lloyd, a team with a great deal of talent, but Jim Rose wasn't able to get 100 percent out of his players like Roland did. Jim Rose ran lackadaisical practice sessions, but playing for Roland was like boot camp in the military. I adjusted to it. I realized that Roland wanted to win more than any coach I ever played under. He instilled that desire in us. Due to his influence we pursued excellence at all times.

I was married when I came to Berea. Talking to Roland for the first time, I didn't know how he would take that. He wanted total dedication, and I had the feeling that he thought I was too young to be married and wouldn't give him the effort he expected. In the end, though, I think I convinced him.

At Berea I lived in married student housing. Phil Perry, Mike Robinson, and Joe Rosselot were also married, so the four of us hung together. We didn't see the other players as much. We had classes with those guys, but we didn't have the relationships with them which we would have if we'd lived with them in a dorm.

I'm six feet tall. I was one of four guards who were roughly equal in ability. If you added the minutes up, each of us averaged about half the game, going in and out a lot. Roland expected 100 percent for our twenty minutes. I knew that if I didn't give that to him, there were two other guards who could come in and replace me and my running mate. Roland emphasized defense, and I guess that was the best part of my game.

It's hard for me to call him by his first name even after all these years, because he was a father to us really. The team was like a big family. We realized that we weren't great players. Some of us weren't even good. Berea gave no scholarships, and we were playing against scholarship athletes on other teams. Roland understood that, but he put the idea in our minds that even with average talent we could do something if we had above-average desire.

My fellow guard Mike Robinson was a good example. He had a great heart. He was an average ballplayer but had a tremendous desire to play. Mike was a joy to play with. He had a positive outlook on life. When you're young you need that, and he had it.

Phil Perry was probably the most athletic of the guards. He was a lot stronger than the rest of us and a little taller. He was very serious, very dedicated. In practice sessions he gave it 100 percent at all times, and Phil played like he practiced.

I had played against Tony Jones when he played for Hazard High School. He was a real competitor. It's unusual to play head to head against somebody in high school and then play with them in college. I'd also played against Charlie Turner when he played for Breathitt County. He wasn't that tall in high school, but he played center for them. They were a rough bunch who played to win. Charlie had that mentality and brought it to Berea. He was a very tough, hard-working individual.

Center was Charlie's position at Berea also. People on other teams would look at him and say, "This guy's not tall enough. There's no way that he's going to be able to perform." But after mixing it up with Charlie they realized that he had something. He gave it extra effort and in most games outplayed his taller opponents. He couldn't jump high, but he was very strong, had tremendous hands, and knew how to position himself.

Union College had a player named Carlos Combs whom I knew well. I played against him for four years in high school. He was an all-stater. Then Carlos went to Alice Lloyd Junior College and we started at guard together. He became one of my best friends in college after being a bitter enemy in high school. After our two years at Alice Lloyd, Carlos chose to go to Union while I chose to go to Berea. I hated it that he went to Union. I almost went to Union with him before deciding to go to Berea because of its academic program.

In the next two years Berea played Union four times. Before each game Carlos would tell me, "There's no way you guys are going to beat us." But we beat them each time. We didn't have more talent than they did, but we won on defense and heart. That was a memorable rivalry for me. It was an odd situation to play against Carlos, play with him, and then play against him again.

I loved playing at Seabury Gym. It was always packed. Anybody who went out of bounds usually ran over some-body and ended up in the crowd. The floor at Seabury

Gary Ferguson: "We pursued excellence at all times"

wasn't regulation size, and we beat many teams there simply by intimidating them. We were in shape, and Roland liked to put on a one-two-two zone press. When we went to play in a gymnasium like Cumberland's after playing at Seabury, we tired out. It seemed like we couldn't even see the other end of the court.

Cumberland was the team we all wanted to beat. They had tremendous athletes who really challenged us. In every game with them we were the underdogs. Once we played at Cumberland and in the first half I hit eleven for eleven. Then I came out for the next half and was one for nine. I'll never forget that, eleven in a row from all over the court, and in the second half one for nine.

If you missed a final exam at Alice Lloyd Junior College, it wasn't a problem. You made it up. Berea, however, was known for its academics, and I knew it was going to be tough when I chose to enroll there. Obviously I wasn't going to play pro basketball. There was life after basketball, and I wanted to come out of college well-positioned to enter the business world.

In my first semester at Berea I took business law with Dr Daniel Yang. We were about to go to an away game which conflicted with one of his tests, so I talked to him about it. I hated to take a makeup test anyway because they were always so much more difficult. I told Dr Yang that we were going to play Xavier up in Ohio, so I couldn't take the test with the rest of the class. He said, "I'm sorry, but you have to be here."

"I can't be here. I play basketball."

He said, "I'm sorry."

That was frightening. I didn't know Dr Yang very well, and I didn't know if his response was indicative of all the Berea professors. I went to Coach Wierwille and said, "Coach, how can we play basketball at Berea if we can't make up tests?" I was ready to tell him that I couldn't play if it meant I'd get a zero on a test.

Roland said he would talk to Dr Yang. He worked it out, and Dr Yang let me take the makeup test before I left. I don't know what the problem was. All of the college sports, golf or soccer or baseball, required the athletes to be away sometimes, so I don't know what Dr Yang's thoughts were.

Later I got to know Dr Yang very well, and that's what I liked about Berea, being able to get to know many of my professors on a first-name basis. Some of them I could call at home if I had a problem. If you played basketball you didn't get preferential treatment, but you were known by everybody. If the professors saw that you were dedicated to academics as well as sports, they would work with you.

Robert Johnstone: "He supported the program"

My major was business management, but my labor assignment was in the Agriculture Department. I worked under the department chairman, Robert Johnstone. One of my duties was to run the tests off, and some of the agriculture students would come in and say, "Hey, Gary, let me have a copy of that." I was offered a few bribes, but I knew better than that. Besides, if I ever did that, Dr Johnstone would have crucified me!

Dr Johnstone was a fantastic guy. He wasn't interested in basketball or athletics until he met me. I was the only basketball player working in the Ag Department office. He said, "I never have followed basketball."

"Why don't you start coming?" I replied "It would mean a lot to me."

So Dr Johnstone started coming to every game. He sat right in the front row. I got to know him real well. He was like a father. My wife and I would stay in his house to watch it when he went on vacation. Now when I go back to Berea and go to a game, Dr Johnstone is still sitting right there in the front row. He supported the program and still does, although he has retired now.

I took no classes under Dr Johnstone, but he influenced me greatly by his demeanor and the way he conducted himself. I got to know all the guys in the Ag Department because I was in there every day. Dr Claude Gentry, Dr Ed Hogg, and Dr Noel Stephens were all influential in my life. I worked for them all. Anything they needed done, I did it. I even worked on the college farm for awhile. They tried to get me to change my major to agriculture, and I thought seriously about it.

After graduation I worked for eight years for a textile rental company, Means Services. After that I spent nine years with Frito-Lay, a division of PepsiCo. I was the district sales manager over southeastern Kentucky, with fourteen route salesman working under me.

I got my master's degree in business administration and thought I would stay in the private world all my life. Then I changed careers. You might think there's no way you can do that at age forty, but an opportunity presented itself to me, and I put forth the effort. Under Roland Wierwille at Berea College I learned that if you have the desire, if you have confidence in yourself, there's no limit to what you can do.

So now I'm working in a government agency. For the last five years I've been the Director of Environmental Health for Blount County in east Tennessee. I handle any environmental issue in the county that has to do with solid waste, air pollution, or water pollution, either at the local level or in conjunction with a state agency. Any development activity in the county, I have to approve the building site.

A lot of issues are confronting Blount County because it has the second-highest growth rate in the state. 100,000 people live here now, and I'm probably as well known as anyone because I'm in the health care field and talk to a lot of people and attend many community meetings. I work with the planning commissions and the homeowners association.

I have a flexible work schedule without much supervision, and that's what I like. I work a lot harder when I don't have someone looking over my shoulder day in and day out. With Frito-Lay it was entirely different.

PepsiCo is a well-run company, but they have a tremendous turnover rate because in some situations they expect too much. In private industry you see a lot of people come and go, but you don't see that in government. I enjoy my job very much. I may not stay in it for the rest of my life, but at this time I'm completely satisfied. I'm outdoors all the time, traveling the county and meeting with different people.

I played competitive basketball for probably fifteen years after I got out of college. At one time I was playing in an industrial league and a city league and a church league all at once. Finally I got too old for that, but I still love to play the occasional pickup game. I'm in great shape. I jog, I lift weights, I work out.

Roland Wierwille taught us that there was something we could learn in winning and also something we could learn in losing. I'll never forget one of his meetings after we lost three games in a row. He said that there were physically handcapped people who would give anything to be able to play basketball for Berea College. At the time I didn't fully understand what he meant. Now as I reminisce I realize what a great learning experience it was to have him as a coach and a mentor.

I think about Berea every day. Yes, it was a struggle to be married and try to study and work and play basketball. I had average intelligence, but I studied hard, and that's why I was able to maintain a 3.5 GPA. Learning the discipline it took to do those things made life easier for me and still does. I'm thankful I was able to go to Berea. When I was a student I couldn't wait to get out, but sometimes I wish I were playing for Roland right now, knowing what I know as an older and wiser man.

July 28, 1998

Tony Jones   1973-77

My objective in college was to succeed in both academics and athletics. Accomplishing that took a lot of hard work. Life for me at Berea was a continuous cycle. I went to my classes, I went to practice, I dragged myself over to eat dinner, and then I focused on my homework. I enjoyed sports, but I recognized that academics came first.

If I had it to do over again, would I go to Berea? My answer is yes. It was a great experience, one I would never trade for another. Young people who are motivated to achieve certain things in life will succeed no matter where they go to school. But Berea provided a perspective on the right things to do, the right kind of effort to apply.

Berea offered a good education, a multicultural environment in which to get an education, and outstanding support, not only from the professors and the coaches, but from the community as well. That made a big difference in my life, knowing that there were people who believed in what I was were trying to do and would get behind and support me. And I enjoyed the company of the many friends I made among the students at Berea, not only basketball or baseball teammates but also people I met in classes and social situations.

There were six kids in my family, four boys and two girls. I was the oldest. My mom and dad did whatever they could to take care of us. My dad had many different jobs. His mission in life was to see that he got his kids educated. Four of us ended up at Berea: me, my brothers Steve and Willis, and my sister Emily.

I attended Hazard High School in eastern Kentucky. My high school coach knew about the Berea program and contacted Coach Wierwille. When I visited Berea he came across as very professional. It was his first year as the Berea coach, and he told me about the program he was trying to build. I liked what he was saying and wanted to participate.

In college I found myself playing with guys who were taller, more skilled, and more focused on the game than my high school teammates had been. The challenge was to understand that I was now competing at a different level and to elevate my game accordingly. Two of the upperclassmen on the team were Larry Bruner and Phil Perry. They were very competitive and always wanted to win. Their attitude impressed me. I knew that they had played most of their careers for teams with losing records, but they continued to play hard and to show people that even if you're losing, you can still feel good about what you've accomplished as long as you're playing your best.

The first game I played was junior varsity, and that was the last game I played as a junior varsity player. I guess my initial showing convinced Coach Wierwille that he had made the right choice in recruiting me. After that I was on the varsity, and after four or five games I ended up starting.

Although I'm five-ten, they used to list me as five-eleven. They gave me an extra inch. My freshman year I was pretty much a shooting guard, but I migrated to playing more on the wing. As Coach's developmental efforts brought us a higher caliber of player, we started rotating roles. We started to jell as a team and understand each other, and as we did we turned from the losing side to the winning side.

The whole team was close, but the player I was closest to Mike Moore, whose room was near to mine in Bingham Hall. Mike was a very religious person, and he was also the type of person who gave a full-out effort. Whenever he had the opportunity to come into a game, he worked hard every second he was on the floor. It was inspiring to see a person with that kind of desire to do well.

In my junior year four freshmen joined the team who added a new dimension. Their names were Ed Flynn, Craig Jefferson, Bill Nichols, and Arno Norwell, and they became the four who would carry the program to the next level. I wish they had started at the same time I did. They were great to play with. Coach Wierwille did a wonderful job of developing them into All-Star players by the time they were juniors and seniors. Before they were through they terrorized the whole conference.

All four of them were big, and they all played a lot even as freshmen. That didn't surprise me. Coach Wierwille had four years worth of potential he was trying to develop. He wanted each of them involved for most of the game, so the guards found themselves playing fewer minutes. That was a difficult adjustment for me, but you do what you do for the sake of the team. The coach decides how the game is going to be run, and you've got to go along with that. I tried to provide some leadership. In a game like basketball everybody has to understand what he can contribute to the team. Coordinating the various roles and making sure that everyone had the opportunity to play his role was something I liked to do.

Charlie Turner, for instance, knew that his role was to get as many rebounds as he could. He was one of the biggest people we had, although he was far from being the tallest player in our conference. Nevertheless, because Charlie could control his body around the basket he did a great job of getting rebounds and putting missed shots back in.

Dallas Leake was a small player, but he assumed a leadership role early on. Dallas added a lot to the team in the areas of motivation and morale. He was also a very good scorer and ballhandler. Another guard, Cluster Howard, was a tough-minded player with the desire to do whatever it took to win. Coach had a good nose for finding guys like that.

Coach Wierwille and I got along fine. I respected him as someone who had a mission, someone who would use all his resources, all his players and their various skills, to develop a winning program. He let us play our game, but he made us work hard.

Union College was the team I most liked to beat. One of my high school teammates, Mike Sammons, went to Union. He was a year behind me, so we played six games against each other. Most of them went down to the wire. They were nail-biters, but Berea won all six, so I got to rub it in. I usually found myself on the free throw line with Mike out there laughing at me, trying to get me to miss my shots. My whole desire was to make those points so we would beat them.

As a team our goal before each season was simply to go as far as we could. In both my junior and senior years we came very close to making it to the national tournament. The teams that beat us, Kentucky State and Pikeville, had a lot of talent. I think we played better as a team and had more desire and spirit than they did, but we just couldn't get over the hump. Sometimes I think about those games and would like to go back and do some things a little differently. But games play out as they play out. You make your choices during those games and can't look back. Still, on the right night with the

Tony Jones: "You do what you do for the sake of the team"

right set of players feeling good on the floor, I believe we could have beaten them.

Pikeville recruited some big men and some fast guards in the Lexington area. They had exceptional talent. I don't know how many of those guys graduated, but if you look at the percentage of Coach Wierwille's recruits who graduate you'll see it's not just winning an individual game that counts at Berea College. That's just a moment in time. A coach really wins when he graduates people who have learned the lessons of playing together as a team and go on to do well in life.

What Coach Wierwille has built at Berea College is something that continues to shape players' lives after they've graduated. They learn that it's not just in sports that teamwork is important. They carry the lessons of teamwork into their business and family lives. They learn to respect other people and work with them to achieve a common goal.

I knew these things before I came to college. My parents instilled those values in me, and my high school coach did the same. I had a lot of the right direction when I came to Berea College, both in sports and academics. But at Berea those values were consistently reinforced, day in and day out. In the newspapers today you read stories about students who don't follow the right track and fall out somewhere along their journey. Well, Coach Wierwille is a man who helps people stay on the right track. That's a proven fact. Look at all the people he has graduated.

I had a great time playing two sports at Berea, basketball and baseball. I played four years of baseball, primarily in center field, although occasionally I pitched. Elvin Combs, in the Athletic Department, was a good counselor and supporter. It helped me simply to know that he was from the same neck of the woods, Perry County. You always want to play hard in front of people from your neighborhood.

Business management was my major. The business program was a good one. Each class was challenging. The instructors not only provided the right kind of classroom environment, but also personal assistance if you needed it. For my labor assignment I was dormitory monitor in Bingham. I was responsible for providing linen and janitorial service to maintain a clean environment in the dorm.

During my junior year General Motors came to campus to recruit. They made me a job offer at that time. After graduation I went to work in their college-graduate-in-training program at a Chevrolet truck stamping plant in Indianapolis. I worked there for two years before concluding that they were too large for me, that the program I was in was designed to focus people on too narrow a specialty.

I wanted to learn how to run a business. That's what I went to school for. My idea was to gain some general management experience in a smaller operation while retaining the option to join a larger organization. So I found a job with Rea Magnet Wire, a subsidiary of the Aluminum Company of America. Rea Magnet Wire was a self-contained business which was responsible and accountable for its own profit and loss and all its own business functions.

I worked at first in the accounting department, where I was responsible for two manufacturing plants from a cost standpoint. I went from there to another assignment in a business start-up for the same company. Then I began working at the parent company in internal audit, looking at policies, procedures, and compliance at several of the Alcoa plants and subsidiaries. After three years of that I became cost accounting manager at a subsidiary called Alcoa Composites. I was eventually their controller, then director of finance and administration. Alcoa sold that business in 1996, so now I'm back with the parent company. Presently I work in the various human resource disciplines of industrial relations, compensation, benefits, planning and administration, and staffing. My role is to offer support to the human resource group in the form of financial analysis. I help them to quantify so that they can decide whether certain strategic directions are sound from a financial perspective.

For about ten years after leaving college I played basketball on company teams in competitive industrial leagues that featured many former college players. I still play, but not with teams at this stage of my life. Just with my kids!

September 2, 1998

Dallas Leake   1974-77

I was born in North Carolina and moved to Vero Beach, Florida, when I was thirteen years old. Both my JV and varsity coaches in high school were from Pikeville, Kentucky. They knew about Berea College and made a couple of calls to Coach Wierwille. The next thing I knew, I was there.

I didn't play on the varsity during my first year. Once I came close, though. Often during the holidays I didn't go home because it was so far away, and as a freshman I got to travel with the varsity team to a Thanksgiving tournament in Tennessee. Coach Wierwille let me dress so he could have even pairings for the warmup drills. I dressed out for one of the games. At halftime we had a lead of sixteen or eighteen points. Coach told me that if the lead held up he would try to get me some minutes at the end of the game. We ended up blowing the lead, so I didn't get to play.

Our JV coach was Charlie McIntyre. He didn't get any pay or anything, but he devoted his time and energy as a volunteer. I appreciated everything he did for us. He and his wife made us feel at home. They invited us out to their house for cookouts. John Cook and his wife did the same thing. He let us stay at his house during the holidays when the players had to remain in Berea for practice and tournaments. A lot of people did many nice things for us.

I'm five-nine. My game was running the team like a coach on the floor. I had a lot of assists. Although I didn't have tremendous of physical ability, I got myself in position to make a lot of defensive plays. I tried to be smart. That's how I got by.

At first I lacked strength and stamina, but after our preseason training program I was in the best shape I'd ever been in my life. It was during a preseason practice session that I broke my nose. I was running around a pick, and my face hit a shoulder. I went to the hospital. They stuck a metal prong up my nose and pushed it back where it was supposed to be. This was preseason, so I didn't have to miss any games. Toward the end of that second year I was starting some games, and I started as a junior and senior.

Another guard, Tony Jones, was the same age as I was. He played varsity as a freshman. Tony was built like a fullback, very muscular, but he had great leaping ability. Tony was a real good shooter from outside, and he shot free throws well. Once in practice I saw him hit twenty-five or thirty of them in a row.

Cluster Howard was another great-shooting guard. He had perfect form. Cluster was always joking and kidding everybody. He kept the team laughing. When he played defense he would tap the shooter on the elbow, and the ball would always be short. He was hardly ever caught at it.

Our big man was Charlie Turner, who was six-five and weighed about two thirty. Charlie couldn't jump a lick, but he could play in the post with anybody. He was a very intelligent player. He could get off his shot against

Dallas Leake: "If he was out there, something was going to happen"

guys who were much taller and had more leaping ability. He was an excellent passer, too.

On offense we ran what we called the double-low, with a forward and the center on one side down on the block, a guard and a forward on the other side, and a point guard out front handling the ball, usually me. In my junior year we had a tremendous freshman class come in: Ed Flynn, Craig Jefferson, William Nichols, and Arno Norwell. They were big young guys who could rebound and shoot. Coach Wierwille threw them in right away. Craig came off the bench, but Ed and Bill and Arno played quite a bit. The offense opened up.

We had a fine season, but we would have gone a lot further had Charlie Turner not been injured. That set us back quite a bit. We were finally eliminated by Kentucky State. We played them close the first twenty minutes but got blown away in the second half. They were a powerhouse with two guys who were later drafted by the NBA. Billy Ray Bates played for a few years for Portland and a couple of other teams, and Lewis Linder was drafted by the Celtics.

We usually packed Seabury Gym, where the crowd was right on top of us. It was a sweatbox, but I loved it. In my junior year the fans really got behind us and began to follow us all over. They chartered some buses to go to Pikeville, a school we could never manage to beat, although for some reason I seemed to play well against them.

Pikeville was loaded. They had some kids from the big high schools in Lexington, Tyrone Dunn and Terry Hawkins. They had a couple of good guards in Mark Myers and Jimmy Kent Kerr. They also had Danny Moses, who was the biggest thing in the conference at that time. Nobody else had anybody who was six-eleven. Pikeville was the best team in the KIAC, and they were the team that eliminated us my senior year. I remember the president of the school congratulating me after the final game.

We never defeated Pikeville, though we came close a couple of times. To prepare us to play tough teams like Pikeville, Coach Wierwille would tell us that they thought of us as "little old Berea," a team that couldn't play. "I've seen you guys work in practice," he'd say. "I know what you can do. I know your abilities. Don't be intimidated, because you can play with them."

Coach Wierwille knew basketball. He knew his x's and o's, and he knew how to prepare us both mentally and physically. I had never been through his kind of training regimen before. He was a tough guy, strict, no nonsense. That worked, because discipline was something we needed. I was never the kind to get real close to a coach, but he and I had a decent relationship.

Once I got gouged in the eye in a preseason scrimmage game, and to protect the eye I wasn't allowed to participate for a while. In preseason training we had to run a certain number of laps. As my eye got better I had to go in and run in the gym during the day. I had to run my laps in front of his office so I didn't get away with not doing something the others had to go through. That's the way Coach was.

After we turned the basketball program around, we were kind of like stars on campus. Everybody thought we were hot stuff. Business administration was my major, and one of my economics teachers, a Georgetown graduate, would always tease me about the games. Coach Bob Pearson, who was head of the Physical Education Department, said I was the best thing to come out of Florida since the orange. I enjoyed all that stuff.

One time my roommate was going home for Thanksgiving, and I wanted to go with him. He was leaving on the day I had a class with Coach Pearson. When I talked to Coach Pearson about it, he told me that life was about choices. I could take off with my roommate and enjoy myself, or I could stay in Berea and take care of my academic responsibilities. He said, "Even if you go, you're going to pass the class. But I guarantee you won't get the grade you would if you stay here. I will leave the choice up to you. That's what college is about, growing up and making choices." I ended up staying and getting a good grade in the class.

Coach Wyatt was one of my physical education teachers. He was a lot of fun. When we first got there he would kick us into the swimming pool, and if we could swim we didn't have to take swimming. I said, "Sure, I can swim." When I got to the gym and they were going to throw me into the pool, I said, "No, no, I'll take the class." On the day I passed it, Coach Wyatt told Coach Wierwille right before basketball practice started. Coach announced, "Dallas passed his swimming test." Everybody got a big laugh out of it.

As a freshman I helped serve in the cafeteria. Later I was assigned to the stockroom in the basement of the cafeteria. Every morning I would go in, check the meals for the day, load up the cart with supplies, and bring it up to them. Eventually, though, I became the intramural manager. I was responsible for all the intramural programs and hiring and scheduling the officials.

If I had it to do over, I would probably change majors. I would either major in sociology or take more physical education classes so I could become a coach on the junior high or high school level. I went into business simply because some of my friends were doing that. I ended up as a retail manager for a few years. Eventually I got into law enforcement, and that's what I'm doing now. I'm a juvenile probation officer in Fremont, Ohio. After hours I coach kids' baseball and softball. I find it rewarding to make a difference in young people's lives.

Berea College is very well-known, but a lot of people in the North who have heard about it don't realize where it is. We have an African-American college club here in town. One club activity is to travel to historical black colleges around the nation. They came to me the other day and asked if I wanted to put Berea on the tour list. They were traveling to Atlanta, and they wanted to stop at Berea on the way because of the College's unique history. I'm proud of that history. Some people don't know I went to Berea, but they're starting to find out now.

June 30, 1998

Charles Turner   1974-76

Basketball is king in Kentucky. I grew up playing basketball. I played basketball in high school, and basketball was the reason I attended college.

I grew up in Breathitt County and went to Breathitt County High School. My dad was a coal miner. If you worked in eastern Kentucky years ago, that was just about the only employment there was. After high school I went to Lees Junior College in Jackson and played basketball for two years. From there I chose to transfer to Berea College. I loved the campus when I visited, and my interview with Coach Wierwille went well.

Although Berea had not had a recent winning tradition, that was also true at Lees Junior College when I enrolled there. We had a great two years when I was at Lees, and I believed I could make a difference in the Berea program. I'm proud to say that we started a winning tradition while I was at Berea College.

I'm six-five and played center-forward. I had never really been in shape before I came to Berea, but under Coach Wierwille I got into the best shape I've ever been in my life. As part of his conditioning program he had us running eights: up and down the floor seven times, touch the lines and turn around. Two weeks prior to practice we ran eights three days a week for two weeks. Berea College teams were known for their conditioning and discipline.

Charles Turner: "He could play in the post with anybody"

As I got into better shape, my all-around game improved. I played against bigger guys all the time, but I led the conference in rebounding two years in a row and was at the top of the scoring list. If we needed a basket I got the ball inside and managed to put it in the hoop.

We scored a lot of points as a team, but our game wasn't simply up and down. We were pretty good shooters. Our field goal percentage was high. We weren't really a pressing team, but when we got the ball off the boards we went with it.

After my junior year we lost Jerry Harris, who joined the Army. Jerry was a guy we could have used my senior year. He was a strong player, a good rebounder and outside shooter. If he had been back with us, we would have been a great basketball team. We were joined by four big, talented newcomers out of high school. Coach brought them along slowly. They were still developing, so Coach worked with them a lot, and I helped.

We had to come back from Christmas vacation a week early to get ready for our next game, which was Transylvania at Transy. We practiced for two weeks, and then in the first half of that game I tripped and fell and broke my left wrist. I'll never forget that if I live to be 100 years old.

It was a close game all the way. Any time we played Transy we had a heck of a ballgame. I was a rugged player who got knocked and banged all the time. My hand hurt, but not enough to get me out of the game. I didn't pay any attention to it, and we went on to win.

I didn't realize the wrist was broken until we got home from the game and I went to bed. About two o'clock in the morning I woke up. My wrist was killing me. I waited until eight the next morning and went to the hospital. The doctor x-rayed it and said it was broken. I couldn't believe it, and neither could Coach Wierwille.

We had a good team and were getting better. I thought we had a chance to win the KIAC tournament, and I had been looking forward to that ever since I arrived at Berea. After I broke my hand I was wild with disappointment. I didn't want it to be in a cast. I wanted to play the rest of the year, but the doctors wouldn't go along with that. Coach Wierwille thought it might injure me for life if I tried it.

I attended all the practices even though I couldn't play. Arno Norwell replaced me at center. He was young and not very strong, and he had a lot of adjustments to make. I worked with Arno on his inside game. We became good friends.

I wasn't supposed to play for the rest of the season. I could hardly handle that. I was determined to play again. After seven weeks I had the cast removed, and I got to play in the tournament. I didn't start, but I played.

The wrist was very weak. I'm right-handed, but inside I shot the ball left-handed. In my first game after the cast came off, I got the ball inside in the low post and turned around to shoot, and it rolled off my fingertips because my wrist was so weak. That was disappointing.

We were the fourth or fifth best college team in the state of Kentucky that year. I believe that if I had been healthy we could have won the KIAC tournament and earned a shot at the national tournament. We beat Campbellsville and Georgetown, two tough rivals, in the KIAC tournament before Pikeville stopped us. They had some great players, especially Danny Moses, who was six-eleven. At six-five I was a lot shorter than he was, but he and I had a little thing going against each other. Berea played the tournament game at Pikeville, which was a disadvantage, but we felt we had the kind of team that could beat Pikeville at Pikeville. Unfortunately, it didn't happen.

I got along great with Coach Wierwille. He treated all his athletes the same. He made sure that we were all going to class and making the grades, because he wanted us to graduate. It was not easy to get through school and work and play basketball at the same time.

Elvin Combs, our equipment manager, was one of my best friends at

Berea. He was a friend to everybody. I worked with Elvin in Seabury Gym.

I majored in physical education, and I was hired as the head boys' basketball coach at Owsley County High School fresh out of college. I coached the Owsley County Owls for eleven years. I loved it. I took a program that was very low and won over 200 games in those eleven years. My 1983 team was my best team. We won twenty-nine games that year, won the district, and were in the finals of the regional.

Coach Wierwille influenced my coaching in a lot of ways. He taught me that success isn't possible without discipline. A lot of stuff we did in practice each day at Owsley County, I learned from him at Berea. I probably ran both his offense and his defense.

I'm not coaching now. I'm a physical education teacher and director of the summer work program at Owsley County High School. I retired from coaching because I love to hunt and fish. I'm an outdoorsman, and I wanted some spare time to do some serious hunting and fishing before I got too old. I hunt different places, different states. Right now I'm setting up an elk hunting trip to Colorado. In the wintertime I fish for stripers, in the spring I fish for walleye and crappie, and in the summer I fish for bass.

Our school is grades seven through twelve. I know every kid here. It makes me feel good when I see these kids graduate and get a job or go to college. We've had many students go to Berea College. A bunch of them are down there right now. Berea's a great school. I wouldn't exchange my Berea College degree for a degree from any school in the United States.

June 23, 1998

Cluster Howard   1976-78

After graduating from Breathitt County High School in 1974 I enrolled at Lees Junior College. Playing basketball at Lees opened up several options for me. Coach Jim Reid at Georgetown College offered me a scholarship. Drew University in New Jersey offered me a scholarship. I also talked to some Division I schools.

My coach at Lees was Paul Davison. He called Roland Wierwille, who was a friend of his, and that's how I was semi-recruited by Berea College. Berea had a good academic reputation, and I had a girlfriend who was attending Eastern Kentucky University, not far away. Berea seemed like the best choice. I had worked all through high school and while I attended Lees, so the idea of working at Berea didn't bother me.

The quality of play was good in junior college in those days. At Lees I had been a scoring guard, but I was asked to convert to point guard at Berea, and that was an adjustment. But the biggest adjustment I had to make was academic. Moving into upper level courses was tough, as I expected. Although Lees was a good school academically, at Berea there was not as much leeway. If an assignment was due at a certain time, we had to have it done at that time. At Lees we had a bit more flexibility.

But I was happy at Berea. I had a job in the gym, and I was a good student who enjoyed my classes. I was on the Mortar Board Honor Society at Berea. I majored in history. Warren Lambert was my adviser. I had an excellent relationship with him, having many conversations with him and visiting him at his home. Frank Wray and Gary Sykes were also good instructors. What impressed me about those individuals was the easy way they communicated with me and treated me as a fellow human being, rather than set up a mentor-student kind of thing. They treated me as an equal, and you don't see a lot of that on some campuses.

I got to be friends with Robert Johnstone, who taught agriculture and some economics. I took a course of his called The Economic History of the United States. Dr Johnstone was a basketball fan, and when I arrived in his class the morning after a ballgame on the road, he was nice enough to say that it was good to see me there at eight o'clock.

Once Dr Johnstone asked me where I was from. When I told him Breathitt County, Kentucky, he said that Breathitt County always interested him because when he traveled through there he saw little red buildings being used for classrooms, with outhouses nearby, while basketball was played in a big modern domed building. That told him what Breathitt County's priorities were. I had never thought about it, but he was right. We did have classes in clapboard buildings with outdoor bathroom facilities, and right beside those classrooms was a state-of-the-art, 4000-seat gymnasium with all the amenities of a coliseum. But while I was growing up there and playing basketball in front of sellout crowds, it never occurred to me that there might be anything wrong with that.

In my first year at Berea, my junior year, the starting point guard was Dallas Leake. I backed up Dallas while sharing time with Tony Jones at the two guard position. Dallas was a phenomenal passer and had a lot of assists. As a shooter he didn't have a lot of range, but he was adept at scoring on close-in leaning shots or drawing fouls. Tony was more muscular than Dallas, but he was not as good a passer or penetrator. He was a good shooter from the outside.

In that year the Berea community's enthusiasm for the team escalated significantly. We were winning, especially at home, and Berea basketball became something that people really looked forward to. Almost every game we played was at Seabury was a sellout. I enjoyed playing there

Cluster Howard: "Hard-nosed and aggressive"

because of the intimate atmosphere. The fans would pat me on the leg when I took the ball out on the side.

We suffered a tough road loss to Covenant College down in Lookout Mountain, Georgia, when one of their players threw up a shot from mid-court at the last second to beat us 106 to 105. That was one of just eight games we lost that year. Unfortunately, four of those losses were to Pikeville College.

Pikeville had better talent than we did. They were quicker, shot the ball better, and had a stronger bench. Wayne Martin, their coach, had recruited some very good players out of Lexington and had also obtained a couple of transfers. The team traveled around in a nice bus, and rumor had it that the school was spending a lot of money on them. The third time we played them was in their building in the finals of the KIAC tournament. The game went right down to the wire before we lost. It was played on a Thursday, and then we had to turn around and go back to Pikeville Monday and play them again in the NAIA District 32 playoffs. In that game they beat us decisively.

After Dallas and Tony graduated our team looked a lot different. In my senior year our best players were inside people: Charlie Turner and four freshmen, Arno Norwell, Bill Nichols, Craig Jefferson, and Ed Flynn. Coach moved Ed out to be a kind of guard, but it was really a one-four alignment, one guard and four men around the basket. I was the guard. The difficulty for me was the pressure of having to handle the ball almost all the time. There wasn't anybody on the floor who could give me any relief. But I had no trouble learning the system. It wasn't complex, and that was part of the reason we ran it so effectively.

We did a lot of pick and roll. Arno set very good picks. He was good at positioning his body, and he became one of the country's best rebounders and a pretty good scorer as well.

Bill was quick, athletic, and a good jumper. He shot extremely well and had good range. Craig could also shoot, and he took good shots. Ed was a tenacious defensive player who got a lot of steals. He was also a good rebounder.

The two primary people who relieved me at the guard position were Tracy Thompson and James Burchell. Tracy was an intelligent player, and of the two, he was the better ballhandler and passer. James was the better scorer. James came to Berea from Sue Bennett College. He was a solid, loyal individual and an excellent student, always between a 3.5 and a 4.0.

We had extraordinarily good talent for a nonscholarship school. In my opinion we were a Top Twenty-caliber team in the NAIA. We played against Georgetown and Cumberland and Campbellsville and Pikeville and defeated all those teams to win the conference and then the conference tournament. We were in better condition than our opponents and probably had better teamwork.

That year we beat finally Pikeville, first in their building and then at Seabury. The game at Seabury was more difficult for us. Pikeville held the ball and led most of the game, but we came back at the end and won 52 to 49.

In the finals of the KIAC tournament I had an extremely good game against Cumberland. I scored twelve points and had quite a few assists, and we won in overtime. Cumberland had a fine team. They had both height and quickness.

After we beat Union in the District 32 tournament we met Cumberland again in Lexington. The gymnasium was full. A lot of fans from Berea came to the game. We played well, but we had trouble with one of their guards, Larry Gorman. I guarded Gorman, but in the second half he was just unconscious with his shooting. Ed Flynn and I switched off toward the end of the game, but Gorman was still scoring with Ed on him.

With less than a minute to play we were up by one. I had the ball, but Gorman made a clean steal at midcourt. He came in behind me and pulled the ball back. I fouled him as he was going in for a layup. He made both free throws to put Cumberland ahead by one. I got the ball again and dribbled it the length of the floor before throwing it to Bill Nichols on the right side. Bill made a beautiful half-turnaround shot from about fifteen feet. We were up by one again with about four seconds to go.

Cumberland threw the ball in to Gorman. He took a couple of dribbles to midcourt and threw up a shot. Bill and I were both in the area, but neither one of us was very close to him. The ball went over the backboard as time expired, but the official called a foul on Bill with no time left on the clock. Gorman had had no chance of making a shot, and no one really touched him. But everyone fell down trying to get out of each other's way, and to the official it may have looked like a foul. At any rate, Gorman made both his free throws to beat us.

We had defeated Cumberland three times that year. They were good, but we were better. It was awful to lose that game after we'd worked so hard to become the great team that we were. I've looked at the teams Berea has had over the years, and I believe that our 1977-78 team was the best of them all.

Coach Wierwille was distraught and didn't say a whole lot. But he told us that we had to display a good attitude, win or lose.

I always appreciated the job that Coach Wierwille did. He believed in hard work. Coach Wierwille was an autocratic coach, but although I sometimes disagreed with him I accepted that. I understood that his goal was to win, and he believed the way to win was to formulate teamwork. He wanted to make his players the best they could be.

I graduated in December 1978, and right at that time the coaching job opened up at Lees. Paul Davison had decided to resign, so I started coaching the team in the middle of the year. I coached at Lees for sixteen years while teaching almost full-time and serving as athletic director.

One thing I learned from Coach Wierwille that I tried to emulate was organization. That was his greatest strength. At Berea everything was organized. When we came to practice we knew exactly what we were going to be doing. We had specific plans for specific games. We knew what defense we were going to play and what we would try to do offensively. As a coach I tried to be structured, too. If you're that way, your players respect you more.

Our record during my tenure was 303 victories and 156 losses. We played in one national tournament and thirteen regional playoffs. We had a lot of success without giving full scholarships.

We had several players go to OVC schools like Morehead State or Murray State. We had a few players who went to Berea. Evans Mitchell, one of the first players I had, played at Berea. Another was Tim Shelton. We had others who could have helped Coach Wierwille, but Berea couldn't recruit them because they didn't qualify academically or financially.

In 1995 I took the job of Dean of Student Affairs for Lees College. Then when we merged with the UK system I became Dean of Student Life. That's my present position. What I enjoy most about this job is helping students who have behavioral or other problems. By talking with them and helping them to be more structured, I've helped a lot of them stay in school. That's very rewarding.

I'm still athletic director, but I've relinquished my coaching duties. I haven't missed coaching as much as I thought I would. What I miss most is the camaraderie that a coach establishes with his players as he gets to know them. I also miss hearing the many compliments a successful coach receives. In my job as Dean of Student Life I don't get many positive comments because all I deal with is problems: discipline problems, parking problems, any and all student problems.

Although the job is doable, the constant struggling with problems burns out deans of students. Any person in this field will tell you that. If you're a successful coach you get accolades. People say nice things to you. You get immediate gratification when your players improve or when they get a degree and get a job. The sort of job I have now doesn't give you that. It's a five- or six-year job, and my fourth year is coming up. Eventually I'll have to do something else.

I'm forty-one. By the time I'm forty-five I'll probably leave so I can coach again someplace. I'd like to coach at a school like Berea, a private school that has some academic standards. Players at those schools are easier to coach because they're academically oriented. They're not looking ahead to a pro career. At a bigger school, a Division I school, I'd make a lot more money, but that doesn't tempt me. Besides, to get a job like that I'd probably have to work as an assistant for awhile.

I had a reputation as a coach who put academics first. If one of my players wasn't going to class, I wouldn't take him on a trip, no matter how talented he was. That was the Berea in me. Many people who graduated from other colleges don't value education as much as I do.

July 8, 1998

Arno Norwell   1975-79

I grew up in the Mount Lookout area of Cincinnati, Ohio. In my neighborhood the thing to do was to go out and play some type of athletic sport. If it wasn't whiffle ball, it was softball. If it wasn't tackle football, it was touch football. We always had some kind of athletics going on. Back in the sixties when television wasn't as big, athletics was a driving force.

I'm six-nine. While I was attending Withrow High School I received recruiting information from several small colleges, mostly in Ohio and Indiana. Coach Wierwille contacted my high school coach and said that he was interested in me making a visit to see what Berea College was about. So early in the spring of 1975 I came down. I really liked the beautiful campus, and I was treated very, very well. The personal touch, the individual attention, was the difference between me coming to Berea College and going to another place. All the people I met acted as if they wanted me to come, and that made my decision easy.

As a freshman I played just a little bit, coming off the bench, until Charlie Turner, our regular center, fractured a bone in his wrist. That gave me an opportunity to enter the starting lineup, and I was a starter from that point on.

Every area of my game improved at Berea. I learned how to be an inside player, whereas in high school I was more of a shooter from outside. My ballhandling skills also developed. In our practices everybody did ballhandling drills. Most important of all, I learned to be aggressive. The biggest difference between high school and

Arno Norwell

college basketball is the level of physical play.

Early in my career I had problems with twisted ankles, which would sometimes cause me to miss games. I also had my nose broken in a game at Cumberland, a big rival of ours. It was a heated game, a very tight game. I took an inbounds pass and their center, Steve Banks, came over and pushed his hands into my nose. I was bleeding and my eyes were watering, so I had to leave the floor. I was awarded two free throws, but somebody else had to shoot them.

Fortunately the doctor got my nose straightened out, and I didn't have to wear anything to protect it. I could practice as usual and didn't have to miss any games. I might have babied it a little for a week or so, but the incident didn't leave anything permanent in my mind.

Ed Flynn, Bill Nichols, Craig Jefferson, and I arrived in 1975. The four of us averaged about six-six in height, and we all got to play quite a bit. Coach could see that we clicked very well together, so we'd often be on the floor at the same time with just one guard in the lineup. Ed could handle the guard position too. He was a very good ballhandler and had quite a few assists.

Our teams were very strong rebounding teams. We had size, of course, but we also had aggressive players who would go after rebounds. Bill, for instance, was a good rebounder as well as a good shooter.

Bill could score from anywhere. At one time he held the record for most points at Berea College, and he'd probably still hold the record if we'd had the three-point line back then. Craig was also a good shooter and a good ballhandler. Craig was very even-tempered, a guy who got along well with everybody. His manner added a lot to the chemistry of the team.

Cluster Howard was a hard-nosed point guard. Cluster was a great communicator. He was very well-liked and fit in well. He knew his role: to bring the ball up, be the feeder, get the ball to people in the right position. Tracy Thompson was our next point guard and did the same sort of thing, handle the offense out front and get people organized so we could get into our offense.

Steve Ridder joined the team when I was a junior. You talk about a good assist man, he really could dish the ball out. Steve was a great individual. I could tell that he was going to be a leader. He got along very well with people. He was the type of person who people would go to, would look up to.

We were a group that got along real well. We liked to joke. There was always laughter in the locker room. I can't remember specific things, but we would have a good time. We meshed very well on the floor. We were all competitive. If you want to win you've got to have some competitive spirit, and everybody on the team had that. Those factors, and the guidance of Coach Wierwille, were the keys to our success.

All the KIAC schools were so competitive at that time. Whether we played Georgetown, Cumberland, Union, Campbellsville, or Transylvania, it was a dogfight every night. The intensity made every game a special event. We didn't go into any game thinking, "Hey, we want to knock this team off by twenty points." The games always went down to the wire.

One game that was especially memorable for me was one we played at Transylvania. We were down the whole game. With ten minutes to go we were probably down twenty, and we came back and won. What made it special was doing it in a game that was broadcast on television throughout Kentucky.

I loved home games because it was a packed house very night. It was intimate. Everybody was on top of us. They were so close, we could hear the screams. That made such a big difference. Our home crowd was a sixth man, no doubt about it. They helped us win many a game. That's probably my fondest memory, the closeness of the fans.

We just missed going to Kansas City in both my junior and senior years. Losing to Cumberland in Lexington in 1978 was heartbreaking. With seconds to go a Cumberland player was taking a near-midcourt shot, and there was a foul called. It always makes me wonder. I'm not the type of person who wants to bring up the officiating because it sounds like sour grapes, but I had a question about that game. If our guy came across and hit their guy, okay, there would be no qualms about it, the foul was made. But I did not see anything that would indicate a foul there.

Arno Norwell: "As good a small-college center as there was in America"

To lose the game like that made it all the more hard to take. Here we were on the edge of going to Kansas City, with Cumberland taking a desperation shot which went nowhere near the goal, and then it was taken away from us in one second. I don't know if anything was said in our locker room. Our season was over, and there was just stunned silence.

Against Kentucky State the following year our destiny was in our hands, and we didn't take care of it. That's all that can be said. We had the game won, but we didn't take care of the ball in the last two or three minutes of crunch time. I give Kentucky State credit. They hit every shot. If we turned it over, they got the ball back and hit the shot. They came back and won it.

I've told Coach Wierwille that he didn't know when he was recruiting me that he was going to have a lifetime project on his hands. Coach and I are very close. To this day we do things together. He helps me if I have to call him for advice. I owe a lot of my success to him.

Coach made a big impact on my life. During my freshman year my father passed away, so I was basically on my own because my mother had died about ten years previously. Coach gave me a lot of direction in my life, got me focused on what I needed to do and how to get myself on a career track. He took a personal interest in me, in my grades, in what my plans were.

But Coach worked with everybody. He tried to improve everybody. He cares about his players. That's evident in the number of students who come into the program who graduate. And that caring is not just for four years. In my case it's been twenty years.

Coach Wierwille runs a class program. Any team coming into Seabury Gym can see that the little things get done. He makes what is not a very large budget go a long way. He's very organized. He knows what he wants to accomplish in his practices. And he's a good disciplinarian, very fair. I think all those qualities make him successful.

I could have been a much better student than I was. I liked to have a little fun. But I did enough to get by.

I was a physical education major. Growing up and doing all the athletic things with my brothers and sisters and all the kids in the neighborhood, I knew that I wanted to be a physical education teacher and a coach someday. All my coaches, in grade school, junior high school, high school, and college, were very nurturing. They taught me a lot. They were the most influential people in my life. I'm glad that athletics was there to give me an avenue to fulfill my goals.

My first labor assignment was as a janitor in Seabury Gym, sweeping floors, mopping floors, general cleanup. When I came back an extra semester as a senior to do my student teaching, I helped Coach Wierwille with the junior varsity team. So I started out as a custodian and moved up to teaching assistant, which gave me some valuable experience.

After I was certified I spent one year at Berea Community School before moving into the Madison County system. I've been at Foley Middle School for seventeen years.

After coaching for fourteen years I found I wasn't enjoying it as much. I thought I wanted my life to go in a different direction, so I resigned coaching and decided to work on a certificate in administration. It so happened that as I finished it that the assistant principal's position came open at Foley Middle School, and I was lucky enough to be selected for it.

I love it. Every day is different and there's never a dull moment. I like helping kids, and I like helping teachers.

Middle school was not my goal when I started. When I was young I was simply looking for a job. Initially I was hired as an elementary PE teacher, then I went over to Foley to coach. When I got there I found that I really enjoyed the kids. They have a high energy level, and they're good people to work with. Of course, I heard the horror stories. People asked, "Why do you want to work at a middle school? It's a time of turmoil for kids." That's true, but I find that to be exciting. I can make more of an impression on them, teach them the right things.

June 16, 1998

Ed Flynn   1975-79

I believe that Coach Wierwille has tapes of most of our games. I'd like to watch them to see if my memories of how things were are anywhere close to reality. What was my role on the team? If Coach had a defined role in mind for me, he had a tough time getting the concept through to me! I played some defense and got some rebounds and scored some baskets, but generally I went where my mood and circumstance took me. I had free rein, and I don't think any other other coach in the country would have given me that kind of freedom. The man was awfully good to me.

I grew up in a rural community in Anderson County, Kentucky. My family had eleven acres and a couple of cows and horses and some tobacco. It wasn't really a farm, but without having any specific plans I made up my mind to go to college and study agriculture. My high school basketball coach knew I didn't want to leave Kentucky, so he set up a meeting for me with Coach Wierwille at Berea.

The meeting went well. Coach Wierwille impressed me. When he talked with me his words were direct, and he looked me right in the eye. He reminded me of my older brothers.

I enrolled at Berea and liked it. Everyone worked at Berea. I don't think anybody was impoverished, but none of us had money to throw around. We were all on a budget. We didn't have hundred-dollar tennis shoes, just whatever we could get on our feet.

At Berea there was a camaraderie and a sense of unity. It was a kind of closed community. We stayed on campus with each other for company. We weren't sequestered, but we were probably closer than students at other schools. There weren't many cars around, so we didn't have to worry about running all over the place. There were no fraternities. We all knew each other and did things together, like Mountain Day.

Coach Wierwille didn't let any trash hang around. He did things first-class and demanded that we do things first-class, from how we dressed on our way to the game to how we behaved on the court. He didn't want us to embarrass ourselves or the school. My teammates were a pretty good bunch of guys, and I don't remember anyone getting much out of line.

We had an old gym, but Coach had it painted. He made sure it was the best-kept facility in the conference. Our example inspired some of the other colleges to upgrade themselves. Cumberland did a major upgrade, and so did Georgetown.

You hear about coaches today who cuss out their players or physically abuse them. I never heard Coach Wierwille say a stronger word than "ass," as in "get your ass in gear." He wouldn't stand for harsher language. As far as getting physical, he'd kick a wall or beat up a locker, yes, but I never saw him lay a finger on a student. I have tremendous respect for him.

To begin my freshman season we made a swing through Tennessee. We were a pretty young team. Coach had and me and another freshman, Bill Nichols, starting. Charlie Turner, a senior, was our leader. He told us we could beat our first opponent, Tennessee Temple. We didn't, but then we turned around and defeated Covenant College. Charlie was one of those guys who didn't jump very well or run very fast, but he was always at the right place at the right time. He knew how to get the ball in a crowd. I guess being mature helped Charlie, but he simply had good hands and instincts.

When Charlie got hurt late in the year, Arno Norwell, a freshman, replaced him. A fourth freshman, Craig Jefferson, was getting a lot of minutes. Our main guard was junior Dallas Leake. Dallas was something else. He was short and slow, but they couldn't stop him. If Dallas didn't have an open shot, he would pass it to somebody else for an easy basket. Had Dallas been with us all four years, we would have been even tougher to beat.

I was close to Ron Rodgers. I think he came from Casey County High School, where he was the main player on his team. We had no room for Ron inside, and he had to make the transition from high school center to college guard. That was very tough. He played just two years.

We had a well-rounded team. Arno was a big presence in the middle and took care of business under there. Bill had a scorer's mentality: for him there never was a bad shot. He'd get twenty a night. Craig could also score. I didn't have to worry about concentrating on any one thing.

Arno was my roommate, and he was like a brother to me. He was a really intelligent guy and a gentle soul off the court. Arno never had any-

thing bad to say about anybody; he'd either say something good or he wouldn't say anything. He remembered the name and face of each new person he met. He was a good student, worked hard at it, and did well in his classes.

Arno developed as a player. At six-nine he may have weighed 180 pounds when he came to Berea. He put on a lot of weight over the four years, and by the time he graduated he was as good a small-college center as there was in America. Good hands, good nose for the ball, and a real competitor.

Craig's shot was a line drive jumper that you're not supposed to be able to hit, but he was accurate with it. He didn't say a whole lot, but he was

Ed Flynn: "He got the job done"

effective. Even coming off the bench, as he did for part of our first year, Craig always got his points and rebounds.

Craig had great hands. He was a fine defensive player. He would hang around after we scored and get a couple of steals a game when our opponent threw the ball in. In our final game that first year Kentucky State was beating us badly until Craig started stealing the ball for some easy baskets. That turned the game around. Late in the second half we built up a big lead ourselves, and he was the main reason for it, but ultimately we lost.

When Bill and Arno and Craig and I were freshman and sophomores we weren't the best team out there, but I think we proved that we were as good as anybody except Pikeville. Pikeville was loaded. We couldn't beat them, although we came close a couple of times. Their players were older and stronger and better. But after the coal boom money dried up down there, so did the team.

By our junior year we could play with anybody in the country. We lost a tough game to a good team, Cumberland, to keep us out of the national tournament. We played well in that game, and I would like to have had the chance to go to Kansas City and see what would have happened. I don't think anyone was playing any better. That was our best team. We were a little stale when we were seniors.

In our junior year Cluster Howard replaced Dallas Leake in our lineup. Cluster had been a shooter in junior college, but we already had a shooter in Bill Nichols. Cluster was joining a team where all the roles were filled except point guard, the man who was supposed to get the ball up the court and into somebody's hands. That was out of character for Cluster because he wasn't a true point guard. He would have made a better second guard, but he worked hard to adjust and helped us. Cluster was succeeded by Tracy Thompson and Steve Ridder, who were both steady ballhandlers.

I got married over Christmas break my junior year. She was a Berea College student from North Carolina, Mary Richards. Ron Rodgers had introduced us. We were married on December 23, 1977, between our last pre-holiday game and our first post-holiday practice. I'm not sure if Coach approved, but he never interfered. As a matter of fact, he helped find her a job at Berea Community School.

I majored in agriculture as I'd intended. Pat Shugars was my first adviser. He was like a father to me that first year. He sat me down and talked to me a couple of times when I needed it.

I worked at various ag-related jobs. I worked in the greenhouse. I watered and weeded. I helped with the crops like asparagus and broccoli that we harvested and sold to Boone Tavern. I did a lot of mowing in the fruit orchards. I plowed and maintained the community gardens, where people could rent individual plots.

I was a junior in college before I learned how to study. I took a chemistry class with Dr Thomas Beebe. It was conducted according to the Keller method. The teacher didn't lecture, and the students didn't proceed at the same pace. You were given a book, you read it, you talked to a tutor if you needed help, and when you thought you were ready to be tested, you took the test. Well, I was halfway through the term waiting on somebody to tell me to read this or do that before it finally dawned on me what was going on.

The way that class was taught made a real impact on me. The "here it is, get it or don't" approach forced me to pursue knowledge actively. I had several talks with Dr Beebe and began to realize that being fed the material you're supposed to learn is not the same as learning the material. I hadn't been a good student. I'd relied on rote memory to absorb just enough to get through. After this experience, things started to click for me in the classroom.

After I graduated I joined the construction business that my brothers had started in Louisville, Flynn Brothers Contracting. I'm with the paving part of the company. I'm more or less a freelance troubleshooter, just like I was when I was playing basketball. I attend to whatever needs to be taken care of in the field.

July 15, 1998

Craig Jefferson (1)   1975-79

I grew up in North Middletown, near Paris, Kentucky, and I went to Bourbon County High School, where I played basketball and ran track. In the summertime after I graduated I went to a basketball tryout at Lees Junior College. They had a lot of ballplayers come down there. The coach at Lees thought I needed to be at Berea College, for academics and basketball too, I guess. He knew Coach Wierwille and told him, "This is a good guy, and you should take a look at him." Coach Wierwille got in contact with me, and I came up to Berea College. I had a cousin, William Carter, who had gone to Berea.

Two standout players at Berea when I came were Dallas Leake and Tony Jones. They were guards, and both were good shooters. Dallas was heady. He was small, but real quick. Tony was strong, and a good shooter outside.

I probably could have started my sophomore year, but Coach liked me coming off the bench as the sixth man. He said I brought more spark. Then he experimented my junior year with four big men and one guard, and it went real well. They called us the Big Four: Arno Norwell, Ed Flynn, Bill Nichols, and myself. Arno was six-nine, Ed six-five, Bill six-four, and I was six-four. Cluster Howard was the guard one year, and then Tracy Thompson.

In us Coach Wierwille had four big guys who could all start. One practice he put us in, and we did pretty good playing as a team. We had come in together and knew each other. I think Coach had it in the back of his mind that it would work. It did. All four of us are in the 1000 point club and the 500 rebounds club.

I usually matched up with the best forward, and Bill or Ed would match up with the other guard. Arno was the center. Other teams had trouble rebounding with us. We could all post up, we all ran down the floor pretty well, and we were good shooters. We could go inside

Craig Jefferson: "Our teams were fun to watch"

with it or kick it out. It was a hard matchup for a team. A lot of teams tried to zone us.

Bill Nichols was probably my best friend on the team. We were real close. Bill was a good shooter from long range. Everybody thought he was mean, but he had a joking streak about him. He'd laugh in the locker room. One day we were playing a rival, Transylvania or somebody, at home. Coach came in and gave us our assignments. I was a pretty good defensive player, so Coach would put me on a pretty good offensive player. Coach would say, "You got him," but Bill would sit behind me and chuckle. When Coach went out of the room for an interview, Bill went up to the chalkboard and imitated him. He got us all loose. He was a character, a jokester, a laid-back guy. He kept everybody in stitches.

Ed Flynn was the Dennis Rodman or Charles Barkley for our team. He did the dirty work. He got the job done. When we needed somebody to clamp down on somebody, he would do that, or rebound. He would get in their face. Ed was nice off the floor, but in game situations it was time for business with him. Ed could bring the ball up, could handle the ball real well.

When Arno Norwell first came in, he couldn't walk and chew gum at the same time. But when he left, he was a player. He could rebound, he could score, he could do about anything. He was a good big man.

Arno got his nose broke, it might have been his sophomore year. He played with that broken nose, and after that his demeanor changed. He just went to war. He had been timid, but after that when we needed a rebound or a score, he took over.

In high school I was a center, playing with my back to the basket, but at Berea I was a forward and could go out on the floor more. I rebounded well. I was a quick leaper off the floor, that first jump. I had good hands and passing ability, and I could score, too. I could shoot a ten or fifteen foot jumper pretty well. I was the leading field goal percentage shooter, just under sixty percent. I had the school record until Dester Terry broke it.

I used a line drive shot. I shot it straight, but it would go in. We had a lot of mismatches underneath, so we got good shots. We were unselfish and looked for each other. We averaged eighty-some points per game.

We had good guard play. Cluster Howard was hard-nosed and aggressive. He got after people. Cluster was a good leader on the floor for us. He could penetrate and shoot, but he could also distribute the ball real well. We were all down front, so he had to distribute the ball. Tracy Thompson was another good leader and good distributor. Tracy could penetrate, too, and he had a good jump shot. He could score when he was open, and he was a good free throw shooter.

Later Steve Ridder came in. He was a ballhandler. He dribbled high, but nobody could get the ball away from him. He was a great passer, too. Steve was a tall guard. You see the five-nine guards, but he was six-four and could handle the ball.

Cumberland was probably the rival. They were real talented and matched up with us well. When we played them it was just like a war. We went down there once when they were ranked ninetenth in the nation, and we beat them. Tracy got in foul trouble. Coach brought Steve in. We pumped him up. I went up to Steve and grabbed him and said, "Get in and play defense." He gave us a real spark.

Beating Cumberland at Berea in the KIAC tournament, that's a great memory. It was hot in Seabury, a lot of people. We were ready to play, and they were kind of shocked at us. We beat them pretty good.

Our teams were fun to watch, a real good show. We had a great coach and played real hard. Loved the game, all of us did. We respected and cared for each other. And Old Seabury was the best place to play basketball. Hot, with the fans right on the floor. We didn't have to warm up, because once we hit the floor we were already sweating. There was standing room only, upstairs, downstairs. We had great support from the students and the townspeople.

The road trips were fun, too. They were more relaxed, more laid-back than they are now. For a while, Coach even let us take our girlfriends on the bus with us. Our group was mature enough to know that we were there for one purpose, to play hard and win a ballgame.

Play hard, that was Coach's main thing. Everything else would take care of itself if we'd just play hard out there. Nothing cheap, no cheap shots, but play hard and play intense and see what happens.

Coach ran hard practices that got us ready for the next game, or at the first of the year developed our fundamentals. Nothing really extravagant, just ballhandling, passing, rebounding. He loved to work on all that. Bear down defensively, block out, go to the boards strong, take it to the hole hard, look for your teammates. He wouldn't center on just one person, but on the whole team.

He was a tough coach, and he was The Coach. We looked up to him and tried to do what he said. He was intense, and that helped us in our play on the floor. We were a good defensive team, we would go to the boards. Coach was always thinking about the game, in his office or at home. He implemented the three-two zone for us, although we played a two-three a lot, too.

Our team was very much a family. Coach would take up for all of us. One time we were playing Scotty Baesler and some people over at Ashland Oil or Marathon Oil in a preseason game. They were big, rough. Bill and I got in a shoving match with one of them, and Coach came out there and got in the middle of it. That guy was six-eight, six-nine, but Coach was standing up for his players. He said, "I'll run you out of here!" The funny thing, Bill was right behind Coach, putting up his dukes, like "I got my man, I got the coach out here now!" Bill got brave when Coach came out there! We always talk about that.

I remember my first game. We went to Tennessee Temple, and they beat us pretty handily. They were real good, and we knew they would be coming up to Berea for Homecoming. That's when we really turned on. We beat them at Berea and played well after that.

But we never did make it to the national tournament. We got beat my senior year by Kentucky State, and my junior year by Cumberland. In that game we were up 74-73 with six seconds, and they called a foul with one second to go. I think the two refs who reffed that game never did ref again. Nichols hit a baseline jumper with six seconds left. Cumberland took it out and tried to run it up, and the refs called a foul. They said Bill Nichols fouled Larry Gorman at halfcourt, but looking at the film, he didn't touch the guy. Gorman went up one-and-one and won the ballgame.

Craig Jefferson: "He always got his points and rebounds"

Everybody was just stunned, speechless. There was nothing we could do or say. It was a shocking loss. We beat Cumberland three times, but we played them four. That's what hurt. It's hard to beat a team four times in a row in one season. It should have been a win for us, and we should have been in the national tournament.

We were favored to go to the nationals in both years, but one thing hurt us. We'd earned home court advantage at tournament time, but we had to play on a neutral floor because Seabury was not big enough, not long enough. We knew we would have won if we were allowed to play at Seabury.

Gorman was one of the best players I played against. Pikeville had two tough players in Tyrone Dunn and Fred Walker. I think they were from Lexington. We never did beat Pikeville until my junior year. They were always tough. Wayne Martin coached them.

One especially memorable game was Transy in 1978. I guess they thought they could beat us, so they played us on TV that year. It might have been the first game that they put on TV. They had a great team, and they were leading by fourteen at halftime. Coach came in and chewed us out. We went out and were a totally different team in the second half and beat them. That was a great feeling. Seeing the headline the next day in the *Lexington Herald-Leader* felt real good.

Coach taught me a lot. He taught me to look people straight in the eye when they shook my hand. He taught me not to be late for meetings for anything. On our away trips we would always to get to the bus five or ten minutes early, or he would leave us. That stuck with me, so I'm never late for anything. I'm always early.

I was a physical education major. Berea's tough, but I could have done better, studied harder. I didn't take my studies seriously at first. But the teachers were good, and we had small classes, not those big lectures, so we got that one-on-one attention. That was good right there. With classes and working and convocations, we had to learn how to budget our time, and I did.

I was happy at Berea. I was raised in the country, and at Berea I was around more people, different cultures and different things, learning about other things in the world. Berea gave me good friends, people I still talk to now.

I lived in Dana, and I was the janitor there. Ed FitzGerald was a good influence on me. He was the dorm director. He'd come up to you and talk to you, tell you different things, keep you positive.

After I graduated I went to Charleston, West Virginia, and managed some shoe stores up there. Then I came back to Berea to work for Berea College in sales, in printing. I knew Owen Presley, who was in business in Berea, and he said it was a good opportunity. They did all the printing on campus, but they wanted to do commercial printing, so they needed a salesperson. Mitchell Tolle was the manager then, and he hired me to get business outside of Berea, in Lexington. We did a lot of work for UK and different places. I like sales, and I did that for a long time.

May 5, 1998

Bill Nichols   1975-79

The main thing I got out of Berea was discipline. I could have gone somewhere else to get a degree or somewhere else to play ball, but I doubt if I would have got the same type of discipline I got at Berea, or met the same type of people. I cherish that. I still think about Berea. I ask myself, "If I had a chance to do it all over again, would I go to Berea?" I always say yes. Berea was good to me.

Wherever you are, somebody's heard about Berea College. The first thing that comes out of their mouth is, "Oh, that's the college where you have to work your way through." People think that if a guy can work his way through college and pay back his tuition that way, he has to be a pretty decent person to accomplish that, because most people couldn't do it.

I played high school ball in Kentucky. I heard about Berea from Mutt Varney, the Scott County High School coach. I went to Georgetown High School, and they were our big rivals. Mutt was a Berea graduate, and he introduced me to Berea.

I don't know if you'd call it luck or fate or what, but Coach Wierwille had an outstanding recruiting year in 1975-76, when the Big Four came in. We had some size and got some good guard play, and we started winning games. That opened a lot of eyes. Berea started to make a name for itself.

I knew Craig Jefferson before we were classmates at Berea. When he played at Bourbon County High School we met on the floor a couple of times. I didn't know Craig was planning to go to Berea. One day we just happened to meet over in the Alumni Building. We got to know each other really well. The Big Four all got along, no problems whatever.

Craig was a good shooter. He shot close to sixty percent throughout his career. If you needed a loose ball or a defensive stop, Craig was there. Ed Flynn was probably the most valuable player on the team. He and Craig were alike in a lot of ways. Ed would come up with a big steal, a big block. We always looked up to Ed as the captain. He calmed everything down when things got out of control. Arno Norwell was a heck of a rebounder, a big man

Bill Nichols: "He could score from anywhere"

in the middle.

We all teased each other, especially Craig and I. In the locker room before the games Coach Wierwille would give us our defensive assignments, and he always seemed to put Craig on the biggest, meanest, toughest guy out there. I'd look at Craig and grin a little bit, and he would look at me as if to say, "What are you laughing at?" We got a kick out of that. Arno kept it going. He'd do some things I shouldn't say! Ed would laugh and cut up, but not as much as the rest of us.

I'm six-four. My strong point was shooting. I liked to shoot the ball and developed a pretty decent jump shot, one that was comfortable for me. The weakest part of my game was ballhandling. I was an okay ballhandler, but I needed to work on it. How would I rate myself as a defensive player? On a scale of one to ten, I'd say a seven.

People talk about the Big Four, but throughout my years at Berea the guard position was probably the strongest of all the positions on the floor. Dallas Leake was our first floor general. We called him the Little Man, but if he was out there, something was going to happen. When we ran a fast break with Dallas in the game, he would get us the ball where we needed it to score. He was a heck of a passer. If you weren't ready, Dallas would hit you in the head with the ball.

Cluster Howard took over at point guard after Dallas graduated. Cluster was bigger than Dallas and a little stronger. He wasn't the ball handler Dallas was, but he was a good solid player. He didn't make many turnovers. With his size he could post up some of the smaller guards, and that was a big asset to us. Cluster was succeeded by a trio of steady guards, Tracy Thompson, Glen Drury, and Steve Ridder. Glen wasn't real flashy, just a hard-nosed guy to have on the floor. Steve was a wonderful passer. It seemed like he had eyes in the back of his head.

Coach Wierwille was a big, impressive guy, real stern. He got everybody to listen to him. What talent we had, he got the most out of it. He and I got along well. I respected him. We always had a good relationship.

The team I wanted to beat the most was Cumberland College. My freshman year, I think they were nationally ranked. We knew we had our work cut out for us when we went down there to play them. Everybody was a little nervous about it. They beat us, but not by much, and when we beat them at home a week later we gained a lot of respect from all the teams around. I loved beating those guys more than anything. They had a whole lot of talent and played hard, but we weren't going to back down. We tried to meet that challenge. When you play against people who are good, you try to rise to the occasion. After we beat them that first time, we wanted to play them all the time.

I always seemed to play well in the Cumberland games, both home and away. But the one game that stands out most for me personally was a game at Transylvania. We were down by a point with five or six seconds left on the clock. The play was designed for me to take a shot out of the corner, which was where I liked to shoot from. I got a good screen from either Ed or Arno and shot it from the corner. It seemed like the ball was in the air for five whole seconds, and then it went in. We won by a point.

In both my junior and senior years we were just one play away from going to the nationals, against Cumberland College my junior year and the following year against Kentucky State. We took both teams right down to the wire but couldn't get over that hump. To get so close, that was the hard part, the frustrating part. I've never been able to get that out of my mind.

Two twins refereed that Cumberland game. I can't remember their names. They made a call on me on the last play. They said I fouled Larry Gorman. There's no way it was the right call. I wasn't even within touching distance. Larry Gorman went to the free throw line and hit both shots, and we lost. There was quite a raucous scene. I don't think those two ever reffed one of our games again. To this day I think about it. It was something we all had to live with and go on.

For my labor assignment I was assigned to Seabury Gym, working under Elvin Combs. I took care of the balls, took care of the equipment, made sure everything was working, whatever needed to be done around the gym.

If it wasn't for Mr Combs, I don't know if I would have made it through school. I looked up to him. He was like a father away from home. When things weren't going so well I could talk to him. He called me Brother Bill. "Cheer up, Brother Bill, things will get better." Just little small talk, but every time I talked to him, I walked away feeling good.

My major was physical education. I could have worked a lot harder in the classroom. I didn't do as much studying as I should have, but I did go to class and listened in class. I got most of what I needed by listening. And I always turned in my work and did my assignments.

My health teacher was Mary Lou Pross, and I liked her a lot. She was a simple, down-to-earth person who seemed to be on my level.

I married a girl I met at Berea, Donna Calfee. The guys used to sit by the Alumni Building and check out all the girls when they first came in. I spotted her. She had rollers in her hair. I don't know what did it for me, but I said, "I'm going to go and talk to that girl." We hit it off.

Donna was from Radford, Virginia. After I graduated I went to Florida and worked in construction for three or four months, then found my way to Radford and married her. I got a job selling burial insurance, but that didn't work out too well.

I"m now employed by the Kollmorgen Corporation in Radford, working with epoxies and resins and different materials. We manufacture motor components. Our work is about seventy-five percent military. We do a lot of work for General Electric, Raytheon, Boeing. Remember the Gulf War? Our motor components were in those Patriot missiles.

Sometimes I go down to Radford University and play basketball with the college kids. I try to get in about three games a week. They're half my age, but I don't do too badly.

July 23, 1998

Tracy Thompson   1977-80

I've been working at Deroyal for fifteen years, and I'm president of the company now. We are a world-class manufacturer of medical products and a provider of information and systems and services to the health care community. We have 2500 employees, and there are many tough situations I get into where I have to do the right thing for 2500 people. There are days I walk out of here thinking about an individual I had to get on, or cutting

Tracy Thompson: "An intelligent player"

some things out or doing something in regard to performance. We've gone through those things as a company. But every day I tell myself that I've done the right thing for 2500 people. Coach Wierwille helped me with that.

A few years ago I called Coach Wierwille on Christmas night. I told him that I definitely wouldn't be doing what I was doing had I not attended Berea College and had a chance to play under him. I needed his discipline. I was your typical young guy going to school who didn't focus on academics as much as I should have. I needed somebody who was very powerful to keep me in line, and he did it. To this day I try to run my job like he did. He was such a class act.

The real reason I went to college was for the athletic side of it, initially. Coming out of high school I thought I wasn't finished playing basketball, and my goal was to continue to play basketball.

My family had a farm in Ewing, Virginia, a very small rural community. I grew up there until the fifth grade, when we moved to Richmond, Kentucky. I went back to Ewing to play at Thomas Walker High School during my junior and senior years. It was a small high school, graduating fifty-two from my class. I knew Coach Wierwille's family. He started talking to me about coming to Berea. My family lived in Richmond, and it was intriguing to me to be close to home so my parents could come to see me play.

I get emotional talking about Coach Wierwille because he did a lot for me as a young guy trying to mature in college. My mind was about 110 percent on basketball and about 50 percent on academics. Coach Wierwille had a remarkable impact on his players, not only from an athletic standpoint but academically. He got that in. He wasn't real obvious about it. He didn't sit you down and have a conversation with you about your grades. He just made sure everybody understood that more than basketball had to take place at Berea College.

Coach treated everybody fairly. He made the tough calls and stood behind them. When he told us what we were going to do, we did it, like it or not, and some people didn't like it. But he has great integrity. He's very honest. If he told you something was going to take place, it did.

He's done a lot for me. I modeled myself after him. My dad had a great influence on me, so I had two people, Coach Wierwille and my dad, who had big impacts on my life. Today when I have to do something with people, I do it right. I treat them fairly. I'm honest with them. I try to do everything by the book. Maybe I would have anyway, but it's nice to be able to reflect back and say, "How would Coach Wierwille have done that?"

Here's an example of what I'm talking about. I had a car at Berea College, and we weren't supposed to have cars. It was a little MG convertible. It sounds like a nice car, but it wasn't. It ran, but it was very old. It had Indiana tags on it. I used to park it on a hill outside of Dana dorm. I couldn't get the thing started unless I could could roll-start it, kick-start it. Well, every day they'd put a ticket on there, and I'd take that ticket and throw it away because the car had Indiana plates and I thought they'd never know it was mine. One day I left a book in there. They saw my name on it and went to Coach Wierwille and said, "This guy's got twenty-some tickets."

When I walked into practice Coach Wierwille met me at the door and said, "Son, as soon as practice is over, you're in my office." For the next two and a half hours I thought of everything I'd ever done wrong at Berea College. I thought, "Oh, what does he know?" I had the worst practice of my life, and as soon as it was over I walked into his office. I knew I was getting ready to catch it. He's a big guy, and he was up over that desk. He asked me about my car.

I told him the truth. "Yeah, Coach, I've got a car. It has Indiana plates. I've had it here."

He said, "Here's what you're going to do. You're going to pay every ticket. You're going to get the car off campus like you're supposed to. You're going to do the right thing."

I said, "Yes, sir." I paid the tickets and got the car off campus. I did exactly what I should have done in the first place.

Maybe that wasn't that much of a tough call, for him to say, "You're going to do the right thing." Just to give you another example, there was a time in my senior year when I didn't start. That broke my heart. I couldn't understand it, because I'd been a starter my entire junior year. In my first four or five games my senior year I did real well, but after that the team slipped a bit. Coach realized he needed to do some other things with that team, and the best decision was for me not to start, because there were better players.

Yes, as tough as that is for me to say because every young guy playing basketball thinks he's Michael Jordan, there were better players, and it was time for them to get some seasoning. Some of the younger guys had developed, and putting them into games was the right thing for Coach Wierwille to do. But it was a tough time for me, and I had some serious conversations with Coach about it. He told me exactly what was happening and why.

I was fine after that. I thought, "This guy's doing his job. He's doing what he has to do to get ready for the next year and the next year, and I'm going to do the best I can to help out." I actually ended up having a better last five or six games than earlier in the season, because I worked so hard to make sure that everybody was coming on and that I was competing in practice. Toward the end of the year I ended up starting again.

That was a tough thing. I had a great relationship with Coach Wierwille, so I think it was hard on him. But it was the right thing to do, and I told Coach that the other day when I came to Berea for a banquet. I was sitting in his office and he brought it up, because he hadn't talked about it much. I said, "You did the right thing. You did exactly what you needed to do."

"Well, that really bothered me."

I said, "It shouldn't bother you." Because there were some players who were better than I was, and he needed to make that move. It's easy for me to say that now, but it was not when I was twenty years old.

Some players he had to let go. In practice we'd run the lines and do the things that qualified us to compete, and some players could not do those things. We had a player one year, Ray Lakes. I think Ray was in his upper thirties, but he decided he was going to play college basketball. Ray was a good player, but you could definitely tell that he was a little beyond his prime. Coach Wierwille finally set Ray down and said, "You need to be my assistant coach." Here was an older man wanting to play with the right spirit and right attitude, but physically it was tough for him. Coach Wierwille let him down but made him his assistant coach. I thought, "What a great way to handle that!" Ray Lakes couldn't perform at the level Coach needed, but there were a lot of good things he had behind him in terms of coaching ability, so Coach made him his assistant. Ray Lakes went on to coach at a high school.

Coach Wierwille's greatest strength was in getting us ready. I don't think there's a coach in America who could have a more focused, disciplined, serious, practice than Coach Wierwille had. He made the practices as intense as the games. Most coaches don't accomplish that. That's another reason he's had a successful career. We didn't walk in there saying, "I can't wait to practice." Those practices were serious. When we walked into that building we had to have our heads on right. We had to be ready to try and perform and dedicate the entire two and a half hours to Coach Wierwille and Berea College basketball, not anything else. Coach not only demanded it, he got it. It was incredible. Every single day, 110 percent.

When I was in high school we'd shoot a jump shot, go and get the ball, walk back out, and shoot again. At Berea, we'd shoot that jump shot, run and get the ball, dribble back out, dribble into the shot, and shoot it, just like we would in a game. When we did passing drills, we didn't throw wild passes. We came down and did a two-handed chest pass or a bounce pass, and we did it fundamentally correct. Coach ran a real serious practice. It was very competitive, too. He kept that spirit going.

The practices were very structured. There wasn't a dead minute in those two and a half hours. We didn't come in and run a few drills and then take a break while he decided what we were going to do next. The practices were lined up just like something in the military.

The joy of victory: Tracy Thompson

That made it a little less fun sometimes, but the end result, what he was trying to accomplish, happened because of the way he conducted his practice sessions. They were tough, they were serious, they were needed.

I learned how serious during my freshman year. I'm six foot tall, and I walked in the gym and saw a lot of players who were taller and stronger, so I thought, "I'm going to outhustle everybody. I'll wear them out!" I was pretty quick.

We ran to the foul line and back, to halfcourt and back, to the other foul line and back, and to the end of the court and back. We ran eight of those with two other groups behind us, so we got a few minutes to rest between each eight. After about five I was leading my group every time, and I was feeling good about it. But after the fifth one I knew I was going to get sick. I slid out the door at the end of the old gym and got sick in the bushes. I didn't think anybody saw me. It only took about thirty seconds.

As soon as I got my composure I walked back in that side door, and sure enough Coach Wierwille was standing there. He looked at me and said, "Son, get back in line." I thought, "Boy, this guy's tough! It's going to be a tough situation here." At that particular moment I did not think, "This guy's going be a great mentor for me someday," although he turned out to be. I was just a young guy going beyond his limits to try to compete, but the next three years when we ran those eights I paced myself better, finished fine, and did not get sick.

I played guard. When I was a freshman I played only on the JV squad.

My sophomore year I started some on the varsity, and then started my entire junior year. During those two years we had four big guys, the Big Four. We ran what was called a double-low, with a lot of picking and rolling and that sort of thing. We didn't have a three-point line back then. The point guard's primary responsibility was to get the ball down the floor and then work the offense. The makeup of our team demanded that we run it with one point guard and the Big Four. That happened my sophomore and junior years.

The double-low was real simple. The point guard was above the top of the key and the other players lined up on each side of the goal down low. As the point guard, I could set a pick for either man on the side I was on, or I could rotate over and set a pick for one of the two on the other side. Sometimes we would rotate someone over and set a double screen for a good shooter. The shooter could shoot off to the right or the left. There was constant motion. If it didn't work, if I threw the ball out to someone on the wing and the play was broken, if he couldn't get a good shot, that man would dribble the ball up to the top of the key, and I would take a position down low. Just a constant rotation. The guard generally ended up back up front. It was a real simple plan, and if it was worked to perfection, which is what Coach taught us, we were going to get an open shot. We had to be patient. If it didn't happen the first time we just set up and ran it again.

If you do a pick fundamentally correct, somebody's going to be open. Most people don't do it. Most people sort of walk up, and you hope to run your man into him. Coach spent a lot of time teaching us exactly how to set a pick, and exactly what the offensive player is supposed to do and the player who's setting the pick is supposed to do, so they're working in conjunction against the one defensive person. We ran that double-low a lot when I was there. The opposition could study it, they could practice against it, but it was going to work if we did it right. Of course the game's changed a lot. You have the shot clock, you have the three-point line. So there's different strategy now.

We did every kind of defense. If we matched up well, we did a man-to-man. If we didn't match up well, we did a zone, two-three or one-three-one. We did some full-court pressing. We did quite a bit of pressing my junior year, because we had four tall guys who could get their man into a corner. That helped out a great deal.

All those things a coach has to have during a game, Coach Wierwille was fabulous at. He knew when we needed a timeout, when we needed to take a break. He knew when we needed to change an offense or defense. At halftimes he was great at depicting the situation during the first half and making some adjustments and getting us ready for the second half. He was very aggressive on the bench, very aggressive with the referees. When I played, eighteen years ago, he was much more aggressive than he is now. We did not have an assistant coach, and we needed one to help balance Coach a little bit. He could get so verbal and aggressive that it could rattle us sometimes.

To be the one guard was very demanding, and it was very exciting also.

The good thing about our team with the Big Four and the one guard was that everybody knew his role. I knew the ball was going to be in my hands most of the time. It was a comfortable position for me. All of the Big Four were very good athletes and handled the ball well also. I enjoyed the one-guard rotation.

When I came out of high school, I was a little, quick guard who shot the ball a lot. I averaged twenty-one points a game. When I got to Berea College, my role changed to more dish the ball out to the other players on the team. I had to adjust to that, get focused on getting the ball down low to our bigger players. I worked very hard on passing and improved there. I was good at some fundamental skills for a person in my position, like free throw shooting and things like that. Coach Wierwille was an incredible coach with fundamentals. For instance, when we came out to shoot layups, we didn't go in and flip them over our head. We ran, went off the right foot, shot with the correct hand, and banked it off the backboard. Coach was a real strict disciplinary-type person about fundamentals, and fundamentally I improved greatly after I got to Berea College.

The guard ahead of me was Cluster Howard, a very competitive, hard-nosed player with good leadership skills. He was terrific. Cluster was the most likeable, pleasant person, always in a good mood. He was very gregarious and got along well with everybody.

The four big guys all played a unique role in leadership. Bill Nichols was one of the best scorers in the history of the College, and he had a wonderful personality. Bill was very quiet and serious, but before the game started he made sure that everyone's head was on right. Craig Jefferson was more vocal, and he showed good leadership skills. Ed Flynn was on a mission every night to win those games. We all rallied around his attitude. Then there was one other guy who was not real vocal but fit in on the Big Four: Arno Norwell, the tallest of all our players. The spirit of our team my junior year was fabulous.

Steve Ridder was a guard a year younger than me. There was definitely a competitive environment with him and me, but I respected him because of his athletic ability and his seriousness about school. Steve really stood out. He was the most charismatic guy you'd ever meet, a motivational person who could charge you up. My senior year I was the captain of our team, and when I felt that we needed to rally the team together, Steve was one of the individuals I would go to to help support what we were trying to accomplish. After I graduated he became captain. I knew he was an individual who was going to make an impact somewhere beyond Berea College. He went on to coach, and he's having a tremendous career.

I enjoyed Steve's personality. He was a happy, well-balanced individual, and I had a lot of fun with him. Steve lived in my dorm, and we were always playing pranks on each other. One night I snuck in his room after he went to sleep and put peanut butter all around him, so if he rolled to the right or left it would be in his hair or in his face. A few hours later he got up and came in my room, angry. I said, "Look, buddy, don't yell at me! The guy that did it is Chris Freeman." Chris Freeman lived right between our rooms, and of course Chris Freeman did not do it.

"Oh, I can't believe he did it!"

I said, "Look, I've got this pitcher. Why don't you take it and go get him?"

So Steve took my pitcher, filled it with water, opened the door to Chris Freeman's room, and walked right up to him and dumped it all over him. Chris woke up and yelled, "What are you doing?"

"That's what you get for putting peanut butter all over my bed."

"I didn't do that! Tracy did that!"

I was standing there looking at both guys and feeling pretty good about my little prank. I will assure you of this: they both retaliated in much greater measure. I don't want to tell you what they did to me.

But we were doing things like that all the time. It was a good group of guys. We had a lot of great times. There was a group of us who would go to Richmond occasionally. There were a lot of college kids there from Eastern Kentucky University, and we'd run around there a little bit.

The bus trips were fun. We had a great time on the road trips when we spent the night out. That was a nice chance for the players to spend a little special time together out of our environment. Coach wanted it to be first-class for us. He put us in places that we could afford, but we always ate well and were treated well everywhere we went. On a lot of our road trips, of course, we'd go to the game and come back that night. If we won, we had a little more fun coming back than if we lost. It was usually pretty darn quiet if we lost.

That's because our players were serious. Berea's a small school, but I tell people that the game meant as much or more to us as it would have if we'd been playing at Duke or UK or anywhere else. We practiced as hard or harder. So when we didn't win we really took it tough because we knew we could win. My junior year we had a fabulous team. We knew we should win every game we played, and we won most of them. But if we lost it was tough, especially if it was a road game. Then it was tough coming back.

We had great rivalries with Cumberland, Georgetown, and Transylvania. Coach Wierwille used to coach at Transylvania, so when we played them, it was special. Two of my best games were at Transylvania. They were televised games. When I was a sophomore I shot free throws that won the game at the end. When I was a junior the exact same situation came up again, and I shot free throws at the end of the game and won it again. There was a nice little article in the paper, and I still have it, sort of like "Same place, same time, same outcome." It meant more for me to see Coach win at that school than the fact that we won or I made some free throws at the end of the game. I was so happy for Coach Wierwille, because that was a big deal to him.

At home the support we got was incredible. My sophomore and junior years were very successful. We won over twenty games both years, and we won the KIAC both years. The gym was packed every time we came out. It was rocking. There were people in the hallways, in the rafters. There were no seats available. It was a small gym, but when we walked out there and had them hanging off that track upstairs and had the band playing, it had a big feel to it.

I loved my whole career there. There are so many games that I recall. I remember playing some teams where we clearly were at a disadvantage, and then our team just rallied, a burst of points and we were back on top. I can remember specific moves and passes and situations. I can remember a comment that a player made to me at a certain point in a certain game. I had this little free throw record there, a little over ninety-one percent my junior year. When I'd go to the free throw line the four big guys would say, "Money time!" Because it was like money in the bank. I remember things like that.

The game I remember most was one I dreamed about for years afterward. It broke my heart, it broke my coach's heart, and it killed my father. I don't mean that literally, but he was devastated by it. In 1977-78 we had the greatest season. It would have been the first time ever for Berea to go to the national tournament, and we knew we had it. But when we played Cumberland College in that last game, we fell short.

They were a good team, but we outplayed them. With about four seconds to go they had the ball out on our end of the floor, so they had to dribble the length of the floor to get a shot. We were up by one point. They got the ball to Larry Gorman, a guard and a great player, one of the best players I ever played against. He dribbled just beyond halfcourt and went up to shoot. The odds were low that he would make the shot. Bill Nichols, the best player on our team, an all-America candidate, fouled him on the shot. It was a tough call on the referee's part, and it was a tough thing for Bill, great player that he was. But Bill fouled him, and Larry Gorman went to the line. If he made one free throw, it was going into overtime. If he made both, they'd beat us. There was one second left when he shot. That little guy stepped up there and drained them both.

I was on the floor most of the night, and losing that game absolutely crushed me. Coach told us we had a great year, great season, we should be proud. He said all the right things. There wasn't a guy on our team or in our stands more disappointed than he, but he knew he needed to make sure we got over it. It was tough, though. There was dead silence for what seemed to be hours, probably for minutes. We were all bewildered and devastated by it. Coach was so supportive. He had prepared us to go out and compete and give it our best, and when we came up short with all the effort we put into it, he was the most supportive, decent guy. He really wanted to make us feel better.

Then the next year we were in the same situation against Kentucky State in the District 32 final. We were up twelve or thirteen points in the second half, on our way to our first-ever trip to Kansas City. They started pressing us, we fell apart, and they ended up beating us by a few points. Again we missed our opportunity. We had played a great caliber of competition and outperformed them except in those two most important games of each season.

In my sophomore and junior years we expected to win everything. In my senior year, we lost four starters, the four leading scorers. We went into every game saying we were going to win, but realistically we did not expect to go undefeated. So when we didn't go to the nationals my senior year it wasn't as much of a letdown for me as it was the other two seasons, although that ended my college career.

That year we ran two guards again. Steve Ridder and I played a lot together. There was another little guard, Glen Drury, who came in and out, and Steve Caldwell played a lot at guard. Vance Blade and Marcus Crawford were very good players for us.

Our playoff opponent was Campbellsville, in their gym. They had been averaging right around 100 points a game, so we talked about slowing the ball down to frustrate them a little bit and get into our game. When we tipped the ball off, we got the ball and held it. A few minutes went by. I remember making eye contact with Coach, and he was just like, hold it, keep it going. So we held it a little while longer, and all of a sudden we'd played half of the first half. We called time out, and Coach said, "Guys, it's on. We're holding it. We are going to wear them out."

I was the primary ballhandler in that game. As long as I was penetrating in and out, I kept it. I dribbled, moving up and down. I would touch-pass the ball, hand it to somebody, and they'd get it right back to me.

We won 8 to 7. It was the most exciting game I ever played in my life. People say, "Gosh, how boring." It was not boring! There was constant pressure. It was the most physically demanding game I've ever played. It was the most high-energy game I've ever played, and the most stressful. It was intense because we knew if we turned the ball over one time and they scored, we could no longer hold the ball. If they got up by four points, we could not afford to hold it. So we kept it within winning range the entire game. At halftime we felt real good. It was as if we knew we were going to win.

When we came out for the second half, the fans at Campbellsville College lined up on the out-of-bounds line on our half of the court and booed and shouted obscenities to us the entire warmup session. And we liked it! We thought, "We've got them! We have completely frustrated this entire gym." Of course they didn't realize it, but we actually felt like that was an indication that what we were doing was effective. So it gave us more confidence to keep it going.

The Campbellsville players were in shock. I think they were just baffled. It was such a cat-and-mouse chase game the whole night. No one ever stood back and said, "Well, let's let them dribble for a minute." They were constantly trying to steal the ball. Some guys on that team probably had a scoring average of twenty-five points a game and were thinking, "I'm going to score just one or two points tonight." So they were chasing us with relentless pursuit, but they couldn't get the ball. No shot clock, of course, so you'll never see a game like that again. Steve Ridder, who did not average many points, was our lead scorer. He had four points in the game.

I was physically exhausted when it was over, but that game was a lot of fun. I'm really proud I got to play in it. When we played Thomas More, our next opponent, I don't recall us specifically saying, "Let's hold the ball." The lesson we learned at Campbellsville was to control the game, but we never took that same strategy into another game. We may have just slowed it down against Thomas More. We beat them, but then Pikeville eliminated us, my final game.

My first Berea College job was at the Log House. I was in sales over there, and I loved it. I thought, "This is the easiest thing in the world!" I could be myself. I love being around people, just talking to people. People would come in, they were buying all kinds of little gadgets, and I'd talk to them. It was fun for me.

But I ended up as a janitor for my Dana third floor. I did it because it was the easiest thing with basketball and school. I could clean that third floor in the morning, in the afternoon, in the evening, at any time, but at the Log House I had to go over and clock in and clock out. Trying to play basketball at Berea, a lot of the athletes had positions where they could perform their labor duty and still get on to practice. That was effective time management, but I could have done a lot better job on my floor. All I did was exactly what was expected.

My major was business, business management, but academically I was a coaster. If today I was going back through, I'd work as hard on my academics as I did my athletics. When I was there I spent 110 percent of my energy on athletics, and when I got to the academic side I did only what I needed to do to make good grades and graduate. Berea was a tough school, and I had to work hard, but I should have worked harder on the academic side. Today I have a little son. I want him to learn and be competitive and enjoy that process, but not just pass, not just graduate. Probably everybody in my age bracket looks back and thinks those things.

I had wonderful teachers at Berea, but one professor I never had a class with was a big influence on me. That was Dr Beebe. He was a chemistry professor, and I didn't take chemistry.

Dr Beebe came to the basketball games. He was a photographer, and he would take pictures that would go into the paper sometimes. I saw him around and started talking with him. We became friends. He was a good man.

Dr Beebe had me come to his office and talk to him about what it was I wanted to do. He used to get on me about potential and performance. He would tell me that he was disappointed in me. I had good potential, he said, but I was more focused on athletics than I should have been.

One summer he called me and said, "I want you to go away with me for the summer with a couple of other guys. We're going to go on a camping trip to Colorado, Wyoming, and Idaho, and you're going to go with us."

I said, "Dr Beebe, I can't go. What would it cost?"

"It will cost about 200 dollars for thirty days."

"I don't have ten dollars. I can't do it."

Dr Beebe said, "I'll tell you what you're going to do. You're going to come out to work on my farm. I need a fence, and doing some things. You can work the 200 dollars off."

I said, "I want to know what I'm going to do." Because I wanted it to be fair. I didn't want him to give me 200 dollars.

He said, "Here are the things I need done."

So I went out there and worked for Dr Beebe. He wasn't there that much. I dug ditches and all the other stuff he wanted. Then I went on the camping trip and got to know him real well. He was important to me.

A friend of mine in Virginia, Kyle Rosenbaum, was the principal of a grade school. After my junior year at Berea he said to me, "If you don't have something you really want to do, I would like you to come down here and teach at my grade school."

I said, "I don't have a teacher's certificate."

"You go in the summers and get a certificate, and you can work on it once you get down here."

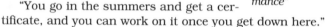

Thomas Beebe: "He used to get on me about potential and performance"

I had some interviews with companies, and I didn't like some of the sales things I heard about. It just didn't seem at the level that I thought it would be. I couldn't find anything to work at where I was going to bounce out of bed with a chill in my spine and a bounce in my step. I called Kyle and said, "Look, I'll do it. I'm going to come down there and teach and coach for awhile."

So I went to Ewing, Virginia, where I played basketball and knew everybody in that little community. I coached and taught PE and special education. I finished two complete years and was getting ready to go into my third when an opportunity came up at Deroyal. It was by a fluke that I ended up there, but I've been there ever since.

The mother of one of the players on my sixth grade team was the vice president at Deroyal, and she kept encouraging me to get into the company. I did not want to. I was not the least bit interested. I was already doing something of quality in terms of returning something back to society, and I felt good about it. But I finally had an interview, and then about a week later I had the opportunity to meet Pete DeBusk, the owner of the company. I was impressed. There was real excitement in his talk about the medical industry.

Robert McCoy was the school superintendent. I think he got a kick out of me because I was a young guy just getting into that teaching thing, and he was getting close to retirement age. I went to his office and said, "I've got to talk to you. There's a job, this is what it is, I'm seriously thinking about it, and I want to know what you think about it."

He said, "I would go do it, Tracy. I wouldn't look back. It sounds like a great opportunity." Then I went to Kyle Rosenbaum, the principal, and he said the same thing. So I took the job.

I was a sales rep in the Appalachian-region mountains. I had Hazard,

Pikeville, Whitesburg, Harlan, Middlesboro, Corbin. I covered those hospitals with what we had back then, mainly orthopedic-type products and some sterile products for surgery. I did that for less than a year, and then they asked me to move to Lexington, Kentucky, a bigger territory. That really started my career, when I made that first move.

I did a good job in sales, and then I started training people. I loved that. It was like coaching. Then they asked me if I would be a manager. I said, "Absolutely. I'm your man."

"We want you to move to Detroit, Michigan."

"Not a problem. I'm there!"

They asked me if I'd ever been to Detroit. I said no. They said, "We're going to fly you up there. Look around for about a week, then come back and tell us."

So I went up there and looked around. I did not like it at all. I came back, and they said, "What do you think?"

I said, "I'm your man."

"You're ready to go to Detroit?"

"Tomorrow. I'm packing, I'm gone. I'll be the cheapest move you ever had. All you have to do is move my desk. I own nothing."

"Well then, it's yours."

Three days later the vice president called and said, "Something's come up. A division just opened up in Dallas. So you can have your choice."

"Not a problem. I've made up my mind."

"That's great. So you're going to Detroit?"

"No, sir. I'm going to Dallas!"

"But you've never been to Dallas."

I said, "I haven't been to Dallas, but I've been to Detroit!"

"Are you sure? Don't you want to go see it?"

I said, "Don't waste your money. I'm on a mission. I'm going to Dallas!" I told them not to even fly me out to look at it.

"How do you know you're going to like Dallas?"

"I'm not going out there for Dallas. I'm going out there for this position. So don't even worry about it!"

So I moved out there. I lived there for six years and became our first regional manager, with everything west of the Mississippi. Then they wanted me to be a regional vice president, which was a nice honor. Then they asked me to take over as vice president and general manager of the orthopedic companies. Then about a year later they asked me to become the vice president of all sales, and then they asked me if I would take vice president of sales and marketing. Each time I said yes. I went from there to the position of executive vice president. We'd never had one before, so that was a step up for me. Then last year I accepted this position as president.

When I took the job as vice president of sales, I told my wife, "I'm really proud of this honor. It's about as high as I'll ever go at Deroyal, and I feel good about it." When I became vice president of sales and marketing, I said to her, "This is it. This is the highest I'll ever go here. It's a family-owned company, and this will be it." When I became the executive vice president, I told her the same thing. But now I'm president, and I'm really proud of it.

It is an honor for me because Pete DeBusk and his son Brian, who's the CEO, didn't need to put me in this position. Brian could be CEO and president. A lot of companies do that. So it says a lot about my relationship with them. I'm real proud that they saw enough in my contribution to put me in this position. I take it very seriously, and it gives hope to our people who come in and work their way up, showing them what can happen even at a privately held family business.

I believe the Berea College experience gave me this opportunity to compete. I was good at juggling basketball, academics, and my labor job. That prepared me. I get resumes across my desk every day from people who say they worked their way through college, but most people haven't had to juggle what we did. Being an athlete at Berea was demanding. At a larger university athletes have an easier situation sometimes, but at Berea it's just the opposite. You play sports, but you'd better keep the academic side up, or you're not playing. There are no short cuts. In addition, you make sure you do the labor side.

There are no social fraternity/sorority things at Berea College. Berea keeps you well-balanced. It keeps you focused on the right things. It prepares you to go out for the next forty-five years of your life and be a productive part of society. Other colleges do too, but Berea gives you a leg up because you're doing things that get you prepared. In your labor job you learn discipline and dedication. You have to get a performance review, you have to make sure you're there on time. Those things are important at that age. We hire young people today who don't have that experience. They don't understand how important it is, and sometimes it hurts their careers.

I'm glad I went to Berea. It helped me a great deal, and I hope I get to do a lot of nice things for Berea now. My younger brother went, Tyler Thompson. I think he went there because I did, and he had a great career there. He played golf at Berea. Now he's a lawyer.

I'm forty years old, and I still play competitive basketball. We have a league at Deroyal, and we play in our own gym probably two days a week. Today at lunch there'll probably be fifteen people down there playing ball. After work there'll be a lot of people. I brought a certain level of enthusiasm to all that. I got it organized, and there are a couple of young guys now who have taken it over.

Last weekend I played in Chattanooga in a three-on-three tournament, and our team won that tournament in the best division. The weekend before that I played in a tournament in Knoxville, and the weekend before that I played in a tournament in Nashville. I'm about done with that, though. The guys I play with are younger than I am, and I'm at the point where I hurt more than I used to. But I'm looking forward to a tournament we're going to play in Louisville. Craig Jefferson's going to be in that one, I understand. He sent an e-mail to me, and I replied that I hope we can play each other.

May 7, 1998

The Eighties

Coach Roland Wierwille's success with his teams of the late 1970s had demonstrated conclusively that he knew what to do with talent when he had it. But the graduation of the storied "Big Four" in 1979 left an enormous void, and the 1979-80 Mountaineers descended to the .500 level. Nevertheless, that team was responsible for the most jaw-dropping upset in the annals of college basketball in Kentucky. Of all of Coach Wierwille's victories, which would total well over 400 by the end of the century, Berea's conquest of heavily-favored conference champion Campbellsville College in the opening round of the 1980 KIAC tournament would be the most renowned.

The final score was 8 to 7. Newspaper readers thought they were looking at a misprint. They weren't. It is possible that this contest was the lowest scoring game of college basketball consummated in the twentieth century. No one knows for sure, because neither the NCAA nor the NAIA will admit to keeping such records.

The low score was the outcome of Wierwille's plan to negate Campbellsville's advantages in size and speed by controlling the ball and playing the game at a deliberate pace. Wierwille's starting five — Vance Blade, Steve Caldwell, Marcus Crawford, Steve Ridder, and Tracy Thompson -- played the entire forty minutes without a substitution, and they executed the whole audacious scheme to perfection. Dribbling and passing in endless, clock-eating patterns, the Mountaineers kept the ball for almost thirty-two minutes and took just five shots, four of them successful. (The team's eighty percent field goal percentage set a school record that is not likely to be broken.)

Eyewitness testimony reveals that the contest was anything but the dull affair it was assumed to have been by sportswriters and fans who didn't witness it. Berea's ball-control strategy, enacted before a howling multitude of Campbellsville partisans, generated almost unbearable suspense. Had Campbellsville been able to open up a lead of more than two points, Berea would have been forced to play a less deliberate style in order to catch up. But it never happened. Trailing 7-6, the disciplined and unruffled Mountaineers controlled the ball for the last three minutes before Steve Ridder put an end to the agony by scoring the last field goal of the game with eight seconds left. Campbellsville's final shot caromed off the rim.

A plan this bold and a performance this masterful will not be seen again. The NCAA and NAIA introduced a shot clock in 1985-86, forcing the team controlling the ball to shoot within forty-five seconds or relinquish control to its opponent. The time was reduced in 1993-94 to thirty-five seconds. No game nearly as low-scoring as the Berea-Campbellsville duel of February 21, 1980, has been played since, and if one ever is, it will be the product of ineptitude, not design.

Seabury Gym: "The best-kept facility in the conference"

By mid-decade the Mountaineers were a power again. Berea's 1983-84 team won twenty-three of the twenty-eight games it played. Their .821 winning percentage was the best of the Wierwille era. The team was so loaded with talent that its bench players could have held their own in the KIAC, and it featured a charismatic sparkplug in sharpshooting, ball-stealing guard Tommy Owsley. The Mountaineers fashioned win streaks of nine and thirteen games and by late February were nationally ranked by the NAIA.

Berea won the KIAC regular-season championship to secure homecourt advantage for the tournament. After subduing Alice Lloyd in the opener, the Mountaineers faced, in succession, Union, Cumberland, and Transylvania, the three teams who had beaten them during the regular season. The Union game was a walkover, but Cumberland, a Top Twenty team in its own right, won the tournament by outpointing the Mountaineers by eight in the finals.

Needing a victory over the Transylvania Pioneers to advance in the NAIA District 32 playoffs, Berea trailed by a point with possession of the ball and seventeen seconds on the clock. They had four shots at the basket and missed them all. It was a heartbreaking end to a superb season.

This time, however, the cry of "Wait till next year" proved prophetic. Surviving the graduation of five seniors, among them kingpins Donald Hairston and Kevin Mullins, and nine losses, including a quadruple-overtime marathon at Pikeville, the 1984-85 Mountaineers overcame Cumberland and Georgetown in the district playoffs to earn at last a long-sought berth in the NAIA national tournament in Kansas City. The win at Cumberland was especially sweet, for the Indians had beaten Berea twice that season, were ranked eleventh in the nation, and had not lost at home in more than three seasons. In the afterglow of victory Coach Wierwille proclaimed it "the greatest win ever in Berea College history."

"Most teams were not expecting us to do anything in the district tournament," remarked senior center David Moeves. "Since we don't have scholarships, I think some teams think, 'These guys are just a bunch of walk-ons,' and they overlook us. About a week before the district we started to jell." Moeves cited the motivational skills of Assistant Coach Steve Ridder as a key factor. "Coach Ridder sat us down in the locker room about two weeks before the end of the season and told us that we had the chance to do something no other Berea team in history has ever done."

Qualifying for the national tournament provoked intense interest in the team on and off the Berea campus. Ed Ford and his staff at the Berea College News Bureau worked overtime to prepare 250 press kits and arrange radio and television coverage throughout the state of Kentucky. The publicity value for the school was incalculable. On the opening day of the tournament the *Kansas City Times* ran a feature story about the College's unique athletic program on its front page, and local radio and television stations vied for the privilege of interviewing Mountaineer players and coaches.

Although Berea lost to Rio Grande College in the opening round in Kansas City, congratulations were very much in order for the 1984-85 Mountaineers. Shortly before the beginning of the next season, Roland Wierwille observed:

> When we walked out on the court at Kemper Arena, I can't describe the thrill I experienced. I don't believe the coaches of the NCAA Final Four teams could feel any better. I was really proud of our program and the way we won the right to be there.
>
> It means a lot when alumni I don't even know write to tell me that they're proud of the team and what we accomplished and how much this means to the College and its overall program. That kind of respect really means something.

The Mountaineers were a force throughout the rest of the decade. In 1987-88 senior forward Jay Stenzel, overcoming a serious Achilles tendon injury that had sidelined him the entire previous year, contributed a season that would earn him KIAC Player of the Year honors. In so doing Stenzel became the first Berea College athlete ever designated a first team all-American by the NAIA.

Coach Roland Wierwille was notably unenthusiastic about the three-point field goal, which was introduced in 1986-87. "We're not going to use the three-point play unless a special situation comes up, especially at the end of the game," he declared, adding, "I've never talked to a coach who was in favor of it." But the role of King Canute did not suit the Berea mentor, and after a few seasons the Mountaineers were firing in shots from long range without waiting for "special situations."

Roland R. Wierwille (2)   **Coach, 1972-**

At Berea College our practices are organized. As a coach I have to figure out what we need to be working on. Are we going to emphasize offense or defense? Or, what kind of offense or defense are our opponents going to use, and what can we do to break those things down to get prepared for that team? We try to vary our fundamental drills. We don't do them all every day, but take this one this day, another one that day. We make sure our practices don't get boring.

On defense, we work in practice on the basic fundamentals. But if you ask if I'm a man-to-man or zone or pressing coach, I say it all depends on who we play. Some teams you can zone. Some teams you can press and really hurt them, but other teams you'd be crazy to press, because they'd go right around you.

The worst thing you can do is try to run something that the players can't execute. I'm not really a pressing coach, full court, half court. I want more of a surprise. I can't have a team that presses every time there's a made goal. I'd have to have ten or twelve guys who could do that, and our teams are never that deep. Let's say I'm a pressing coach and I've got three guys who don't have good foot speed. Am I going to press? Well, some coaches would probably do it, but I'm not going to.

I think some coaches overcoach. They think they're responsible for

Coach Roland Wierwille: "A class act as a coach and a person"

everything, they're going to call everything, and if they win, it's because of their coaching. Well, I don't believe that. If we lose, I blame myself. I'll never badmouth a kid after a loss.

Our offense has been very, very good to us, and I have used variations of the same offense since my second year at Berea. I'm not going to take credit for developing the double-low offense, but we were one of the first college teams to use it, and it's amazing the number of people who use some form of it today. I designed that offense for us because on those first couple of teams I didn't have forwards who could handle the ball, and I wanted them to pop out and throw it in. It was simple then. Today we have ten or twelve different variations of that same offense.

In the double-low you have a point guard, you have a guard and a forward on one side low, you have a forward and a center on the other side low, and they pop out. It's a motion offense where you screen away and you interchange on the perimeter. You've got to have motion in an offense, and we have motion, much more motion now than when we first started. It seems like each year I put something else in.

The double-low is a quick offense. You can shoot the perimeter shot or you can shoot the underneath shot. You can have penetration. It involves a lot of things, but it's a simple offense. You see, generally we can't come in and practice three or four hours. For us it's two hours, and the simpler we can make it, the better our players are going to understand it and execute. Repetition is important. If we practice five days one week, four of those days we're going to run offense, just go through it over and over.

Most of the time, under control, we want to run with the basketball. You've got to let your players play. It's much more enjoyable then. Of course, I don't believe in an offense where they turn it over and over, out of control. If you have good ball movement and you get a good shot, you should take it. The open tempo, the fast break, letting them play, under control, moving the basketball, boy, it's a beautiful offense.

The dunk is an exciting thing. The three-point shot is an exciting thing. Winning is an exciting thing. And I like an up-tempo game because I think it's very enjoyable, not only for our kids but for the people who watch us. I feel good about it.

Speaking of exciting basketball, it's hard to top the night we beat Campbellsville 8 to 7 in the 1980 KIAC playoffs. I've never seen, heard of, or coached in another game like it.

We were an average team that year, and we were playing the best team in the conference in their building. They had very good personnel, especially James Boulware, their tough underneath pivot man.

We didn't go down there with the idea of holding the ball, and we didn't hold the ball. We simply wanted to control the game. We wanted to take good shots. So we had an offense that was three out, and we spread the floor, getting that big guy away from the basket so it would open up. Our offense controlled it like a little figure eight.

People who saw the final score thought that we went out and held the ball, and Campbellsville stayed back and let us hold it. That was not the

Coach Roland Wierwille: "He has never lost his intensity"

case. I'm disappointed that nobody taped that game, to show that Campbellsville had people after us. They were trying to get the ball, but they couldn't do it. At one stretch we actually had the ball for eighteen minutes and thirty-seven seconds without turning it over. You can't even do that when you're practicing without a defense!

We wanted to penetrate the ball, but it happened that we didn't get the drive we wanted. The score was 4 to 0 in their favor just before the half when Steve Ridder hit a shot, just threw it up and it went in, so it was 4 to 2 at halftime. The people were booing me, really after me. I walked in and said, "Fellas, one thing about it, we're only two behind!" I told them we were going to do the same thing in the second half, and if we got a good shot, take it.

So we still controlled it, and the score with ten seconds to go was 7 to 6 their way. Steve Ridder had the ball. I can still see him looking over at me. I said, "Take it in!" He took an off-balance shot from the baseline, and the game was over. They were stunned.

We beat a very good team and coach, Lou Cunningham. I hated to do it to him, but that's part of our profession, to do what you have to do. He said, "Good game," and I got out of there. I said to the team, "We will leave here together. I don't want anybody going out one at a time."

I received phone calls all the next day, great game and all that. I'll never forget it. Three nights later we went to Thomas More and did pretty much the same thing, controlling the ball. We won 34-33. Thomas More is a Catholic school, and there were nuns in the stands yelling at me, telling me I was a cheater!

Then we went to Pikeville and got beat bad. Pikeville was tough, and it finally caught up with us, but winning two playoff games like that made our season successful.

Steve Ridder later became my first real assistant coach. He played for me for four years, then was my right-hand man for eight years. He was truly an asset to our program. He is now the athletic director and head basketball coach at Embry-Riddle University. Steve has developed one of the finest small-college programs in the NAIA.

In the summer of 1982 I got a call from C.M. Newton, who asked, "Would you be interested in coaching in the pre-Olympic sports festival in Indianapolis this summer?"

"Coach, I don't know. That's for Division I players. I don't know if I can handle them."

"Roland, you can do it, and you need to do it in your professional career."

I said, "Coach, I'll do it if you want me to."

In each sport the athletes were divided into a south team, a north team, an east team, and a west team. I was with the south team as an assistant to Nolan Richardson, who coaches at Arkansas now. We won the gold medal. Those were college players, but in our team picture you can see six or seven future NBA millionaires.

That was really a proving ground for me. If I didn't do a good job, I wouldn't be asked again. But after working with Nolan Richardson I was invited to make two overseas trips. In 1984 I was asked to go as an assistant to Taiwan with a team of Division I players coached by Lute Olson, head coach at Arizona. And the next year I was fortunate enough to coach with Lee Rose in the World University Games in Japan. Those were three great experiences for me. I felt very pleased that I was given that much respect. It was a great honor.

I enjoyed seeing those different countries and cultures, and I enjoyed being around great athletes, who ended up, some of them, making millions in the NBA. Somebody asked, "Would you treat them any different than your own players?" I said no, I wouldn't. If they know that you know what you're doing, you're going to get respect. Our Berea College players were good players, and I used pretty much the same philosophy with those Division I guys that I was using at Berea.

I enjoyed just the idea of sitting in a packed house at the finals of the World University Games. Here I was a little guy from Berea College, and I was on the bench for the United States of America while we played Russia. That gave me goosebumps, I'm telling you! We lost on a three-point shot with no time on the clock. It happened right in front of our bench. Lee Rose and I watched the guy get the ball, shoot it thirty-five or forty feet, and beat us.

At Berea College we didn't practice the three-point shot for the first couple of years after it came in. I played underneath in college, so I didn't like the idea of the three-point shot. I thought, "Why should they get three points for a shot from out there, when a nice underneath basket only counts two?" But guess what? We do it now!

I didn't think it would make a real difference, but boy! After about two years I figured out that it does. I saw teams beat us with it. So about the third year we started shooting the three-pointer, and now we shoot it every day. On the day of the game we'll come in and shoot free throws and three-pointers.

It's an exciting shot, and we'll shoot it if it's there. But we're careful that we don't have our people standing around on the perimeter shooting it too much. We don't want to isolate our underneath men. We do pretty good at kicking the ball in if they're there and kicking it back out. We're a much better three-point shooting team if we move the ball and then shoot the three. These days a practice will not go by when we don't shoot the three-point shot.

In 1984 we had a tremendous team, but we lost to Transylvania by one point in a game that kept us out of the national tournament. That was very hard on me. Once again we couldn't play the game at Seabury Gym because it was not regulation size, so the game was played at Eastern. We had 2000 over there, one side all full. It was a great game, but I was really disappointed at how it ended. We had three referees from Lexington, and I felt that our kids didn't get a fair shake with the officiating.

I was hurt at what went on late in that game. I felt that we were not treated right. We had some townspeople who were irate. What happened was not fair to our team, but I didn't bring it out in the paper or anything because that sounds like sour grapes. I was disappointed that our twenty-three and five team had to end our season that way.

But those calls were judgment calls, and nobody wants to hear complaints from a coach. I don't want to hear them from another coach, either. I've heard it so much over the years. If I hear one of my players complain, I say, "Easy!" I don't want to hear it. It's over, and we can say we didn't get a good deal, but nobody wants to hear it.

I've had people leaving our gym thinking they got messed over. I've left places thinking we got messed over. That's the game! I can talk to the referees, but I know when to lay off them, because I don't want to get a technical to cost us a basketball game.

The next year, 1985, we qualified for the national tournament the hard way. Cumberland had a fifty-three game winning streak at home, and we went down there and beat them. Not many people gave us a chance. They were nationally ranked, but we beat them. That was on a Monday, and then Wednesday we went to Georgetown, another team ranked way up there, and beat them. That had to be the highlight of my career at Berea College. We'd had a lot of good wins and some tough losses, but when we went to the Cumberland and Georgetown gyms and beat two teams of the caliber they were in 1985, that was a great, great experience for me and the team and Berea College.

Before the Cumberland game one of our guards got hurt. I decided to start Cliff Blackburn, a six-four freshman who had very little experience. We went down there and zoned them the whole game. Cliff had long arms and covered the middle. We played our standard three-two zone and never came out of it. That zone was the factor that won the game. In Cumberland's fifty-three game win streak, they hadn't lost at home in about four years. I think they were looking ahead to Georgetown.

Georgetown was thinking that their reservations were already made at the national tournament in Kansas City. We played our zone again with the freshman in the middle, and once again it was the biggest factor in our victory.

We had a good team. Decent size, and we played very well together. We went to Kansas City and lost by only three out there. We had a chance late in the game. We were behind but we came back, a typical Berea College team. It went down to the last minute.

It's a shame that that was the only year Cliff Blackburn played. He was a very nice young man from Lexington. Those playoff games were really the only two games that he played in.

In 1986 we had another very good team, but this time we were eliminated by Georgetown in a game we led at halftime. They thought they were going to destroy us. We played very well, but we came up short.

Steve Ridder   1977-81

I grew up in Bellevue, Kentucky, right across the bridge from Cincinnati, Ohio. My mom was a full-time mom with four kids. Dad was a general maintenance man. He worked for a meat company for several years before joining the Kroger grocery chain.

I visited several colleges before choosing Berea. Mom and Dad came to all my high school games, and they thought it would be an ideal situation

Steve Ridder as player: "A great passer, a great assist man"

to be able to see me play on weekends at a school just two hours away. Furthermore, they regarded the Berea labor program as a great opportunity for me to develop an intense work ethic to go with my classroom education. The two of them accompanied me on my visit to Berea. We were all impressed by the quality of the basketball program and the level of spectator interest on the part of the faculty, staff, students, and townspeople. Dad saw in Coach Wierwille a man like himself, a disciplinarian who was always concerned about doing things the right way.

Although I'm six-four, I played guard. In high school I averaged twenty-two points a game, but at Berea I had to adjust my style of play. We didn't need another scorer because we already had several outstanding offensive players. With Ed Flynn and Craig Jefferson and Bill Nichols and Arno Norwell on the team, the job of our guards was to control the tempo and distribute. We needed to be unselfish, to get the ball down the floor and select which all-conference player we wanted to feed the ball to. I adapted to that role because Coach felt it was best for our team.

It's important for every team to have role players. I'm proud to say I put the team first. Getting the ball to the scorers was what I did best as a college player.

My height was an advantage for me as a point guard because it helped me see over opponents and read the defenses. On the other hand, many of the other point guards were quicker at getting up and down the floor. I needed to work on my strength. Now I can see that I thought I was a better player than Coach thought I was.

In the area I came from, high school basketball players were treated like royalty. When I decided to enroll at an NAIA school after averaging over twenty points a game, I actually thought I would go to the NAIA school for a year and then maybe transfer to the University of Kentucky! I thought I was that good. So when I saw that I wasn't going to play that much as a freshman at Berea, I asked myself what Coach could possibly be thinking.

My first response was to sulk and show my disappointment. With Coach Wierwille you can't do that, so we didn't hit it off that well at first. You won't be around Coach long if you sulk and feel sorry for yourself. Although I didn't agree with some of his decisions, I liked the program and thought we had a good team. I respected Coach from day one because he said it the way it was. Not every decision was going to go in my favor, and I had to learn to handle that. It was an important lesson.

Cluster Howard was the returning point guard, with four or five of us switching on and off as his backup. Whoever could get the ball down the floor and to the right people got to play. Cluster did a great job of quarterbacking the basketball team. He had been a scorer in junior college, but as good a shooter as he was, Cluster didn't score a lot of points at Berea because of his role. I admired Cluster's willingness to sacrifice and his intense desire to compete.

Arno Norwell and I became the best of friends, although he was two years ahead of me. We did a lot of things together off the court. Arno was from the same area as I was, and he and I would try to get rides back home together.

Arno let his game speak for him. He was not the type of person who would go around saying, "I'm six foot eight, and I'm the best player in the conference and the greatest rebounder ever to play for Berea College." But in my opinion he was. He averaged fourteen rebounds a game. That's a ton of rebounds. He pulled down over 400 one season. Arno liked to compete, and he very seldom lost. He was big, he was strong, he had great hands, and he knew how to play. He was also smart, which seemed to surprise some people. Opponents saw Arno as big, but they didn't realize how smart he was. He was a smart person, period.

Those teams had great chemistry. I liked Bill and Craig a lot, their personalities. They were very popular on campus, but they let me hang out with them as a freshman, which is rather unusual. It was neat for a freshman to hang out with upperclassmen. When Arno and I became friends, it became easier for me to establish good relationships with the other guys.

I was fortunate that Ed Flynn liked me, because if Ed didn't like you, well, he was one intense player. If Ed got mad at one of his teammates for boxing him out too hard in practice, he would come at him. I saw Ed rip the practice jersey off one of the freshmen, and there wasn't much said to him about it. He was that intense.

Ed could shoot and rebound, but he could also dribble, and he liked to bring the ball up the floor. One night we were playing at Wilmington College. I was standing on the free throw line when a Wilmington cheerleader looked over at Ed. He said, "Number Forty, you are the ugliest thing I've ever seen." When I heard that I thought, "Oh my God, anybody but Ed Flynn!" The ref threw the ball in to Ed. Ed threw it back to me, and I knew then that something was up, because he usually wanted to bring up the ball himself.

After Ed got rid of the ball, boom! He took off and was all over that cheerleader. He made a forceful point that the guy's remark was not appropriate. The rest of us had to break everything up. That incident tells you something about Ed. He was not the type of person to start a fight in the middle of a game, but he wasn't going to tolerate anybody making a comment like that.

The teams with Ed and Arno and Craig and Bill were the best I played on. We were very disappointed not to reach the national tournament. In my freshman year our season ended when a foul was called on us with just seconds to go, putting Larry Gorman of Cumberland on the free throw line. We had already beaten Cumberland three times that year, and we were in position to win that final game. I can remember thinking, "Here we come Kansas City, we're going to fly out there." But we missed doing that by a hair. It's hard to defeat any team four times. I think we would have had some success in the national tournament had we won that final game with Cumberland.

The following year we had Kentucky State where we wanted them. They were a talented team, but we had a good lead going down the stretch. Then we made some costly errors and poor decisions on the floor that spoiled another opportunity to get to the big dance. We were devastated, but I don't think as a player I truly understood the level of disappointment Coach must have felt, not to make it to the tournament after the special years we had with those wonderful players.

When the Big Four graduated we lost eighty-five to ninety percent of our scoring. Our dominating inside players were gone. We were spoiled because all four of those guys were premier players, not just in the conference but in the country. They weren't good; they were great! After they left we had to change our style of play.

We had some people who could dribble and score, but because we lacked size we no longer enjoyed a rebounding edge. If Arno had been able to stay one more year, or if we'd been able to replace him with an impact inside player, we would have been very good. We had quality players, but not that go-to, six-eight guy. Keith Riley did a fine job, but he was a year away and four inches short of being that kind of player.

So we did the best we could. We were a close team, good friends off the court. We spent a lot of time together. On the court we overachieved. We won some games we probably should not have won. We weren't big, but often we found a way to win because we were used to winning.

We had balanced scoring. Vance Blade was six-three but played much larger. He could play above the rim. We could alley-oop to Vance, and he could catch it and dunk. Marcus Crawford was slick. He could find holes in a defense and score. Steve Caldwell and Keith Riley could score. Tracy

Thompson was a threat from the perimeter.

Tracy and I had similar personalities. We developed a close friendship that was tested at times because we were competing for each other's playing time. I started a lot of games at point guard, but sometimes I played small forward. I never thought I was big enough to play small forward effectively at the collegiate level, where I needed to guard people six-five or above and play inside. I was a better perimeter player. I liked handling and distributing the ball or scoring from the outside. Even so, my attitude was "Just get me out there." Ultimately I didn't care where Coach wanted me to play, because I simply wanted to play.

We had another good guard in Glen Drury. Not many players could play college basketball at five-nine, but Glen was a hard-nosed competitor. He did some great things for us. Glen was captain with me my senior year.

That was the year we drew Campbellsville as our tournament opponent and beat them 8 to 7. Nobody realizes that we did not plan to go into that building and play a delay game. That's the truth about it. We talked about how we needed to be patient on offense and let them come at us, but there was no whole week of preparation to take one or two shots in a half of basketball.

The way I remember it, we scored first. When Campbellsville didn't score on their possession, on our second time down we decided to be very patient. With the game at 2-2 right before the half, we had the ball and shot a thirty-five or forty-footer which seemed like it shouldn't have gone in but did. At halftime we were almost in disbelief that we were up 4 to 2. We were excited to be in that position, and Campbellsville was frustrated. Their fans were booing. They were not happy about us coming in there playing that way.

In the locker room at halftime we all agreed that we liked what we were doing and didn't want to change. During the regular season Campbellsville had beaten us badly, so we would have been foolish to get the idea that we might be twenty points better than they were. Our first-half strategy had worked. When they had the basketball they were hesitant to shoot, because they didn't know if they were ever going to get it back. It was fun to watch them start to panic. If they didn't adjust, we knew could frustrate them again in the second half.

That second half was very much like the first. We were very selective. When they went up 7-6 with about ten minutes to go, we decided not to change our tactics. With their slim lead Campbellsville did not stand back and let us toss the ball. They were chasing us the whole time. But we had good ball handlers in Tracy, Steve, Marcus, Vance, and myself. We kept the ball, and probably took a couple of timeouts during the next seven or eight minutes.

It was so intense. The people in the stands were standing up the whole time screaming. Campbellsville had three or four guards in. They pressured us, trying to steal the ball. With under thirty seconds left we were still running our weave and handling the ball. I could see Coach signal that it was time to take it to the basket. I saw an opening in the lane and took a couple of dribbles. I wanted finish it up with a nice easy layup. Of course they cut me off. I was off balance, but I used the board and the ball went in.

The crowd didn't go wild. The place was quiet. I thought that I must have missed the shot. For a split second I'd forgotten that we were playing in their building. There were four or five seconds left on the clock, but Campbellsville did not get a timeout to set up a final play. They just froze, and I don't recall them getting a good shot at all.

Campbellsville was a bigger team, a quicker team, a better team than we were, and we had beaten them in their own building. It was tough for us to get out of that gym because their fans were so hostile. It was one of the best wins in Berea College history, and certainly one of the most exciting games I ever played in.

We realized that we had found a style that fit our personnel very well. If we could continue to execute the same patient offense, we had a chance to be a pretty good team. Our next opponent was Thomas More, who had beaten us twice. They had a great player, Brian O'Conner, who was very difficult to stop, especially on their home court.

That game was especially fun for me because my family was there and a lot of people I had known in high school. It was another exciting yet low-scoring game. With just seconds left, Glen Drury drove to the basket and hit a shot that enabled us to knock them off 34-33. Their fans were mad. The nuns were yelling at us. Later I read in the paper that the nuns had a real problem with us coming up there and playing that kind of basketball. They did not think it was fair for us to do that. But it was a style that gave us a chance to beat Thomas More, so it worked out great for us.

Pikeville beat us in our next game. Early in the game we missed a couple of shots we should not have missed, and Pikeville got control of the tempo. We were in a position where we had to try to catch up, and things didn't go our way. I give Pikeville credit. They did a nice job of taking away our game plan. We didn't execute as well as we did the two previous games. That's unfortunate, because the Pikeville game was another chance for us to go to the national tournament. We fell short, and that was tough to take. But we were happy we had won some games that no one believed we could win.

Our problem in my senior year was our inability to win the close games. If you look at the scores you'll see eight or nine games that could have gone either way. All you have to do is figure out the math on that.

Close games can be won in different ways, but whoever gets or prevents offensive stickbacks usually comes out on top. The offensive team needs the second shot. The defensive team needs the big stop. If your opponent has the ball down the stretch and you get an initial stop, but they're big and strong enough to grab that offensive rebound and put it in, it breaks your back.

We had good role players inside, but we still didn't have that dominating inside player. When you don't have that kind of player you don't get offensive rebounds, and you don't have a good post defense. Your opponents spot that, and all of a sudden they start going inside. Some nights we'd be okay. We could knock off a Cumberland or a Transy if we were shooting the ball well. To win without shooting well, on each possession you have to get two or three opportunities to score. And you've still got to play great defense and not allow second shots. We weren't able to do that consistently.

I played my last game of basketball against Thomas More as we closed out that 1980-81 season. It was ironic that I completed my college career just fifteen minutes from my hometown, with my family and many of my friends in the audience. The Thomas More point guard was Dave Faust. He and I had been the best of friends in grade school and competed against each other all the way through high school and college. Berea lost the game, so Dave got to finish on a winning note while I was disappointed. I stayed at Berea for another eight years as assistant coach, and we made many more trips to Thomas More and enjoyed great success.

I also played baseball at Berea. I was a pitcher. That was the best thing for me because the everyday position players were practicing while I was playing basketball. Playing both sports was challenging. After finishing a very intense basketball season I'd get to rest for maybe a day or two before reporting to baseball practice.

I had a lot of off-speed stuff. I had been throwing a curve ball since I was ten years old, but I didn't understand about setting up hitters and throwing fastballs to get ahead of the count and not walking people. I was one of those guys who was either going to walk you or strike you out. I never did learn that I didn't need to strike out every batter. Sometimes I'd pitch both games of a doubleheader. That's unheard of at the college level, but I did it more than once. We had some success, but not as much as I hoped we would.

My first labor assignment was helping out Elvin Combs in the gymnasium. Elvin was the kindest man in the world. He was never impatient, and he would do anything to help us. Elvin was never an I-I-I guy. With him it was always We-We-We. His presence made it easier for all of us to be away from home.

Later I worked in financial aid, and then I became a student coordinator for career development. That was a good job. I had the chance to meet the employers who came to interview our students. I set up the interviews, and I got the chance to talk about Berea College. On a couple of occasions I also worked as a teacher's assistant for Coach Wierwille. That helped strengthen our relationship, and it led directly to the opportunity I had to stay at Berea after I graduated.

My major was business administration. I was a conscientious student. David Hall, my roommate my first two years, was studying pre-med, and I tried to keep up with him. David helped me get off on the right foot academically. He took notes in blue ink and wrote certain key words in red ink. When I looked at his notebook I could not believe the organization. It woke me up. At Berea there was a much higher intensity level in the classroom than I was used to in high school. Playing sports also helped me do better academically, because it kept me focused. If I hadn't played sports, I would

Jim Holloway: "He introduced me to different ways of thinking"

probably have just goofed off.

I had several outstanding teachers. One was Phil Spears, who taught Organizational Behavior in the Business Department. When we came to his class we needed to be ready to participate. Whoever wasn't ready would get embarrassed. I recall him going at me hard about things we had been assigned to read the night before. If I wasn't prepared, he would say, "Here I come at you with a full-court press. You can't handle it. You're turning the ball over. You're not ready to get it done today." We needed that kind of wake-up call. Once we left college, anyone who wasn't prepared would be eaten alive. That was the message he was trying to send. He did a good job, and he knew how to compliment us when we did a good job.

Jim Holloway taught philosophy and religion. He and I really hit it off. I helped him one semester as a TA when I was a senior. I spent some time with him outside the classroom at his home. He introduced me to different ways of thinking. For instance, I read Thomas Merton's *Raids on the Unspeakable* and had discussions with him about it. That sort of thing was very important to me.

During my sophomore year I lost my father to lung cancer. He was just forty-eight, and I was nineteen. People like Coach Wierwille and Jim Holloway and John Cook helped get me over the devastation of losing my dad. I needed that. I needed mentors who would make sure I stayed on the right course.

I'm loyal to Berea College today because I'm so grateful for what it gave me. The people I met. The value system. The great education. The labor experience. Discussing important topics, playing sports, reading Thomas Merton, working in the gym or Financial Aid Office. So many things that helped to shape what I'm about today. Nobody's going to outwork me. I get up every day and get after it.

Vicky Taylor was a student math tutor who helped me and several of my teammates with probability and statistics and that sort of thing. She was a lot smarter than we were. She wasn't interested in coming to our basketball games, but she and I became good friends anyway. We got married shortly after graduation.

I started to get interested in coaching basketball when I was named captain in my senior year. Coach Wierwille expected a lot of me, but I enjoyed the responsibility of helping to get the team ready to play. If our guys weren't ready I felt I could say, "Coach, we need five minutes by ourselves because something's wrong." I could shut the door and get in somebody's face a little bit and say, "I don't know where your mind is, but it's not here." I didn't know a lot about x's and o's then, but I knew I had found something I was good at and enjoyed. As the season came to an end I realized that athletics was over for me unless I chose to pursue it as a profession. I had to decide whether I wanted to take a business job or try to teach and coach.

After I graduated Coach invited me to stay at Berea College as his assistant. I also had a chance to join the Goodyear Aerospace Corporation in Akron, Ohio. I had met their recruiter when I was student career development coordinator. Goodyear flew me up to Akron and made me a wonderful job offer. I turned it down. Vicky and I were newly married, and that was our first big decision in life, what direction I would go in.

It was not an easy decision. After all, I had a business degree. But I had taken all my electives in education, which would enable me to earn a teaching certificate without too much difficulty. So we stayed in Berea, and I enrolled in grad school at Eastern. During the next eight years I served Berea College in several ways. I was dorm director in Bingham before moving over to Danforth. I was a financial aid analyst specializing in Pell Grant verification. I taught activity courses like racquetball and soccer. I was the head baseball coach. And, of course, I was the assistant basketball coach.

I have the privilege of saying that I know Roland Wierwille better than anyone outside his family. We had a player and coach relationship, then an assistant and head coach relationship, and since then a wonderful friendship. I've seen him change over the years, but he has never lost his intensity. He has always taken losing hard. As his assistant I received many two-in-the-morning phone calls. "What went wrong tonight? Where did we come up short?" After Saturday night games I wouldn't get to bed until twelve or one, but win or lose, the phone might ring at seven on Sunday morning. "Steve, you're up, aren't you? Come over and have some coffee and doughnuts." We'd watch the videotape. I loved getting those phone calls.

It was fun in my years as his assistant to go to clinics and talk with other coaches. The game of basketball is always changing, and I'd learn new

Steve Ridder: "He was already one of the brightest young coaches in America"

Steve Ridder and Coach Roland Wierwille: "We laughed and cried together"

ideas to bring to the Berea program. Coach never felt that he had all the answers. He welcomed new ideas, new plays I'd find out about. He gave me the chance to coach some, for which I'm grateful. Coach never said his way was the only way. He asked how we could adapt to each new era of basketball.

I wanted to look at our personnel and innovate to fit what we were good at. When I was playing we didn't run many set plays, but later we had guys who could score on set plays. With Jay Stenzel in the game we weren't going to sit back and hope he'd get the ball. We designed set plays for Jay. We weren't going to hope that Tommy Owsley could create a shot. We had plays for him.

I did all the scouting, and we started using plays I took from other teams. Georgetown ran a play we couldn't stop. One day I said, "Coach, we haven't stopped this play. Why don't we just run it ourselves?" We put it in, and Berea still runs that play. It's a back door alley-oop play. Transylvania runs it now. There's nothing wrong with that. We all copy off each other.

We wanted to make things happen with our defense. When we had Tommy Owsley and Donald Hairston and Kevin Mullins and John Small, we could press. John was six-five at the point. He would get out there and intimidate. Tommy in the middle was quick, steal after steal. Donald and Kevin were smart and aggressive. We had Jay Stenzel or Bubby Napier to protect the basket. At times we just would humiliate a team. Once we led Union College 53 to 16 at the half. They could not get the ball up the floor. Our defense attacked them. We had our kids believing that our best offense was our defense. They liked it. We didn't do that when I was playing because our personnel was different.

I was at Berea when the three-point shot came in. I didn't care for it initially. But we needed to get away from having a bad attitude about the three. Like it or not, the three was there. Some coaches were slow to adapt to the difference in the game. If you didn't have people who could knock down threes, you had to build your team accordingly. Eventually we realized that the three-point shot was there to stay and made adjustments.

When I became close enough to Coach to be able to say just about anything to him, I pointed out that there was always a distance between him and the players. That same distance had been there when I was a player. As his assistant I kidded him about it a bit. I'd ask, "Why don't you let your hair down more often with some of your players? It's okay to do that. We can get closer to these guys." I was always the go-between guy, and I felt that the players didn't get a chance to know him. He has a heart as big as this room. The players would only respect him more if they knew him as a real person. It wouldn't mean that we were softies who wouldn't prepare just as hard for Transylvania.

In my eighth year as Coach Wierwille's assistant I had the chance to become Berea's head baseball coach. We didn't have a lot of funding, but we turned the chicken farm into a winter training facility. We built some mounds so the pitchers could start throwing in January. They'd go out there three nights a week. Then we built a new baseball field, the whole thing: infield, pitching and bullpen mounds, warning track, press box. There were a couple of talented kids on campus who hadn't intended to play baseball. We got them excited about playing, and they joined us.

We had a great pitching staff and finished one game away from winning the conference championship. We won sixteen and lost seven, the first winning season in several years. That was when the bug bit me: I could be a head coach! I liked calling the shots, having my own team, giving out the trophies at the banquet. I thought, "This is what I need to do. I'll stay at Berea and build one of the best baseball programs in the country."

Then I was approached about coaching basketball at Embry-Riddle Aeronautical University. I was enjoying the baseball deal at Berea, and I wasn't sure I wanted to leave Kentucky to go to Florida. But I figured I should at least fly down and take a look at Embry-Riddle.

When I got there I saw potential. Embry-Riddle was a school of 5200 students with a beautifully landscaped campus, professional people walking around, a lot of class. But there was no gym and no interest in basketball. I thought that if I could come to Embry-Riddle and get people excited about the game and bring in the kind of kids who would fit in as students and athletes, the school would be able to compete one day. I was twenty-nine years old. I loved Berea College and was happy there, but perhaps it was time for me to step up and do something different. So I accepted the challenge.

I'm still basketball coach at Embry-Riddle. We're a technology-oriented university that offers only an aviation curriculum. Because we have extremely high academic standards we get a high caliber of student. We've been fortunate to attract some good athletes.

Our basketball team has had seven straight winning seasons, and in six of those years we've won twenty or more games. We've made it to the national tournament three straight years. We think we have one of the best programs in the country. We've had good teams year after year with kids who know how to get up every day and go to class, and who know how important it is to graduate. They know that although basketball is important, life after basketball is more important. We're very popular on our campus right now. People like and enjoy the type of kids we're winning with.

I've been athletic director for the last five years. It has been a very rewarding experience. We've had a lot of success in all of our sports. We have a nationally ranked baseball team that wins forty-something games year after year. Our volleyball team was thirty-three and six last year. Our tennis team has gone to the national tournament two out of the last three years. We've built a new arena and a new soccer complex. We've started women's sports. It's been a tremendous challenge for me, but we've made a strong effort to grow our athletic program at Embry-Riddle.

When my team and Coach Wierwille's team both made it to the NAIA national tournament in Nampa, Idaho, I asked Coach to talk to my players. He said he didn't know if he could do it, but when I told him how much it would mean to me, he said yes.

I stood up before my players and said, "You guys have shown your loyalty to our program, but you may not always understand why I ask you to do things like keep your hair cut, tuck your shirttails in, be on time, thank people, and look people in the eye when you shake their hands. I learned all those things from this man right here. I want you guys to welcome Coach Wierwille. I've asked him to say a couple of words to us."

Coach couldn't do it. I was emotional, and he got every bit as emotional and couldn't get the words out. We got through it, but as we left the locker room he said, "If you ever do that to me again, I'm going to kick your ass!" It was a tough on both of us because it was so intensely emotional.

I had played for him and coached for him, and now I had coached my own team to the national tournament. We'd had so many moments when we laughed and cried together, and it was extra special for us to share the next phase of our relationship there in Idaho. My team had won a lot of games, but I think the biggest thrill for Coach was to see how my players looked. They were doing things right, and he knew he'd had a tremendous influence.

When Coach brought his team to our Embry-Riddle holiday tournament in 1997, Hope College beat them pretty good. The next night my team played Hope College. The Berea players were in the stands yelling just like Embry-Riddle fans. They were cheering for every basket we made. Hope College had an excellent team, but we upset them by two points. As we went into the locker room the Berea players followed us in, pounding on us like we were all one great family. In the exhilaration of the moment I told the whole group, "This is what it's all about."

August 4, 1998

Glen Drury   1978-81

Berea College taught me that in order to do a good job, a man's got to have a lot of good people helping him. On the first day I walked onto that campus I could see that Berea was a place where everybody chipped in for the good of everybody else.

I'm the head basketball coach at Anderson County High School in Lawrenceburg, Kentucky. When I took over we hadn't been to the state tournament in twenty-four years. In the twelve years I've had this job we've been to the state tournament, and we've won over seventy percent of our games. It isn't Glen Drury doing all this work. It's Glen Drury and all the good people I have working with me.

I had already decided before I came to Berea that I wanted to become a coach. I learned a lot of things from Ron Reed, my high school coach, and I went on to learn a lot of things from Coach Wierwille. Putting their two philosophies together with a little of my own has helped me to be successful.

I graduated from Anderson County High School. I was very fortunate to have the kind of family I grew up in. My parents were kind-hearted, family-oriented people. My dad worked at the Kentucky Overall plant. My mom worked odd-and-end jobs. We also raised twenty-five or thirty acres of tobacco to earn money to help put me through school.

As I was finishing high school Ron Reed, trying to find a place for me to play college ball, got in touch with Roland Wierwille. I went over to Berea for a visit and a semi-tryout. Coach Wierwille showed me around campus. I liked the people, the atmosphere, the friendliness. It was like a family.

Coach Wierwille was

Glen Drury: "One guy who really stepped up"

very organized. He was also very demanding, but I'd played for someone very demanding. It didn't bother me because I knew he could make me better. I thought I'd feel comfortable at Berea, and I believed, correctly as it turned out, that I was going to be part of a successful team. Luckily for me, Coach was looking for a couple of point guards. That description fit me and Steve Ridder. As things worked out, Steve played in front of me at Berea. During the time I spent on the bench I was always thinking, "What can I learn? What can I contribute even if I'm not playing? How can I help the team?"

I'm only five-nine. As a freshman I didn't get into any varsity games, but I did play as a sophomore. I wasn't a great athlete. I had less physical ability than Steve or Tracy Thompson. My strengths were court awareness, vision, and an understanding of where people should be and when they should do things. I developed good camaraderie with the other players, and I knew who needed the ball and when. I was a good passer and ballhandler. I could hit an open shot. I was a pretty good defensive player, too. I had been taught a lot about defense in high school.

Coach Wierwille was very aware of my ambition to coach. Sometimes he talked to me about it after practice. On several occasions he asked me, "Do you think we're doing the right thing here?" He was putting my mental ability to work, and that was good.

One night we were playing Union, and they were using a one-three-one zone that was giving us trouble. We were attacking in a two-one-two set. It was not effective. I'm a very vocal person, and I was talking on the end of the bench. That disturbed Coach, but he responded by putting me in. He said, "If you think you can do it, do it!" When I went in we switched to a one-four high and were very successful with it. From that point on we played a one-four high. I thanked Coach for giving me the chance to help the team. My study of the game made that contribution possible.

A high school player who comes to college is usually accustomed to being the best player on his team. Then in college he finds himself playing with fifteen guys as good as he is or better. With Tracy and Steve ahead of me at Berea I was obliged to become a real good cheerleader. I had to sit back and critique the situation and try to understand it. It worked out for me, because playing with good players made me better, and when they got hurt I ended up playing a little.

Tracy wasn't a better shooter than I was, and he wasn't any stronger; however, he was quicker and taller. Coach felt more comfortable with him against presses. As a small man I had a harder time if opponents pressed me. Tracy could see over the top.

Steve was even taller, and that helped make him a more valuable commodity than either Tracy or me. Steve was a very good teammate because he wanted the team to be successful. He made sure that we all stayed together. Even at that age he knew that success is achieved through other people, not just oneself. Steve thought pass before score, and he was an excellent passer, especially in the dribble penetration, where he could really kick it off.

Those two guys made me the third point guard. Once they were both hurt, and I got to start about five games in a row. One of them was against Campbellsville. Campbellsville guarded the Big Four instead of me that night, and I scored twenty-five points. That was unusual for a little bitty guard like me.

Coach Wierwille and Coach Tom Bryant at Centre didn't see eye to eye. When we went to Centre that year I played a lot and had a real good game, but we lost by two points. The following year we went back there and beat Centre, but I didn't play. When I got to know Tom after my college days, he asked me why Coach didn't use me in that game. "We thought you kept Berea in the game the year before," he said. "So we did all our preparation to make sure you didn't handle the ball to set them up for their shots."

"The guy who played in front of me was better. He showed he was better because we won that game."

Tom said, "That darn Wierwille! He'll do anything to beat you!"

That's not the end of the story. Later I went to watch a Berea-Centre game. Coach Wierwille said, "That Bryant guy, if you ever talk to him, I don't know if I'll talk to you again." That was competition! They're both good gentlemen, but I got tickled at the two of them.

My sophomore season was the last for the Big Four. We thought we were the best team in the conference, the team that should go to the national tournament. We put pressure on ourselves. The monkey on our back got so heavy that we forgot to have fun. If we had reached our goal we would have been jubilant, but when we didn't, we felt a tremendous letdown. In our sorrow we got down on ourselves. I learned a big lesson there: expectations notwithstanding, you should never take the fun out of any working situation you're involved in.

Two of the big four, Bill Nichols and Craig Jefferson, were among my closest friends, along with my roommate, Jerome Simmons, who only played JV basketball. They were black and I was white, but they didn't mind. They liked me because I distributed the ball well. I knew what cuts they were going to make and could get them the ball, so they wanted me on their team even in pickup games. Those guys were so accepting, so friendly and kind and easy to talk to, that they made it easy for me to fit in.

I found that I loved to play at Seabury. Not many of the other colleges supported their team the way Berea did. Night in and night out we had a lot of people there. We were rarely beaten at Seabury. It had a mystique about it. It was so unique, so different. You couldn't shoot out of the corners because of that overhang. When I started analyzing why Coach had us playing a three-two zone, there was the answer: to force the ball down the baseline.

The next year was tough on Coach as he tried to decide who should be out on the floor. Now I understand what he went through, because I've had heavy graduations too. At first you try to refill roles in the same system, but sometimes you have to adjust your system to fit the personnel you have. So in 1979-80 we stopped playing as much three-two. We played some one-three-one. We played some man. We pressed more. All the experimenting was difficult for him. He couldn't get the double-low offense working well after we had lost so much strength in the lane when Ed Flynn and Arno Norwell graduated.

Vance Blade moved into a starting role. He had great hands and good eyes. I knew as a point guard that the more Vance touched the ball, the better he was going to play. One of my goals was to set the offense to get it to him.

Marcus Crawford was a transfer, and it took all of us a little while to understand him. Marcus was a heck of a shooter. We knew that if he popped open, he was going to make his shot. In that double-low set we had to figure out his cut, where he was going to be. It took me half a year to learn what his offensive mindset was, and that was longer than I wanted, but I was determined to learn everything I could. I was still playing behind Tracy and Steve, and I wanted to make sure that if Coach used me I knew what made our two main guys, Vance and Marcus, go.

For me as the third guard it was still five games in, five games out. I'm very competitive and my will to win is strong, and when I didn't play I lost some of my confidence and didn't perform well when I got the chance. That was nobody's fault but my own. I had to try to maintain a positive mindset.

I thought, "If I'm going to play a reserve role, how can I make my teammates better?" As the season went along I began to take pride in figuring out a way to get my group to win when we scrimmaged in practice. The first and second and third teams usually scrimmaged a half every day. I asked myself what positions I could put people in to help them improve their game. For instance, Tim Shelton was often on my team, and I put him on the right block, saying, "If you'll be there, I'll get you the ball." That move made us more competitive, and in turn the other team had to step up in order to beat us. So everybody got better.

At the close of the regular season we went down to Campbellsville. Campbellsville had dusted us in both games that year. They were coached by Lou Cunningham to be a running team. They liked to speed the game up. They had an ultra-quick guard in Cecil Ellis, and neither Tracy nor Steve nor I had his kind of quickness. They had beaten us by pressing and forcing turnovers.

Preparing us for our playoff game, Coach Wierwille was determined not to let Campbellsville press us. As he analyzed that team he observed that they couldn't guard in the halfcourt. He figured that the more we kept the ball and made them guard, the less chance they had of getting into their full-court press.

Their fans booed us, of course. They didn't like the slowed-down game we were playing. But in their minds they still thought their team was going to win. And Campbellsville could have won if they had taken more risks, fouled us more, and doubled us in the half. But they hadn't practiced those things. They were caught by surprise, and being surprised made them worry.

Steve hit a last-second shot to win the game 8 to 7. Although I didn't play at all, I had a great time. I congratulated Coach Wierwille. I understood what he had managed to do, and I was very proud of him and happy for him. My mind works strategically, and in the locker room and on the bus back to Berea I asked myself, "What would I have done in Lou Cunningham's shoes?" I concluded that Campbellsville should have forced us to shoot the basketball. I wrote down all my thoughts.

Our next game, at Thomas More, was a whole lot more of the same. Thomas More managed to force the tempo more. They had seen the 8 to 7 score and called Campbellsville, so we didn't surprise them. But Tracy and Steve and I were pretty good dribbling and timing guards. I got to play against Thomas

Glen Drury and Ed Flynn with Coach Wierwille.

More. Both Tracy and Steve fouled out, and I ended up with the ball on the last shot. It wasn't my objective to shoot it myself. I intended to drive toward the basket and throw it to Jim Royer, but Thomas More let me go. I took a little jump shot in the lane, it went in, and we won by a point. I was very happy that Coach had enough confidence in me to put me in at the finish of a close game.

When Pikeville beat us to end our season, I was disappointed in all of us, including me. We seemed to be satisfied to simply be playing in the championship game. Pikeville was more talented than either Campbellsville or Thomas More, but I still believed we were capable of taking them out of their game and beating them. I'm not saying that Coach didn't do his job, but the mentality of the players seem to be, "We've done all that we can do." I was disappointed in myself because I always tried to get everybody ready. I thought, "Why didn't I pick us up? What should I have done to prepare us to play our best game against Pikeville?"

Tracy graduated after that season. I knew that Steve and I were going to be playing a lot together the following year, the final year for both of us. I was ready. I started the first six or seven games, and then I got hurt for the first time in my career.

I broke my right foot. It happened during a game. I didn't realize I had broken it. I was a very determined player, so I kept on playing. The next day I couldn't walk. Coach sent me to the hospital for an x-ray, which showed a break. For the rest of the season I had to sit and watch. I might not have started the entire year ahead of Donnie Harper, who had a real good shooting eye, but I was terribly disappointed.

I still came to practice, still tried to utilize what I had. Coach sent me on some scouting trips for him, to watch other teams and bring back information that would help us. One of those teams was Cumberland. Cumberland introduced their players like UK or the Chicago Bulls are introduced today. "Jumping Joe" Dallas, what a buildup he got! The atmosphere at Cumberland made us especially eager to beat them. We didn't do it, but we gave it everything we had, and that made me proud.

I came back at the end of the year and played my last game. I didn't like the way my career ended, but when it was over I said to myself, "Glen, look at what you've gained. Look at how far you've come and think about far you're going to go."

I started out in the labor program as a broom maker. It was good for me even though I didn't like it. It was the lowest paying of the jobs and probably the hardest, but it was okay with me to have the hardest job. I was an old tobacco cutter anyway.

I had to dye the brooms, take them out of the heat, and lay them out to dry. Johnnie Reed, my supervisor, was a very demanding man and not the greatest communicator, but he got the work out of me. He was always saying, "Get it done, Glen! They've got to have those for tomorrow." That stuck in my head. At the time it upset me a little, but one thing I've always been good at is thinking, "What's he trying to do? What's he trying to accomplish?" Finally I understood him.

I went from there to janitorial work in the dorm. I had to clean the hall and the bathrooms on Dana Three. I liked that job better because I was allowed to set my own hours. At that time my main focus was still basketball, so I started to neglect my job. What I needed was somebody to kick my tail, and they did it! I didn't like that, but it helped me. The next semester I did my job much better. I ended up supervising janitors in Dana and the education building. Then I stayed a fifth year and coached JV basketball. In those jobs I gained valuable leadership experience.

Physical education was my major. I wasn't a good student at first. I didn't use my mental energy in that area. In high school I had done just enough to get by, so when I got to Berea I didn't know how to apply myself.

Many people helped me with my academics. Mary Lou Pross, a health teacher, was very understanding. She talked with me a lot. Bob Pearson, who was head of the Athletic Department, showed me how to keep myself organized. Among the advice he gave me was to take notes, read over my notes, re-read them, and read them over one more time just before going to class.

Coach Wierwille checked up on me a lot, making sure I kept up with my class work. My dorm director, Ed FitzGerald, talked with me. He'd say,

"Glen, how are things going? Are you applying yourself?" He saw my grades one day and got a little worried.

Berea gave us something that most colleges couldn't or wouldn't. I felt it from the first. It was a kind of caring or nurturing, and it was just what I needed. I ended up on the Dean's List my last two years. That made me proud of myself.

I was very happy at Berea. My parents didn't make a lot of money, so at times I needed to go home and work tobacco over breaks. But I always returned to school. Like everybody else, I started off homesick, and that contributed to my academic problems. After I got over that, I had fun. Sometimes I was learning and didn't know I was learning. That's what I consider some of the best education.

To teach and coach at the high school where I'd played was not my original goal. At first I wanted to go into college coaching. When I was offered a job as an assistant at Anderson County, I took it. I did that for three years, then became head coach at Western Anderson, a small school. Two years later Anderson County hired me as head coach.

During my years at Berea I'd come back in the summers, Glen Drury, a big college player now. Even though I'd led my high school team in scoring, people realized that I wasn't a great athlete. And as coach I had to prove that I knew what I was doing. Through the first few years there were a lot of questions, but the best quality I've got is determination. I looked back into my past, thought about what I could do to help these kids, and ultimately became successful. Anderson County has been good to me. Maybe the Lord sent me back here.

Sometimes I still use what Coach Wierwille called the double-low offense. I came to Berea with a guard-oriented mindset, but Coach Wierwille was an inside man when he played at Eastern, and he taught me how important it is to establish an inside game. He helped me understand that if you can establish inside, you can establish outside. So we use the double-low when we want to force our opponents to guard our inside game, when we're bigger in the lane and trying to make an entry pass quickly to the block to get a quick hitter.

How long do I plan to coach? Until I decide it's time to quit! Coaching is fun here. I love kids, and I love the game. It looks as if I'll stay in public education. I've still got twelve or fifteen years left.

July 22, 1998

When my mother met Coach Wierwille, I knew that in the back of her mind she was thinking, "This man will continue to do what I have done." I was one of five kids growing up in a one-parent household with only her to raise us. She ruled us with an iron fist. We were all big, but she intimi-

Vance Blade: "Great hands and good eyes"

dated us. She made us shake all over. We were too scared of her not to listen when she said something. We were fortunate that she dealt with us the way she did. With the exception of my older brother, who got hooked on drugs, we all got good educations and good jobs after we left home. He could have done the same, but he didn't.

My mother saw in Coach Wierwille a person who would keep my butt in line. She was right. I came to Berea College after spending the first eighteen years of my life in a dictatorship, and in college there was no escape. Coach Wierwille pounded on us constantly. I didn't agree with some of the things he was on us about because as a young man I lacked foresight. But I respected him because he was the coach. Nobody of my generation ever thought about hitting or choking a coach.

I'll tell you a story I call "Seven Minutes of Hell." On the day before Thanksgiving in 1978, my freshman year, Coach said, "You guys can go home tonight, but I want you all back here in the gym tomorrow at seven o'clock. Eat dinner and come back."

I got a ride home to Eminence, Kentucky. The next day I asked my granddaddy to take me to Georgetown to meet Steve Caldwell so I could ride the rest of the way back with him. I got there at five o'clock, and Georgetown is about an hour's drive from Berea. Steve's sister, who was going to take us to Berea, was hugging and kissing with her boyfriend in the car, and she wouldn't let that boy go. Steve and I we were seven minutes late getting back.

When we walked into the gym, Coach had steam rolling off him. He didn't say anything to me. He didn't say anything to Steve. I asked the players, "What does Coach do to you when you're late?" Nobody knew. Nobody had ever been late.

Coach ran both of us out of the gym. He told us to hit the locker room, get our street clothes on, get out of there. I didn't know what was going to happen. He came down and raked us over the coals. He asked us if we really wanted to play basketball at Berea. He was tough on us. Then he said, "Get your clothes back on and get upstairs. I want both of you, dressed, in this gym tomorrow morning at eight o'clock."

When we showed up the next morning, Coach made us run seven suicides. When you run suicides you start on one end of the floor. You run up and touch the foul line, then run back to the out-of-bounds line where you started. You run up, touch the center court line, and run back. You run up, touch the other free throw line, and run back. You run up to the last foul line and run back. We ran seven of those and ran them hard.

This was on Friday. Saturday we went to Louisville for a tournament. That wasn't far from Eminence, so my family and my pastor were there. That was the first time they'd seen me play. Coach put me in the game. I was thankful for that, because he didn't have to. But my legs were jelly. They ached. I couldn't move, and I was very ineffective. We lost the game. I was in excellent shape, but my body wasn't prepared for what it had just been through.

That seven minutes of hell taught me something. After I thought about it I realized that when a coach is responsible for a player and that player doesn't show up, a million things race through the coach's mind. "Was there an accident?" Did my player get injured or killed? If he did, what do I tell his parents? Maybe I shouldn't have let the players go home for Thanksgiving break. If I hadn't let them go home, he wouldn't have had an accident. And so on. Remember, Coach Wierwille had never had anybody late before! I didn't know why I had to run those suicides, but now I fully understand. I have young children of my own, and I worry about them all the time. So while I respected Coach then, I have a greater appreciation for him today than I did yesterday, just as I do for my mom.

Coach was brilliant at knowing everybody's attributes, what they could do and what they couldn't do, and putting the right mix together. He was a master of preparation, too. We did everything in conjunction with conditioning. We didn't walk into an offensive set, we ran into it. We ran constantly in practice. Coach believed that if we were better conditioned than the other team, we could probably overpower them at the end. He was right, too. I was in top shape. On Saturdays I reported at five-fifteen for the junior varsity game, played the whole game, and then played half the varsity game. I could have played more if I had to.

As Coach conditioned us, he made sure that we understood our offenses and defenses. We always knew what play to execute. We didn't always execute flawlessly, but that wasn't because he hadn't prepared us.

I played a couple of years of football at Eminence High School. In both those years I had bad basketball seasons. I had trouble making the transition from the gridiron to the hardwood, and basketball in November and December was disastrous for me. I decided that any athletic career I might have beyond high school was going to be in basketball, so as a senior I skipped football and played only one sport.

In the summer before my senior year in high school, Warren May, my industrial arts teacher, moved to Berea. I helped him move, but I had no idea at that time about going to school there. But I had several high school business courses under J.T. Stinson, a Berea College alumnus and former basketball player, and he took me to visit the College. That was my first time on the campus. I met Coach Wierwille and some of the players along with some faculty members and administrators. I liked what I saw and decided to enroll there.

I played power forward. At six-three and a half, I could compete with people who were six-eight or six-nine. I didn't believe in blocking out. I simply used my quickness to beat people to the ball. I had outstanding leaping ability, and it wasn't something that came naturally. I worked on jumping. A lot of people didn't believe I did that. They'd say, "All you guys can jump." But that's not true. My brother and I spent long hours after school lifting weights, doing toe raises, anything we could do to make us decent competitors. I developed a strong inside game, rebounding and scoring underneath the basket.

I wasn't tall enough to play power forward even in the KIAC. There were guards as tall as I was. I had the skills to go inside, but I needed confidence. I had to prove to myself that I could compete consistently and effectively against guys who were four or five inches taller. I wasn't sure about that at first, because in high school I only ran across a guy that tall once in a while. Night in and night out in the KIAC in those days, the caliber of player was excellent, much better than it is today. Everybody was big and strong. But once I gained confidence, I was all right.

Ed Flynn was a guy who made the freshmen earn their stripes. Ed and Arno Norwell, the two big guys in the middle, were hard on us in practice. We realized only later that they did that to make us tough. They succeeded in that purpose. The upperclassmen served as mentors to the young players. They were all decent human beings.

Ed and Arno and Craig Jefferson and Bill Nichols were established stars who should have had huge egos, but they didn't. They worked together. The person who probably had the hardest job was Tracy Thompson, because he had to direct all those guys. He dealt with four players who were all-conference and held them together. Tracy was a great point guard.

Bill was an excellent shooter. He mastered the art of shooting from the corner in Seabury Gym better than anyone I ever saw. Bill was also a very comical individual. He lived on one end of the third floor of Bingham Hall, and I lived on the other end. The telephones were in the hallways then. One day Bill tapped on my door and said, "Hey, Blade, telephone! I think it's some girl!" I didn't know that he had half-filled a thirty-gallon trash can bucket with water and tipped it toward the door. When I opened the door, all the water rushed into the room. That was his idea of a joke. But there was a serious side to Bill. He could break away from his silly mode and talk seriously.

In my freshman year I was the sixth or seventh person off the bench. I could count on being able to play because Craig Jefferson was always in foul trouble. Coach didn't like Craig getting all those fouls called on him, but I loved it.

Although we had high hopes of going to the national tournament, we had to stay home after losing to Kentucky State. We had to play the game in Lexington because we didn't have a regulation-size floor. If that game had been played at Berea College, it wouldn't have been close. Berea fans generated a tremendous amount of energy. They'd follow us on the road, but putting Berea fans in an arena-type setting on the road was not the same as having them at Seabury. Still, we should have won that game, regardless of where it was played.

It was a terrific game for me as a freshman. I can still remember Ed Flynn taking the ball to the middle, drawing everybody to him, and laying it right in my hands so I could score. I played well that night, but for some reason we had trouble playing up to our full potential as a team. Kentucky State wasn't a better team than we were. We gave the game away, and I couldn't understand it. The upperclassmen had lived through the Cumberland loss the previous year when Larry Gorman hit his two free throws at the end. I don't want to say that we were snake bit, but that might have been in back of some folks' minds. After we lost to Kentucky State, Ed and Arno and Bill and Craig were devastated. So was Coach. I was hurt, but I knew there would be a tomorrow for me.

Although we lost those four big seniors, when the next season began we refused to believe that we wouldn't be just as good. We worked as hard, but the year we had was frustrating. We simply weren't as talented. The gap between us and the schools that gave out athletic scholarships was starting to show. They could go out and recruit talent. Berea had been very blessed to have Ed and Arno and Bill and Craig at the same time. I don't know how our school pulled it off, to attract four guys like that in one year. We've never been able to do it since.

We were just a .500 team in 1979-80, but the fans hung in there. However we performed, we always had the 100 percent support of our fans. They always came to the games. A fan named Owen Presley once said to me, "I don't expect you to win every game. You're competing against schools that offer scholarships. But when you guys walk onto the floor, you play hard and put it all on the line. That's what I come to see. If you do that enough, you're going to win some games."

Our missing ingredient was a big man. A six-nine player like Arno Norwell could have helped me with rebounding and set picks to give us good shots. We had Jim Royer, but he played sparingly. Jerry Harris was a big guy with a good shot, but he had knee problems. He was a nontraditional student who came back from the military to finish his degree.

Marcus Crawford and I did the best we could in the frontcourt. Marcus was a tremendous asset who helped filled the scoring void. We lost fifty or sixty points a game when the Big Four left, not to mention what we lost in rebounding. There were times when Marcus and I played hurt, and Coach knew it. When we looked in his eyes they seemed to say, "I know you're hurting, but get yourself ready! We've got to keep going!" We played as hard as we were capable of playing.

To open the KIAC tournament we had to go down to Campbellsville. Those guys had beaten us twice. We couldn't run with them. They had quick guards and a tough player inside named James Boulware. Today his brother works in the same building I do. I show him the scars over my eyes and say, "Your brother did this."

We knew that in order to win the game on Campbellsville's floor, we had to slow it down. We had to take very few shots and make their guys work hard on defense. We ran an offense designed to put the ball in the hands of the guards, who would dribble and penetrate, dribble and penetrate. We would hold the ball as long as we could, then break for the basket and try to get a good shot.

Those were the days before the shot clock. Although few shots were taken, the game was exciting. It took a tremendous effort by Coach Wierwille to keep us composed and settled down. We were fired up, playing hard, and as we began to realize that we could beat Campbellsville, Coach had to work hard to keep us focused. It was our strategy that enabled us to play with Campbellsville, and if we got out of it, we'd find ourselves in trouble fast. Because we stayed with our strategy the whole game, we won. The final score was 8-7. Steve Ridder was high point man with four points. It was a magnificent win for us.

Our next game was at Thomas More, and we weren't sure we could pull off another victory. Thomas More had also beaten us twice. We employed the same style against them, although not as deliberate as in Campbellsville. There was a little more output in terms of points. It was a close game and a hard-fought one. They had a huge crowd. But things were working well for us, and in beating Thomas More we did something we didn't think we could do. That was a good night. When we got back to campus, everybody was happy and excited.

Our next trip was to Pikeville. That's when the wheels fell off the train. We ran up against the Newsome brothers, Robert, Greg, and Steve. Their whole team was good, and their building was a tough environment to play in. Our luck ran out.

If there was anyone who believed that we could do anything, it was Steve Ridder. Steve was one of the best motivators I've been around. Everything he said was positive. Even if we were going up against a giant, Steve would say, "We can do this, you know."

Steve was someone we needed and Coach needed. He was a perfect person to have on the team because he was a good bridge from Coach Wierwille to the players. There was only so much Coach could do. Coach couldn't go into the dorm and live with us. He couldn't see us on campus all the time. But a fellow player could, and Steve was always there for all of us. I considered him more than a teammate. He was a good friend.

Steve had excellent peripheral vision. He knew where everyone was on the floor, and he could pass the ball right where he wanted it. He often said to me, "If you would just take that alley-oop pass I throw to you and dunk it, it would be so much easier than putting the ball in off the glass!"

I was a short guy who could jump, but I never had any intention of dunking one of Steve's alley-oop passes. My main goal was to catch the ball. It was hard for me to focus on the rim while receiving his pass. I knew he was going to throw it when he looked away from me and looked down. All I wanted was to get my hands on it. Then I'd figure out where the rim was. Steve was a great passer, a great assist man, but sometimes he thought he was throwing to a seven-footer.

Keith Riley and I were both freshmen the same year. Keith was a guy who was determined to work hard to become a good player. In high school he might have been an average player, but he was a guy who wanted more out of his ability than he'd been getting in the past. He became a true competitor.

Because both of us were tenacious inside, we had a terrible collision at a game at Clinch Valley when we were seniors. I grabbed a rebound and came down looking for an outlet. Keith was right next to me, and my elbow hit him just below his nose. When I turned around he was on his hands and knees with blood coming out of his mouth. At first I thought I'd merely busted his lip, but my elbow had broken the bone that holds the upper teeth in place and shoved his teeth halfway down his throat.

Keith went over to the sideline, and Coach took one look at him and said, "Oh my God." There happened to be a dentist in the audience, and he came down and assisted. Everything had been going great up to that point. We were routing Clinch Valley by twenty points. But I was terribly upset. We were all in a shell, and we didn't want to play any more. Forget the game, we were all worried about Keith! Coach was too. He wanted to get out of there just as badly as we did. We lost the game, and it was a long ride back. By the time we got Keith to the hospital, six hours had passed. It was a nightmare. Luckily he recovered and rejoined the team later in the year.

I met Tommy Owsley when he came to campus for a visit one spring. He joined us in a pickup game, and afterwards in the shower I noticed that two of the toes were missing on one of his feet. When I asked him what had happened, he explained that he'd had an accident on a riding mower when he was young.

"How in the world can you keep your balance and play basketball like you play without those toes?"

Tommy said, "I've got this little piece." He had a device that he slipped into his shoe to give him the balance he needed. That was the most amazing thing about that guy. He was so quick and could steal the ball so easily. What's more, he was a great shooter.

Tommy was one of several excellent players who joined the team when I was a junior and senior. Donald Hairston was a superb athlete. He was about six feet tall, but we always told him that if he could straighten out his bow legs, he'd be six-six! Donald was physically strong and a tremendous jumper. Speaking of jumpers, Kevin Mullins was a guy who could jump right out of the gym. We always accused him of being a soul brother. I don't know what Kevin's vertical was, but he was a great athlete.

I scored my thousandth point against Thomas More on a last-second shot that won the game for us. That was a memorable occasion, but the most memorable game of my senior year was one we lost. Our opponent was Cumberland, and it was my last game at Berea College. It was a tremendous game for me as an individual. I felt like I was in control of everything. I don't remember how many points I scored that night or how many rebounds I got, but it was a lot. I heard someone say, "He played like it was his last game."

That was good, because it meant that I went out the way I came in. I got into our Homecoming game when I was a freshman and played very well. Everybody knew after that game that I had a vertical leap of forty-plus inches. My first and last games stand out more in my mind than any of the others.

When I was a junior I became obsessed about doing just one thing: graduating from Berea College. The mistake I made when I came to campus was placing basketball above academics. In middle school and high school I was a so-so student. With my mother doing all she could to raise us but sick all the time with high blood pressure, I had to work. I started working when I was nine years old. I worked two, three jobs, all kinds of things. I spent more time working than I did studying simply because we needed to eat.

When I got to high school people started telling me that I was a good basketball player. When they started talking about college, I started clicking. In my small K-through-eight school I was near the bottom of the fifty students in my class, but by the time I graduated from high school I'd worked my way up to number thirteen. I was proud of that. I was motivated to pull myself out of poverty, because if I could do it, maybe I could pull my brothers and sister out of it. So by the time I got to Berea College I was an average student.

I wasn't sure I could get into college. My high school guidance counselor, Ruth Collins, worked very hard to help get me where I needed to be academically. In my senior year I was scared and nervous about the whole college thing, and I said to her, "Do you think I can do this? I don't know if I can."

She looked at me and said, "Vance Blade, I know you can do it. You can do anything you want to." Her words have stayed with me to this day. I've learned the value of hard work and preparation.

When I got to college I found that I was smart enough to survive, even thrive. But first I had to do two things. Number one, I had to study. Number two, I had to believe that I could do it. And we all get by with a little help from our friends.

Soon after I enrolled at Berea I took a test that showed I had a few aca-

Boone Tavern

demic deficiencies. My math skills and reading comprehension level weren't sufficient, so I needed to take some non-credit classes. I spent the first semester of college getting ready for college! But I made the best of that first semester because I had the right people helping me. I had people like Steve Boyce, a super guy who worked hard with me in math. I had a good tutor by the name of Steve Dillard. He worked day and night with me. Vicky Taylor, Steve Ridder's fiance, was a math major who was very helpful to many of us who were struggling in that area. While Vicky worked with us, Steve had to give up a lot of the time he could have been spending with her. You don't forget things like that.

Beth Baber, who taught English, helped me improve my grammar and punctuation. Bobby Fong took me to another level of ability to express myself in writing. Jim Masters, my adviser, put pressure where it needed to be. He guided me.

I had the time, because at Berea I had to work only ten hours a week, not forty. But I still had that basketball thing. Most of the professors at Berea didn't give a diddley squat whether I played basketball, soccer, or what. They had just one thing in mind: that I learned enough to earn a degree. I couldn't make it at Berea if I kept basketball above academics, and besides, Coach would boot anyone off the team who didn't have the grades.

In my sophomore year the team didn't win the way it did when I was a freshman. Consequently, basketball got tougher. There was a lot of pressure on me and Marcus Crawford. If the two of us didn't produce, our team had little chance of being competitive.

I came close to being booted that year. I had personal problems with a young lady. I can't believe that I let somebody mess me up that badly, but I did, and it affected both my studies and my basketball season. It took a lot of help from John and Becky Cook and Coach Wierwille to get me back on track. They did a lot of talking to me. I'm very glad I got back on track, because I almost fell off. I remember working at Boone Tavern and gazing out the window and asking myself, "Why am I doing this? Why am I here? I should go home." But I didn't. I stuck it out.

By the time I was a junior my whole attitude had changed. The basketball thing was there, but I no longer had the drive I'd had when I was a freshman. I don't know if Coach sensed that in me or not. I'd made up my mind to put the classroom first.

The College always closed the dormitories during Christmas break. Because the basketball team needed to keep practicing, the players stayed in the homes of various people around town. When I was a freshman, Lamar Frederick and I stayed with John and Becky Cook. I stayed with the Cooks every year after that.

The Cooks were people who were down to earth. It was their home, but they made me feel as though I'd lived there all my life. They didn't mind leaving me there by myself. Once they went to New Orleans and trusted me enough to watch their two teenage boys, Steve and David, while they were gone. When they came back, the house was in order. There'd been no wild parties or any of that stuff!

John and Becky are two of the lovingest people I've ever known. One year I got real sick. I was sick the whole short term and lost twenty pounds. They let me stay at their house for a week. David was sick at the same time, and Becky took care of both of us. They were like parents to me. When I visit Berea today, their house is the first place I go, and they know that if they're ever in Louisville, where I live now, my door is always open to them. They're special people, and they mean a lot to me and my family.

I was a bellhop and porter at Boone Tavern, "Boone Saloon," the entire four and a half years I was a student. It was a good job. It was also a lucrative job, which maybe I ought not to confess. I made a lot of money as a bellhop. People came to the hotel with all kinds of wild perceptions about the poor Appalachian kids at Berea College. They'd look at me and my size sixteen feet and say, "Where are you from?"

"Eminence, Kentucky."

"Where do you get your shoes?"

They were just waiting for me to say, "The shoe library!" But the truth was that I had to order them, and that's what I said.

"Well, we'd like to give you a tip and help you out, but there are 'No Tipping' signs all over the hotel."

I'd say, "Ma'am, if they didn't put those signs up, every student on campus would want this job. They can't employ all the students over here. They have to work other places too."

"I hadn't thought of that. Here you go!"

It worked every time. But I was grateful for everything I got. If my mom sent me five dollars, I knew that was all she had. Getting five dollars from her was like getting 1000 dollars. It was big, important, special. At Boone Tavern I made enough money to help my sister Valerie when she enrolled at Berea. When I went home I could give a little money to my two younger brothers. I believe in miracles, and that job was a miracle to me. It was a gold mine. And I went the extra mile for every guest, no matter what they gave or didn't give me.

I majored in business administration. I had many fine teachers who helped make me what I am today. They didn't treat me differently than they treated anybody else; they exercised tremendous patience with all of us young folks, which is not always easy. In addition to the ones I've mentioned, I have fond memories of Mary Lou Pross, Orville Boes, William Schafer, Robert Menefee, and Robert Johnstone. And I can't forget Phil Spears in the Business Department. He'd sit there and tell us the way it was. He'd worked in corporate America, and he knew what reality is all about.

Studying came easier for me in college than it did in high school, where they separate students into below-average and average and superstar groups. But if some of the students who are average or below-average get in with some of the superstars, they learn more while they're drowning than they do back on the sand. That's what happened to me in college. I thought, "These people don't have anything on me. Their opinion is no better than mine."

There are blood, sweat, and tears on my Berea College degree. Success as a student didn't come naturally for me. I had to work at it real hard. In Business Law, for instance, I was borderline between a C and a B. I knew that if I did real well on the final I could get a B. I studied all night, then took the test and did well enough to earn the B I wanted.

The elite group at Eminence High School who were predicted to achieve everything looked back at the rest of us and said, "You guys are never going to be anything. You won't amount to a hill of beans." Well, I'm one of those guys, and I graduated from Berea College. I wasn't ever supposed to have anything, and I still don't have anything. I don't have anything because there are so many people to give to. There's family, church, United Way, and Berea College. I and my wife and two kids will never be rich, but we'll always survive. I grew up in two rooms with no running water, no nothing. But what I've learned over the years is to give and give and give. We'll always have something. Everything comes back to us. That's the way we live.

When I was a senior I met the woman who is my wife today, Vivian Hairston, Donald Hairston's cousin. Five of her older sisters graduated from Berea. When I met her my whole life settled down, my confidence soared, and I was able to do what I needed to do to finish out my basketball career and graduate.

Vivian was a freshman when I met her. I'd just got out of a devastating relationship with a girl who was still on campus. That girl was going to marry another guy, so she was on cloud nine while I was still drowning in my miseries. Then I met Vivian, and everything turned around.

I've known Vivian for seventeen years, and we've been married for eleven. I had to wait six years for her to finish undergraduate and graduate school. Her mom said that Vivian couldn't get married until she got her master's degree, and I said that was fine. But it's tough for a future son-in-law to be on his best behavior for six years.

What happens is, "Vance, can you do this?"

"Yes, I can paint your house, no problem." And I painted the house, believe me. It was a two-story, wood frame house.

Vivian and I got married in Berea. She had her bachelorette party at the Cooks' home. Becky and John took care of a lot of things for us and helped us in every way they could.

I've worked for the Kroger Corporation for sixteen years. Currently I am the assistant distribution manager at our Louisville distribution center. We receive all the merchandise here and disseminate it out to the stores. I'm in charge of all the logistics. It's a big job.

At one time I was human resource manager. Now I've got the human resource responsibility back in my lap because my successor, Frank Polian, just got himself promoted to assistant produce merchandiser, the same level of management that I'm at. Frank is a Berea College graduate I recruited.

With everything I've been able to do for this company, one of my greatest joys is to step back onto the Berea campus and recruit people to work for Kroger. I've been accused of favoritism, but Frank and Greg Osborne and I have all risen to top-level positions in the company. Berea graduates have done extremely well. There's no other college in the state of Kentucky that has the representation in this organization that Berea has.

September 23, 1998

Keith Riley   **1979-82**

I played basketball at Walton-Verona High School in northern Kentucky. My father was a cement finisher and had his own business. My uncles all worked in construction. I would probably have wound up in either a construction job or a factory job had it not been for the father of Mary Cheesman, one of my high school friends. Layne Cheesman was an accountant for a construction business and a big basketball fan. One day

he asked me where I was going to college. I said, "Nowhere." No one had contacted me, and I had made no plans.

Mr Cheesman called Coach Wierwille, who made a trip up to Walton a week later and invited me to come to Berea. He told me he couldn't guarantee anything, but he'd let me try out for the basketball team. He had the school send me the paperwork. I filled it out and was accepted. Mary Cheesman and I came to Berea College together and graduated together. She and I never had a boyfriend-girlfriend relationship, but we were close friends. Her whole family was very nice, and I still stop and see them when I go back to Walton.

When Coach Wierwille came to talk to me he was very direct, very firm, very straightforward. He didn't beat around the bush. He didn't sugarcoat anything. He just told me how it was. My father and my high school coach were exactly like that, so that was something I was used to. I appreciated a person who told you what

Keith Riley: "He became a true competitor"

they expected and you were supposed to go do it. That's why I thought I'd like it at Berea. Some people can't handle that coaching style. They want to be babied or pampered. But Coach liked to smack you on the back and tell you to get out there and do what you can do. That's how I felt things should go.

In high school I used to get up early, milk and feed the cows, go to school, practice basketball, go home, strip tobacco till dark, come in, eat supper, and do my homework. My days were long. I was accustomed to a busy, hectic, full schedule. So to come to Berea and work and go to school and practice didn't bother me. I really enjoyed college, although I realize now that I could have done better in the classroom.

I thought my high school practices were hard and physically demanding. After graduation I continued to run every day and came to college in excellent shape. But I've never been so tired and worn out and physically beat as I was after my first week of practice at Berea. My muscles, my bones, and my whole body ached. I thought I knew what demanding was, but I knew nothing about what it was. Coach Wierwille's practices were a nonstop rotation of activities. We never stopped, never took a break. Our practices lasted two and a half hours. After about an hour and fifteen minutes he would let everybody get a drink of water. Then we went right back into it. I couldn't believe that I could go through so much more conditioning than what I thought I was already in. But I did, and after a week or two I was okay. A lot of people don't realize the physical condition his players are in, to be able to go up and down the floor like they do.

I began a weight program to gain strength. You don't understand how weak you are as a freshman in college until you go up against the senior who's been there and has built up the strength and endurance you need to play at that level. I was a freshman when Bill Nichols and Craig Jefferson and Ed Flynn and Arno Norwell were seniors. What a powerful group of players! I'm six-four, but as a freshman I weighed only 175 pounds. In practice I had the thrill of guarding Arno. He could blow me out of the way and do whatever he wanted to do. That year of experience showed me what I was going to have to be like if I wanted to play. Here was a guy six-nine and 230 who was all-dominating inside, and I had to practice against him every single day of my first year in college. When I stepped up to the varsity the following year, there was nobody I played against who was ever as good as Arno Norwell was.

As a freshman I played solely JV ball, and I started my sophomore year as a JV player. During Christmas break the varsity team had to come back early to practice for tournaments, but as a JV player I got to go home to do some farm work to make some extra money to help pay for my bills at school. One evening my dad told me that Coach Wierwille had called and I was supposed to call him back. I did, and as usual he was very direct: "Practice is at such-and-such time, I need you back here for that practice, and I'll see you when you get here." I had to hustle to finish the work I'd promised to get done so I could get back to school when he wanted me. Coach had also called Dwayne Tate, my roommate, and said the same thing to him. Dwayne lived in Richmond, and his mom and dad let me stay with them for the rest of the break. From that point forward I was a varsity player.

After I graduated I asked Coach, "Why in the world did you ever keep me as a freshman? There were far better players than I was." When I first tried out there must have been sixty guys out there! His reply was that he felt I was coachable. So he gave me an opportunity, and he worked with me and developed me. He put me on a three-day-a-week weight program that I did religiously my first two years. He knew, I now realize, that if I was going to play it would have to be in the middle, and if I was going to play in the middle, I would have to be strong. I was the only player in the weight room the whole two years I did that. I got a lot stronger, but in my junior year I quit lifting weights because it was affecting my shooting.

Arno Norwell had been a rebounding, put-back guy who scored a lot of points, but I wasn't a big enough center for us to gear our offense around and pound it down inside. So what Coach wanted me to do was offset the opposing center, who usually was their scorer. My main job and responsibility was to play defense inside, keep their big man off the boards and keep him from scoring.

There was no particular guy who dominated our offense. Our scoring was well-balanced. Vance Blade, Marcus Crawford, Kevin Mullins, and Tommy Owsley all scored a lot of points for us, and in a few games I was the leading scorer. Steve Ridder was a big assist person for a couple of years. He could score, but he would rather make a move and get the ball to an open player somewhere else. One year a couple of guards got hurt and Glen Drury got to play. Glen came in and averaged twenty-something points for several games. It was remarkable what he did when he got the opportunity to play, how he could shoot the ball. He was one guy who really stepped up when Coach asked him to.

Marcus and Vance and I developed a close relationship when the three of us stayed in Berea one summer to take some courses. I was the monitor in Bingham dorm, which was emptied out and used for visiting groups in the summer. I was the host who made sure they had everything and cleaned up after them. Marcus and Vance had an apartment together. Marcus was pretty quiet, the kind of person who is not outgoing but once you get to know him is really friendly. Vance was very nice, but a lot more serious about everything, not as happy-go-lucky about things. He was always down to business.

Dwayne Tate was a shooting guard on the team. Dwayne grew up on a farm, and he was just your average, everyday country boy, calm, laid back, easy to get along with. Dwayne did not play his senior year. He knew he wasn't going to get to play a lot and wanted to concentrate on his studies in the Ag Department.

My junior and senior teams did not have winning records, but we were in every single game. We lost a lot of games on last-second shots, shots they made or we didn't make, or last-second turnovers. The one thing that would have made us an outstanding team is one dominating offensive player. Tommy Owsley became one later, but he wasn't when I was a senior. We needed a player like Jay Stenzel, who came along later. We lacked a go-to person offensively who we could depend on time after time, a guy who could make his own shot if it wasn't there and put it in. Without such a player we were a simply a undersized, scrappy, overachieving team, and we were probably fun to watch, because guys were flying everywhere. We had to be that way, or we would have been blown out of every game!

My sophomore and junior and senior teams were a close-knit group of guys who had a good time with each other. Probably the biggest cutup was Steve Ridder. He would always joke and fun and kid, and we had a blast with him around. He was a real trip, and a real leader because he would give his all out on the floor, and everybody else would too. When I looked at him I thought, "Here's a guy who's doing everything he can to help the team, and it wouldn't be fair if I don't give everything I've got." That tie between us is the reason we were such a hustling group of guys. We'd dive or jump across or run over somebody or get run over, do whatever it took to play our best and try to win.

During my sophomore and junior seasons Steve was the guy who led us and motivated us. In my senior year he was too, because he was the assistant coach. He was still the emotional leader of our group, although it was a different relationship with him in the huddle but not on the floor.

Steve was high scorer, with four points, when we beat Campbellsville in the KIAC tournament when I was a sophomore. At the end of the first half he shot a halfcourt shot that went in, and at the end of the second half, to win the game, he drove down the lane, was tripped, fell down, got up, threw the ball up, and it banked in off the glass. Those were the two shots he made, and we won the game 8 to 7.

Campbellsville had James Boulware inside. He was my toughest battle in college, but I could always keep him in check. After a game with Campbellsville my forearms and legs were bruised, and so were his. We played each other like two defensive linemen squaring off. He was about six-seven, an unbelievably talented guy, and I had to keep him pushed out of there and do everything I could to keep him off the boards. It was always a war. But when we went down to play them in the tournament that year I had a sprained ankle and couldn't defend him in any way. So Coach said, "We're going to play a slowdown game."

We had no idea it was going to wind up 8 to 7. We didn't plan it to wind up like that. Our rule was four high, pass, pick and roll. If we got a wide open layup we were going to take it. If we didn't we were going to kick it back out and pick and roll off the other side. And that's pretty much how the whole game went, all the time. When they got the ball they'd come flying down the court and throw up a shot and miss it, and we'd get the rebound and walk it back up and go into our pick and roll offense. We beat them out of the conference tournament they were favored to win, and their fans were not happy.

Our number one rivalry was Cumberland College. They had talent that shouldn't have been there at our level, guys who could do the things you saw on TV, not playing in the KIAC. A couple of times Cumberland came to Berea ranked in the Top Ten in the nation. But we beat them! That used to irritate them royally. They didn't like playing us because we were too feisty, in their face, slapping at the ball, doubling down on them.

Transylvania was also a rivalry because Coach Wierwille had coached over there and always wanted to do well against them. Centre College was a rivalry simply because Coach despised them, and if we didn't beat them we paid for it. There was another reason for our rivalry with those schools. The Transylvania and Centre guys looked down their noses at a bunch of dumb, poor, Appalachian basketball players coming to their elite institutions. They made no bones about it, they were better than we were. That would always get to us. They had more opportunities than we did, but that didn't make them any better. So we'd bust up on them a little to teach them a lesson.

I enjoyed playing at Thomas More. Most of their players were guys I had played against in high school, and I knew a lot of their fans. When I was a junior, Thomas More's Brian O'Conner was touted as the best player in the league. Nobody could do anything with him. I took that as a challenge.

When I worked out my defensive strategy, I always concentrated on the best area of my opponent's game. I'd attack him in that area, frustrate him in it, keep him off balance. If he was a scorer, I'd do everything I could to keep the ball away from him. If he was a rebounder, I'd try my utmost to box him off the boards. In my last game against O'Conner I scored twenty-nine points and held him to twenty-two, this guy who was going to mow us down and run over us and everything else. That was really satisfying, to go back to where I was from in northern Kentucky and play before all the people and reporters who knew me and have a good game like that, my best ever.

In my senior year I had my worst injury as a player. We were playing at Clinch Valley. My man blocked me out, so I pivoted around him to get the rebound. Vance Blade had also gone up for the ball and grabbed it. When I looked up Vance came down and accidentally hit me in the face with his elbow. It broke all of my palate and drove my two front teeth up against the roof of my mouth.

I went over to the bench with my head down and went down on one knee in front of Coach. He was saying, "What's wrong? What's wrong?"

I said, "My teeth."

"Spit them out!"

I told him, "I can't." And when I opened up my mouth, the blood that came out covered the whole floor. Coach turned my head up and asked me to open my mouth. To keep another person from panicking you're supposed to remain calm, but when Coach looked in my mouth the look on his face, well, he went into a panic himself. He put my head back down and told the referee, "We're going to need some time."

They got a dentist out of the stands. He reached up into my mouth and took those two teeth and actually got them hanging back down. They were still attached to the gum. He popped them back into a straight position. The pain then was worse than when I got hit. After that they got me some drugs.

After the game we drove all the way back from Clinch Valley. At three-thirty in the morning they brought me to Lexington to one of Coach's friends, who was a surgeon. He put my teeth back up there as best he could and wired the whole upper row together. Then he stitched the lip and gum and all the surrounding tissue. The idea was for the gum to heal and hold the teeth, and eventually that's what happened. I still have those original two teeth.

This happened on a Tuesday, and that Saturday we were going to play

Cumberland on senior night. I wanted to play, of course, but Coach didn't want me to. Dr McClure, the college dentist, said he didn't feel that there would be any trouble if he made me a special mouthpiece that would cover all the wires. The inside of my mouth, you see, was just like a barbed wire fence. They'd clipped off the ends of the wires when they fastened my teeth, so I had all these wires sticking out of my gums. If I got hit in the mouth the wire ends would come right through my lip. I harrassed Dr McClure to get the mouthpiece made, because he was real busy. On Friday afternoon he got a mouthguard for me to wear, and I finally got to practice a little. Coach let me run before that, but I couldn't practice because I didn't have anything to protect myself.

I was hurting, but I was determined to play on senior night. My brother Ken always said that I was the kind of player who was too nice until I got mad, and then I could play basketball. When I walked out there I heard one of the Cumberland players say, "Let's bust his other lip." That's all it took. I had one of my better games, and we beat them.

In the early minutes I was guarding one of those athletic guys who would show you the Converse star on his tennis shoe whenever he jumped up. Cumberland took a shot, it missed, and this guy went up for the rebound. From a spot near the free throw line I went up and over the top of everybody, grabbed the ball, hit the board, got undercut, and went flying up against the wall on the far end of the gym. Before I could get up, Coach had a substitute off the bench, taking me out of the game. He was scared to death. When I came over he said, "Are you all right?"

"No problem," I said. He put me right back in.

Ken is thirteen months younger than I am, and he followed me to Berea. Ken played basketball and baseball in high school, but when he came to Berea he wouldn't try out for basketball. He felt the talent level was too great and he wouldn't stand a chance, although I thought he would have done okay. Ken did play baseball for Berea, however.

I met Pam Powell my first semester at Berea College. We quickly became close friends working together on class assignments and attending various campus activities together. Gradually we began spending more and more time together.

Pam graduated and moved to Virginia to accept a teaching position. She returned every weekend to attend home basketball games. We began dating. After the season I would travel to Virginia to see her. Pam rented from and stayed with a family in their home. They were very nice to me and especially to Pam. Tracy Thompson was also teaching in the area, and I often visited him on my way to see Pam. Once Pam was very ill, and I went to Virginia with her mother, Imogene Powell, to bring her back to Berea, where her mother nursed her back to health.

On Valentines Day in 1981 I asked Pam to marry me. She said yes, and I thought that was the hard part. I'll never forget the anxiety I felt when I asked her father, Walter Powell Jr. He gave us his blessing, and her mother was very happy for us. We were married on August 1, 1981, the summer between my junior and senior years of college. Pam is my best friend, and we have two wonderful boys, Chad and Brent. I thank God for my wife and family.

My first college job was as janitor on the third floor of Elizabeth Rogers dormitory, where I lived. My job was to keep the floor clean. Later I found out it was supposed to be a cushy job and I wasn't really supposed to do all that much, but I kept everything clean and scrubbed and in real good shape. I don't like messy or dirty things, and if I do something I want to do it the best, not do it halfway.

I wanted to make some extra money, so the spring semester of my freshman year I started working at the front desk at Boone Tavern as a second job. I had to pay my way through school with what I'd make in the summer, and that barely covered my term bills. I needed that little bitty labor check for all my expenses during the school year like soap and shampoo and laundry detergent. After my first semester I learned that I could work additional hours at another job, so I arranged a total of twenty to twenty-five hours a week. I wound up helping out in all areas of Boone Tavern: front desk, bellhop, and dining room. I kept that job all the way through school, and supplemented that in my senior year with a five-hour teacher's assistant position for one of my major professors, James Yount.

My major was industrial arts technology management. Dr Yount, Dr James Hall, and Dr Donald Hudson were wonderful people. As professors they were professional, but they were our friends, too. They gave us real life advice about what we were going to experience in the real world. They were really good to me and everyone in the department.

One professor I'll never forget was Phil Spears. He had his own style. At first I despised him, but soon we got along. On the first day we walked into Accounting One he told us to read such-and-such a chapter and do such-and-such problems, and that was class. We did the assignment, not really understanding it, and in the next class he asked, "Did anybody have any difficulties with that? Do you have any questions?" But as it often is in the early going, nobody said anything. He said, "Okay then, read the next chapter and do these problems. See you later!" And he was gone. At the third class session we started to speak up. That was his way of teaching us a lesson: keep up or get left behind. We expected to be spoonfed, but he taught us that we'd have to take the responsibility for our education upon ourselves.

I started out not liking the guy, and he became one of my favorite teachers. I took Accounting Two with him. Some people would never take him again because he expected us to take the initiative to learn. He wasn't going to stand up there and force stuff into our heads. Phil Spears made a big impression on me. My time with him helped me a lot in my later years in college simply because I learned from him what I had to do.

I graduated intending to go into industry. My goal was to become a factory manager. I figured I could start out in finance or personnel or another area of some company and learn and work my way up. That was my ideal, and I was going to set the world on fire. But the job market was terrible when I got out in 1982. Companies were laying off workers who had thirty years of experience.

I mailed out I don't know how many resumes before I graduated. All I got back were letters that read, "Your qualifications and education are exactly what we're looking for. However...." I got pretty depressed after thirty or forty of those. I'd been married almost a year, I was ready to graduate, and I didn't have a job lined up. As graduation neared I decided I'd have to go around Berea and find a job locally until one of the companies I'd written to sent me a letter saying they wanted to hire me.

I knew several people who worked at Berea National Bank, so I just walked in and asked to apply for a job. They didn't have applications forms or anything like that, but they told me that I could come back later and talk with Fred Williams, the president. As I was walking out the back door Fred raised his office window and called to me. Apparently somebody had told him that I was looking for a job. It just so happened that he was looking to hire somebody. I went back into the bank, and he talked to me. He had seen me play ball at the College, and I had run into him the previous year when I was getting my driver's license renewed at the courthouse. He remembered me from that. He offered me a job and a salary and asked when I could start. I said, "I can start tomorrow." It was finals week, but as luck would have it I didn't have any tests scheduled. So during my finals week I started working full-time as a teller at the bank.

A few months later one of the senior vice presidents retired and a few months after that one of the loan officers left. Fred would have me do a lot of extra jobs in the bank, take care of this or that, then come back to the teller line. When the personnel director and auditor left to take another job, Fred promoted me to that position. He thought I had the qualifications for it and felt I would do a good job.

I wound up doing just about every job there was to do at Berea National Bank. I never looked for a job anywhere else because things kept coming available at the bank, and each time I got shuffled the board would review my salary and give me an increase for added responsibilities. I liked what I was doing because I had studied accounting and economics and many other things that tied in directly with the banking business. So everything worked out really well. I had never considered a career in banking when I was going to college, but the management part of my degree qualified me for the various things I had to do. When Fred decided he wanted some time for himself last fall, he promoted me to president.

If it hadn't been for Coach Wierwille and Berea College, I'd probably be an hourly worker somewhere or maybe a low-level supervisor, just working day to day. Coach made the effort to drive up to see me and say, "If you want to come to Berea, I'll give you every opportunity to play if you show me you can and want to." I had the ability and desire not just to play basketball, but to earn a college degree, and Berea gave me the opportunity to get a four-year college education at a cost I could afford. The work I did cutting and stripping tobacco and installing water lines and septic tanks made me enough money to pay for my school at Berea, but it wouldn't have been a drop in the bucket anywhere else.

I hope Berea College considers me a success story, because what they've done is great. My Berea education helped transform me from a poor high school guy to a person who's successful in business, and I'm just one of thousands. I don't want the people who run the College to get so caught up in money and endowment matters that they forget the needs of their students. The purpose of Berea College is not to become a hugely endowed or rich institution. Its primary mission was and should always be to provide a top-quality education for people who can't afford one anywhere else. As long as Berea College does that it will always be successful, and people will always give the College the money it needs to keep going. But if the College gets away from that, people will close their wallets and say, "You're not doing what you're there to do. You're not there to become a financial giant. You're there to teach people." I hope Berea College will always stay on the right track.

August 20, 1998

Jeff Britt   1980-84

I grew up in the small town of Scottsville, Kentucky, and attended Allen County Scottsville High School. The opportunity to play college basketball was something I worked very hard to achieve. I played four years of high school ball, and in the summers I played all the time with friends. I attended basketball camps, including Transy's. I spent hours and hours practicing. I played pickup games. I practically slept with that basketball. I loved and lived and breathed the game.

There were many high school basketball players, and not that many college scholarships to be handed out. I had a friend who knew how much I wanted to play college basketball. His name was Mike Patton, and he was a Berea College graduate who sometimes scouted players for Coach Wierwille. He took me up there on his own. Coach Wierwille watched me and a couple of other players and invited us to enroll at Berea and try out. I wasn't sure what my chances were, but I was excited to have an opportunity to try out at Berea College. Over forty kids tried out, and it was very competitive. I wasn't sure if I'd made it. A list was posted. I made the cut, and I was thrilled to death.

I'm six feet one and a half. I discovered that the big difference between high school and college ball is that you have to be much stronger and in really good physical condition. That was the biggest adjustment I had to make. Coach Wierwille had an extensive conditioning program that we had to go through before we could even start practicing. We spent a lot of time running. There was a lot of sprint work and a lot of drills. He wanted us to be fundamentally sound in all phases of the game: dribbling, passing, shooting, and defense.

Our practices were very demanding, but I didn't mind. All that hard work allowed me to release some stress. It was good for me to get in there and dribble that ball around and sweat for a couple of hours. The practices helped me to become more disciplined.

The best part of my game was my leadership on the court as a point guard, setting things up. I was a better passer than I was a scorer. I prided myself on looking for the open man and making that extra pass to get the ball inside.

As a freshman I played with guards Glen Drury and Steve Ridder, two great leaders. Even though they were seniors, they showed me the ropes. Glen and Steve were outstanding team players and good people. They were both good passers and played hard-nosed defense. There was room for a point guard on the team that year, and I played a lot. In January I had a good game against Transylvania. I came in off the bench and sparked us with a couple of steals, and we rallied from behind to win by five at their place. That game was one of the highlights of my career. It earned me a starting spot for four or five games.

The next year Donald Hairston and Tommy Owsley joined the team.

Jeff Britt: "He would nag you to death"

They were guards of all-American caliber. Trying to beat them out of a starting spot was rough going. We had another good guard in Donnie Harper. I played a reserve role from my sophomore year on.

That frustrated me, and I had several conversations with Coach Wierwille. He told me he understood that I wanted to play more and wanted to start. He said he would be upset with me if I didn't feel that way, and he encouraged me to try to do my best. So I gave it my best shot. I felt that even as a reserve player I contributed something valuable. I was proud and honored to be a part of the team for four years. There were some disappointments along the way, but never any hard feelings. I always understood that there were good players ahead of me, and I tried to make the best of the role I had to play.

Coach Wierwille was a strong force in my life. He was always a positive influence. He wanted us to be good students as well as achieve on the basketball court. If we needed help in the classroom, he'd help us or try to get somebody who could. He was very supportive. I always felt that I could talk to Coach Wierwille. His door was open. Even if he disagreed with me, he would always listen.

Our team was loaded with talent in those years. There was strong competition for playing time. Among the guards, Donald Hairston was solid all over. He had a great game. He was a good offensive player who could pass or score. For his size Donald could really jump. He was a strong defensive player as well.

Tommy Owsley was lightning quick. He had a knack for being where the ball was. Tommy took a lot of chances when he risked trying to steal the ball, but nine times out of ten he would come up with it. Donnie Harper was a pure shooter, one of the best I ever played with. Donnie really elevated on his jump shot. He had strong legs and got up high. He also had a nice soft touch.

In the frontcourt, start with Vance Blade. Vance wasn't that big, but he could jump out of the gym. I was amazed at how he could score inside. He was a strong player who could do a lot of things with the ball. And Marcus Crawford was a great scorer.

Later we had Jay Stenzel, one of the best scorers I ever saw. He had a knack for it. He could score from almost anywhere on the court. We had many solid players up front: Kevin Mullins, Mark Walls, David Moeves, Mark George, Bubby Napier. They could all score and rebound.

Those experienced veterans formed the core of an outstanding team my senior year. We didn't have a big man, a super-tall center we could go to, but we did have strength inside, depth at every position, and quickness. We played good team ball. We looked for each other and made up any size deficiency with the way we played together.

I don't think anybody expected us to have the year we did and win the KIAC in the regular season. Transylvania was always a big rival for us, and they defeated us in our first game. We thought we had a better team than they did, and we got better and better after that loss. We won nine in a row, lost two of three, and then reeled off another winning streak of thirteen games.

Transy was our opponent in the NAIA district tournament. Because we had the better record we had the home court advantage, but we weren't allowed to play in our gym because our court wasn't big enough for NAIA standards. So we opted to play Transy on a neutral floor in Richmond. They beat us, and I'll never forget that loss. It sticks in my mind today. I didn't get to play in that game. That was one of my biggest disappointments. I thought we should have beaten them. I don't know if I could have made a difference. It was a hard-fought game that went down to wire.

I had a great college life at Berea. It was a dream come true for me. I had a lot of fun, and I worked hard. I learned a lot about self-discipline. I had to, in order to make it with classes and work and convocations and sports, getting everything done, meeting deadlines, making the grades. I had a wonderful time and did a lot of things.

When I came to Berea I requested a job in the gym, but there were no openings. They assigned me to Woodcraft. I got up early in the morning to sand furniture and skittle games. Then I'd have to blow the dust off me, clean up as best I could, and go to class. It was a hard, dirty job, but a good experience. The next year I was a resident assistant, and then in my third year I finally got a job in the gym as monitor. That was a great job because I got to live in the gym. I could swim in the pool, use the weight room, and play ball any time I wanted.

I majored in physical education, with K-through-twelve certification. I had many fine teachers. Dr Robert Pearson had a big influence on me. I made a D in a short term class of his. I intended to slide by with a B, but I got the D because I goofed off. I sat down with Dr Pearson and tried to get him to change my grade. I told him I thought I deserved a C. We looked at it on paper, and he wouldn't change it. He told me he wanted me to learn from the experience. If I'd worked harder and done what I should have done to begin with, I wouldn't have been in that situation. I had to work extra hard to climb out of that hole and keep my average up. Dr Pearson taught me a good lesson, I needed to do my best. He was a good teacher and a good role model.

I got married the day before I graduated. Then I went back home and took a summer job at Barren River State Park, as I did every year. I heard about an opening at Austin Tracy Elementary, a K-through-eight school. They needed a physical education teacher and football, basketball, and track coach. I was hired and stayed there for nine years.

I had always wanted to coach high school, and the opportunity came to move into the position of freshman coach. My principal, Glenn Flanders, talked to me about the advantages of working with junior high kids. He said I was doing a good job teaching fundamentals, and he pointed out that a coach who doesn't win at the high school level may be out of a job. I was secure and comfortable in my job at Austin Tracy and liked working with kids of that age, so I decided to stay with it.

Then they consolidated the junior highs in our county and formed a middle school, which was a good idea. It probably should have happened ten years before it did. They moved the seventh and eighth graders to the middle school level and built a new building, Barren County Middle School. I opted to go there. I teach the seventh and eighth graders and serve as the school's athletic director.

Berea College continued to influence me. Mike Johnson coached track and field at Berea, and I learned a lot of games from him to use in elementary physical education classes to help kids improve their coordination and cardiovascular fitness. In coaching seventh and eighth graders I employed many of Coach Wierwille's fundamental ballhandling and dribbling and shooting drills.

Currently I'm working on being certified as a principal. That's what I'd like to become eventually. I know it's a tough and challenging job, but I'm working toward that goal.

July 13, 1998

Mark Walls   **1980-84**

My father worked for the University of Kentucky extension program, so we lived in and around central Kentucky most of our lives. I graduated from Bourbon County High School in Paris. A friend of Dad's told him about Berea, and I made an appointment to visit and talk to Coach Wierwille.

Vance Blade, who was a junior then, was in the office, and he filled me in about some things. Coach Wierwille looked at me point-blank and said, "If you come to Berea, you'll get no special treatment. And don't think that today I'm going to buy you a Berea College T-shirt. If I loan you shoes and shorts to play in, I want them back at the end of the day." Straight to the point. He told me that in the fall I'd be given a chance to try out and make the team, and we'd go from there.

I asked myself, "Do I want to come to Berea or not?" It felt almost like getting drafted into the Army. As a senior in high school I had torn a ligament and played only ten games, so I didn't have many options. Centre College and Washington and Lee were talking to me, but Berea seemed like the best fit, and I was confident that Coach Wierwille would give me as good a shot as anybody else.

I'm six-three and a half. I had told Coach I was six-four, and after I was measured he wanted to know why I shrunk before the season even started. I lettered all four years. I was a sixth man as a freshman, a spot starter and reserve as a sophomore, a starter as a junior, and then a reserve player as a senior.

The biggest thing I learned when I came to college was that the game was a lot more physical than it had been in high school. I had to get used to that. If I had to pick one thing that Coach taught me that stands out more than anything else, it is the idea of being in position to shoot the basketball before catching it. If you do that, you can release it quicker. You gain about a half second, but sometimes a half second coming off a pick makes all the difference in the world. An average jumper who stands six-three and a half can shoot over a six-six guy if he gets it off quickly enough. That's a tip I've tried to pass on to my sons and to the kids I coach today.

My strongest assets were shooting the basketball and passing. If they had had the three-point shot then, I could have scored a lot more. But I'd say my biggest strength was recognizing what the other team was doing on defense and then making the right choice with the ball, shoot or pass. I was a good scorer when I had to score, but I didn't make that my number one option. If Coach needed me to pass, I passed. If he needed me to play defense, I played defense. I did whatever he asked me to do for the benefit of the team.

As a defensive player I was hard-nosed, although probably not quick enough. Still, I'd stick my nose in there and get it chopped off. In one of my first games, in a tournament down in Tennessee, I took an elbow to the

Adam's apple while standing on the free throw line. I had done a little jawing with the guy. He stood about six-eight and weighed maybe 230. He told me to quit elbowing, and I told him that if he couldn't take it, he could not play. The next thing I knew I was on the floor. I quit talking after that.

The first two years were rough. We were ten and sixteen in each of those seasons. But I could not have been in any better shape if I had joined the Marines. From Monday through Friday we practically ran to death. Coach Wierwille was known for his ability to get his teams prepared. He had us in top-notch condition. If we were going to get beat, it was because the other team was better, not because it was in better shape. Coach always

Mark Walls: "I took my education seriously"

had us ready to play come Friday night or Saturday.

Glen Drury and Steve Ridder were senior co-captains when I was a freshman. Both of those guys took me under their wing. Glen was the consummate team player. He probably didn't play as much as he thought he could have or should have, but you never heard him say a derogatory word or do anything that would cause friction. At an early age Glen knew he wanted to be a coach, and he set an example of what he was going to teach his players to do. He did a great job.

Steve was the most unselfish player I ever played with. He was a great playmaker and understood the game well, but he would rather get the assist than score. He could have scored much more than he did, but he wanted to get everybody involved. Every once in a while a team needs a guy to step forward and take the shot. Steve would give up a layup to give someone else a chance to score.

Vance Blade knocked me around a lot, but I liked and respected him. Vance was as tough a six-three power forward as you could find anywhere. He led the league in rebounding the two years I played with him. He didn't have a tremendous shooting range outside ten or twelve feet, but on the blocks there wasn't a guy in the league who could stop him when he got the ball in position. He was a team player. Even though he wasn't the big scorer, he accepted his role admirably.

Jeff Britt came in with me. Jeff did a good job of setting up the offense, but he wasn't as strong an offensive player as he was a defensive player. He would nag you to death. We wouldn't let the other team hurt Jeff during a game, but in practice we sure wanted to beat up on him ourselves once in a while.

After my sophomore year the team's record improved. We had many talented players, and they were a group of guys who accepted the theory that the team comes first and the individual second. Donald Hairston was one of our leaders. Donald didn't do a lot of talking; he just went out and got the job done. He could score a bunch of points if we needed him to score, but was entirely satisfied if he scored two points and the team won.

My senior team, 1983-84, went as deep as any team I ever played on. As a junior I had started every game, and the next year I was everything from sixth to seventh to eighth man, depending on what was needed. Donnie Harper had redshirted, and when he came back he was in the same position. He started some games, then went to the bench.

When we substituted during games we never missed a beat. Our team concept enabled us to play together as a unit. When we started having success with it, nobody stepped up and said, "I'm more important than the team." In those two years basketball was a lot of fun. We went out there as a team and started winning.

Having more size helped us considerably. We brought in Dave Moeves from Boone County and Jay Stenzel from Erlanger Lloyd, both six-five or better. Bubby Napier was almost as big. As a freshman I had played every position on the floor, and when your backup center is six-three and a half and can't jump, you're in trouble. Once we started getting the size in, we were able to battle on the boards and win more games. Those big players had an immediate impact on our team, and they were good athletes, too. They weren't just big. They could play.

Seabury Gym was the best sixth man in the history of college basketball, in my opinion. I don't think any Division I school could claim a greater home court advantage than we had at Seabury. In my junior and senior years we predominantly ran a three-two zone, and we trapped in the corners. That made the visiting team feel like we had an extra man on them. It would take them almost a half to learn not to go into the corners, just as I had to learn as a freshman that if I shot from there, the ball would come back off that overhead track and practically break my nose.

We'd pull pranks on each other: the balm in the athletic supporter, the missing shirts and socks, all that stuff. We could do just about anything to each other, but if anybody on another team tried to pull something on one of us during a game, we were ready to fight. Jeff Britt, a good guy but a major irritant in practice, had a terrible experience at Campbellsville one night. They had a player named Cecil Ellis who scratched him up badly. Jeff's body had bloody marks all over it where Cecil had stuck his hands up under his jersey and scratched him. Coach called a timeout and took Jeff to the scorer's table and protested, raising his jersey up and saying, "Look what's happening here." After that Cecil ran into some pretty hard picks. If we had a chance to level him, we tried our best to pay him back with a little pain.

Another memorable opponent was Adrian Hayes of Cumberland. He reminded me of Derrick Hord, who played at UK at that same time. One time I was on the back line when Cumberland threw an alley-oop pass over the top of me, and it seemed like all I could see was the bottom of Adrian's size twelve and a half Converse shoes. He could jump out of the gym, absolutely. When I was a freshman we played at Thomas More the night that Brian O'Conner became their all-time leading scorer. He was later drafted by an NBA team. I'll never forget our game at Georgetown when I was a senior. Mark George of Berea played against his brother Mike George of Georgetown, and we won the game.

We thought that year was our year. We were on cloud nine after winning the regular season conference title. We weren't allowed to play a home game in the NAIA tournament because the court at Seabury wasn't regulation size. Coach let the team decide whether we wanted to play at Eastern or borrow Sue Bennett College's gym, which was closer in size to ours. We all chose to play at Eastern. We had more fans up there that night than our opponent, Transylvania, had drawn in any game they had played.

I don't think there was a single person in the city of Berea who thought we were going to get beat that night. Coming up short against Transy was a devastating blow. Everybody thought that 1984 would be our year to get over the hump. We had a senior-laden team that had done very well as juniors, and we were expecting to win it. I don't want to take anything away from Transy, but there were couple of questionable calls in that game, and we had two Lexington officials refereeing. I can look back and say what if, but what it all comes down to is putting the ball in the hole, and Transy did that more times that we did. Losing that game was one of the most disappointing things I've ever had happen.

I was one of the few Berea students who worked all four years in the same job. I was a clerk in the Alumni Office. My major was business and the job fit into my schedule well, so I didn't go looking to change it. Originally I was supposed to be a janitor, but somehow that got messed up, and I was sent to the Alumni Office. I think I was the first athlete to work there. Mary Labus, the office manager, said, "Oh my gosh, I've got a basketball player coming!" She didn't know what to expect.

I liked the job. Rod Bussey was the director, and Ed Ford worked there. I enjoyed talking with the alumni when they came to campus, because that taught me about Berea's traditions. Moreover, the office was air-conditioned. It sure beat working in the cafeteria.

I took my education seriously, and that's something I owe to my parents. In high school I needed just a C average to be eligible to play basketball, but my parents insisted on a B average. Like most freshmen entering college, I played around a little bit and did what I had to do to get by. Thanks to the values my parents instilled, I kept my head above water academically, and when I got into my major courses after my sophomore year I started cracking down. By that point I realized that basketball was going to be over after four years, and I needed to get serious about my education.

I had several professors who were very good. One was Phil Spears in the Business Department. He taught us how to deal with adversity and humiliation. He browbeat us in class. At one point I wanted to drop his class, but as a business major I knew I had to have it. Outside of class Dr Spears was our best friend. In business life I've met very few people who are capable of turning it on and off like he did. All he was trying to do was get the best out of us. In class he treated us as if we were working for him at DuPont, and if we didn't understand or screwed up or didn't perform, he got on us like a supervisor would.

The most enjoyable class I took was one that Warren Lambert taught on the military history of the Civil War. I still have the book and my notes from that class. When Dr Lambert spoke I didn't care what was going on outside, what my next assignment was or my labor job or my schedule for the rest of the day. I gave him my undivided attention for an hour. He was full of knowledge and could pass it along in a way that very few people could.

When I graduated in 1984 I went to work for Peoples Deposit Bank and Trust Company in Paris, Kentucky. I had filled in there the previous two summers. In 1985 that bank merged with what was known as the old Bourbon Agricultural Bank, which is now Kentucky Banks. I've been with the same organization since I left college, although we've changed names and locations due to acquisitions and mergers.

Presently I'm vice president in charge of Scott County. Banking has been good to me, but at the same time it's like any other job in that I sometimes wonder if the other side of the fence doesn't have greener pastures. Banking's changed a lot in the years that I've been in it. We've moved away from the handshake, "Yeah, you're going to pay me back the car loan, no problem." Now we have to request so much documentation that the customer loses some of the personal touch that used to be in banking twenty years ago. I miss that. I understand the regulatory side of the business, but in dealing with the public every day, I wish that part of banking had not changed. The customer can't understand why he now has to supply all his tax return information, but that's just the nature of the business today.

I didn't play any basketball in my first year after college. The next year I played with Glen Drury and a bunch of guys from Anderson County in a league in Lexington. I proved I could still play, but now that I'm older and have kids, my body doesn't bounce back. Now it's time for me to pass along my experience by coaching kids. I've coached youth league basketball, soccer, football, and baseball.

At Berea I took the PE class for coaching basketball that Coach Wierwille taught. I use a lot of what he taught me. I try to set up an outline for practice so I'm organized enough to get from point A to point B. I run a version of his double-low offense because it's simple to teach and hard to defend. It's not too complex for little kids to understand. It gives them some formation for setting up an offense, rather than just running down the floor and shooting.

Berea College's basketball program has a lot of tradition. An athlete who enrolls at Berea will have an opportunity to be part of a program that is proud and well respected. Win or lose, he'll learn how to do things right. He'll get an excellent education, and, most important of all, he'll work with and get to know people who care about him. I'll never forget our Christmas vacation periods. The basketball players got the week of Christmas off, but we came back for practice two weeks before school started. During that time we stayed in the homes of various people in the community. They were willing to take college kids into their homes, give them their keys and say, "If you need anything, just holler. If we're not here, just come on in." I cherish the memory of those times.

July 6, 1998

Kevin Mullins   **1981-84**

Basketball does a lot for a person. It builds you physically and helps you mentally. So much of what Coach Wierwille taught is useful in today's world: teamwork, discipline, punctuality, work ethic. All those lessons carry over into society.

If I had to do it all over again, if I were standing at a crossroads and someone said, "Here's a UK basketball scholarship, or you can go down that Berea College road again," I'd go back to Berea without hesitation. At Berea we got more than an education. We had to work and got graded on it. We were expected to perform both in the classroom and in the work environment, and that was unique. The company I now work for grades me in almost the same way. I get paid according to my performance. I'm used to that. It was great preparation to learn all that at Berea. It was tough, no doubt about it, but I wouldn't trade the Berea experience for anything.

I grew up in Ashland, Kentucky. My dad worked at Armco Steel. My mom was a housewife. There were five children in the family, and we didn't have a lot of money. Often I borrowed my brother's shoes.

Growing up in the city, I ran around with the wrong crowd. I wore long hair and leather wristbands, and I smoked cigarettes. I wasn't on the right track, and that helped motivate my parents to move us out into the county when I was in the fifth or sixth grade.

The very first boy I met at the county school was Mike Meade. He had a basketball in his hands, and he threw it to me and told me to shoot it. I didn't even know what it was. My hair was so long I couldn't see the basketball to shoot. I threw it back at him, but I hung around Mike, and we became good friends.

Mike would say to me, "You shouldn't be doing that, you should be doing this." I started getting on the right track and around the right people. Mike talked me into trying out for the basketball team. I made the team, and I quit smoking and got my hair cut so I could see to shoot. Before every game I'd look for Mike in the crowd, and when I made my first basket I'd point at him to acknowledge our friendship.

Basketball changed my life. Whenever I got in trouble or got upset or got mad, I'd want to go play basketball. It relaxed me. Finally it became part of me. If I hadn't played basketball, I probably would not have gone to college.

Rocky Wallace, a Berea College graduate, came to Boyd County High School and talked to us. He was the one who inspired me to go to Berea. I'd been offered a couple of baseball scholarships at other schools, but I liked basketball better because it's more team-oriented. I visited the Berea campus and talked to Coach Wierwille, and the academic value of Berea was evident. So I decided to enroll there. I played basketball and baseball at Berea and competed in the triple jump and high jump.

Coach Wierwille had a kind heart, but when I first met him he seemed big and intimidating. He could be very stern, and that worked to my advantage. I was an average player when I came to Berea. His discipline and coaching helped me step up my game tremendously.

I'm six-two. In high school most of my game was outside. Coach Wierwille made me tougher mentally, and that enabled me to become more of an inside player. Eventually I became a good man down low.

In my freshman year Coach was always yelling at Vance Blade. When Vance did something wrong like missing a layup, Coach got on him. If I missed a layup, he wouldn't say anything to me. Coach did that on purpose. He wanted me to improve before he'd start critiquing me. I wanted to get his

Kevin Mullins

attention but couldn't. I didn't get into any varsity games as a freshman. During my sophomore year I was practicing one day, and I must have done fairly well in previous practices, because when I missed a layup Coach screamed my name out. "Mullins! Get back in there and do it again!" What a compliment that was! I finally had his attention, and he started working with me. From that day it was all uphill.

Some players didn't adapt well to Coach Wierwille. I remember one player who would hit four or five long shots in a row during warmups, but he'd tense up as soon as Coach walked into the gym. His shooting ability would vanish because he'd worry that Coach would yell at him if he wasn't perfect. It would have been better for him to relax and play his game, and if he made a mistake, he made a mistake. He was intimidated by Coach's presence. Coach's style didn't suit every player, but it helped many more players than it hurt.

It certainly helped me. My high school coach was rather conservative. If we missed a dunk in a game, we'd have to do extra running the next time we practiced. I was an average player, but I was holding back quite a bit and didn't even know it. If I failed to dunk the basketball at Berea, Coach Wierwille would motivate me by saying, "Next time I want you to get up there and slam that ball in the hole!"

Coach Wierwille and I were not the type of people to sit down and talk on a personal level. But I knew what he wanted on the basketball floor, and he knew that I knew. Perhaps we weren't closer to each other because our personalities were so similar. He was a class act as a coach and a person, and he instilled many qualities in me that I'll always thank him for.

I had pretty good ballhandling skills. I was agile enough to bring the ball down the court, and I had excellent leaping ability. I didn't play to the crowd on purpose, but often my leaps or blocked shots got the crowd going . There were times when maybe I should have been a little less unselfish, more self-serving, but I always thought it was better to win as a team and lose as a team.

When I first joined the team the players I looked up to were Marcus Crawford and Vance Blade. Marcus was a flashy player with a lot of good moves. He had a very quick first step. He could go outside, then move back inside and post up. He was a good all-around player. Vance was probably the best rebounder I've ever seen. When he grabbed that ball he would always smack it, and you could hear it all the way across the gym. He never let up, either in a game or in practice. If you were underneath him and got your hand on the ball, you had to get out of the way of his elbows.

As the years went along our team seemed to get better and better. I attribute that to our closeness. Every one of us was an unselfish team player, and we were like a family on and off the court. We were so close-knit that when we went out, to movies or to Richmond or wherever we went, we did it together.

Playing together for as long as we did, we learned what our individual teammates could do and couldn't do. We communicated well. For instance, often if I just looked at Donald Hairston I knew what he was going to do, and vice versa. By my senior year the team was full of confidence.

Donald impressed me a lot as a player. He was bowlegged, and just to watch him walk hurt me. But he could jump like a kangaroo. He was a guard and shorter than I was, but the two of us sometimes had dunking contests. Donald would bounce the ball off the floor, grab the rim, and turn around and do a 360 dunk. I would bounce it off the floor and hit the back-board and grab it. I learned that from him.

Donald was quick, but the quickest guard I ever saw was Tommy Owsley. His quickness was doubly incredible because as a kid Tommy lost a couple of his toes in a lawn mower accident. For a lot of people a big toe is like a thumb; it's impossible to do anything without it. But Tommy didn't let anything stop him. He wore a sort of artificial toe in his shoe. I admired him tremendously, and we became close friends. I was best man at his wedding.

Like Tommy, Mark Walls and Jeff Britt arrived the year I did. Mark was a friendly guy, easy to know, and a real professional. He worked hard on the court and was a classy guy off the court, always dressed nice with his hair just perfect. Jeff was a jokester who kept everybody laughing most of the time. He had a little bit of a temper, but he used it to his advantage by hustling after the basketball. Jeff always played taller than he was.

Dave Moeves was also fun to be around. He was a tall lefthander with a soft touch. He could have been a bit more aggressive, but he was a deceiving player. He was quick in making a move to the basket, which made it difficult for big men to guard him.

Evans Mitchell, "Big E," was another person who made all the players loose. When Coach yelled at us in practice and we all had our heads down, Evans would get us laughing in the locker room with his Roland Wierwille imitations. He was a special individual and a good, hustling player. He was a real good shooter from the outside. Evans worked in the tote box in Seabury Gym and had to be there at six or seven o'clock in the morning. Elvin Combs noticed that Evans was never late for work, not one day, even after road games or the nights we went out. I respected Evans a lot for that, and I was glad when Mr Combs made sure that Evans got a special award.

Mark George was a quiet, reserved person who battled me for the swing forward position one year. Mark and I exchanged a few words a couple of times, but that was typical in that kind of situation. I hope he doesn't have any hard feelings. In my senior year we got along and played together well. Bubby Napier was another quiet one. Bubby worked hard for everything he got. He was a good team player with an effective turnaround jump shot.

Assistant coach Steve Ridder was like one of us. He would get us off to the side away from Coach Wierwille and say things to us that Coach really couldn't. He was a caring person and an excellent motivator.

In my sophomore year Coach Ridder often said to me, "Be ready to play, because you might get your chance." I'd think of his words all night and all day, and then the game would come and I wouldn't get to play. But he kept me alert and ready. Before one particular game he told me as we were waiting for the bus, "Tonight might be your night." So once again I prepared myself mentally, and when I finally got my chance to play that night, I excelled. From there on I started every game.

The first time I ever dunked the ball in a game was against Brescia College in the first home game of my junior year. In high school I didn't dunk one time. I didn't even attempt it. I would jump two or three feet over the rim, and the fans would ask, "Why didn't he dunk it?" I was too worried about having to run suicides in practice if I missed a dunk.

Early in the game we were trailing Brescia by about five points. Coach called time out, as he often did if we were slacking off. A lot of times he wouldn't have to say anything. He would just walk back and forth and look at us with his face red and his veins popping out. That told us that we needed to get out there and start playing.

On this occasion he had designed a particular play. He yelled to Donald Hairston to get underneath the basket, and he came up to me and grabbed my shirt and said, "Mullins, when he throws that ball I want you to slam it through." I was scared to death. I thought that if I didn't dunk that basketball, he would hurt me! On the way to take the ball out of bounds I looked at Donald, and he looked at me. He was about as scared as I was. I told him, "You'd better make a good pass."

My adrenaline was so high, I wasn't going to let anything stop me. That forceful push from Coach Wierwille was just what I needed. In practice I'd showed him I could dunk, but in a game I was timid. That night when Donald threw the ball up to me I felt as if I were walking on air. I grabbed the

Kevin Mullins: "Welcome to college basketball!"

ball and threw it through the hoop, and the crowd, a packed house, went ballistic. Everybody started running around like chickens with their heads cut off. We went on a fifteen-point spurt. I tried to dunk another one, but I was so pumped up that I hit the back of the iron. Coach had to call time out again, to calm us down! We beat Brescia by sixty points.

After I got that first dunk out of the way it was easy from there on out. All I needed was to break the ice, but I would never have done that without Coach Wierwille's help. A couple of days later one of our fans brought me a picture of the dunk that had appeared in the *Richmond Register*. That was a nice memento of the occasion.

Coach Wierwille liked to move the game inside rather than out. He wanted a lot of motion, a lot of passing, a lot of picking. He gave us precise instructions on how to set the pick, stuff I was never taught in high school. He wanted us to fast break whenever we had the opportunity. If we didn't have the fast break, we'd simply flow right into our offense, which we did pretty well, especially in my senior year. We usually controlled the tempo. If we made a basket, we'd press every time. Sometimes we'd back off into a halfcourt press, then we'd mix it up with a full-court press. Coach had us well organized to do that effectively.

It meant so much to me to be named co-captain with Donald. Our team was like a family, and if somebody wasn't happy, on or off the court, it upset me. With as many talented players as we had, it wasn't easy to keep up morale. If a guy wasn't getting much playing time, we encouraged him to continue to work hard. The idea was to keep working together as a team.

We tried to be unselfish. If I was wide open underneath the basket and there was a guy in front of me, I didn't hesitate to pass it off to him. If one of us didn't do that, I thought it was my role or Donald's to say, "This guy, your teammate, was wide open underneath the basket." Similarly, if I was working hard down low to get a pass and a teammate threw the ball in to me and I turned around and scored, the first thing I did was run over and pat that guy on the butt for passing it to me. If I didn't, the ball might not be there for me the next time. If somebody made a steal, we always patted him.

If you look at our stats for the 1983-84 season, almost all of them are team records. We won thirteen games in a row at one point without anybody setting any individual records, because we didn't embrace individual play at all. We had a freshman who came out of high school accustomed to being a star. Sometimes he'd take a one-on-one under the basket when we had a guy open high on the post. Donald and I said to him, "Don't force the ball down low. Throw it out." He got the message.

I got married when I was still a student. The guys decided to hold a bachelor party for me the night before we had a game scheduled with Union College. I don't know what I was expecting. Let's put it this way: it was a rough night.

When we were shooting around before the game I felt good. When I got out on the court, everywhere I looked I saw guys who had been at the party, and I felt self-conscious thinking that they were talking about me. My first shot slipped out of my hand, and after that I couldn't buy a basket. In Seabury Gym if you looked toward the backboard you could see the fans sitting there. In previous games I could either block out the crowd or use them to motivate me, but that night I was distracted by the sight of the spectators waving. I missed my first six or seven shots. Finally Coach took me out of the game, sat me down, and said, "That's the worst basketball I've ever seen you play." I thought, "If he only knew what happened last night!"

When we ran into some foul trouble Coach had to put me back in, but I still didn't do very well. I couldn't hit a basket or even a free throw. Coach took me back out and put somebody else in my place just to punish me. I deserved it, because I wasn't performing.

Something happened, and I had to go back in again with about ten seconds to go. Nobody wanted to throw the ball to me, so I was setting screens to try to help out. One of us shot the ball with maybe two seconds left and missed it, and a Union player got the rebound. I was so determined to do something right that I swatted the ball out of his hands. I knew I had enough time to get one shot off, and I let it fly right at the buzzer. It was good, and it won the game for us. It was the only basket I made the whole game. Before the next practice Coach found out what had gone on the night before the game, and we had to run quite a bit.

Centre College was a big personal rivalry for me. When my parents decided to move out in the county when I was in elementary school, my brother Jeff didn't want to leave all his close friends in the city, so he was allowed to stay with my grandmother and go to city schools. He went to Fairview High School, and I ended up playing against him. Then Jeff enrolled at Centre College, and I guarded him when Berea played Centre. Jeff and Coach Tom Bryant had a personality conflict. Jeff was a flashy player who liked to pass behind his back. Tom Bryant was a chest-pass type of coach, so they clashed. Jeff left Centre, and I sympathized with him. Thereafter I always had a little personal vendetta against that school. Jeff went out to Oklahoma City and played there, and when we talked he always asked me, "Did you beat Centre?"

In one game against Centre I had a little soreness in my foot. I'd had it for a couple of days, but I thought it was just a stone bruise or something like that. I always got so pumped up on the court that I didn't feel it if I got a little banged up. The game was close, and we trailed by a point with three or four seconds to play. In our timeout I told Coach I wanted to shoot it, and he called a play for me to roll up from the top of the free throw line. I got there, Donald threw me the ball, and when I shot it I knew it was going to go in. It did, and we won by a point. After the game my foot was absolutely killing me. I couldn't even walk on it. They had to carry me out to the bus, and I had to go to the hospital emergency room. An ingrown toenail had sent blood poisoning up into my leg. I could have died. I had to stay in the hospital for three days.

My last college game was a devastating loss to Transylvania in the 1984 district tournament. That game was a stepping stone to Cumberland, and I knew we'd beat Cumberland to advance to the national tournament. But all our hard work and sacrifice didn't seem to be enough.

We had to play Transy at Eastern Kentucky University, which was a disadvantage for us. They wouldn't have had a chance at Seabury Gym. We always thought that Transy got a little bit of favoritism from the referees, and in that game there were a few times when Donald got hacked, almost tackled, without a whistle from the officials.

We had a good lead with a couple of minutes to go, but Transy came back, and the game went down to the nitty-gritty. Maybe the refs helped them a bit, but there was no way we should have lost that lead.

We were down by a point with seventeen seconds to go when Donald took the ball out of bounds and threw it to Tommy Owsley. He dribbled it for what seemed like forever, trying to get loose. Mark Walls stepped up and got the ball in the corner, and I yelled at him to shoot it because time was running out. Mark shot, the ball hit the outside of the rim, and David Moeves got the rebound. David's shot bounced off and came right to me. I handled it like a hot potato, thinking I had to get it back up there before the buzzer went off. I threw the ball up, it lay there on the rim, and then it slid off. Transylvania got the rebound and managed to throw the ball to halfcourt before the buzzer went off, which made me realize that I'd actually had time to come down with the ball before going back up to shoot. That hurt the worst. I felt like I had let the team and the whole community down. The winning shots I hit at the buzzer against Union and Centre meant a whole lot less to me than the one I could have, and didn't, hit against Transylvania.

My first labor assignment was in Woodcraft Industries. That wasn't the only job I had at Berea, but it was the best, and I did that most of the time I was there. I enjoyed working with wood. Pat Wilson in Woodcraft taught me everything I needed to know. I got promoted to what they called a piece maker, taking a piece from the rough lumber all the way down to the finished product and getting paid for each piece. That was a good motivation to work hard. We made our furniture with the finest quality wood and used horse glue, the best glue to use on furniture. That was furniture you could be proud of.

My total workload of basketball on top of classes, labor, and convocations was demanding. Sometimes I was too worn out to keep my head up, but I had to. I had to stay up at night and get things done. Sometimes I needed tutoring and had to schedule it for nine o'clock. But that was necessary to keep me in school.

I was very close to my roommate, Bill Murphy. We had many good times together. Bill was a great soccer player, and very religious. He went to church three times a week. Whenever something was bothering me, Bill would sit down and talk to me about it. I regret that I didn't stay in contact with him after I got married. When he called me I told him, "We can't get together. I've got to stay home." Many times he knocked on my door, but I turned him down. I shouldn't have, but I did. Two years after I graduated he died in a tragic accident. Whenever I think of Berea College, I think of Bill and what an inspiration he was to me.

I majored in physical education, with a minor in business. I was torn between the two, and I changed my major three times. While I was in school I worked at Berea National Bank and found that I enjoyed customer service, so I decided to make business my major. There wasn't enough time for me to do that and get my teaching certificate too, so I stayed with the physical education major.

One summer I took Accounting Two, a course I had to pass, with Phil Spears. I didn't know the man when I walked in there, but somehow he knew I had to have a passing grade, and he worked me to death. Right in the middle of class he'd ask me questions about the material before we'd even had a chance to review it, just to make me sweat. He wouldn't ever crack a smile at me. I was certain that he wanted to flunk me.

When it came time to take the final, I needed something like an eighty-five percent. Steve Ridder's wife Vicky tutored me, and that helped me quite a bit. When it came time to give us our final scores, Dr Spears gave out my test last. I turned it up and looked at it and saw a score of ninety percent. Then Dr Spears smiled at me for the first time ever and patted me on the back. He'd been pulling for me to pass the whole time, but he wanted me to work hard to earn my grade. He wasn't going to show me any favoritism because I played basketball. I didn't understand him until the very last day of class, and then I realized how much he'd helped me.

Today I'm a claims adjuster for State Farm Insurance. I enjoy it. I schedule my own hours and control my own workload. I meet new people every day. Sometimes the job can be difficult. Often the people I talk to are upset. Perhaps they've had an accident, and I have to try to calm them down. Sometimes they have to sell a policy at a loss and forget what they bought, and it can be hard to try to explain the specific terms of the policy they paid for. People expect excellent service from us. When we do a good job we rarely get complimentary letters, but if we do something less than perfect we get complaints. So the job can be stressful at times, but I enjoy doing it.

Still, I'm not completely convinced that I've found my niche. Maybe there is something bigger for me out there in the world. A part of me thinks that somewhere down the line I'd like to coach. I think I'd make a good one.

August 18, 1998

Donald Hairston   1981-84

I grew up in Williamson, in Mingo County, West Virginia. My father worked for the railroad. I received an athletic scholarship from Pikeville College in Kentucky, which wasn't far from where I lived. I'd had a lot of advanced math in high school and intended to study mining engineering. I left Pikeville after one semester. I wasn't satisfied with their academic program. I thought I'd get a better education at Berea College.

Donald Hairston

I enrolled at Berea in February 1981. Mathematics was my major. A lot of it came easy to me, and because I didn't have to work hard at it I developed poor study habits. At first I got by, but when I got into the upper-level math courses I had problems. One of my teachers was Phil Schmidt. I went in and talked to him and said, "This stuff is not that difficult, but when it comes time for a test I'm encountering some difficulty." So he sat down with me and explained the proper study techniques. After that I'd stop by his office every so often, and with his help I turned it around.

My first labor assignment was as a "correspondence executive" in the Admissions Office. That is, I opened the mail and filed it. When prospective students sent letters to Berea, I opened them and filed them in a folder for John Cook and the Admissions staff to look at. I recall opening a letter from an Evans Mitchell. I had trouble filing it. Was his name really Evans Mitchell, or was it Mitchell Evans? I had to give it some thought. Finally I filed it as Evans Mitchell. That fall I met Evans Mitchell when he joined the Berea College basketball team!

I worked in the Admissions Office for just one semester. After that I became a teacher's assistant in the Math Department. Eventually I got a job in the mathematics lab in addition to being a TA. I had to be there at certain hours of the night to help other students with their math. For a while I worked in both the Math Department and the Computer Department, spending maybe ten hours a week in each. In my senior year I stopped working in the Math Department, stuck with the Computer Department, and served as a resident assistant at Bingham.

I'm six feet tall, or maybe six-one, somewhere in that area. I played guard, mostly point guard, handling the ball and trying to be a leader. My goal was to become a student of the game. In my junior and senior years I was team captain, responsible for calling the offenses and defenses for the team to execute. Coach Wierwille left it up to me to call whatever I thought we should be doing.

Coach and I got along fine. He was stern, big on the discipline, but I didn't think there was anything wrong with that. He was concerned about our character. Young guys out on their own, leaving high school and their parents, need discipline.

When I arrived we were a very small team. When we beat people we did it by applying pressure in an uptempo style of game. Vance Blade and Keith Riley were our biggest players, and they were just six-three or six-four. They would get in and bang the boards, and if we got the ball down into them, they could score. For men their height they showed ability on the inside that really impressed me.

Tommy Owsley usually played the other guard position. Tommy was a sound ballplayer. He was quick, but he didn't have a flashy game. Tommy could shoot the ball pretty well, and overplaying on defense helped him get a lot of layups.

In my junior year, 1982-83, Tommy didn't play, and our go-to guys were me and Kevin Mullins. We did whatever was needed. Sometimes it was scoring, sometimes it was defense, or maybe it was pushing or a pep talk. Kevin could flat-out jump. He could shoot. He played hard, and he was a good fellow. I don't have anything negative to say about anyone once they got on the court. Everybody played hard, and you can't ask for anything more out of people. That's what Coach demanded from us, and that's what he got. Like everyone else Kevin put forth the effort, and his added leaping and shooting ability made him a go-to guy. Kevin and I provided the consistency, and every night a Mark Walls or Donnie Harper or someone else would step up and bring something to the game.

Our season ended in an overtime loss at Northern Kentucky University. That's a big school, and I think they expected to blow us out of the gym. I was somewhat happy that we took them to overtime, although losing to them spoiled that. They had a big guard or small forward named Brady Jackson, who was supposed to be an all-American. He scored some points, but I think the way we played against him and his team brought a great deal of recognition to Berea.

No one particular person guarded Brady Jackson that night. It was a team effort. We didn't play man-to-man that often. We employed various zones, and occasionally we went into a man or did some full- and halfcourt

Donald Hairston: "His only interest was in helping the team to win"

pressing. The defense we used most often was a three-two zone. We might have tried a box-and-one against Northern Kentucky, where we put a man on Jackson for a short time while the rest of us played a zone. For us to compete the way we did against a team from an institution of that size gave me a lot of satisfaction.

Our record improved in my senior year, although when we started out I thought we were going to have a long season. We were unsettled at first. Transylvania beat us at home, and I hated to lose to them. Transy's attitude made me want to work harder against them. I knew a couple of their players prior to college. Their cockiness didn't sit well with me, and I don't think it did with anyone else.

Losing a game right out of the gate set us back. I was afraid that things might go downhill. But we were able to regroup and pull it back together. We finished the season with twenty-three wins and were nationally ranked. It was gratifying to have that type of season and achieve national recognition. The other schools in our conference offered athletic scholarships and we didn't, so they tended to look down on Berea College and its players. We made people respect Berea College.

Jay Stenzel was a freshman that year, and he exceeded my expectations. When he came to Berea he gave us something we hadn't had for awhile, which was height. I could see that he was a good player, but I didn't expect him to produce or contribute as much as he did. He was able to contribute significantly in his very first year. With the caliber of upperclassman we had, that impressed me a lot. Jay wasn't yet a go-to type of player, but when he was given the opportunity he delivered.

Our season ended just as it began, with a loss to Transylvania. We played at Eastern's gymnasium, down in the pit. It was a hard-fought game. All of us understood its importance, and the effort put forth by everyone on our team was outstanding. Everyone went out and gave it their all. I thought the officiating could have been better. There were some questionable calls. Transy might have thought the same thing, of course. That's what was unsettling about it. In a championship game the officials should let the players play.

I graduated in January 1985. After the ceremony I packed up my clothes, went to Lexington, and moved into an apartment. The next morning I reported for work at Ashland Oil.

I started as a computer analyst working on projects related to automated coal weighing. Now I'm a project manager responsible for all of the information technology and point-of-sale equipment for Ashland's Super-America stores. I enjoy analyzing a business situation and applying technology to it. Technology offers many different solutions to problems, and my job is to determine and implement the solutions that are most workable and cost-effective.

Once I got into the business world, I didn't use a great deal of the upper-level math I learned in college. But thinking in that logical, problem-solving mode has helped me immensely in the line of work I'm in. The labor positions I held in the Computer Department were very valuable, as was a summer job I had one year in Berea helping the Forestry Service develop computer applications. All of these things helped prepare me for life after graduation, for working on real-life business solutions rather than class assignments.

When I was a student, all that study and work seemed like a chore. Once I entered the workforce I began to appreciate my Berea background. Tasks that many people found challenging came easier for me. Ashland Oil hires many Berea College graduates. The company recognizes their academic preparation and work ethic. In my department alone we've got three Berea graduates helping to support the information technology for Super-America.

July 8, 1998

Tommy Owsley

When I was in junior high I was on a riding lawn mower with one of my friends, cutting his grass, when we went into a hole. I fell off, and two of my toes were cut off. After I got out of the hospital and my foot healed up, I wore a special piece in my shoe, so the injury didn't affect me as an athlete. A lot of the players didn't even know I had it, because I could do anything.

I played basketball at Lincoln County High School in Kentucky. I also played football for two years and ran track for a year. I would have liked to continue to play football, but my mom told me that if I wanted to go somewhere to college and play basketball, I needed to cut the football out. Moms know best, and that's what I did.

Tommy Owsley: "The quickest guard I ever saw"

I wasn't recruited that heavily in high school. I accepted a scholarship to go to Lindsey Wilson College in Columbia, Kentucky, but the coach who signed me left. He wanted me to go with him, but that would have been against the rules. I found out about Berea College from a good friend of mine, Shelby Reynolds. He went to school there, and that's where I ended up going.

I'm six-one and played guard. In high school my defensive play was all right, but I was more of a scorer. At Berea College Coach Wierwille emphasized defense, so I worked on my defense and took pride in it. I knew the scoring would come, and it did. What I liked most was to come up with an important steal, because that got the players and the crowd excited. I set three different records for steals, improving every year. As a sophomore year I had seventy-plus steals, as a junior ninety-plus, and as a senior 113. One conference official said I was quicker than a hiccup. I played defense by looking at a player's eyes. A lot of people look at a guy's waist, but I'd look at the eyes, and the eyes usually told me where the guy was going to throw the ball. Then I'd have a steal and two points.

Because I had attended a couple of classes at Lindsey Wilson, I was ineligible to play during my first semester at Berea. I didn't start playing until the second semester of the 80-81 season, but in the first game I played I scored eleven points. I was really excited about that. Then I started as a sophomore. In our first game that year we lost to Rio Grande by two points, but the game sticks out in my memory because I had twenty-five points and eleven steals.

When I first met Coach Wierwille I thought he was kind of tough. I thought he was going to break my hand when he shook it. But after I got to know him I came to regard him as more of a father figure than anything else. He cared about us not just as basketball players, but as people. He wanted us to succeed in life. Not too many coaches are like that.

Coach Wierwille and I never had any arguments. If something wasn't going right, he would let us know about it. If we weren't practicing well, he'd say, "Hey guys, you need to do a little running today." If he had to yell to get his point across, he did. That didn't bother me. I really enjoyed playing for him. He was an excellent communicator and very, very knowledgeable about basketball.

The two upperclassmen who impressed me most were Vance Blade and Marcus Crawford. Vance was an awesome rebounder, one of the best in the KIAC. Marcus was a prolific scorer. He was very smooth and drove to the basket extremely well.

I'd been just an average student in high school, and at Berea I should have taken my studies more seriously. I had some grade problems and left school for a year. Then my mom passed away. I went to work in a shoe store. After awhile I said to myself, "I don't want to do this for the rest of my life. I know my mom would want me to finish college." I grew up a lot that year. After talking to some good friends about it, I went back to Berea.

The team I joined in 1983-84 was one of Berea's best ever. We had a good group of guys who played well together. Teamwork made us successful. Everyone knew his role and responsibilities. If we had the fast break, we'd run it, but no run and gun stuff. It was a set-up offense. If we had a good shot, we'd take it. Certain people had a green light.

My closest friend on the team was probably Kevin Mullins, who was later best man at my wedding. He and I went through a lot together. He was always there for me and vice versa. Kevin was laid-back and almost always in a good mood, but if he was having problems with school work or basketball, he knew he could always talk to me. I felt the same way with him. He was a good person to talk to.

I started at guard that year. The other starting guard was Donald Hairston. I didn't know Donald too well because he kind of kept to himself, but he was very intelligent. Although he was bowlegged, Donald at six-one had a vertical jump of about forty-four inches, just unreal. I remember a close game against Alice Lloyd in which somebody threw the ball up and Donald came from the corner, rose over two or three guys, and slammed it into the basket. He was unbelievable. Donald shot well, ran the offense, and was a leader. He was a terrific player.

I thought we should have gone to the national tournament that year. Transylvania beat us out by one point. Transy was one of our biggest rivals

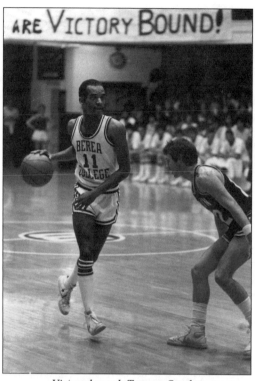
ARE VICTORY BOUND!

Victory bound: Tommy Owsley

because they always thought they were so much better than everybody else. At Berea we had to work our way through school, and I don't think they ever gave us any respect.

That final game with Transy was close all the way through. We had a chance to win it at the end. Somebody shot it with a few seconds to go, missed it, and the ball came back to me. I shot it back up. My shot also missed. Kevin Mullins put up the last shot from just two feet away from the basket, but it didn't go in either. Losing that game was terribly disappointing. If we had won we would have played Cumberland, another big rival, and I think we would have beaten them and advanced to Kansas City.

We had a lot of good players back the following season. Mark George and Kevin Martin played a lot of guard after Donald Hairston graduated. Both of them were slashing-type players. Kevin was another good friend of mine. He was my roommate for two or three years. He was a hard-nosed player who shot the ball very well.

Dave Moeves and I were co-captains that year. He didn't score that much but rebounded well, and he did the little things that weren't always noticed. Dave was a leader, too. Jay Stenzel was six-six and could shoot like a guard. He'd been a starter as a freshman the previous year. Jay could score twenty points a night, but he did whatever the team needed. He was one of the top players I played with at Berea College.

Lionell Miller played a big part in our success that year. He'd been a couple of years behind me at Lincoln County High School, and he transferred to Berea from Sue Bennett College. He jumped very well. Lionell came in off the bench, scored ten or twelve points, got rebounds, and did whatever had to be done.

Our first game in the District 32 playoffs was at Cumberland. We always had good games with them. Coach Randy Vernon did a wonderful job down there. Cumberland had won fifty-three games in a row at home. We were the underdogs. We had nothing to lose.

Before the game Jay Stenzel and his girlfriend had been having some problems, so he wasn't really into it. I went to him and said, "Look, Jay, I know you're going through some tough times right now, but the team needs you tonight." The atmosphere was electric at Cumberland. The game was nip and tuck, back and forth, but at the end we pulled away. With about ten seconds to go I said to Coach Wierwille, "Coach, this game is over."

"No, don't you say that!"

"Yes, this game is over." And it was. That was one of the greatest victories in Berea College history. Beating Cumberland in the playoffs while breaking home their winning streak was certainly one of my best experiences as a basketball player.

Our next opponent was Georgetown, who had beaten us three times that year. They had their luggage already packed for a trip to Kansas City and the national tournament. Knowing that gave us extra incentive to go out and show them what we were made of. We thought, "You've beaten us three times, but it can't happen again."

The game with Georgetown was another tight game. After halftime I picked up my third or fourth foul, so I had to be careful. That's when Lionell Miller stepped up and played a big role. Cliff Blackburn, who was with us just one year, played well, and so did Jay Stenzel, Dave Moeves, Mark George, and everybody else. We came out on top, and we celebrated that night. At Berea College the fans followed us whether we won or lost. Although the game was played at Georgetown, we probably had more people in the stands than Georgetown did. It was an amazing night.

It was wonderful to be the first Berea College team to go to Kansas City. All of us were excited, and we were treated like royalty. We were taken to a real nice steakhouse, very elegant, and we got to see the Kansas City football stadium. It was fun to meet the teams from all the other districts. But we didn't play well in our game against Rio Grande.

The game was close. Jay Stenzel struggled a bit during the first half, but he came on in the second half. At the end we had a chance to win the game, but one of the younger guys had trouble with the ball. I couldn't get it because I had two or three guys on me, so they threw it to him, he kind of bobbled it, and we got beat by three points. I wish it could have ended differently, but that year was a good year for us.

Steve Ridder, our assistant coach, had a big part in our going to the national tournament. He was already one of the brightest young coaches in America. Coach Ridder knew his basketball. He scouted games and looked at films. He was always there for us, very easy to talk to about basketball or anything else. He was also my dorm director in Danforth.

The basketball players had to come back to school early during Christmas vacation. The dorms were closed, so we stayed with local families. I'm grateful to Betty and David Olinger and Carolyn and Max Hughes, who took me in. The Wierwilles, too, were always great to me. Whenever I had problems, no matter what they were, I could always go and talk to them. Mrs Cecilia Wierwille was just like a mom. We still stay in contact.

Like many students, I had several jobs at Berea. I think I started in

St. Gertude's Church, Vastervik, Sweden

the cafeteria. I taught tennis, worked at Boone Tavern for awhile, and was a janitor in my dorm. My major was physical education. One of the most memorable teachers I had was Phil Spears. I took him for a business class. He really enjoyed basketball, but we used to talk about just about anything. He really made you work in class, but he was another person who wanted you to succeed in life.

In my last semester as a senior, I knew that I was going to be a couple of credits short of graduation. But I thought I had a chance to play professionally, and that was something I'd always dreamed about. So I withdrew from school. I went to Atlanta to try out for some CBA teams, and then I went to Florida. I wasn't offered a contract. The fact that I played at a small school like Berea hurt me in the eyes of the coaches. Many of the players at those tryout camps were outstanding, but the coaches had already made up their minds about who they were going to select.

Coach Jim Connor of Thomas More had a son who scouted in Europe. A team in Sweden was looking for a guard, and he recommended me. I signed a contract for a year. The team kept an American for just one year. I would have liked to have stayed over there, but I didn't have any connections. Kenny Smith, who played at Cumberland when I was at Berea, played in Europe for ten or eleven years. I ran into him over there.

My team was in Vastervik, which is about three hours south of Stockholm. We played a fifteen-game season in what was called Division Two. They had four or five divisions. I enjoyed playing in Sweden. The atmosphere was great, and the competition, okay. They had the three-point line over there, which I hadn't had in college. Basketball in Sweden was played by international rules, which are just a bit different from ours. There were several former NCAA Division I players around, including Poncho Wright, who had played for Louisville.

My team lost only three games. When I wasn't playing I coached a junior high team and a girls' team, and I went around to different schools teaching the Swedish people about American-style basketball. I didn't know Swedish. That's a hard language to learn. But most of the people knew English, and they greeted me warmly. Seeing another part of the world was something I always wanted to do.

After my year in Sweden I returned to Kentucky. I tried to get back into Berea College to finish my degree, but by that time I was married, and they said that my wife and I made too much money for me to qualify. I had all my credits transferred from Berea to Eastern Kentucky University and finished there. I consider myself a Berea alumnus, though, because I was there for so long. If I had to do it over again, I would have made sure I graduated from Berea, where everybody treated me so wonderfully. Earning my degree made Coach Wierwille's graduation record record for his four-year players 100 percent.

I've been working at Ashland Oil for eight years. I'm a shipping cooordinator. I've moved up two or three positions since I've been there, and people tell me I'm doing an excellent job. I'm trying to gain more computer experience. I've think I've got a bright future in the company.

I've thought about going into coaching, but I don't have time to go back to school and get a master's degree. I'd have to quit my job and go to school full-time, and with two little ones at home I can't afford to do that. I've been playing in a lot of three-on-three tournaments, which I really enjoy. My wife said she wants me to keep playing until the kids get a little bit older. I try to play as much as possible. That's just about all I do in the summer.

October 12, 1998

Randy Logsdon   1982-84

Basketball brought me to Berea. Although I grew up in central Kentucky, in Crab Orchard and Danville, I knew nothing about Berea College. I didn't even know it existed. My basketball coach at Danville High School contacted Coach Wierwille. I was dating a girl from Paint Lick who was in college at Eastern, and she brought me over to Berea and showed me the campus. Then I visited with John Cook and Coach Wierwille and worked out with the players. It was off-season, but they played every day.

I didn't get into any varsity games as a freshman, but I played a lot as a sophomore. I'm five-eleven, or maybe five-ten and a half. Directing and controlling the team was what I did best. I handled the ball real well and passed the ball real well. I always had the ability to anticipate on the court.

I don't mean that I'm clairvoyant, but I knew who was going to be open before they were open, probably even before they knew.

I had problems with my ankles which cost me some playing time. Then when I was a freshman or maybe a sophomore I got hurt horsing around in the dorm. I banged my right knee into a door jamb, which resulted in some severe hemorrhaging under the knee. For a while it was so tender that I couldn't even touch it. I had to wear a knee pad, but if it got bumped I'd be done for a while. Finally it healed up.

Then I had one of my teeth knocked out in practice, a front tooth in my upper jaw. We little guys are not supposed to reach in for rebounds. Tim Shelton brought the ball down, I swiped at it, and he elbowed me in the mouth and left just a little nub,

Randy Logsdon: "A fierce competitior who wasn't intimidated by anybody"

which I spit out. I've had that thing repaired a couple of times. Tim was big. He may have elbowed me to teach me a lesson, but I don't think he meant any harm. Losing the tooth was just an accident.

I was fairly strong, and I jumped well. I had a nice game down at Clinch Valley when I was a sophomore. I had seven rebounds at the half. We

— 180 —

played a lot of three-two zone defense, which was probably Coach's favorite. As a guard I understood that I had to rebound on the off side. If they shoot the ball from over there, most of the time it comes off over here, and if you clear that side, box out, the ball will come to you. But in that game I was the only player who was rebounding well, and at halftime Coach got all over the inside players. We went on to win the game.

I played well off the bench in the first half of our game against Northern Kentucky University in the district playoffs. I started the second half and played the whole rest of the way until I fouled out in overtime. Winning that game would have put us just one victory away from the 1983 national tournament, but we lost. NKU was a good team, but I thought we were capable of beating them.

That was the year I became close friends with Bubby Napier. He came to Berea a year after I did, but I remembered him from playing against him in high school. Bubby and I were very different people, but we seemed to balance each other out. I was a positive person, one who could hardly ever see why things wouldn't work. Bubby was the opposite, a little pessimistic, although he would say realistic. While I'm an emotionally charged person, Bubby was laid back to the point where it almost irritated me sometimes. He never played with any emotion whatsoever. Never up, never down. He'd give us sixteen points and eight rebounds every night, no spikes or valleys. That can be good, but also bad. I was a guy who came at you, and Bubby wasn't. I thought Bubby could have used a little of my emotion, but he didn't have the swings I had, either.

We were loaded with talent in 1983-84, but it was a frustrating year for me and some of the other guys who didn't get to play. I sat on the bench after playing a lot my sophomore year and starting some. John Small and Mark Walls sat on the bench after starting most of the year before. Donnie Harper was a senior who sat on the bench although he was a good player who had averaged double figures as a sophomore. Bubby sat on the bench, and he was a future 1000 point, 500 rebound guy.

I think that in the beginning Coach Wierwille planned to play a lot of people. Our first game was Homecoming against Transylvania. We had control of the game early, then at the end of the half made several substitutions. With a lot of cold people on the floor we lost momentum, and Transy beat us. That experience might have convinced Coach that he couldn't play that many people.

It was very difficult for me to sit on the bench and watch my junior year slipping away. I couldn't understand it. I felt that I was proving myself every day in practice, but without any hope. Coach never communicated to me the reason I wasn't playing, and I didn't go to him. I should have, but I didn't. I did talk to Steve Ridder, his assistant coach, but I don't think Steve's role at that time was to advise Coach Wierwille about who he should be playing. I was married and expecting a child, so I had a lot to handle emotionally.

We played a game at Pikeville that was not close. At the end Coach put in many of the people who hadn't been playing, me included. I got poked in the eye pretty severely, and I covered it up to try to get my bearings. Coach hollered out at me, "You're on the bench." He was jerking people up to try to get them into the game, but I didn't want to come out, and I hollered back at him. That made him very angry.

Later we talked. Coach Ridder explained to Coach that I had reacted defensively. The incident was supposedly forgotten after we talked it out, but in the next seven games I didn't play one second.

I'm a coach now myself, and I don't know if there's a solution to the problem of too many talented players and too little playing time. Rick Pitino won a national championship at the University of Kentucky with a very talented team, and even he was always questioned. I suspect it's a problem that every coach would like to have. Basketball is a team sport, and most players have little difficulty recognizing their roles or playing them. But a coach needs to find a way to help players understand their roles.

I believe to this day that I was good enough to start at Berea College. I played behind two guards who were tremendous, Donald Hairston and Tommy Owsley. But I could have done some things for that team, that year, that Tommy couldn't. I thought we would have been better if I'd had the ball. I wasn't the scorer Tommy was, but all we did that year was shift points from other people to Tommy. It wasn't until the following year, after a few people had graduated and Berea needed a guy to put the ball in the hole a lot and to do the other things that he could do, that Tommy was instrumental.

David Moeves was not a better player than Bubby Napier, but David brought some things to the team that were a real nice fit. David came to Berea as a shooter who liked to play outside, but he worked hard on the weights, got strong, and became an excellent rebounder. David accounted for a lot of inside baskets, putbacks, that some people call garbage but are essential. A team needs a player who will do that, and he was willing.

Nevertheless, there should have been a place for Bubby in the lineup. Jay Stenzel played a lot that year as a freshman. Nobody questioned that Jay was going to be a terrific player, but he wasn't then. He was weak, and he didn't know when to shoot the ball and when not to. Jay had size, he had quickness, and he worked hard, but he should not have been playing ahead of Bubby and John Small that year.

Donald Hairston, incidentally, was by far the best player I played with at Berea. He wasn't real outgoing, but he was caring. He proved that by sacrificing his own game. He could shoot the ball from anywhere on the floor and could easily have been a twenty-point scorer every time out. But he was only interested in the team, and scoring was not what he was asked to do.

Donald looked like Herschel Walker. His strength amazed me. He never lifted weights. He just did pushup after pushup after pushup, situp after situp after situp. A lot of guards were bigger than he was, but he wore them out. He'd take a guy inside and do what he wanted with him. He didn't have any weaknesses in his game, but his only interest was in helping the team to win.

As I said, basketball brought me to Berea College. Although my career as an athlete was not everything I hoped it would be, I knew that life's difficulties build a person's character. I've always been reluctant to let go of anything, even if it's not going well.

I could have played elsewhere. Ron Reed, who had been Glen Drury's high school coach in Anderson County, Kentucky, was an assistant at the University of Mississippi when I was in high school, and he was interested in me. They recruited four players for two guard scholarships. I was one, another was Phil Cox, and I don't know who the other two were. Phil Cox went to Vanderbilt and I wasn't offered, so I assume the other two played at Ole Miss. Then Ron Reed took over as head man at Millligan College. In my freshman year my roommate was Tim Mefford, a good player but one for whom things weren't working out all that great at Berea. Both of us could have transferred to Milligan.

But I loved Berea College. It was a wonderful place, one I thought would lead me to the better life I always wanted. I grew up with no money. My family was what would now be called dysfunctional. My mother was a wonderful Christian woman, but my dad was an alcoholic, and they were divorced when I was ten. A lot of situations were not real good. When I came to Berea I left that life behind. I never considered transferring or dropping out.

I didn't play basketball as a senior. I didn't think I could handle another year like the one I'd just been through, not with all the responsibilities of working and studying with a wife and child at home. I came to Berea believing and expecting to be as good a guard as ever played there, and I worked hard to be the best I could be. But I had to put my ego aside and evaluate my situation honestly. I missed playing, and today part of me regrets that I didn't play another year. Most athletes don't want people to identify them only as athletes. I was happy to be part of the team, but if I couldn't play, that was all right too.

Roland Wierwille's a great coach. There were times when I didn't think so, for my own selfish, twenty-one-year-old reasons. I gained plenty of insight playing for him at Berea College. I can't imagine a better small college program. Don Lane does a wonderful job at Transylvania, but money is not an issue there, and he's sitting in one of the only two big cities in the state, and the nicer of the two. Recruiting is not a big problem. Berea is nonscholarship, so Coach Wierwille can't get a lot of the people he'd like to have play for him. It's hard to attract seventeen and eighteen-year olds when you can't say the word "scholarship." Coach Wierwille does a wonderful job, especially considering the restrictions he's always had at Berea.

During my years at Berea the contributions of Steve Ridder were huge. He had a real good knowledge of the game. We had plenty of talent, but his coaching improved the quality of our play significantly, especially on defense. He related to the players very well. That wasn't long after his own playing career. Steve was upbeat all the time. He'd high-five us, pat us on the back. That wasn't Coach Wierwille's nature, and I don't know if that's what you want in a head coach anyway.

You can't compete on any level without talent, no matter how good a coach you are. You can get the most out of what you have, but if you're going to win consistently you've got to have talent. Steve Ridder was a tremendous recruiter. Coach Wierwille was more, "Berea's a great place to play, we've got a great program, come or don't!" Steve was an expert communicator and motivator. He was very valuable to Coach Wierwille sitting beside him during games, as they bounced ideas and suggestions off each other.

My campus job was student director of the intramural program. I enjoyed it. It was a lot of responsibility. Like any college job, I could do it 100 times better now, but it was a great learning experience. I spent a great deal of time on it. I was not a person who needed a lot of sleep. Even today, if I sleep eight hours I feel lazy afterward. I was fortunate to have a very understanding, cooperative wife who was supportive of everything I did, even at our young, ignorant age. She was a former Berea College student, Lisa Gray.

I majored in business administration. Although I was sharp enough, I never developed good study habits. Many times I took care of my studies by staying up all night. I could retain what I read, so I did fine. I'm very much a relationship-oriented person, and I'm sure that hurt me academically. When I lived in the dorm there was always somebody who didn't have anything to do, and I was happy to do that with him. So instead of studying I'd go here and there.

After I graduated we moved to Gainesville, Georgia, outside of Atlanta. I spent three years in the furniture business there, working for a company that did corporate leasing. The owner had multiple stores. I started out as a collection guy for him, and that's the greatest job in the world for getting experience, because you learn how to communicate with people. Eventually I rose to a pretty good position in management, but we moved back to Kentucky in 1989.

Today I work for a company called Southeast Service. It's a national housecleaning service company. I ran our Lexington operation for a while, cleaning a lot of UK and hospital property. Now I manage the janitorial service for all GTE facilities in the state of Kentucky, and all the Bell South facilities from Frankfort east. Additionally, Bubby Napier and I own a floor care business together.

Bubby and I are Christians, and our kids go to Victory Christian School in Somerset. One of the reservations I had about a small Christian school was athletics for my son. He's a good athlete, just like I was. God gives us everything we have in life, and athletics was the vehicle He chose for me. I wanted my son to have that opportunity.

Three years ago the principal said to me, "We need to start a basketball program. Do you want to do it?" I didn't have time to do it, but I said, "Sure, and Bubby will help." I volunteered him, but he did it without question, just as I knew he would. We were co-coaches the first year. Not too many people could do that. Usually you have to have one guy as head and the other guy as assistant. Bubby and I never had any problems.

We've used a lot of what we learned at Berea about structure and preparation. We run a very disciplined program. That goes along with the school, but it doesn't go along with society today, although kids still need discipline. Our basketball teaching becomes life teaching. Our kids learn cooperation, team play, responsibility, and hard work. They learn how to win and how to lose. We use some of the philosophies we learned at Berea as well as some of the drills. What we didn't like at Berea, we don't use. Eat the fish, spit out the bones.

When you teach or coach young people, no matter what their age, the best thing you can hope to gain is the satisfaction of making a positive impact on their lives. You can be happy with the team you have or with the athletic skills your players develop, but those things are less important than the type of people they become. I'm sure Coach Wierwille feels that way. I don't know every player he's coached, but I'm certain that as a group his players compare favorably with people who go through programs at other schools. Whether you agree with everything he does or not, he makes you a better person.

October 14, 1998

Nathaniel "Bubby" Napier   1982-87

Coach Wierwille has always asked the seniors to give a speech at the spring athletic banquet. One of the first things I did was recognize the Lord

Bubby Napier: "A clean, honest person, good to know and to be around"

for his protection over me. I never missed a game or even a practice in high school or college due to illness or injury. Like all athletes, of course, I had my share of aches and pains. As a college senior I had a very painful sciatic nerve problem in my back. It didn't bother me at all when I was playing, but often on the bus rides back to Berea it really hurt, because a sitting position puts a lot of pressure on that nerve, which runs down your leg. To take the pressure off my lower back I would sit on the end seat in the aisle, place a rolled-up towel behind my back, put my legs up, and stretch out. In classrooms, too, I often had to stretch out. Other than that I was very fortunate, very blessed.

My dad worked for National Cash Register for thirty years, and my mom was a homemaker. They were very supportive of my playing basketball. I went to Pulaski County High School in Somerset, Kentucky.

Berea College was interested in me, and I met Coach Wierwille when he invited me to the athletic banquet. Berea was a college close to home where I could play ball, so I jumped at the chance. I went up there, took a look at the campus and what the College had to offer, and met several of the players. Coach Wierwille was big, boisterous, and intimidating. That didn't bother me. My high school coach was a small guy, but he was intimidating too, a very stern and strict disciplinarian. I knew I could cope with that.

In the first game of my freshman year we played Brescia College. They were just getting their program off the ground, so we had a fairly easy time of it. I was put in early in the second half. Later in that half Coach Wierwille called a timeout and set up a special play for Kevin Mullins to come down the middle of the lane. I can't recall who took the ball out of bounds, but I was on the block, and I was supposed to go out to the corner, simply to get out of the way and act as a decoy. When I moved out into the corner, all I saw was a flash up the middle of the lane and a guy jamming his hand down through the rim. Kevin was about six-one and a half, and he took that lob pass and threw it right down. Welcome to college basketball! It was exciting.

Kevin was the type of leader who would tell you what to do. I wasn't used to a player who was talkative and directive. Later that season we were playing at Campbellsville. I'd broken into the starting lineup by that time. Something transpired, I can't remember exactly what, and Kevin gave me some instructions. I was a little offended. I expected the coach to do that, because that's the way it was done at my high school. Later I realized that in college basketball it was good to have those on-court leaders. That was a lesson for me as a freshman. Donald Hairston was another kind of leader, a quiet player who led by example. He said, "Do as I do." Then he went out and did it.

I'm six-four. I was a well-rounded player, not exceptional in any one area. I was never a huge scorer, but always a consistent scorer. I was never a huge rebounder, but always a consistent rebounder. I was never a huge playmaker, but I was willing to give the ball up. I was never was a great ballhandler, but I didn't turn the ball over very often.

Scoring and rebounding came naturally to me, but I had to work hard to improve my defense. Defensively, high school and college ball are a lot different. The players in college are much better than the ones in high school, and in college a poor defensive player can't be hidden.

I came to Berea from a winning high school program. I didn't know the history of the Berea program in terms of wins and losses, but I arrived expecting us to win and intending to help the team to win. We had a lot of talent, and we were able to mesh all those individual talents together into a team that won a lot of ballgames.

My first year at college was difficult, as it is for many students. I was not happy about having to leave my family and my high school sweetheart, Jill. My parents came to all of my home games, and Jill came to a lot of them. Back at home the next summer, I was reluctant to return to Berea for my sophomore year because it would mean another long-distance relationship with Jill. I did go back to school, but I struggled in the classroom and on the basketball floor. Jill and I got married during Christmas break, and that kept my mind away from my studies and basketball. As a freshman I'd been the team's second leading scorer and rebounder, but midway through my sophomore season I lost my starting position and found myself sitting on the bench.

I began to realize that there was more in the world than basketball. I wanted to get my marriage on a solid foundation. That was more important to me than ball. My studies were more important than ball. But I still wanted basketball to be a part of my life, so after thinking hard about it I made a decision. I took the 1984-85 season off so I could focus and concentrate on my marriage and my studies. Then I went back to the team, played two more years, and did very well.

It was always my intention to go back and play after that one year off. Coach Wierwille didn't like it, and I could understand that. I think he believed that if I left the team I would never play again. He could see me struggling my sophomore year. It was difficult for me not to be playing. That was partly my fault, of course, because I was not totally committed and focused on the game. I felt that I still had something to contribute to the team, and later that year I was hardly playing at all. That was frustrating.

Coach noticed before the next season that I was no longer coming into the gym. I met with him and told him that I had decided not to play that year, that I would pick it up the following year. He said he didn't think I needed to do that. I said, "I'll go home and re-evaluate it and let you know my decision."

But Coach didn't wait on me. The next day he sent his assistant, Steve Ridder, to find out what I'd decided. My feelings hadn't changed, and I told Coach Ridder that.

It just so happened that the year I didn't play was the year the team went to the national tournament. I lost out on that, but I have no regrets, because my marriage and my studies were more important. I went to watch the team play, and after the final victory over Georgetown I went out and hugged the players. I shook Coach's hand and said, "Congratulations." The team's successful year certainly helped Coach to get over the fact that I sat the season out. There was no tension between us when I came back to the team in the fall of 1985.

In the year I didn't play I learned how to study and organize my time, which was essential if I wanted to stay in college. The biggest part of college or anything else is enduring. You have to persevere. That builds your character.

Being away from basketball for a year changed my perspective on the game. After I came back I felt much more relaxed. The stress of performing was gone. In my sophomore year I was always concerned about making mistakes, and when you're concerned about making mistakes, you make them. For the first time I found myself playing for the enjoyment of the game and the love of the game, not because it was something I was supposed to do.

The best part of my basketball career at Berea College was my friendship with Randy Logsdon. Randy was a year ahead of me. We were both married players, and our relationship blossomed from that shared bond.

Randy was a tremendous ballhandler. He could see the floor better than anybody I played with. I had a real connection with Randy when he was on the floor. We clicked together. Randy was a fierce competitor who wasn't intimidated by anybody. He was a very confident person. He knew what he could do, and he played within his abilities. I don't think he got the opportunity to display his talents that he should have.

All the guys I played with were great people, and many of them were very good players. I'm proud that I scored 1000 points, but I wasn't the only 1000-point scorer among my teammates. I played with Tommy Owsley, who was much more prolific than I was. Tommy could pull up and shoot the ball from anywhere. Not many players could come off the break, stop, and shoot like Tommy could, whether bringing it down or out on the wing. Because he anticipated so well, Tommy often got away with cheating off his man, so he intercepted a lot of passes. At times when he should have been covering his man, he wasn't. Although that sometimes backfired on him, on some nights it paid big dividends. I don't mean that Tommy was slack in playing defense. He was simply more intent on stealing the ball and getting the bucket on the other end.

Our opponents knew that Jay Stenzel could score, but he scored anyway. He was very offensive-minded. When he got the ball, he looked to score. He could do it, so why not? Jay was not a forceful

Bubby Napier: "He worked hard for everything he got"

leader, but a quiet player who went about the business of putting the ball in the basket. Jay was injured during my senior year, and that was the only year we had a losing record.

Willie Hill was a very disciplined ballplayer. I likened him to myself, although he was a better ballhandler and assist person. He was not a tremendous scorer but a consistent scorer, like me. Willie also ended up with over 1000 points.

Mike Sams rebounded the ball real well for his size and jumping ability. He was always around the ball when it came off the boards. As someone who was not a great leaper either, I knew what it took to rebound the ball. It was positioning, timing, and awareness of where the ball was at all times. Mike did that well, and he was another player who could put the ball in the basket. He played with a lot of intensity on the offensive end.

Mike became a minister after he left college, and I wouldn't have predicted that for him. But the Lord has the power to change us all. I was a devout Christian and still am. My faith is very important to me. As a Christian in college I tried to influence those around me by example. One player asked me in my senior year if it was true that I had never been to Richmond. He didn't believe it, but it was true. I never went there to drink or to socialize. He told me he admired me for that.

I scored my thousandth point on the road. Our previous game was at home against Thomas More. We had a considerable lead with three or four minutes to go, and Coach took me out. Apparently he didn't know I was close to the milestone. I think that John Cook, our scorekeeper, told him. Coach called time out, and I will never forget what he tried to do for me. He put me back into the game and said, "He needs six points to reach 1000. Let's see if we can get him the ball." Well, it didn't happen. The guys started forcing things that weren't there and threw a few balls away. Thomas More was able to creep back into the game, although not close enough to scare us. I would have loved to get the thousandth point at home, and Coach knew it, but it didn't work out. Still, in the years I was there I don't think he did that for any other player.

We scored a lot of baskets off our fast break offense. We looked to push the ball up, and if the layup wasn't there, we'd shoot it from the corner or dump it inside. Coach Wierwille designed a little maneuver off the initial fast break that we scored a lot of points off. I scored my thousandth point at Clinch Valley off that particular play. Off the break I came through a screen on the block and shot a little fifteen-foot jumper from the baseline. We set screens and moved the ball around outside, getting it inside when we could. It was just a simple, basic offense, and it was very successful.

Constant repetition in practice made our offense work. We ran it every day, with and without defense. After a while it was ingrained and came naturally. We all clicked at the same time. Nobody had to stop and think about where to go or what to do.

Coach Wierwille was not a real personable guy with the players, but I never had a problem getting along with him. In my senior year we were traveling to a game in two vans. Coach wanted to go in a car, but he didn't want to drive, so he picked me to be his chauffeur. That shows you that we had a good relationship.

He was a very good administrative coach. When we were playing at Clinch Valley one year we came into the locker room at halftime and found no drinks. That really bothered Coach, because he expected drinks to be in both teams' locker rooms. The next year we played there again. This time there were drinks set out for us, but they'd been sitting there awhile. The ice had melted, and they were warm and watery. Coach was upset again. That kind of thing offended him as an administrator. He always took care of our gymnasium and the teams that visited us.

If things didn't go right Coach got upset, and when he got upset he never got a little upset, he got a lot upset. One time at Union College I came out of the game for some reason and took a seat at the end of the bench. Coach hollered down to one of the managers, "Bring me some water! Bring me some water!" They brought a cup of water over to him, and he set it down between his feet. About that time something happened on the court that displeased him, and he reached down and smacked the cup. The water went everywhere. The next thing he hollered was, "Bring me a towel! Bring me a towel!"

Later in the same game the chair next to him was empty. He turned around and kicked it, and it went flying backwards. The kick must have done something to his toe, because he was hopping around for a week. He was a very intense man.

Steve Ridder was Coach Wierwille's link to the players. Coach Ridder was a very good practice coach who influenced our intensity level tremendously. I had a close relationship with Coach Ridder, and Jill and I babysat his kids when the team went to Kansas City. He entrusted us with his young infant.

At my senior athletic banquet Coach Wierwille gave me a videotape of that season's Homecoming game. We lost that game, but I played well and scored thirty-two points. My son has watched that tape over and over.

Although we struggled that year, we defeated Georgetown, a nationally ranked team, on their home floor. I had a very good game that night against an old high school teammate, which made our victory doubly satisfying. Georgetown and Cumberland were always the teams to beat within the KIAC. If we were going to win the conference we had to beat them, and if we couldn't, there was a long road ahead of us. Those teams loaded up with Division I transfers, and we wanted to show them that we could play too.

The last regular season game of my final year was a very emotional game for me and the team. We were playing Centre College at Seabury, and they had a good lead on us. Suddenly I got into what I can only describe as a zone. Everybody on the floor saw it. I started making shots at will and rebounding the ball real good. Keith Smith, our manager, was jumping up and down and shouting, "Get him the ball! He's hot!"

We came back and grabbed a one-point lead with seven seconds to go. We were sure we were going to win. Centre had the ball out at halfcourt, and they scored at the buzzer on an inbounds pass, a lob, and a fifteen-footer. We lost by a point. I wanted to win that game badly. We'd had a tough season, and the seniors wanted the team to finish on a good note to send a message to the players coming up behind us. We didn't want there to be any more losing seasons. We were devastated, but we turned around and beat Union in the KIAC playoffs. That win gave the team something to build on.

My first labor assignment was in the Admissions Office. I spent two years there doing clerical work, filing things, entering data. Once I got more into my physical education major, I started working in intramurals. My duties were to coordinate and run the campus intramural programs. Some other students and I were in charge of scheduling everything from intramural soccer to football to basketball to ping pong to badminton. Students ran it all, although we had labor advisers. That gave me a lot of

Mike Berheide: "He wanted us to find the answers"

valuable experience, exactly what I wanted. I took a lot of business courses, too.

Phil Spears' classes were stressful from the moment we walked in the door. I sat through them on pins and needles. Every day I'd say to myself, "I hope he doesn't pick on me today." Dr Spears put us under his thumb to see if we would fold under the pressure. He knew that if we withstood the experience, it would develop our character. He was right.

College is the place where students are supposed to learn to think for themselves. I enjoyed Dr Mike Berheide's thought-provoking approach. He didn't give us the answers; he wanted us to find the answers. He taught us to stop and think and evaluate. I enjoyed being around him.

I wanted to stay involved with both the athletic and business sides of sports. The Lord worked it out perfectly for me when I graduated from college. I was able to get a job at the YMCA in Somerset, my hometown. I was the program director for four and a half years and executive director for three and a half years. I also served for three years as the head JV coach at Pulaski County High School, which I enjoyed tremendously.

I now teach at Victory Christian School, a private K-through-twelve school in Somerset. When the school opened I shared with the principal the vision I had for an athletic program, and he and I were on the same page. Randy Logsdon and I volunteered to coach basketball. We did very well. I was later asked to teach and serve as athletic director. It has been very satisfying. I enjoy working with kids. We have high expectations, and I'm looking forward to what the Lord has for us to do, athletically and academically and spiritually.

Randy and I are still very close. We attend the same church. We own a business together. He's a very special person to me. Spiritually we're on the same level, and we still play basketball together. I'm thankful that we had the chance to get to know each other as teammates at Berea College.

The more I think about my Berea College degree, the more I appreciate it. During my student days I didn't realize the value of what I was going through. Now the experience means much more to me. My degree signifies that I accomplished something important. I was the first in my family to graduate from college. My sister and brother later went on to pick up degrees after they were married and had jobs. We see the value of education, although we understand that an education is not the same thing as a guarantee.

Berea College made it possible for me to go to college, and I'm grateful. My family earned a fairly good living, but the cost of education was high, and they were limited with what they could provide for me outside the home. Thanks to Berea, I could afford college.

I'll always have fond memories of Berea College basketball. I still play the game. I played in leagues until last year, and now I play in pickup games during the noon hour, although the aches and pains come a little more frequently now and take a lot more time to get over. Every year I go to Homecoming at Berea. I'm glad I had the chance to play college basketball, and I'm glad I took that chance. Had I not returned to the team after the year I sat out, I would have regretted it to this day, because I knew I had the ability to play and play consistently. I'm glad I followed through after I got my life in order.

Berea College basketball is something I tell my kids about. They watch it on film. A couple of years ago, out of the blue, Coach Wierwille sent me another tape of a good game I had. He enclosed a note that said, "I thought you might like this." I was very happy to get that.

I'll never forget the friendships I made. I've always been a reserved person, and basketball has been my link to society. I believe that the Lord has used basketball to help me to communicate and socialize with people. It has been a blessing in my life.

August 31, 1998

Mark George   **1982-86**

Mark George: "He let his playing do the talking"

I'd play basketball every night if I could. I'm going to play tonight. My wife is very patient, very understanding, and I appreciate that. I feel guilty as a husband and father when I'm gone playing basketball too much, so right now I'm just playing pickup games. I haven't played in any leagues the last couple of years.

My experience playing college basketball at Berea was positive. There were some rough times, times when I didn't get to play as much as I would have liked, but I'm glad I had the opportunity I did.

I had my highest scoring game as a freshman. I was playing against my brother Mike, who was a senior at Georgetown. That was my most memorable game, surpassing even our two big wins at Cumberland and Georgetown in my junior year. My parents were there to see it. Of course, Mike and I had played together all our lives, and after college we still played together, until our jobs finally separated us. Georgetown beat us that night, but they had a great team, one of the best of its time. They won the KIAC tournament but couldn't go to Kansas City because the school's whole athletic program was on probation.

My family moved from London, Kentucky, to Shelbyville when I was in the eighth grade. After I graduated from Shelby County High School I looked for a place to play college ball. Opportunities I thought I might have at Georgetown and Union faded away, so I talked to Coach Wierwille to see if Berea was a possibility for me. He acted interested, and that's how I ended up there.

I played quite a bit as a freshman, more than I did as a sophomore. Usually I was the first or second guy off the bench. I'm six-two, six-three, somewhere in there. I played small forward or second guard. I was an all-around player who tried to do whatever I thought was needed at the time. I didn't take a whole lot of shots, and I wasn't a big rebounder or assist man. When I got into the starting lineup my junior year I was a forward. Then I started some at guard my senior year.

I didn't speak much to Coach Wierwille, and he didn't speak much to me. There wasn't a whole lot of conversation going on between coach and player. He did his thing, and I tried to do mine. We didn't have a personal type of relationship.

All four of the teams I played on had good winning records. We won a lot of our games by being prepared, playing smart, and controlling the ball. We didn't turn the ball over very often. We had some pretty talented ballplayers.

In my freshman year we had a good team, but young. I don't think we had any seniors. We were better when I was a sophomore. Unfortunately we ran into another very good team, Transylvania, in the first round of the district tournament. I had some personal bones with Transylvania. I would have liked to go to school there, but I wasn't given the opportunity. They brought in Kip Hagan, an old high school rival of mine. All the way through college we played against each other. Kip was a win-at-all-costs type of player. He'd do anything to get an advantage, push you, cuss you, try to get in your head. Sometimes it was effective. He and Bobby Storie were tough opponents for us.

Losing to Transylvania in the district tournament that year was especially disappointing for all our gifted seniors: Donald Hairston, Kevin Mullins, Jeff Britt, Mark Walls, and Donnie Harper. We lost a lot of good talent when they graduated. Donald may have been the best athlete I ever played with. He was so strong and physical that he probably could have played pro football. I don't know about his baseball game, but he was a great all-around athlete, and very smart. He did real well at Berea. Kevin was another ballplayer who was both smart and physically gifted. He knew what to do to win. He was a great leaper and rebounder, and he could score.

Jeff wasn't blessed with a lot of quickness or speed or jumping ability, but he too was smart, and he could shoot. I ran into Jeff four or five years ago at a three-on-three tournament in Glasgow, Kentucky. He looked like he was in good shape. Mark and I developed a pretty good relationship because we lived on the same dorm floor, the first floor of Dana. Mark was an excellent shooter. He could stick it in from about anywhere. If we had had a three-point line back then, he would probably have played a lot more than he did.

Bubby Napier was probably my closest friend on the team. He didn't say a whole lot, but he was a great guy. He was a clean, honest person, good to know and to be around. Bubby was a scorer inside and a good rebounder.

Tommy Owsley was amazingly quick, not with his feet, although he had speed, but with his hands. He wasn't always consistent, but when he was playing well he was nearly unstoppable. There was no player in the league who Tommy couldn't take the ball away from.

Jay Stenzel knew how to score inside or outside. Jay was built like a basketball player should be, long, thin, and strong. He was a picture-per-

David Moeves: "A steady, consistent player"

fect specimen of an NAIA player. We didn't have any skywalkers in the KIAC.

Dave Moeves had a good basketball body, but he wasn't blessed with a lot of physical skills. He knew how to play inside, though. He worked hard and was very competitive. Once he got the ball inside he could usually score. Dave never got too high or too low. He was a steady, consistent player, night in and night out. You've got to have people you can depend on, and Dave was that.

The most competitive player on the team was probably Kevin Martin. He always gave everything he had, and there wasn't anybody too big for him. Kevin was a great guy to have around because he kept us laughing. Lionell Miller was the same way, a guy who liked to keep things light. Remembering him brings a smile to my face. Lionell was a junior college transfer who arrived in my junior year. He was a great leaper. He worked hard and contributed a lot to the team. Lionell and I graduated together. We were the only seniors our senior year.

At the end of my junior year we beat Cumberland and Georgetown back to back to earn a trip to the national tournament in Kansas City. Those were great moments for Berea College. I relive those experiences quite often, even now.

Both of those games were dramatic. Cumberland always had the great athletes and the great teams. They hadn't been beaten on their home court for fifty-three straight games when we went down there. Most people thought we had no chance to win, but we pulled off an upset. Tommy was unconscious that night, hitting everything. Cliff Blackburn, a freshman, did an exceptional job for us. Everybody played to their utmost potential, which we had to do against the talent of Cumberland. We had great fan support. It seemed as if there were more Berea people down there than Cumberland people.

When we went to Georgetown we were sky-high from beating Cumberland. That boosted our confidence. The Georgetown game wasn't as physically and mentally demanding as the Cumberland game, but in some ways it was more difficult. We lost Jay early. He got knocked to the floor and lost some teeth. Lionell came off the bench and played well, and Jay returned in the second half. Once again we played good team ball.

In Kansas City we played at nine o'clock in the morning. It felt more like a pickup game than a championship competition. There didn't seem to be anybody in the stands. We had a lot of fans there, but the arena was huge. If it wasn't for the Berea people, though, the place might have been empty. Rio Grande beat us, but the game could have gone either way. They pulled away at the very end and edged us out. We played well, but we could have played better.

As I remember it, we spent three days in Kansas City. We went to the stadiums where the Royals and Chiefs, the two professional teams, played. We had a nice meal in one of the clubhouses at the Royals stadium. We went out into the city one evening. We had a great time.

In my senior year we were eliminated at the end by Georgetown. When two good teams play, one of them is going to get beat. That game was probably my worst. I had some bad shooting games in college, but that one was right up there. I missed three or four shots from five feet. I couldn't get one to go in down the stretch when they needed to go in.

When I look back on it now I wish I had another opportunity to play against that Georgetown team. At the time I wasn't tremendously disappointed that my career was over. I tried to stay positive. I realized that I'd had a good career, played with a lot of good players, and had a good time doing it.

I came to college wanting two things: to play basketball and get a good education. I did both at Berea. I don't know if I would have been able to do either anywhere else. Berea was difficult for me, the first couple of years in particular.

I wasn't a great student in high school. That was because I didn't really try. As a young person I had ideas of playing college ball and possibly professional ball. Basketball was all I did or thought about. When I got to Berea I found out pretty quick that I was going to have to work academically to get through. I appreciated the patience of my professors. Maybe they knew that their incoming students hadn't always trained to be hard workers in their studies.

In my freshman year I had some trouble. That was the only time I got a C minus. It was in a sociology class. It was hard for me to balance work, basketball, difficult classes, and a new social life. I struggled with being away from home more than anything else. That's a big adustment for any college kid. Whether you play sports or not, you're in a totally new environment, completely on your own. It can be tough.

My first labor position was janitor at the gym. I enjoyed that as much as you can enjoy working as a janitor in a gym. I got out of the janitorial business in my junior year when I became a resident assistant in Dana. In the last semester of my senior year I was head resident at Bingham.

I majored in sociology and also had a major in history. I enjoyed history and took a lot of history classes. When my senior year rolled around

I noticed that I was close to having a double major in history, so I completed it. The Sociology Department consisted of John Crowden, Thomas Boyd, and Robert Stuckert. They were all great. Cleo Charles, David Nelson, and Warren Lambert were fine teachers in the History Department. Sociology and history are very different disciplines, sociology looking at current social issues, history concerned more with the details of what happened back when. I enjoyed both of them.

Immediately after I graduated I entered the master's program in criminal justice at Eastern Kentucky University. While pursuing my master's degree I worked juvenile corrections in Lexington. I've been in the corrections field ever since.

I developed an interest in criminology and corrections pretty early. I wanted to be in a helping profession. I was less interested in psychology, which is needed in this field, than I was in sociology, learning about institutions and environments and groups. There are always a lot of job opportunities in corrections. That's both good and bad, depending on how you look at it.

Today I'm a federal probation officer. I supervise between sixty-five and seventy-five people who have been placed on probation and/or supervised release from prison. I like the work because I get to help people and, ideally, help society. You don't have a whole lot of successful folks, but those you do have, you remember. It's like basketball, where you remember the victories and what you may have done to be a part of them. A person on probation has to really want to change their circumstance in life if they want to succeed. I'm not one to take credit for another person's success, but I do like to think that I play a part in it occasionally.

August 13, 1998

Charlie Andrews 1983-88

Charlie Andrews: "A wiry guy who played bigger than he was"

Players like Donald Hairston, Tommy Owsley, and Jay Stenzel were more than great athletes. They were great guys, great friends. We still get together.

I played one year with Donald. He was like a big brother to all the players. I'd see him working hard in practice, and it rubbed off on me. I wanted to get to the level he was at. Donald was a brain, too. He assisted in the computer lab. If anyone had a problem with math, Donald was the man to see.

Players on other teams would look at Tommy Owsley and say, "I'm going to have an easy game." Tommy was small and thin, but he was a player. I think he was honorable mention all-American a couple of years. Tommy was fierce and played great defense. Off the court he was an easygoing guy. We hung out and had fun.

Jay and I came in together. He could do it all, inside or outside. Jay got hurt and had to sit out a year, but when he came back he picked his game right up where he left it. He had a lot of dedication. We hung out somewhat, but Jay was quiet and hit the books.

I'm six-five and played forward and center. We had players who could score, especially Jay and Tommy, so my role was rebounding and defense. Often I guarded the other team's best player, trying to contain and stop him.

I grew up in London, Kentucky. Sports were important to me. I played football for a couple of years, but after I broke my leg in eighth grade playing football, I decided to stick with basketball. My Laurel County High School team won the state championship in 1982.

Bubby Napier, later my teammate at Berea, played for Pulaski County, the second-best team in the region that year. We beat them by one point in the tournament. Bubby was a quiet guy in college, but when you needed him he was there. He got the rebounds, and he did the little things. Bubby wasn't flashy, but Coach Wierwille could count on him. He was a Kevin McHale-type of player.

I went to Berea for several reasons. Larry Bruner, who coached me in high school, was a Berea graduate. I wanted a small school that offered a good education, and Berea was close to home, just thirty minutes away. My cousin, Paul Andrews, was going to UK, so at Berea I'd be in between. My family could drive up from London to see me play at Berea, and whenever I wanted to see Paul I could go north to Lexington. A lot of people think Paul and I are brothers because we played ball together all the way through school.

Coach Wierwille was very intense, but I think that he and I had a pretty good relationship. He hollered at me, but he knew I could take it. Some guys couldn't. So if we weren't rebounding, for instance, Coach would say, "Charlie, you need to get more rebounds." The other players would get the message. The way I looked at it, Coach hollered at me because he cared about me. If he didn't care, he wouldn't have said anything to me.

I started my first games in my second year. Unfortunately, I hurt my back. It was a slipped disc. I had to visit the chiropractor in Berea from time to time. I didn't miss games, but conditioning exercises were difficult. When we ran the eights I couldn't bend down to touch the floor, so Coach made me run past the lines and then turn around. Coach figured he was going to need me, so before the season started he arranged for a lady from Eastern to come down and help me with some special drills and exercises.

Coach liked to stick with his five starters. Once I twisted my ankle real bad and couldn't make a road trip to Pikeville. After I rehabbed he put me back in the starting lineup right away. You could look at that as either bad or good. It was bad for the bench guys who didn't get to play, but it was good for the starters, who gained confidence because they didn't have to worry about losing their positions. He knew what we were capable of doing.

On the road everybody had to concentrate on the game. Nobody joked around. On the bus we slept or listened to music or studied. Classes at Berea were tough, so we took advantage of any chance we could get could get to squeeze in a little study time.

I enjoyed our trips to Pikeville because we got to stay overnight in a nice hotel. It was a chance to get away. On most trips we'd go somewhere and come back that night. I had some of my better games against Pikeville's Todd May, who I had to guard. He was a great player, and our battles brought out the best in me. I have pictures of me blocking his shot.

In the NAIA district playoffs my senior year we played Alice Lloyd at Sue Bennett College in London. My grade school and high school coaches were there, and my family was sitting behind our bench. They put banners on the walls. I wanted to play well in front of them, so I was nervous. But I played hard and finished with nineteen points and nine rebounds as we beat Alice Lloyd to advance to the district finals. That was the highlight of my career.

Our next game was at Transylvania, and it was on TV. I stole the ball at the beginning of the game and thought about dunking it, but I laid it in. Everybody asked me later why I didn't dunk it. We gave Transy a good game, but we lost to end our season. We had beaten them at our place, but they beat us at theirs.

I worked in the gym and later as a janitor in Danforth, where I lived. I vacuumed and took out the trash. Those weren't bad jobs. When I was a freshman my roommate got stuck in food service and had to get up at five o'clock in the morning, so I was lucky.

I majored in physical education with a minor in health. School was difficult for me. To make the grades I had to take responsibility. If I wanted to stay in bed, there was no one to tell me I couldn't.

Mike Johnson taught in the Physical Education Department and coached track. He knew athletes. He pushed me, and I'm glad he did. It mattered a lot that people cared about me not just as a basketball player but as a student as well. Another person who helped me was Steve Ridder, the assistant basketball coach. He had just graduated a few years before, so he wasn't too old to know what it takes. He got me to change my attitude, to work at getting my education. He explained that I would need the things I learned. After four years basketball would be gone, but nobody could take away the knowledge in my head. I chose Berea because I wanted a good education, but it was Coach Ridder who taught me to value my education and make it work for me.

Berea's most important lesson was to work hard. Today I never do nothing: I'm always working. I teach school. School was finished for the year last Friday, but I didn't take a break. On Monday I was working at a day care center, which I do every summer. I'm with the seven to twelve-year-olds right now, but I've worked with kids of every age. I've worked with the babies. I try to go into all the classrooms occasionally. If one of the staff calls in sick, I may have to spend a day with the two and three-year-olds, for example, and I don't want it to be a big adjustment for them. If they've seen my face they'll be familiar with it, and they won't get frightful and cry.

During the school year I work at Fayette School in Lexington. It's different than a regular school. It's for kids with behavioral problems. It's a challenge. I enjoy the kids and try to help them so they'll have a chance in life. I'm hard on them, but I hope they realize that I love them. I didn't always appreciate Coach Wierwille, but now I understand what he was doing. Some of my kids at Fayette School may hate me now, but I hope that ten years from now they'll respect what I've tried to do for them.

June 1, 1998

Lionell Miller   1984-86

After graduating from Lincoln County High School in Stanford, Kentucky, I enrolled at Sue Bennett College in London, which at that time was a junior college. I played basketball there for two years. Morehead

Lionell Miller: "I'll take the challenge on"

State and Kentucky Wesleyan were interested in me, but I hurt my right knee in my second year, and after that my production went down. I realized that basketball wasn't forever, so I thought I'd better go someplace where I could count on getting a good education.

My cousin Alphanso Miller was attending Berea College, and Tommy Owsley, a friend of mine from my home town, was playing ball for Coach Wierwille. They encouraged me to come to Berea, and I thought I could play there. When I first talked to Coach Wierwille, he told me that he didn't really like junior college transfers. He wanted players in his system all four years. But he'd had some junior college players before, and they'd done well. So, he said, it was up to me if I wanted to pursue it. He was straightforward with me, and I dealt with it. I said, "I'll take the challenge on."

I'm six-four. At Sue Bennett all I did was score, but we didn't win a lot of games. The team I joined at Berea had guys who could score. Our idea was to play as a team. If I had the opportunity to score, I scored. If I didn't, I rebounded and played good defense. What I brought the team was fire coming off the bench. I worked with weights to strengthen my knee, and after that I had no more problems with it. I didn't need surgery.

In my first year at Berea we won twenty games and advanced to the national tournament in Kansas City. We won those games in practice. We had ten or twelve guys who could all play, and in practice we challenged each other. We had a first team and a second team. I played a lot on the second team, and often we kicked the first team's butts. We made them play hard. That made us a better team at game time. The practices were harder than the games.

Jeff Royce was a typical story. He was a quick player, and a winner. Jeff was a starter for part of the year and then dropped down to the second team. Many of us were interchangeable. That's what made us so good. We were all vying for that first team position, so we pushed each other. Everybody wants to start, but everybody can't be a starter. So all of us tried to find a way to contribute.

Tommy Owsley was the quickest of us. He had the offense, and he had the confidence, so he got the green light. Tommy was a jokester, always playing around. He hardly ever got serious until it came time to play ball. Then he was all business. Kevin Martin, who was mostly a backup guard that year, was always pushing, hustling, wanting to play, wanting to start. He gave it all. Off the court he was another outgoing guy, joking all the time.

Kevin was a tough, hard-nosed player, but we were all tough. We used that toughness to make each other better. Jay Stenzel had a lot of talent, but he, too, was a tough guy. Jay brought a lot to the table. He could shoot, he could rebound, and he didn't back down.

Charlie Andrews was a wiry guy who played bigger than he was. He had long arms and big hands. Charlie was a lefty with an unorthodox shot, but it was good. Another lefty, David Moeves, was an uncanny scorer. Often I played against David in practice. We were always challenging each other. Sometimes I thought he wasn't giving 100 percent, but he could get it done. He knew what Coach Wierwille wanted, and he knew the offense.

Mark George was another player who knew what Coach wanted. He was a leader who helped keep us together. Mark wasn't outspoken. He let his playing do his talking.

Mark always kidded me about something that happened in one of our Homecoming games. I had a breakaway dunk right at the end of the game. Both coaches had their mouths open on the sidelines. Mark said, "You took off from the free-throw line! You were flying forever." But I missed the dunk! Coach hated it when we missed dunks, but he never said anything to me about it.

I got along fine with Coach Wierwille. I was a physical education major and had him for a lot of classes. He was a disciplinarian who got respect from everybody. If we were running drills in practice, he made us do it until we did it right. His assistant, Steve Ridder, did most of the instruction. He was the one who got down on our level. Coach Ridder was fiery, and he helped make us a better team.

I would love to have played in Berea's new gym, but I liked the old gym. In those days Berea College basketball was it! The fans came out. We were competitive. We were winning, beating some major teams, and getting a lot of press.

Transylvania was always a big rivalry because Coach Wierwille wanted to beat them so badly. We had several scuffles with them. They were a Lexington school, and their players were city kids who looked down on us "Mountaineers."

To get to the national tournament in 1985 we had to beat Cumberland and Georgetown, in their buildings, in the district playoffs. Cumberland had defeated us twice, Georgetown three times, but we were sure we could beat them if everybody stepped up. In the Cumberland game Cliff Blackburn came off the bench and stepped up real big. In the Georgetown game I got to step up. Jay got hurt. He fell and knocked a tooth out. I came in and played the whole second half. I had eight points and eight or nine rebounds and three or four blocks. It was my turn to shine, and I was very happy.

Knocking off Cumberland and then Georgetown was the best feeling ever. I had a friend at Cumberland, a cheerleader. We went to high school together. He said, "We've got our bags packed." Better unpack them! We knew we could beat them, and we just stuck it to them.

In Kansas City we played Rio Grande early in the morning, and it was hard for us to get loose. We'd never played in a gym that wide open, either. We got behind, but we played better in the second half to get within reach. Unfortunately we had a bad turnover at the end that cost us the game. Had we had won that game, I believe that we could have won three or four or five games. We were new to the national tournament, and we just couldn't get over that first hump. Not to take anything away from Rio Grande, who had a good team, but we could have beaten them.

We were supposed to fly back to Kentucky that day, but Coach let us stay. He said, "This is a once-in-a-lifetime opportunity." We got to watch some of the other games in the tournament. Taking my first plane ride to a big city to play in the national tournament with the big boys was very exciting. I had a blast, and so did everybody else.

We thought we could get there again the next year. We knew that the other teams were pretty stacked, but we thought we could beat all of them. We won a lot of games, although we missed Tommy. Willie Hill joined the team that year and got a lot of what had been Tommy's minutes. Willie started some games as a freshman. Some of the older guys might not have liked that, but players who had good practices expected to play and start. Willie was out there doing it. He was the right size for an off guard and handled the ball real well for that spot. He wasn't a big scorer, but he was an excellent defensive player.

I thought I should start that year, but I didn't. Coach and I talked about it. He thought it was best for the team if I came off the bench. I tried to do whatever was best for the team. I went from a losing program to a winning one, and I knew that winning was a team effort.

After Georgetown defeated us to end our season, I was prepared for life after basketball. It was time to move on. Although my eligibility had expired, I needed another year to finish my degree, and I became a better student after I stopped playing ball.

I didn't mind working because I had a pretty good job. I worked in security. On Sundays I sometimes worked a whole seven-to-three or three-to-eleven shift, and during the week I usually went in for a couple of hours a day. I worked many more hours than I was required to.

I had some excellent teachers. Mike Johnson was a super guy who would do anything for his students. If I were a teacher I'd want to be just like he was. I thought Joy Hager was tough at first, but she had a good side. I always enjoyed being around Mike Berheide. Whether we were in class or out on campus, he always had plenty to say.

I threw the javelin at Berea College. They wanted me to try it, so I said, "Why not? It might be fun." I couldn't do it well at first. I watched another guy do it, and after studying his techniques I knew I'd been doing it wrong. When I started using an upright position I found that I could really fling it. At the track meets I went up against some big-time boys, but I won three first places and a District 32 championship. It was awesome, and I could have been even better if I had started earlier.

My first job after I graduated was working security at Kentucky State University in Frankfort. That was a big adjustment. At Berea we were all in a little protected world, black, white, Asian, most of us with rural backgrounds. A lot of the kids at Kentucky State University came from the inner cities of places like Atlanta and Detroit, and they had an attitude. Here I was in uniform, having to tell them what to do. That was tough for me, coming straight out of Berea College. Finally I understood that my Berea experience was important because it had taught me how to give everybody respect. People of different backgrounds and nationalities have to respect each other to get respect.

I spent a year working at Kentucky State, and since then I've been working for United Parcel Service. I drive a package car. The money is good. It's hard work that keeps me in good shape. You can do this job if you can deal with people. I like it.

August 12, 1998

Kevin Martin   **1984-87**

I did everything the coach said and gave 110 percent on every play. Some of the players could have given eighty percent and done better than me, but they didn't, and I was glad. That meant I got to play. That's as honest as I can be. I had some talent, but I played because I outworked the competition.

Kevin Martin: "The best leader we had"

Nobody goes 200 miles an hour like I do. I'm nonstop. When we ran eights in practice, nobody beat me in the three years I played on the varsity. Probably half of my teammates were faster than I was, but I wouldn't let them beat me, and when they stopped I was still running, still pushing, still going hard. When they were tired, I was laughing and joking. Hyperactive, that's the way I am.

Some of that is natural, and some of it is growing up in a broken home and seeing all my friends with things that I didn't have. I grew up wearing different colored socks to school and the same pair of tan corduroy pants to church every Sunday. Nobody made fun of me. Although I was small, I was strong. I beat up kids bigger than me, and I beat up groups of kids. I couldn't tolerate embarrassment.

When I was seventeen I slept in the same bed with my two brothers, twenty-five and twenty-two, in a 700 square-foot home. My brothers raised me. My father never had anything to do with us, and my mother worked sixteen hours a day. Anything I wanted I had to earn. I was fortunate to go to a small high school, Walton-Verona High School in Walton, Kentucky, where I could be a big fish in a small pond. I liked getting awards and recognition. At home I didn't get anything. We were all just trying to survive.

I applied to Berea College but wasn't accepted. Before I graduated my mother remarried, and my stepfather made too much money for me to qualify financially for admittance to Berea. I was working tobacco when my family doctor, who was a member of the Berea College Board of Trustees, asked me what my plans were. I told him I wanted to go to Berea but couldn't get in. He talked to somebody down there and explained my situation. After I met with admissions director John Cook I enrolled for the spring term in February 1983.

I'd never met Coach Wierwille. I came to Berea just to go to school. I played varsity baseball that spring, but I didn't sign up to try out for basketball. Some friends from northern Kentucky planned to try out and asked me why I didn't. I said, "I don't know. Maybe I will." So I did.

I didn't make the varsity team that year. That was an excellent team, the Donald Hairston-Kevin Mullins-Tommy Owsley group. Jay Stenzel barely made that team. My sophomore year, the year we went to the nationals, I started six games and was the sixth man when I wasn't starting.

I'm six feet tall and played guard. I was a good shooter. In my junior year I shot fifty-five percent from the field, pretty impressive for a guard, and led the district in assists. They didn't bring in the three-point shot until my senior year, but I led the team in three-pointers that year.

As a freshman I looked up to Donald Hairston. He was strong, mature, and smart. I respected Donald for more than his play. He was a leader. He didn't say much, but when he did say something it made a big impact.

Tommy Owsley was my roommate for three years. He was a super guy who became one of my best friends. Tommy liked putting on a show. He liked the notoriety. I never played with or against anybody else who had his quickness and savvy. He had a knack of being where the ball was.

Jay Stenzel and I bonded from day one. He and I hit it off because neither of us backed down from anything. Jay was just like me except he was taller and weighed more. He never let anybody one-up him. If you were walking to the Alumni Building with him, he wanted to beat you.

Jay was the most ferociously competitive player I ever saw at Berea. There was no one even close. He was determined to get the most out of his abilities. He was an average jumper with an average build, but I'd take him on my team against anybody. There were people who could jump higher, people who were stronger, but they couldn't stop him. Todd May, the six-eight Kentucky recruit who played for Pikeville, couldn't stop him. Jay schooled him every time. Jay had bad knees. He'd often have to rub them, or I'd rub them for him. He worked harder than anybody. He was the first one to arrive at practice and the last to leave.

Cindy Stenzel, Jay's sister, was a lot like Jay. She didn't have the shooting touch that Jay did, but she was very competitive and laid it all on the line when she was in the game. She was very aggressive and held nothing back. Cindy was an inside player. She'd get twelve points and fifteen rebounds every game. As a person she was very organized, very responsible. She excelled in the classroom.

Keith Smith, our basketball manager, was another good friend of mine. Keith was a big part of the program. As the manager he was one of the guys we abused and made fun of, but he was an important interface between us and Coach Wierwille. Keith was the kind of guy I could have called at night and said, "I'm a hundred miles away. Can you come and get me?" He would have done it without asking why. I was best man at his wedding, and I think of him fondly.

I loved it when we beat Transylvania. I saw them as a cocky bunch of rich kids. I was very proud and couldn't stand to have anybody put me down.

I was involved in several altercations with that team. One of the most notable was with Kip Hagan at Transy in January 1985. I was sixth man that year. From the bench I watched Kip put his finger in the face of Mark George and a couple of other guys, taunting them. Jeff Rippy said, "Kevin, if you get in there, clean his clock!" That wasn't what I was thinking about. I wanted to get some minutes and play well, not go in and mess up and get pulled right back out. But as I watched Kip taunting our players, I took that stuff personally. My teammates were like a family to me.

At halftime Tommy Owsley yelled at us about what was going on. He said, "Mark George, don't ever let those guys make fun of you!" I'm a guy who doesn't start anything, but I don't walk away from anything. With about fourteen minutes left in the game we were down by eleven points or so. I was picking up Kip full-court, putting pressure on him. I was going at him and he was coming, and I fouled him. I didn't hurt him, but I fouled him.

Kip ran into me and pushed his finger right up against my nose. When he did that I grabbed him by the throat and started choking him. The emotions that had been building up the whole game came out. The benches cleared, and when order was restored I was removed from the game. We came back and won it.

I'll never forget it that incident. It was on the front page of the paper. Am I proud of fighting? No! Berea College got some bad publicity, and I got a reputation as a troublemaker, which distressed me because all I did was stand up. I did what I thought Coach Wierwille would have done when he played. When he talked to me on the bus on the way back to Berea he kind of told me that without saying it in as many words.

A month later Transy came down to our place. With two minutes left in the game they led us by maybe thirteen points. Bobby Storie of Transy came running down and pushed Tommy, my roommate and best friend. I jumped off the bench and hit Bobby, took him right down to the ground, and the whole place cleared. So the rivalry built over that kind of stuff. For years after that there was taunting. Those guys were on scholarship, they had cars, and they didn't have to work. They thought they were better than us, but we beat them more often than not.

In the 1984-85 district tournament we beat Cumberland College in the best game I've ever been part of in any sport. Cumberland had defeated us twice that year, and they were heavily favored. They had recruits from all over. Before the game began I thought that our chances of winning were about the same as the U.S. Olympic hockey team's had been when they played the Russians in 1980. Tim Hartig and I were shooting thirty-footers in warmups and laughing. We were all loose, thinking we had nothing to lose.

Tommy put on a show. Cumberland had their best defenders on him, but he was unbelievable. He carried us. I didn't get to play a lot. Coach Wierwille put me a couple of times when Tommy got cramps. I'd be in for a minute and a half before Tommy would come back out. We played a flawless game and surprised Cumberland.

After the game the Cumberland players were very sportsmanlike. They encouraged us to beat Georgetown, our next opponent, saying, "You're not finished yet."

Cumberland was a finesse team. Georgetown was bigger and stronger, but plodding and slow. We played a heck of a game and beat them handily. Jay got his teeth chipped, but he still played. We used a three-two zone with Cliff Blackburn, who had a long reach, up in the point. Cliff couldn't shoot, but he played great defense. Putting him out there was a good move.

Our game against Rio Grande in the national tournament was not one of our typical performances. Maybe we just couldn't believe we were there. Whatever the reason, we weren't sharp. We lost by three. If Jay Stenzel had had half of an average night we would have won by double figures. Rio Grande didn't contain Jay. He simply had an off game.

I was just a sophomore that year, and I was a still a role player. I wasn't one of the catalysts. I was almost a spectator. I don't think I appreciated 1984-85 as much as I would have after I'd worked my way into the starting lineup.

In my junior year I finally earned my starting job. I started every game at point guard after battling for playing time with Jeff Royce. We had a real good team with a lot of depth, and it was tough for us when we didn't make it to Kansas City again.

Jeff and I never developed a friendship, but we got along well. He knew how to break down a defense. He was quick, with slashing moves. He could kick it out to the open man or finish himself. He had a flair for heroics at the end of a game. The day I had the fracas with Kip Hagan, Jeff hit the last-second shot that won the game for us. He had done the same thing in the state high school tournament, and Coach Wierwille said, "I was waiting to see when he was going to start doing that for us."

The second guard my junior year was Mark George. He was very gifted, but very quiet. He and I were total opposites. Mark was reserved, and I was loud, a "what you see is what you get" kind of guy. We were very good friends, though. Mark was good at every facet of the game. He could dribble, he could shoot, and he could 360 dunk.

Willie Hill was a freshman that year. He and I had a good relationship. Willie was a character, just like me. We had a lot of fun in the locker room. Coach loved Willie from the day he came to Berea, and so did everybody else. He was a favorite on the campus. He was very nice to people, and he could play ball.

When Willie first came he was a slasher. He was quick, he could jump, and he could dunk. His outside shooting got better every year. His defensive play was excellent from the start, and that was what we needed.

Jay was injured my senior year and couldn't play. When that happened I didn't want to play either. Jay and I did all our drills together in practice and before games. I didn't want to spend my last year on a team without Jay. Without him we weren't equipped to win, and the fun was gone for me. But although I was disappointed, I played.

In Jay's absence some people stepped up and got opportunities they normally wouldn't have had. One of the highlights of my career was our Homecoming game that year against Knoxville College. Callen Cheesman and I, two guys from Walton, started that game. Callen's father, Layne Cheesman, was the person who talked me into applying to Berea. All his kids went there. Callen and I were good friends, and Layne was almost like a father to me. I hadn't even thought about college, but Layne convinced me that a college education was something worth pursuing.

Callen was a shooting guard, I was a point guard, and I had hoped that we would play together a lot. That didn't happen, though. Callen was one of the purest shooters we had, but too much may have been expected of him. Sometimes Coach would put Callen into games when we were seven or eight points behind and expect him to make several shots in a row to close the gap. That was unfair pressure, and Callen struggled. His attitude was affected, and he never turned out to be the player I hoped he'd be.

Without Jay we were forced into playing a smaller game, running up and down and shooting the three-pointer, which Coach had us do only because he had to. Coach Wierwille's idea of a three-pointer had always been to work our butts off to get the ball inside, then score and draw a foul. We had some good players, but we didn't have a team like we'd had the last three years. I got an opportunity to show what I could do, but it was disappointing to finish with a losing record.

I'd never been injured in all my life, so I never dreamed that would happen to me in my senior year. After the Homecoming game I played some baseball on a cold day. I swung at a ball and missed and felt something go tight in my back. I didn't think much about it at the time, but my back was never the same. For a while I couldn't even stand up. I missed some classes and couldn't play basketball again until after Christmas.

Nobody ever determined what the problem was. I went to an orthopedic surgeon, I got CAT scans, and I went to a chiropractor twice a day. For weeks I was on my own, just trying to get well enough to play again. When I finally came back I had to take it game by game. What had always made me effective was my endurance. Nobody could outrun me or outlast me. After I hurt my back that was no longer true, and my quickness and shooting ability suffered too. It was a tough year. I still have a bad back.

Our season ended with a loss at Cumberland. After the game Coach Wierwille talked to the team and congratulated the seniors, and then we got onto the bus to return to Berea. After a losing game Coach was always very somber and closemouthed. We didn't do any goofing around. But on that occasion I was very aware that my career and our season were over, so

I decided to have a little fun.

The bus had a toilet in the back and a rubber cord to wrap around the door to keep it closed. I was sitting in the back with Jay, who was a big practical joker. When Robbie Taylor went into the restroom we wrapped the cord around the door three times so he couldn't get out. We left him in there all the way back from Cumberland. When we got to Berea we gathered up our stuff and got out, and the driver brought the bus all the way over to the physical plant and parked it before he heard Robbie's shouts and let him out.

I was co-captain my senior year. I got along with Coach Wierwille very well, although he never brought me into his office to ask me my thoughts about things. I was different than what he traditionally looked for in a player. He wanted big, strong guys who would pound the ball inside. I excelled in a transition game, running up and down and shooting the three-pointer. When I played well, we got along great. If I hit two shots from the perimeter and then missed one, I'd hear, "Let's get the ball inside." I worked within his system, but it wasn't what I would have preferred to play in.

Coach Wierwille was not a loving type of coach who put his around me and said, "Poor Kevin, what's wrong?" I didn't have that kind of relationship with him. Part of that was him, part of it me. My relationship with him now is completely different. When I go to see him with my kids, you'd think he was an uncle to me. I can kid with him and laugh, but back then I would never have done that. We'd kid a little, sure. He'd say something if I had a big game. I scored twenty-three points against Pikeville once, a heck of a game for me. Afterwards he smiled at me and asked me what happened. I said, "I have some new shoes." But then he didn't talk to me again for some time.

I was a talker, and Coach didn't do a lot of talking. But I loved the discipline. I liked things regimented. I liked the hard practices. I liked looking people right in the eye when I talked to them. I liked saying "Yes, sir" even if I didn't like what I heard. If Coach Wierwille had been a guard coach, he would have been my favorite person I ever met!

He made sure that all his players understood the specialness of Berea. "You're no different than anybody else here. You've got to work, you've got to study, you've got to bust your butt, and guess what? Everyone you play against has a scholarship and has it easier than you. But we're going to take care of them." That kind of talk motivated and drove us.

Coach Wierwille knew the game of basketball. He knew what he wanted to do, and he didn't steer from it. Our opponents knew we were going to run the double-low offense and the three-two zone, but we still beat them. Coach drilled us until we executed perfectly.

Before I graduated I received the Coach Wyatt Award, which is given every year to the senior letterman who exemplifies sportsmanship, academic achievement, and community service. It's not just for basketball players, but for any athlete. I shared the 1987 award with Darrell Baxter, who played baseball. My getting it was a surprise. I never even thought about it, but once I got it I treasured it. People thought of me as a very aggressive person, and yet here was proof that they also considered me a valuable member of the College and the community.

I played two years of varsity baseball. Baseball was actually my better sport, but I was disappointed in the baseball program at Berea. In my first year Jack Hall was coach. He did it as a volunteer. He was a great gentleman, but he didn't have the same presence as Coach Wierwille did in basketball.

I was a righthanded pitcher and did some catching. In the first game I played I threw a shutout against Centre. I've still got the game ball. I could have been a heck of a pitcher, but I had no one there to work with me. They were a good group of guys, but the program wasn't professional enough for me. I disgrace myself to admit this, but I was so upset with the program that I stopped going to practices.

One day one of the players said, "We're going to Pikeville for a game. Are you coming?"

"I haven't been to practice for two weeks."

"So what? Get on the bus."

I went, and I was the starting pitcher in that game! A lot of players were upset, and in their place I would have been too. But that was the way it was. Nobody took it seriously. In one game I went up to pinch hit and the coach said, "If you strike out, we're going to laugh at you." I hit a triple off the right field fence. The program disappointed me, and I stopped playing. It's too bad that the school didn't put the same energy into baseball that they did in basketball. Steve Ridder helped revive the baseball program when he took it over after I left Berea.

When Coach Wierwille yelled at us or made us run at the end of practice, Steve did the damage control. He was the one in the locker room telling us not to take it personally. He was Coach Wierwille's assistant, but he was close to our age and could relate to us. He demanded respect and got it, but he could goof around with us and laugh. I'm biased towards Steve because he's my brother-in-law. I married Anita Taylor, his wife Vicky's sister.

My first labor position was trayman at Boone Tavern. I carried trays of food that had been ordered and set them on tables for the servers to present to the customers. I didn't like that job because I was looked at every second and wasn't supposed to talk while I was working. Later I became a bellhop, and that was better because I could meet people and talk to them. After a year at Boone Tavern I worked my way into the intramural program and finished up as the head intramural manager, one of the top-paying jobs at the College.

I majored in biology because it was my favorite subject, not because I had a plan to be a doctor or work in research and development. I never had a plan for what I was going to do with it. I was the only member of my family to go to college, and I was so proud just to be there that I never strived for high grades. Having fun was more important to me than an A in history. If I had to do it over again I wouldn't change my social life, but I'd take my studies more seriously and formulate some idea of what I was going to do after I graduated.

One of my brothers was a warehouse worker for Levi Strauss. I worked there the summer before my senior year and swore I'd never go back. I said, "I'm going to finish my education and do something better than unloading trucks." But after I got out of school, married and without a car or a place to live, I took a job unloading trucks at the warehouse in Florence, Kentucky. I thought I might get on at Procter and Gamble. I said to myself, "If I get my foot in the door, they'll see that I'm a heck of a guy." But it didn't happen.

When I went to Homecoming a year later Jay Stenzel asked, "Why aren't you using your major? Why are you unloading trucks?"

I said, "I'm making a good living. I'm working hard and getting a life started."

Eventually I got an opportunity to be a supervisor. Then I became night manager and warehouse manager. After that I was a warehouse manager in Nevada, which was a promotion. When I had the opportunity to make a lateral move back to Kentucky, I took it. Professionally it wasn't the best decision, but my family was too important to me to see just once or twice a year. I've been with Levi Strauss for eleven years now. Today I'm a process leader at a million square-foot warehouse, setting the vision for what the facility is going to do.

My Berea College degree indicated to Levi Strauss that I was capable of learning at a high level. It's the only reason I got my job. How else could I get a business management job with a biology degree? I told them, "I can learn. I got through one of the top academic schools in the country with no problems."

Interestingly, though, everything I use in management I got from sports. I know what it's like to be on top in high school and not even make the varsity team in college. I know what's like to be on good teams and bad teams. I remember those experiences and ask myself how I handled things in the good times and the bad.

We all have a role. We all have to work together. As a manager I think in terms of a team. Here's the guard, here's the forward, here's the center. Here's what you bring to the party. Let's use everyone's skills and ideas. Let's try to form a consensus we can all live with. That's how Levi's works, and that's what I excel in.

July 22, 1998

Jay Stenzel   1983-88

Berea College gave me a great education, and all they asked of me was to work a little bit for it. It was difficult to work and keep up academically while I was playing basketball, but it was manageable. I learned how to organize my time and get things done. I had a great basketball career and

Jay Stenzel: "I'd take him on my team against anybody"

wound up with a great wife and a great career at Ashland Oil. I wouldn't change anything.

Sports was always a part of our family. Both my mom and my dad were very athletic. My dad was a two-handicap golfer and pitched professionally. I played baseball because my dad played it, and I enjoyed it. But in my freshman year in high school I decided to give all my time to basketball.

As a senior at Erlanger Lloyd High School in northern Kentucky I was recruited somewhat, but not highly. It was mainly by letter. Recruiters didn't come to see me play. Layne Cheesman, whose son Callen became my teammate at Berea College, knew about me and mentioned my name to Coach Wierwille. He and John Cook contacted us.

Berea was just an hour and a half away and it was a good academic opportunity, so things just fell into place. My twin sister Cindy also wound up going there. We didn't want to stay around home, but Dad was getting older and we didn't want to go to a place that was too far away, either.

Cindy and I both played four years of basketball at Berea. Rebounding was her greatest strength, but she could also score. I got to watch her play and enjoyed it. She watched me play also. She was a big fan. So were my mom and dad. They would drive down to just about every one of our home games.

I was the only freshman on the varsity in 1983-84. The upperclassmen were nice to me, but I felt a little awkward because I didn't know them very well. On road trips I used to talk a lot to Coach Steve Ridder. He was from northern Kentucky like I was, and we related well to each other. His

— 214 —

personality was a lot like mine. He hated to lose, and he would do whatever it took to prepare himself to win fairly. As a coach he has the total package. He understands the game, he knows how to motivate people, he can recruit, and he's both a good practice coach and a good game coach.

All the upperclassmen impressed me. That was one thing about going to Berea: the people down there were outstanding people for the most part. If you're going to play four years for Coach Wierwille you've got to have a good work ethic or you're not going to play. If I were a coach, that's what I would demand of my players. So in practice or in games there was never a problem with anybody slacking off or not trying or not giving their all.

I think the world of Coach Wierwille. He taught me a lot about life. Whatever you do, you do it right. A lot of teams we played had bigger gyms or nicer gyms, but ours was always the cleanest gym, because he wanted it that way.

To me his greatest strength is his truthfulness. He tells you exactly what he needs to tell you whether you want to hear it or not. I respect someone like that. I wouldn't want to play basketball, and I wouldn't want to work, for someone who would tell me only what I wanted to hear. Coach always knew who he could push in certain ways and who he couldn't. Some players respond well to being yelled at. I was like that, but another player might respond by going into a shell. Coach knew how to handle that type of player too.

I'm six-six. My skills weren't lacking when I came to college. My high school coach, Bill Code, spent a lot of time on fundamentals. But my body needed to mature for me to play college basketball. It's a big transition from high school to college, and the talent level in the KIAC was high. Coach Wierwille wanted me to take it strong when I was inside, so I needed to develop my body with weights and get in better condition.

I began starting by Christmas of my freshman year. I was more of a support player at that point, just trying to do the little things like get the rebounds and take the charges, but I progressed. Tommy Owsley was the predominant scorer, but as I got my confidence I began to step up a little bit. I played forward. The center was Dave Moeves. With the offense we ran, the double-low, we didn't have a traditional swing man, power forward, and center man, so I played all over the floor.

The 1983-84 team was the best I ever played on. We played tremendous team defense, and we had so many talented players that someone would always pick up the slack if an individual had an off night. Donald Hairston was an unbelievably intelligent basketball player. If he saw a teammate becoming unnerved, he would always say a few words to calm him down. As I went on in my career I tried to use what I learned from Donald about the mental part of the game.

Tommy Owsley was a great leader, competitor, and teammate. I have nothing but good things to say about him. He did a lot of things well. He was a defensive threat with his quick hands and quick feet. That's probably how he got most of his points. He'd slap the ball up, beat the guy to the ball, and get a layup. Then again, he had good range as a shooter.

I was very disappointed when Transylvania beat us in March to deny us a trip to the national tournament in Kansas City. I thought we were very capable. We had every opportunity to beat them, but they were a capable team too. I remember it being a good game with a couple of key opportunities missed.

The next year we earned a trip to Kansas City by beating Cumberland and Georgetown in the district finals. I didn't think we were going to do it, and I don't think anyone can honestly say they thought it was going to happen. A lot of things went right for us. We played on emotion. Both Cumberland and Georgetown were favored by quite a bit because they stood high in the national rankings. I remember all of us going in there real loose. We had nothing to lose and everything to gain, unlike them, so we just had fun and played good basketball.

We played a lot of man-to-man defense that year, but what got us to Kansas City was our three-two zone. We put Cliff Blackburn in the middle, and he was so quick and had arms so long that it was like adding an extra man out there. That was especially true in those final Cumberland and Georgetown games. We just shut those guys down, and the main factor was Cliff. He was a tremendous athlete. I didn't know Cliff well, and I have no idea why he didn't come back after that year.

Kansas City was great. We got to see some of the city. I remember going to the football and baseball stadiums. But we weren't there too long, because we lost in the first round. We played terrible. Beating Cumberland and Georgetown was such an emotional high that when we were warming up in Kansas City it seemed like we were satisfied simply to be there. I mentioned that before the game, but we played flat. Still, it was a good experience.

In my junior year I was counted on to score more and make things happen offensively. I tried to do as much as I could defensively too, but I spent most of my energy on the offensive end. I think I was a very good defensive player when I needed to be, but you can't do everything all the time. You have to pace yourself. To contribute my utmost on offense I had to slack down a little bit on defense.

We hoped to go back to Kansas City again, but we were eliminated by Georgetown. Losing to them was especially disappointing. They started the trend of loading up with NCAA Division I transfers who for one reason or another decided not to stay at the schools that recruited them. In that final game I got hit in the throat. I was lying on the floor unable to breathe, and that was scary. I wasn't actually knocked out, but I was knocked out of the game. I couldn't talk for four or five days. We looked at the film, and it was an inadvertent elbow that just happened to hit me in a bad spot.

I injured an Achilles tendon before my senior year. We were running eights for conditioning purposes in practice. Maybe I didn't stretch enough, I'm not sure what happened, but I strained my Achilles. It wasn't torn, it was what they call strained. There was a big knot on the back of it. I'd rest two weeks, then come in and try to practice, but I couldn't practice. Coach Wierwille did not want me to risk hurting it further, so for the sake of my health we decided to put a cast on it and wait till next year. There was no operation.

Sitting out that year was rough. That was the year Kevin Martin was a senior. Kevin and I were always close and played real well together. He was also from northern Kentucky, and we played in the same summer leagues. There was nothing I could do but realize that things could be worse, and work on trying to get better.

We had a lot of talent on the last team I played on, 1987-88. Mike Sams was an excellent player, and Dester Terry really stepped up. We missed Kevin Martin, but Willie Hill was another good player. I think that team could have achieved more than it did. Our season ended sooner than I thought it would. We lost to Transylvania in a game where we were up by thirteen or fourteen points at one point. They were hungrier, or something happened, because at the end we weren't hitting the shots we needed to hit.

Jay Stenzel: "He could shoot, he could rebound, and he didn't back down"

Ann Bane was a cheerleader, but we actually met at a dance. I was a freshman and she was a sophomore. Ann lived in Kettering, and my friends and I went over to the dance. There were three or four guys and three or four girls just talking as friends, but for the two of us one thing led to another. We started dating sometime after Christmas.

I always promised my mom that I wouldn't marry while I was still in school. Ann and I ended up getting married the day before I graduated. We got married on Saturday and I graduated on Sunday. That weekend wore me out!

Incidentally, Ann's brother Joe played basketball for Campbellsville. I didn't ever want to lose to him. Ann's dad, my father-in-law, always gives me a hard time that I played better defense against Joe than I did against anyone else in the league.

When I first came to Berea I didn't have Mom and Dad to answer to, of course, so I fooled around a little and didn't do well in a couple of my classes. Dad sat me down and said, "If you're going to go to school, you're going to study, or you're not going to go to school." At that point I started to take my academics more seriously. I majored in business management and minored in computer science.

I worked at first as a janitor at Bingham, the dorm I lived in. I did that for two years, worked for a while as Coach Wierwille's teaching assistant, and then got a job in the the computer center working for L.D. Montgomery and Chuck McIntyre. I loved working there, and it was a good opportunity that opened the door for me at Ashland Oil, where I got a good job as a computer programmer after I graduated. I'm still working for Ashland. My title now is senior systems engineer. I design computer systems, write and implement and maintain them.

I spend most of my spare time coaching. Anything my kids are involved in, I coach it. We have two boys and a girl. My boys started playing basketball when they were three! I couldn't believe that. I coached them at the Y when they were three years old.

July 14, 1998

Willie Hill   **1985-89**

I grew up in Cincinnati. My mom and dad were divorced, and I lived with my mom, who worked for the Postal Service.

On my Western Hills High School basketball team we had at least three players who were capable of playing college ball. I was one of them. I played well in an AAU tourna-ment in Cincinnati, and a man named Layne Cheesman approached me and asked if I was talking to any colleges. I told him there were a cou-ple of schools in Ohio who were interested, Ohio Dominican and Witten-berg. He asked me if I'd ever heard of Berea Col-lege. I hadn't, but he arranged with Coach Wierwille for me to visit Berea.

What sold me on Berea was the fact that I'd get an opportunity to play ball, plus a quality educa-tion. None of my friends knew about Berea, but the school had a good reputation among the teachers I talked to. I was a little reluctant to go to Berea because I had to turn my back on a partial scholarship at Witten-

Willie Hill: "Defense was his specialty"

berg. If Wittenberg had offered me a full scholarship, I might have enrolled there. Fortunately I didn't have to pay much at all to go to school at Berea, and everything worked out.

Ironically, when I got to Berea I found myself competing for playing time with Layne Cheesman's son Callen, along with Mark George. When the season began Kevin Martin played point guard, Mark played second guard, and I played forward. It almost seemed destined that I come to Berea, because the person who'd been playing my position as a three man left school. He could rebound and jump better than I could, but I had the passing skills of a guard, and I was his equal as a defensive player. At any rate, he left and I replaced him.

I was a starter my whole career at Berea, first at forward, later at guard. When I came we had Jay Stenzel and some other good scorers. My role, as it was in high school, was to do whatever the coaches asked, and at Berea they wanted me to pass the ball and play defense. I usually guarded the other team's toughest guys. I could score, but I wasn't a great shooter.

My height was an advantage when I played guard. I'm six-four, which helped me see the floor. I was tall and also quick, so I could guard other guards or guard a forward my size. The guys who guarded me were usually shorter than I was. I knew the game and enjoyed the game, and I tried to be a leader.

In Coach Wierwille's early years he had Arno Norwell and all those big guys, and they just pounded it in and took their time. But the game changed. I was there for the transition. In my freshman year we didn't have the three-point line, but the next year we did. The pace of the game became faster. I don't think Coach was totally ready for it at first. We ran a break, but it wasn't like we pushed for a fast break. We ran a controlled break.

Our point guard, Kevin Martin, was a fireball out there. He gave us great energy, nonstop. Off the court he was a very funny guy who kept us laughing. Kevin kept everything in perspective.

I looked up to Jay Stenzel because he had such a good work ethic. I often guarded him in pickup games, and he was one of the hardest working people I played against. Jay was always moving. He understood what he needed to do and did it.

Charlie Andrews was a guy with defensive skills. He anticipated things. If Charlie gambled and made a mistake, well, we had to take the bad with the good. Charlie was lefthanded, and on offense some of his moves were unorthodox. He could play, but Coach's system did not allow a lot of creativity at that time, and Charlie was a creative person. It was bad timing for a player like Charlie.

Jeff Royce was another player who didn't fit into the mold perfectly. He was a good player, but as a point guard he didn't have a great handle, and as a shooting guard he didn't defend as well as he needed to. Jeff was a great scorer in high school, famous for hitting some big buckets in the state tournament. He hit a couple at Berea too. That's what made him dangerous for the opposition.

Two guys who came in with me were Dester Terry and Terry Tapley. Dester was the most deceptive six-six player I ever saw. He was big around the middle, so people thought he'd be slow as molasses. But he might have had the best offensive moves of anybody who ever played at Berea. He wasn't flashy, but he got the job done. Dester played some my freshman year, then decided he didn't want to play any more and took a year off. That was devastating to Coach, because Dester had some good talent.

We were happy when Dester returned to the team. One of my favorite plays was to find him on the delayed break. Dester was the fourth man or fifth man down on the break. I'd push the ball up, then drop it back to him. He'd score on a jump shot from twelve or fifteen feet, something he could do all day. Knowing what Dester and the other players could do was a big part of my job.

Terry Tapley became an anchor for Coach at the end of games. Terry wasn't offensive-minded, but he rarely turned the ball over, and he hit his free throws. He stayed consistent, and that's what Coach wanted from him.

Mike Sams had a scorer's mentality. He joined us in my sophomore year and waited for Jay Stenzel to leave so he could be The Man. One of the things he had to deal with was the fact that he wasn't Jay. Mike could score, but he didn't work as hard as Jay and wasn't as fluid. Mike could be rather mechanical, and sometimes that limited his offensive game. Once I saw Gerald Osborne of Pikeville strip Mike four or five times on the post with the same move. But we fed Mike the ball, and he was our leading scorer after Jay left. Mike could be a little cocky on the floor, but he respected me enough to listen to me when we were out there.

Mike was sometimes in trouble for being a partier, so we were shocked a few years later to read in *The Berea Alumnus* that he'd become a minister. For him to flip like that is beautiful. What an extreme contrast!

Mike was a funny guy, and so were Kevin Martin and Robbie Taylor. One night Kevin locked Robbie in the bathroom of the bus when we were coming back from Cumberland. We had lost the game, so we all had to be quiet. Another time Robbie hid in my locker before practice. He had all his clothes on, just waiting for me to appear. I don't remember exactly what I was doing, but I didn't go near my locker for about thirty minutes, and all the while Robbie was in there waiting to scare me. When I finally opened it up, he popped out.

The team we most wanted to beat was Alice Lloyd. Coach didn't like them and did not want to lose to them, and we never did. They were the epitome of what we did not like. They had an attitude that was at least partially racially motivated. When we went down there we heard some things we didn't need to hear. Our games with them were always nasty battles.

In my junior year we played Alice Lloyd in the District 32 playoffs at Sue Bennett College in London. A girl walked up to Jay Stenzel and me and asked for our autographs. We were surprised, but we signed them. She tore them up right in front of us, then went over and hugged Michael Smith, one of the Alice Lloyd players. Apparently she was his girlfriend. Michael Smith was a big kid, and country strong. He didn't look like he lifted weights, but he was as strong as all outdoors. I disliked him because he played dirty. He'd hit people with his elbows without a care.

I remember the Alice Lloyd players well, guys like Michael Smith, Tom Setser, Robby Russell, Jeff Sizemore. Some of them could play. I'm not going to take anything away from them. We didn't like their style one bit. We didn't retaliate with cheap shots or dirty play. We simply played hard and gave it back to them double in terms of effort. We pounded them as much as we could, and most of our victories over them were by double digits.

Berea, unlike most schools, had no fraternities, but our basketball team was a sort of fraternity. We were brothers in the sense that we shared many things. There were a lot of us who hung around each other, although we also hung around non-basketball players. I was friends with everybody, but the one guy I really got close to was Robert Phillips.

Robert was one of the nicest guys you would ever meet. He grew up in a small town, so he had a twang in his voice that you don't hear from a lot of African-Americans. It was certainly new to me, coming from the city. Robert was pure, a good person through and through. He always tried to do the right thing, and he would talk to anybody. Additionally, he was a pretty good ballplayer. His build was not typical for the position he played, power forward, but he could jump. He had great jumping ability off two feet. Coach expected a lot of Robert, and he gave a lot for a six-three guy, doing the things he did.

My senior season was my most disappointing at Berea. We started off winning ten in a row, then went nine and nine the rest of the year. We had a pretty good nucleus. We had everything we needed but consistency. We were ranked eighteenth or twentieth in the nation earlier in the year, and we could have improved on that. I still ask myself where we went wrong at the end of that year. I don't think we had the right attitude. I've always felt bad about that because I was the captain and leader of the team.

We didn't have the killer instinct. We didn't put people away. You have to have that cockiness. When we played Georgetown or Cumberland, there was always a cockiness about them. We didn't have the attitude of, "We're not going to lose this game, because we're champions."

One thing I regret about my college career was that we never beat Cumberland. We came close a couple of times, but we never defeated them, not once. They always had quick players, they always had three or four guys who could get out there and flat-out play defense, and they always had two big men, six-six or better. In the NAIA you could dominate with a couple of guys like that. Jay Stenzel was six-six, but he was not a power player. His game was finesse. We didn't have anybody who could bang, and that hurt us. Coach always wanted another Arno Norwell, a big guy who could bang around with people.

The closest we came to beating Cumberland was a game we played at their gym in 1988. We had a play we had taken from Georgetown and put into our arsenal. With the score tied I made a perfect backdoor lob pass to Jay. Jay shot it, and it banked in and came right off. Cumberland got the rebound with two seconds left. They beat us by three points in overtime. Jay's shot was a good shot, a good opportunity, but it just didn't go in. We should have had that game, but I guess it wasn't meant to be.

I believe now that I should have worked harder in the summer before my senior year. I didn't go out and shoot 150 jump shots every day. I played a lot, I always played, but I didn't truly have the work ethic it would have taken for me to improve my scoring. Each year I contributed more on offense, but I could have been a lot better, and that would have made the team better. We definitely could have used more consistent outside shooting that year, but I didn't feel that scoring was a big part of my game. My role, as I saw it, was to put the ball in the hands of the other players when they needed it.

Coach Wierwille and I got along very well. When I was a senior the guys on the team joked with me before practice, asking me what we were going to be doing that day, because they thought Coach and I were so tight that he consulted me on those matters. I thought that was pretty funny, but it tells you about the relationship Coach and I had and the way others saw it. Coach respected the effort I gave. He rarely yelled at me, and I can't remember even two times when he needed to put me in my place.

Coach set the tone whenever he shook hands. He made sure that you looked him in the eye. That was always a requirement of his. We knew we were talking to a disciplinarian. Coach had a burning desire to win and do well, and he pushed us to give our best effort. If we didn't, he got upset.

I'll tell you a funny story about Coach, the dribbling story. We dribbled before every practice for maybe two minutes, and then we started our layup drill. As the captain I led the dribbling. One day Coach was mad at us, I don't remember why. We started dribbling, and two minutes passed, three minutes, and he didn't say anything. I looked over there, and he still didn't say anything. Usually he gave me a nod or said to go ahead. So we dribbled and dribbled, and the next thing we knew fifteen minutes had passed. Everybody was wondering what we were doing. We just kept dribbling and dribbling. Finally I looked over at Coach, he looked at me, and he said, "What are you waiting on?"

I said, "I was waiting on you!" Then, at last, we went into our layup drills. We were worn out from dribbling the ball around the gym for almost twenty minutes.

Coach could be stern, but he had a lighter side. He came into one practice wearing our mascot's great big Mountie head. He sat there in silence while Coach Ridder directed practice. All of us got the biggest kick out of him showing up in that Mountie head. We laughed about it for a long time.

Coach Wierwille produced good people who cared about the world, not just basketball. The people who came to Berea interested only in basketball either grew out of that while they were there, or they left.

My relationship with Coach Ridder was very special. He was a great person. He was younger, closer to my age. I knew what he'd done as a player and respected it. Our personal games were a lot alike. He taught me a lot, and he motivated me to do the things he taught me.

My senior year was Coach Ridder's last year at Berea. His departure was hard on Coach Wierwille. I served as a student coach the first year Coach Ridder was gone. When Coach Ridder played he was a coach on the floor, and I think I was the same way in the last couple of years I played.

During my year as student coach I became very close to Antonio Woods. He was a nice guy, and we were both from the same city and grew up in the same kind of environment. When we were teammates Antonio was cool people, but we didn't hang out that much. After I graduated I got to know him better, and now we're best friends.

Antonio was a couple of years behind me in school. He was aggressive in those days, but only as aggressive as Coach Wierwille let him be. Antonio didn't think he had the freedom to do what he needed to do, and that hurt his confidence. During those years Coach was more restrictive than he later became. He wanted people to stay within the strict confines of the game. Getting over that was a hard transition for him. In Antonio's senior year Coach let the team play a little more loose. They started shooting the three a lot more than we were ever allowed to when I played. Antonio arrived at Berea at a time when he needed to play loose, and he was always worried that Coach would take him out if he made a mistake. In Antonio's senior year he was The Man, and Coach just let him play. That season Antonio averaged over twenty points a game, and I'm certain that he could have averaged close to that in my years.

Antonio and I have been playing together for four years in an open league in Cincinnati. I got him to play on my team. We hold our own against the young guys who are going to colleges in Ohio and Kentucky. Antonio's game has evolved so much since the time I played with him at Berea. If at that time he'd played anywhere near the level he plays at now, there's no doubt that we would have gone to the nationals.

I majored in business management. Basketball was time-consuming, but it didn't hurt me academically. Many of the nonathletes simply wasted the two hours a day we spent at practice. If you asked Berea students what they did from four to six every day, I guarantee you that most of them weren't studying.

Phil Spears in the Business Department had an influence on me. He was not a book teacher. That is, we didn't go to the book, read exactly what we needed to read, and take a test on it. Dr Spears was more of a reality-based teacher, and that helped us learn to think. Scholars might not approve of that approach because there isn't a lot on paper. I thought it was good. We had to make decisions and talk about those decisions.

Dr Spears gave me a bad grade in one of my classes, one I didn't totally agree with. But he gave me what he thought I deserved, and that was a reality check for me. Perception means a lot in the corporate environment. That experience helped me understand the importance of communicating effectively to control how other people perceive me.

I worked as a clerk in the Development Office mail room. Eventually I became a student supervisor there. John Jennings, my labor supervisor, helped influence my style of management. I was already a personality person who enjoyed life and tried to have fun. As long as we weren't breaking any rules and were getting the job done, I saw nothing wrong with having fun on the job. John was young, maybe twenty-six, and he kept the atmosphere fun. Some people might have thought he was too much of a buddy, but we handled business and had a good time. Everyone who worked under him enjoyed it. Today at work I tell people, "I want a fun environment to work in. I spend more time with you than I do with my family, so I'd better like you. If I don't like you, I am not going to want you around."

After I graduated I returned to Cincinnati to enter Star Bank's management training program. I actually got that job before I graduated. I interviewed for it in February or March. I spent a whole fifth year at Berea although I only needed three classes to graduate, so I was pretty much cruising.

I was very naive about the corporate world. There are a lot of things that go on that aren't acknowledged. Another guy from college and I were the youngest people in the class of trainees, and I made some mistakes at first. It took a while for me to understand that I was no longer at Berea, where people knew me and knew my work

Philip Spears: "A reality-based teacher"

ethic. Entering a corporate environment of 3000 employees was a big adjustment for me. I was just a Social Security number starting off.

I still work for Star Bank. It's been challenging, and I've grown a lot. My present title is assistant vice president. I manage a forty million-dollar branch office. There are very few African-American managers at Star on the higher levels, and I do a lot of mentoring of African-American management trainees and management personnel. I want to help people below me move up.

That's something I took upon myself informally, but I made it formal, and the company has responded well. They know they'll benefit from it. My goal is to groom decision-makers who can go anywhere they need to go. They need to be well-trained and understand their environment to be able to make decisions.

Star Bank is making progress in this area. The number of African-American management trainees has increased, and the retention rate is better. Having too few African-American decision-makers can have a bad effect on where the money goes to support things in the community. Without the African-American perspective, Star Bank might not be able to make sound decisions about areas of concern to African-Americans.

Berea College is in a similar situation. They want to retain African-American students. There's a high dropout rate for African-American students everywhere. The creed of the United States is, if we help the less fortunate, we'll all be better off. Lifting up those who are struggling will make everyone stronger in the end. It's the same on the basketball floor. Helping the least skilled player to improve strengthens the whole team.

August 10, 1998

Terry Tapley   1985-89

I grew up in Stearns, Kentucky, which is in McCreary County. My mom worked in the school system as a teacher's assistant, and my dad was a coal miner. My mom still works for the school system, but the coal mines in McCreary County have shut down. There's not a lot there. The education system employs more people than any business in the county, if that tells you anything.

Terry Tapley: "A dedicated team player"

Dester Terry and I were born on the same day, and we played basketball all the way through grade school, middle school, high school, and college. Dester's game improved every year he played. We've been best friends all our lives. There's not much he can't tell you about me and not much I can't tell you about him. We've had two arguments since we were six years old, and both of those were minor. Our likes and dislikes are almost the same. I doubt if you could find two brothers who agree on more things than he and I do.

When Dester and I were seniors in high school we started looking for a college where we could enroll together, participate in basketball, and get a good education. Our coach and our guidance counselor both recommended Berea College. Toward the end of the school year we visited Berea and talked with Coach Wierwille. I had planned to visit David Lipscomb University in Tennessee, but Dester and I were so impressed with Berea College and its basketball program that we made our decision right then and there. At the time we thought there would be a new gymnasium built in a couple of years, but it turned out to be a longer project than that. The new Seabury Center wasn't opened until long after we graduated.

Coach Wierwille was very straightforward. He didn't beat around the bush. I liked that, because I've always wanted to know where I stand with people. Early on Coach let Dester and me know that Berea College was a lot more than just a place to play basketball. He spoke about the quality of a Berea education, and that was extremely important to us.

My freshman year was very difficult, but they were all difficult. There was never an easy time. I was glad to be able to get out in four years. Looking back on it, I probably should have stayed a fifth year and taken fewer hours and made better grades than I did. My grade-point average wasn't bad, but I probably could have been a half letter to a letter grade better if I hadn't been so tired all the time. It took a special person with a very strong will to cope with labor assignments and demanding classes while feeling exhausted from playing ball. I was a bit of a procrastinator, and I always had to stay up late to study the night before an exam. Many students did that, of course, not just basketball players, because classes were tough at Berea. I learned to organize, to make every minute count.

I'm six-one. I was mainly a JV player my freshman year. I was one of two or three guards on the JV team who took turns dressing out for the varsity. It was not easy for me to come from high school, where I played every minute of every game, into a situation where I wasn't even allowed to dress for the varsity much of the time. I struggled with that, but I didn't say anything to Coach Wierwille about it. At the end of the year each of us had a meeting with him during which he told us what we needed to work on in the coming months. My weakness was defense.

I vowed to work every day that summer to improve my game. Before I left to go home I told Steve Ridder, the assistant coach, that if I was not good enough to play in varsity games my sophomore year, I wouldn't play, period. Coach Ridder, as always, was positive and encouraging. He could tell I was serious. He knew what my work habits were, and he never doubted me. He knew I would do whatever it took to become a player who could contribute on the varsity level. Under Coach Wierwille even the most talented players had no guarantee they'd get playing time. Whoever worked hardest and played best got the minutes.

I spent much of that summer of 1986 doing defensive slides in the gym. In preseason conditioning in the fall I started to get noticed, and I played a lot that season. The strongest part of my game was running the team. I knew when to set up certain offenses and when to speed the tempo up or slow it down. I was good at recognizing which players needed to be more involved in the game and getting them the ball.

We'd had a competitive team my freshman year. Jay Stenzel was our go-to guy, and he usually delivered. Jay was a very satisfactory defensive player, but the best part of his game was offense. As a scorer he was as good as any player in the NAIA. If he decided he wanted to score, he could. Jay and point guard Kevin Martin were big pals. There was a lot of passing between those two players. Kevin got Jay the ball, and Jay finished.

Jay was injured my sophomore year and didn't play. It was a very long season. We didn't make much progress. We lost several close games and got blown out in some others. We played defense and played as hard as any other team, but we couldn't get the job done on the offensive end of the court. Coach Wierwille struggled with his temper the entire year. The morale of the team got down. I wasn't used to losing, and it was not a pleasant experience. Coach Ridder had many conversations with us after practice, urging us to hang in there.

Kevin was a senior that year. I couldn't understand why Coach Wierwille didn't start Kevin at the beginning of the season, because Kevin was obviously the best leader we had. Jeff Royce shined in preseason pickup games because he was quick, flashy, and a gifted penetrator and scorer. Kevin was more a "let's get a play set up" type of player. But Kevin was tremendously aggressive and hard-nosed, and there was no question in the minds of ninety percent of the players about who should be starting. Yet in both my freshman and sophomore years Jeff was the starter when the season began. After a few games Kevin would be back in the starting role. Kevin was a serious guy on the court, ready to do whatever it took to help the team win, and that included sacrificing his body. But outside the gym he was always cutting up, telling jokes, keeping us laughing.

Our dismal 1986-87 season ended with a loss at Cumberland College in the KIAC tournament. We'd struggled so much that year that no one was shocked when Cumberland beat us. But none of us ever laughed or cut up after a loss. We took every game seriously.

As we were getting undressed in the locker room, Coach came in for the last talk of the year. When Coach walked into the room the players, as always, stopped doing what they were doing and sat up straight to listen to what he had to say. He told us that he wasn't satisfied with the results of that year, and he'd have plenty to say to the returning players when he talked to them individually. He expected us to keep coming into the gym to work out. He liked to see players working to improve their game in the offseason.

Finally Coach thanked the seniors for their effort. He said, "I fully expect all you seniors to graduate this year, and if you're not going to, I want to know why." Then he went around the room pointing to the individual seniors, asking them if they'd be graduating. Every one of them said, "Yes, sir." Kevin's answer was slightly different. With a straight face he replied, "Yes, sir! With honors, sir!"

All of us who knew Kevin knew that the honors part was almost certainly not true. As Coach continued to go around the room a couple of the players started snickering. When Coach heard that he exploded. For about five minutes he lectured us on how important it was to earn good grades, how you carried those grades with you the rest of your life, and how important it was to graduate. As long as he coached at Berea he didn't want to hear anyone laugh at or make fun of a player who was graduating with honors. Finally he said, "Stand up, Kevin. You ought to be proud." Coach congratulated him in front of the whole team.

Coach looked at our grades at the end of every semester, so he had to have known that Kevin was not an honor student. But he was so caught up in the game that he took Kevin at his word. The way Kevin replied, so serious and straightforward, would have fooled anyone. He hadn't hesitated for an instant. But that was Kevin. We never knew what he was going to come up with. He had nothing to lose at that point, because with his senior season concluded he wasn't going to be in the gym running sprints if he got caught in a lie. But when Coach left the locker room we all jumped on Kevin and tried to thump his head, especially the players who had done the snickering.

I started almost every game my junior year. We had a very good team with many capable inside scorers. I was never told not to look for my shot, but my first thought was always to get the ball inside. If our opponents collapsed and I had an open shot, I was free to take it.

Mike Sams was a sophomore that year. As a freshman Mike got a lot of playing time because he was a scorer and Jay Stenzel was injured. When Jay came back there was some conflict between the two. Both of them wanted the ball. I could tell when one of them was beginning to get out of sync because he wasn't getting enough touches, and I'd call a play to get that man the ball. He'd score or get fouled and go to the line and hit a couple of free throws, and that would rejuvenate him. Jay started slow that season, but eventually he reclaimed his position as our go-to guy. He got more touches than anybody on the team. However, if we didn't get Mike involved he was no good to the team in any part of his game. Get Mike the ball and he'd contribute all the way around.

Willie Hill and I had a very good junior year together. He was the two guard, and I was the point guard. Willie was tall for a guard. His ballhandling was probably the weakest part of his game, but he did it adequately enough to play the two guard position. He wasn't really a shooting guard. He wasn't a big threat from the outside. He was more like a small forward. He got a lot of assists on the fast break, which he could lead or finish if necessary.

Willie was a superb defensive player, and he had a great attitude. We never had to worry about Willie coming to practice or a game and not giving us 100 percent. He was very confident in his abilities. He and I didn't always agree on the play calling that year, but ultimately he learned to respect my decisions, and I learned to respect his. After that we got along great. We bonded together our senior year when we were named team captains. Willie and I were the only seniors to graduate in 1989.

Speaking of confidence, Chad Tate was the most confident guy I've ever played with or against in any sport in my entire life. He was offensive-minded and was never shy about standing up and telling everybody what a good game he'd had. Chad could be a little loud, but everybody accepted that because that was just the way he was. He was a good guy.

Chad was definitely a guy you wanted on your team at the end of a tight game. He'd do whatever it took to win. He was very hard-nosed. You can always spot a player who isn't a winner. You've got to have players who believe it's not acceptable to lose by one point even when you're expected to lose by ten. Chad was one of those players. He didn't go out there to lose.

Antonio Woods was the guard I competed with for playing time in my last two years. Antonio and I never said a negative word to each other, but we competed hard. If I was having a bad game and Antonio came in and played well, I was happy for him but at the same time upset with myself, because I wanted to be out there.

At the end of my senior year Coach went to a three guard lineup, putting Willie, me, and Antonio in the game together. That took some getting used to, but it ended the competition between Antonio and me. There was nothing wrong about our competing. Every team needs competition at every position, because that makes the whole team better. Antonio was a very good defensive player, certainly better than I was, and he was quicker, stronger, and a better jumper. I was better at running the game and getting everyone involved.

Robert Phillips had a great attitude. He was a muscular power forward with good athletic ability. I met Robert in high school when my team went over to Belfry to play in the Mountain Schoolboy Classic. Like Dester Terry, Robert was a player who continually improved from his freshman year to his senior year. When Robert was a freshman some people questioned whether he'd ever be a contributor. He worked hard and had some very good games as a junior and senior. He could clean the boards with anybody.

We had many players who gave everything they had all the time, but I don't believe they developed that attitude at Berea. They brought it with them when they came. Anyone who had that attitude didn't lose it playing for Coach Wierwille. Shane Lakes was like that. Whatever Coach told Shane to do, he did to the best of his ability. Score, rebound, dive on the floor, Shane would do it. He, too, was a winner.

Shane was the same every time you met him. If you saw him on his worst day, you couldn't tell. He was always friendly and courteous. He told the corniest jokes imaginable, so corny that you couldn't help but laugh. We might stop for a drink of water in the middle of practice, and Shane, gasping for breath, would pat one of us on the back and tell a little three-line joke.

We all got along wonderfully. We had black and white players on the team, but there was never a bit of racial tension. We had a tape player in the locker room so we could listen to music before and after practice. A small group of players controlled the type of music that we listened to, and finally the rest of us said, "We can't have that stuff every day." So the team made an agreement to rotate the music. Every day a different player would get to choose what kind of music we would listen to.

The selections ranged from country to soft rock to hard rock to rap. We started out with country artists everyone knew and rap that was so mainstream that even a country boy like me could understand what was being said. From there the gap between our tastes widened. Eventually it was the banjo and twangy voices of bluegrass versus the hardest hard rock and rap that was almost impossible for me to comprehend, although Willie and some of the other guys knew every word.

As the music got more extreme the atmosphere in the locker room became more comical. People would come in and hold their ears in horror at what they heard, but it was all in fun. The whole thing became a learning and bonding experience for the team. The rock and rap lovers came to appreciate the country stuff, and vice versa.

The team I wanted to beat more than any other was Cumberland College, but we never did while I was at Berea. In both my junior and senior years we had golden opportunities to beat them but couldn't come through. In my junior year we had them beat on their floor. We had a play set up, but one of our players missed a wide-open layup, and Cumberland came down and hit a three-pointer to defeat us in overtime. Cumberland was our opponent in my last game at Berea. We lost to them by seven points. It was close all the way, but we didn't do a couple of things right at the end and fell short again. Cumberland was the more talented team from top to bottom, and we knew we'd have to play a perfect game to beat them. Unfortunately, we didn't.

I resented a comment that Cumberland's coach had made while I was in high school. When I was a sophomore he recruited one of our seniors and told that player that there was no one else at my high school who would ever play college basketball. I saw that coach in camps occasionally and heard him talk about the importance of academics. He said that nobody would play for him who didn't have a 2.0 grade-point average, but he recruited a player who had flunked out of Eastern. When Dester and I were seniors he came to watch us play a few times and talked to us after the games. I was polite, but I wouldn't have gone to Cumberland to play for him if he'd offered me a scholarship and fifty thousand dollars.

I never had any problems with Coach Wierwille. Although I didn't always agree with him, he was always honest. Sometimes I heard players who had graduated say, "You may not think that he cares a lot about you because he's so stern, but if you give him 100 percent and play for him for four years, after you leave Berea he'll be somebody you can count on to help you in any situation the rest of your life." Today I know that's true. How many players can say that about coaches they've had? I have total respect for Coach Wierwille.

He didn't hand out a lot of compliments. Often when we won he'd simply say, "It was a good game. We played hard. Let's get our showers and get out of here. Hit the books, get in bed, and get some rest." He might not say anything to a player who had the best game of his life.

I got just two compliments from him the whole time I was there. After I broke the school record for consecutive free throws he congratulated me in front of the entire team. And early in my senior year I got hurt and wasn't able to play, but later I came into a game we trailed in the late minutes and helped us come from behind to win. He noticed my contribution and complimented me on it.

Coach Wierwille was a winner. That was the greatest thing about him. He knew that some teams had more talent from top to bottom than we did, but he never accepted losing. I agreed with that. When we played for him we always knew what we were there for. We went out there to win, not to play close with somebody.

Coach Ridder contributed a lot. He was a great motivator who made marginal players like me better. Coach Ridder took over the baseball team my senior year. I played baseball in high school but didn't play at Berea because the baseball program had been weak for several years. When Coach Ridder took over I agreed to help out with the field. When I played in high school we did a lot of work on our field, and I knew about infields and pitchers' mounds and home plates.

One day Coach Ridder needed somebody to throw batting practice, and I did that. Then he needed another player for a scrimmage, and I did that too. A week into the season he came to me and said, "I want you to play." I ended up playing about half the year at shortstop, second base, and pitcher. I was starting to get back into it when I pulled a hamstring and had to stop playing. Our team had the best record in the school's history that year. Right after that Coach Ridder left Berea to coach at Embry-Riddle.

As a freshman I performed janitorial duties at Seabury. I helped clean and maintain the gym, the racquetball courts, the pool, and the toilets. I made such a good impression on Coach Ridder that he asked me to interview for a resident assistant's position in one of the dorms. As a sophomore I was hired as an RA in an upperclass dorm and allowed to pick a single or double room of my choice. I picked a double room and brought Dester, my best buddy, with me.

In my junior year I kept my RA job and picked up additional hours in the art building doing some janitorial work and building some looms for students who wanted to do some weaving. In my senior year I wanted some experience related to my major, business management, so I worked fifteen to twenty hours a week in the Accounting Office.

During my sophomore year I had a computer math class that was required. It was taught by J.P. Lee, the kind of professor who always gave us our money's worth. The class was scheduled for one hour, but he kept us for an hour and two minutes. He was very thorough and very concerned about our grades. We had to play close attention, because his English was far from perfect and he wasn't always easy to understand. That made a tough class even harder.

Dr Lee gave two-hour exams. He scheduled them at night because we couldn't get them in during the regular daytime class periods. One of his tests conflicted with a basketball game we were going to play out of town. I'd been playing better and getting more minutes. I told Dr Lee that I had a very important game on the day of his test and was willing to do anything I could to make the test up. I offered to come in two hours before we left for the game or the night after we got back. Dr Lee opened his assignment book and calculated my average, which was in the low nineties, on the borderline of A minus and B plus. He said, "Mr Tapley, you good student. You stay good student! You come and take test!"

He shut his book and walked out the door. I was floored. I couldn't believe it, but there was no questioning it. He'd made his decision, and there was no sense in arguing with him about it.

Now I had to explain all this to Coach Wierwille. I thought Coach Wierwille was going to die. He couldn't believe that Dr Lee wasn't willing to work something out. Coach didn't expect us to be granted special privileges, but most of the professors accommodated those situations in some way, perhaps by administering a harder test, which was very common.

"Young man, I can't believe that you couldn't convince this professor to let you make up his exam. I'm disappointed in you."

"Coach, if you can come up with a way to negotiate with this professor, I'll be shocked."

"I can't come up with anything. You'll stay here and take the test."

So I stayed and took the test, and after that I saw little playing time for a couple of weeks. I had to work really hard to get back in Coach's good graces. I didn't like that, but there was never any question with Coach. If Dr Lee told me that I had to take his test at that particular time, that's what I had to do.

Coach Wierwille was always clear with us about what our obligations were. Dr Phil Spears was a lot like Coach Wierwille, very intimidating, and like Coach he helped get me ready for life after college. Dr Spears prepared us for what it would be like to be interviewed for a job, for instance, or what it would be like to be chewed out by a supervisor in front of everyone for not getting a job done. He taught us how to respond to real-world business situations. Dr Wayne Tolliver was another teacher who showed us practical skills we could use in the business world.

I was interested in entering the insurance business, and when I was a senior I walked into a State Farm claims office in Lexington with no appointment and asked to see somebody. Luckily I made a good enough impression for them to call me back for a second interview. The person who interviewed me that day was Carl Sumner, the divisional manager. He looked at me and said, "You were Number Eleven for Berea College." I was amazed. I had no idea how he knew that, but he looked familiar. It turned out that he was an NAIA official.

The interview went well. Carl was very sports-minded, and he knew all about Coach Wierwille and Berea College. After he told me I was hired he said, "Anybody who can go to Berea College, graduate with decent grades, and play basketball for Roland Wierwille for four years can do anything he sets his mind to."

I've been with State Farm Insurance ever since, going on ten years now. Six months after I was hired Carl came to me and asked whether I knew Kevin Mullins. Kevin graduated from Berea before I arrived, but I'd played against him in alumni games and pickup games in the summer and early fall.

I said, "I don't know much about Kevin's background or personality, but I know how he plays basketball. He's hard-nosed. If he does other things like he plays ball, he's a hard worker. And I'll remind you of this: Kevin went to Berea College, he graduated with decent grades, and he played basketball for Roland Wierwille for four years."

Carl said, "A man can do anything if he can do that, can't he?" The next day I saw an announcement that Kevin had been hired.

Several months later I ran into Robert Phillips. He was assistant manager of a Kroger store in Lexington. We had a thirty minute conversation.

Robert said, "Do you like your job? Let me know if there's ever an opening, because I'm not sure I'm liking mine."

"Robert, there's an opening right now. If you can get off work before five o'clock, go over to State Farm and fill out an application. Make sure you put my name down as a reference. Let them know that you're serious about an interview."

The next day Carl asked me about Robert. I knew a lot about Robert and talked about his great personality and strong work ethic.

"And by the way," I concluded, "Robert went to Berea College, he graduated with good grades..."

Carl said, "And he played for Roland Wierwille for four years!"

Carl hired Robert, too. He and Kevin have done very well, and I have to believe that Carl has been happy with those decisions.

Today I'm a claims specialist working in a special investigative unit. Every insurance company in Kentucky is mandated by law to have such a unit to investigate possible fraud situations. I like the work. It's never boring. Every day is different. I paid claims for seven years and felt good about helping people in their time of need. Now I'm doing something I hope will stop our insurance rates from continuing to go up. They'd be half of what they are now if there were no insurance fraud. It's a huge fight.

I still play competitive basketball, but I probably won't do it much longer. I'm getting too old. I can't get to the places I used to be able to get to. My mind knows where I need to be and when I need to be there, but my body won't get me there quick enough. It frustrates me to know that we may lose a game because I can't do the things I want to do. I don't like losing.

There's a summer league in Berea every year, and Dester and I have played in it just about every summer since we graduated. We've won the championship every year. Last year we won it by one point in overtime, which I regarded as a sign that it was time to pass the torch to the younger guys. The team we beat after we graduated was stacked with players like Arno Norwell and Craig Jefferson. They'd won the league for several years, but we were younger and in better condition, and after we beat them they hung it up. Now it's our turn to hang it up, but I let the guys con me into playing again this year. We've got a good chance to win it again, but I'm basically through. I like to hunt and fish. Those are things I missed out on when I was growing up because I was so dedicated to basketball and baseball. I'm trying to make up for that now. These days I'm hooked on golf, a sport that's not as physically demanding as basketball but still very competitive.

July 30, 1998

Dester Terry   **1987-90**

Coach Wierwille is definitely one of my mentors. I have the utmost respect for him. Coach Wierwille gave me a second chance to play at Berea College, and I can't give him enough credit for that. I can never stress that enough.

When I was a freshman I had a little bit of an injury in preseason that nobody knew about, and right then I felt that I wasn't physically capable of playing at that level. The game was a little too fast for me at that time. I had to approach Coach Wierwille after I went through preseason and tell him that, and he was not a happy man.

Maybe he saw it as me giving up. He thought I had some potential, and he was very upset. I can see why he would be. We were just about ready to start playing. I'd done decent and was obviously going to make the varsity level, and when I stepped down, there went six weeks of preparation when somebody else could have been in there. That's why I felt guilty about it.

I should have shared some more with Coach

Dester Terry: "Unselfish to a fault"

Wierwille or Coach Ridder, his assistant. I just let things get out of hand until I thought leaving the team was the only thing left for me to do. After I had done it, I knew within three months that I wanted to try to play again. It was just a question of whether the opportunity would be offered.

When I approached Coach Wierwille a year later to come back to the team, he was gracious enough to give me a shot. He let me know right away that if we had twenty-four people trying out, I was the twenty-fifth in line. All I could ask for at that time was a shot. He was gracious enough to give that to me, and I'll always thank him for that.

I grew up in Whitley City, in McCreary County, Kentucky. I played basketball from third grade all the way through high school. I tried to play baseball, but basketball really dominated my sports life. After high school I was looking for a competitive college team at an excellent academic school. Berea College had both to offer. My high school coach and I actually approached Berea. Coach Wierwille never pursued me at all because he believed I'd already signed with a Division I school. Our meeting went well, and I ended up at Berea.

I thought I knew what hard work was coming out of high school, because I'd played on some successful teams. I had no clue. Not many people know what it takes just to get from October 15, when practice begins, to the first game. Coach Wierwille would start out every year by having the practice schedule, the drills, what we were going to do, typed up and posted on the board so everybody could see. He did that so there would be no wasted time going from drill to drill. Coach never wasted a minute. That's the one thing that sticks out in my mind more than anything else, the organization. Coach Wierwille was the most organized coach I've ever been around.

Screens and movement were the keys to his offense. The offensive sets were simple sets, but as long as we executed them, we got every shot we ever needed. On defense, Coach Wierwille stressed effort. He taught the mechanics of defense, but once we got those down, it came down to desire and the effort to play. We took it as a personal challenge to stop the guy in front of us. It was also very clear that anyone who didn't play on the defensive end wasn't going to play, period.

The pregame preparation was tremendous with Coach Wierwille. He was terrific on scouting reports. We knew what was going to happen before the game ever started, so once the game began, it was simply a matter of execution. We knew what they were going to do, when they were going to do it, and who was going to do it. Then it just came down to effort, to getting it done. Coach Wierwille could stomach a loss as long as he was convinced that we gave 110 percent effort. If we didn't, we cheated him, the school, and ourselves. I couldn't agree more!

Some players need hugs and a pat on the back. Some need a little scolding sometimes. Other guys, you can sort of look them in the eye and they get the message that they're not performing up to par. Coach knew how to push a player's buttons. He knew who he had to get a little vocal with. That comes from knowing your players.

I happened to be a versatile player. I'm six-six, and although I never played center, I played every other position in college, including point guard. I wasn't always tall; in middle school there were several players taller than I was. Because I was average size, I had guard skills. Then I grew all at once, five inches over one summer. I became more of an inside player then, but I was able to go both ways.

At Berea I was able to break the starting lineup the first year I played, as a sophomore. When I came to Berea I didn't know how to play defense. In high school you're looked to for offense and to stay out of foul trouble, so I had to learn how to play defense in college. Not only did I learn how to play it, but it became my favorite part of the game.

Coach Wierwille asked me to play both forward spots and a lot of two guard, and now and then to bring the ball up the floor as a point guard. During my first year I was able to play with Jay Stenzel, one of the all-time best. I didn't look to score much then. I just wanted to be a smart player and keep everybody else involved, do my part. After Jay graduated, I had to step up scoring, so my role changed.

A couple of words come to mind to describe the teams I played on: unselfish and intelligent. Jay Stenzel was a good example. Jay was a very solid player and very much a team player. He was an incredible offensive force. Jay scored a lot of points but rarely took a bad shot. He did everything within the framework of the offense. And he felt it was important to keep other players involved. Even though he knew and everyone knew that he was our main man, he made sure the ball was shared enough to keep everybody happy.

Another player everybody looked up to was Willie Hill, the point guard, who was a year ahead of me. The things Willie did started at practice. He kept everybody loose and low-keyed, but he was definitely a big motivator on the team. As point guard he always made sure we were in the right sets, made sure the right people had the ball in the right situations.

My closest friend on the team was Terry Tapley. Terry and I came from the same county and grew up together. I played with him on my high school team. He and I are like brothers even now. We have the same values. I would classify both of us as low-key, conservative people who do not have to have the limelight to be happy. We just wanted to play on good, competitive teams.

Terry was also a point guard. He did a wonderful job of keeping everybody in the right sets and the right frame of mind. He knew what plays to call for in what situations. There's an art to that without a doubt. Certain things work in certain situations, and other things don't. Terry was very good at knowing what would work and when.

After Willie and Terry graduated, Antonio Woods was our point guard in my senior year. He was a big part of the team in the other years too. From the first time I saw him until the time he left, Antonio improved more than anybody. He always had the athletic ability to run down the floor and shoot the ball, but in handling the team and knowing how to get everybody involved, he improved a lot through his career.

Robert Phillips was maybe the best athlete and certainly the strongest player physically I had a chance to play with. Robert was a lot stronger than he appeared to be, strong from top to bottom. If you could get his attention or if he got upset about something, you could forget about rebounding. He got every one that came off the boards. Nobody else was going to get near them. At times he could dominate like that.

Two players who could shoot the ball were Chad Tate and Mike Sams. Chad was a fun-loving guy who liked to talk in games. I think he did that to get himself motivated. Mike was a born scorer. He didn't have the prettiest shot in the world, but it was effective, and that's all that mattered. Mike hated to lose. He was a big-time competitor from practice all the way to games.

Robbie Taylor had the unfortunate luck to have a major knee injury early in his career. He would have been an excellent player for Berea. He was still a very fine player, but he lost probably a step and a half on his quickness and had to wear a bulky knee brace the rest of his career. In practice he would put it all out. Toward the end when you were thinking to yourself that you were dying, Robbie would still be beating people up and down the floor, wearing a thirty-pound knee brace after going through major reconstructive surgery. You sort of felt guilty watching him. When he came into games it was always motivational for us. He might be out there only five minutes, but he would turn the game. It never failed.

Shane Lakes was another guy who suffered a major knee injury. That slowed him down, but he worked extremely hard. He didn't get into games on the varsity level until my senior year. I can remember one game in particular, in the tournament at the end of the 1988-89 season when we were playing Alice Lloyd at Eastern. One of their big guys was eating us alive. None of our regulars could stop him, but Shane came in and did a wonderful job. Had it not been for Shane Lakes, we would definitely have lost. He always gave a great effort.

Bob Cowie was a big man who was a rough, tough competitor. He was a freshman when I was a senior. In practice he banged me around a lot. I can remember thinking, "If he keeps improving and getting bigger and stronger, he's going to be hard to handle!" Mike Sams, another senior, took Bob under his wing. They were pretty close. Those two were always up to something. You had to watch out for them all the time.

Very seldom did we have an overnight trip. Mainly we were just going there and coming back. On the way to wherever we happened to be going it was serious business. There was no joking around. If we were fortunate enough to win the game, everybody had a good time on the way back. But if we did not win the game, it was not a lot of fun driving back home. In my years the road trips were serious all the time.

Overall the campus and the students and the town supported us very well. I loved it when Seabury was packed, standing room only. When it was like that it sometimes felt like 105 degrees on the floor, and you couldn't hear yourself think. You could almost feel your head vibrate. In my junior year against Georgetown, a great rival always loaded with Division I transfers, we put on a little run in the last three minutes to knock them off. I stole the ball and put us ahead, and I can still see Antonio Woods in front of me, yelling at me from about three feet away. I could not hear a word he was saying. The intimate setting of that place was great.

Transylvania was another great rival. Both of us had success at the other's place. We had success at Lexington, and they had success at our place. We liked to play in Lexington because there was always a lot of media there. Everyone knew that those were important games for Coach Wierwille, who used to coach there. They meant a lot to him, so in turn they meant a lot to us.

Orbrey Gritton played at Transylvania. He was about my size, but he was totally an inside player, so he and I didn't hook up a lot. Yet the two of us had a great rivalry. We could beat on each other physically, bloody sometimes, but it would never go over the line. I can remember officials talking to us. Orbrey and I both got T'ed up one night for what they called flagrant fouls. But as soon as they did it, he and I just looked at each other, patted each other, and walked off. Every time we hooked up we were like that. I've never had such a relationship with an opposing player, where we could just kill each other and never have any ill feelings toward each other at all. I think it was mutual respect for how hard we were trying to play.

During my senior year I injured my left knee in the Berea Lions Club Tournament. We were playing an inferior team, which made it even worse. I had to miss four or five games. When I came back I came back healthy, but missing four or five games and over the Christmas break, I was out of game shape. It took me a long time to get back to the shape I needed to be in.

One of the games I had to miss was against Alice Lloyd at Berea. We had never lost to Alice Lloyd in history, but they beat us that night. I had to sit there and watch it. Then on the way downstairs after the game, their coach put his arm around me and said, "I guess if you'd been playing, there would have been a different outcome, don't you think so?" He may have meant it as a compliment, but I took it as sarcasm. It stuck with me. I knew from that night, as we went down to the dressing room, we had thirty days until we played them again. I could not wait to get over there for that game.

We beat them in that rematch, and I had the best offensive game of my career with thirty-seven points. But the thing I'm more proud of is that it was the best defensive effort of my career too.

In my sophomore and junior years, we had good, competitive teams, but we lost in the postseason tournaments to Transy one year and Cumberland the next. We gave our best efforts but came up just a little short. Anytime you lose in a tournament situation it's tough to take, but as long as you can leave the floor and know you did everything you could, you'll eventually get over it.

Injuries held us back when I was a senior. What would have been the starting lineup that year started just two games. One of them was against Transylvania after Christmas break. That was when I came back from my injury. We blew them away. If we hadn't suffered so many injuries that year, we would have had a much better record. When we were all intact and had everybody there, we were a good team.

There was also a bit of an adjustment because that was the first year without Steve Ridder. We definitely missed his enthusiasm and motivation. Coach Ridder never gave up, no matter what. He's a great head coach now at Embry-Riddle, but then he was a terrific assistant. In practices Coach Wierwille might work with the big men on one end while Coach Ridder would take the guards on the other end, and we could get a lot more done in our practice time. After Coach Ridder left, Coach Wierwille needed to be involved with everybody. Even though the same amount of practice time was available, we didn't get as much accomplished. That affected us.

Several times in my career I heard Coach Wierwille tell us, "Put it all on the line, because before you know it you'll wake up one morning and this will be over." That might have been the truest statement he ever made to us. It all happened so fast. I was pretty depressed for a week and a half after my final game, knowing that after my last class I would never have to be in practice again. The team is your extended family from October 15 until late March. I missed the friendships with the players. I could still be around them, but it wasn't the same.

But I took my studies seriously too. I enjoyed playing basketball and loved it to death, but I knew that after the last game of my senior year I would have to make it in the real world. The only way I was going to do that was with my academic background. Coach always checked up on us individually. Around midterms each player would have to go in and discuss his academic performance with Coach Wierwille. We heard rumors that if we were on a road trip during the week and didn't get back to campus until two in the morning, Coach checked up on who was there for those eight o'clock classes and who was not. I never knew that for sure, but I always heard that.

Playing basketball at Berea College took a lot of discipline and a lot of dedication. You gave up a lot. Your social life went to nothing. You had to be extremely disciplined to put the hours into the program and keep up academically. With that labor program, you couldn't let anything slide. If you could go through all that, each of your days was a full day.

There were some jealousies on campus, but Coach Wierwille was very careful to make sure the basketball players got no favors. As a matter of fact, he wanted to be rougher on us to set examples. He never wanted anyone saying we got a break because we were basketball players. Everyone on the team agreed with that, too. There was never a problem.

I majored in business administration, with a political science minor. I had coasted through high school, so Berea College was a challenge. I welcomed that challenge. I had to apply myself, but as long as I did, I had pretty good grades all the way through.

The head of the Business Department was Clifford Sowell. I admired him. He taught college classes the way they should be taught. In my first class with him I saw that he didn't just teach out of the book, even though he was one of the authors of the book! When exam time came we needed to know what was in there, but his teaching went beyond what was in the book. I enjoyed that a lot.

When I first arrived I worked as a janitor in Seabury. After that it was sort of like the real world, where you have to go out and interview for something else you may want. From there I worked security at the Art Building, and in my last year I was a resident assistant at the Danforth dorm.

Right after I graduated I joined the Westfield Insurance Company, and I've been working for them ever since. I interviewed for the job while I was still at Berea. I had to go to Cleveland to train for about eight months. They have offices everywhere, including Lexington, Louisville, and Bowling Green, Kentucky. The whole time I was in Cleveland they would put up on the bulletin board at the end of every month where the specific openings were. I knew I was going to have to go to one of those places, and I was hoping, praying for one of the Kentucky offices, but they were never posted. Then two weeks before we were to be sent out, Bowling Green and Lexington came open. I was fortunate enough to be sent to Lexington. So I came back home.

Westfield came and approached us at the College, so my Berea College degree got my foot in the door of a very nice company. While getting through a liberal arts college, you become a well-rounded person whether you know it or not. Now that I've got a little bit of age on me and I can look back on it, I'm very appreciative of the different classes I had to take at Berea, classes I wouldn't have taken if I had had a choice.

For instance, I had music-oriented classes in which we had to study opera. I personally would never have chosen those classes, and I won't tell you that I enjoyed them. But looking back on them now, I'm thankful for that experience, because with an education you can fit into any situation in society.

I'd like to stay with the same company and continue to move up. That may mean some more moves. I had to move to Florida for a while, but now I'm back in central Kentucky, and I'd love to stay here if I can. My wife and I are Lexington-and-south kind of people.

After college I played in some men's basketball leagues in Richmond, and I played on a team when I was in Florida. Now I'm getting to the weight and age where I'm starting to find something else to do. I miss the competition a lot. We go to the Berea College games whenever we get a chance.

Coach Wierwille is a great basketball coach, but if you stay in his program you become a better person, and I think that's what's important in the long run. He puts his heart and soul into every minute of his life. That's one thing I picked up from him. If you're going to do something, do it 110 percent and do it right, whether you're playing basketball or going to class or sweeping the floor. I've tried to take that and apply it to my professional career now. Being around him has helped me a great deal.

May 15, 1998

Chad Tate   1986-90

At the beginning of the 1986-87 season we played a couple of games in Louisville. We played Bellarmine at Indiana University-Southeast, then played IUSE at Bellarmine the next night. I was a freshman. Coach Wierwille called me in and said, "Normally you wouldn't get to go on this trip, because we can only take so many. But Coach Ridder told me you deserve to go because you've played really hard on the JV team, so I'm going to take you. You won't play, but you're going to Louisville." I was glad to go.

My parents lived in Richmond. They liked to come to my games, but I told them that I wouldn't be playing against Bellarmine, so they didn't travel to Louisville. Bellarmine was tough. They had a great big kid, Jimmy Crawford, who looked like an NFL lineman. I watched from the end of the bench as Bellarmine went ahead of us. A couple of our guys got into foul trouble, and Coach put me in.

I played the way I always played, shooting the ball as quick as I could. I had a little guard on me. I posted him up twice, drew a foul, and scored. I got an offensive rebound and put it in. The next time we came down the floor, Crawford pushed me and got a technical called on him. I got to shoot two free throws and hit them both. Later I attempted a three-pointer and shot an air ball. Opposing fans always loved to get on me, and by this time they were really hollering. I got the ball back and put it in. I ended up with eleven points.

I called my parents after the game. They said they had listened to it on the radio. They could hear the people in the stands yelling at me, and my dad wanted to get in the car and drive up there and make sure I was okay. He didn't do that, but they came the next night. Because I'd played well against Bellarmine I got to play against IUSE. I scored ten points as the second guy off the bench, and we won the game in overtime. I almost won it in regulation on a tip-in, and I hit two free throws in the overtime. It was a big win for us. I was on cloud nine. I got into quite a few varsity games after that.

I never got along very well with the other team's fans. I played hard, and I knocked. I was always a shooter and scorer from outside, but I could go inside and knock a guy down to get a rebound. I was very animated. If I was happy people knew it, and if I was upset people knew that too. I showed it on my face. I never could manage the stoic look of a Dester Terry. I was a little on the heavy side, too, and I got name calls for that. I knew what the fans were thinking: "This kid, the way he looks, he's shouldn't be able to do the things he's doing. Let's get on him about his physical appearance and see if we can get in his head." They didn't realize that I enjoyed their taunting. It inspired me to play better.

My mom and dad came to almost all my games from the time I was eight years old. All the way through college they probably didn't miss five games, not even the long travel games. They wore out two brand new Suburbans while I was in high school and college. In my freshman year at Berea they drove all the way down to Clinch Valley, where they were the only two Berea fans in the stands. They were Mom and Dad to a lot of kids on the team.

That was great, but I felt bad whenever they traveled a long distance and I didn't play. They couldn't understand why I got upset about it. My dad and I had always been friends. When I was growing up he never had to discipline me much because I was a good kid who rarely caused any problems. He and I were buddies. Finally he said, "Look, Chad, you're our son. If you're playing tiddlywinks, we want to be there for you. If you play, fine, and if you don't play, that's fine too." That made me feel a

Chad Tate: "He didn't go out there to lose"

lot better. I think my dad is the greatest guy in the world, and I never mind telling people that. A lot of stories I tell are, my dad did this, my dad showed me that. I got a lot of kidding about that, but it didn't bother me.

I'm an only child. My dad is Kenneth, and I'm Kenneth Chadwell. Dad played basketball at Eastern Kentucky University and coached at Madison High School. Sports was a big part of my life from day one. Some kids feel they're forced into athletics, but I never did. It was there, and I enjoyed it. It was a family thing for us. My dad played softball in the summers. I had the opportunity to travel to many big-time basketball tournaments and games and meet a lot of people.

Dad knew Coach Wierwille and helped him with his camp for years. I attended the first Wierwille camp. I grew up watching the Berea College players. Guys like Arno Norwell, Bill Nichols, Craig Jefferson, Ed Flynn, Steve Ridder, and Keith Riley were my heroes. Many kids idolized UK, but I was more interested in Berea because I could get close to their players and meet them personally.

When I graduated from high school I had some opportunities to go to other schools, but I felt Berea College was best for me. I knew I'd get a good education, and my dad was certain that I'd get a fair shake athletically. He said, "You can walk on at a big school without a scholarship, but you'll be competing with guys who have scholarships. You may be as good a player as one of them or even a little better. But will the coach say he was wrong in recruiting the other guy and give you an opportunity over him? That just ain't going to happen!" Coach Wierwille said he'd give me the opportunity to play at Berea. Furthermore, he told me that if I didn't want to come to Berea, he'd help me get into any school in the United States other than a school Berea played.

I'd known Roland Wierwille since I was seven or eight years old. People watching him coach during a game got the impression that he was mean. I had a tough guy at home, so Coach Wierwille's actions on the bench didn't faze me. I looked up to him. In the summers he was a personable guy who always talked to me, a young kid who admired the program. When I was considering enrolling to Berea he said, "As a coach I'm nothing like you know me. I'm a lot tougher."

"I realize that. I've got my dad at home, and he can be tough too. I've learned what to listen to and what not to listen to."

Coaching me was difficult for him. He wasn't sure at first about how to handle our relationship. I knew that he and I couldn't be the buddies we'd been every summer. It had to be different. I think that on occasion he felt the need to demonstrate that we weren't buddies. Sometimes he yelled at me worse than he did the other guys, like a father would at his son. He knew I could take it. I was proud to play for him.

I was a late grower. Right now I'm about six-five, and that's an inch and a half taller than I was in college. I played a little bit of forward at Berea, but mostly guard. I was tall for a guard, but I could handle the ball a little bit. I'd go inside if there was a smaller guy on me or stay outside of a big guy.

Coach was always telling me I needed to improve my defense. Nobody likes to play defense. Defense is mostly setting your mind to it. On offense you can improve your skills if you shoot, shoot, shoot. Defense is a matter of getting down and doing it. I needed to concentrate to monitor where my man was. I was slow for the position I played, so I tried to eat less and run more.

My freshman year was the year Jay Stenzel sat out with an injury. Jay and I were different in a lot of ways. He was older, and I was a young guy trying to fit in. He could be difficult to work with. If he thought you weren't doing what you needed to do, he didn't have a problem telling you about it. But I had a world of respect for Jay, because he was a heck of a player. He was aggressive on offense. He wanted the ball, and he put the son of a gun in the hole. He was able to get his shot off against bigger defenders. He was a very tough competitor.

Jay did one thing I'll always remember. In my freshman year I played well in one of the games I got into. Soon after that Jay saw my mother in Richmond and made a point of telling her that I had done a good job. That was very gentlemanly. But he and I didn't hang around a lot. We've probably talked more since we graduated than we did then.

Bubby Napier was a hard worker and a quiet leader. He hardly ever said anything, but he was a force. I have a funny story about Bubby that I'll tell until I die. We were getting ready to practice one day when Coach Wierwille walked in wearing that great big Mountaineer head the cheerleaders had. We wondered what was going on, but we didn't have the nerve to ask.

We stretched, did all our drills, and started running our offense up and down the floor. On that round I was with the first team with Bubby, and we ran through on a fast break offense. Bubby didn't set a pick or something, and Coach didn't like it. He started getting on Bubby, talking real loud out of that big head. Finally Bubby burst out laughing right in his face.

"You're laughing at me?"

Bubby just said, "Yeah."

Then Coach started laughing, and we all laughed. Coach wore that thing all through practice.

Willie Hill taught me a lot about the game. He and I were at the same position a lot of the time, so we battled. We knocked and fought and scratched and kicked, but off the floor if there was anything I needed, Willie was there for me. I appreciated that.

Willie was a leader. Defense was his specialty. He was fast, had long arms, and read the passing lanes well. He made his teammates better because he was a passer who would look for the open man. Willie helped me a lot when he was the point guard and I was the off guard. He'd do the penetrating, and I'd spot up and shoot.

Willie was a year ahead of me in school. When he finished he stayed at Berea and assisted Coach Wierwille for a year. That was our hardest time together. He'd been a friend and teammate for a long time, and now he was in a position of responsibility. But we got through that. Today Willie is one of my closest friends.

I played with Robert Phillips for four years. He was there for me through hard times, good times, whatever. My liking for him might have been a lit-tle selfish, because Robert was a heck of a rebounder. He knew I could shoot, and he read my moves so that if I missed the shot he could get the ball and throw it back to me.

Another player I got close to was Carlos Verdecchia. Carlos was from Argentina. The high school he attended, University Heights Academy in western Kentucky, had about fifty students, and most of them were athletes. University Heights was notorious for stocking up with transfers and foreign players. Carlos was six-nine. He came to Kentucky as a foreign exchange student and lived with a great family in Hopkinsville, a doctor and his wife. He'd only been in the States a couple of years when he came to Berea.

Carlos Verdecchia

I lived on campus, and Coach Wierwille asked me to room with Carlos. Coach knew me and my family, of course, and he thought I would be good for Carlos, take him to Richmond and help him continue his adjustment to life in the United States. I met him, and he was a wonderful guy. His English wasn't real fluent, but he had a great sense of humor. Carlos could have been a comedian if he'd been born American and talked regular, so add his accent and he was hilarious. We roomed together for four years.

Carlos was an excellent athlete. When he came to Berea he'd only played basketball for a couple of years. Coach Wierwille wanted a six-nine guy on the block, which is where Carlos needed to be. But Carlos wanted nothing to do with the block. He wanted to run the fast break and shoot the three-pointer. That was his type of game. He never really understood what Coach wanted. He ended up quitting basketball and played soccer, where he broke the school scoring record.

There was a lot of humor in our locker room. Guys were always making fun of people and their actions. Mike Sams and Robbie Taylor were like Laurel and Hardy, mocking everybody from Coach to the team manager. I talk a lot, and they got on me about that. The only guy who got any slack was Bubby. They didn't know how Bubby would react. They'd never seen him get mad, and they didn't want to make him mad.

Mike is a minister now, and all my love goes out to him for that. My grandfather was a pastor, and I've been around the church for years. The Lord is there to forgive our sins and give us another chance. Mike probably needed a lot of forgiving. He really enjoyed his time at school. As a player Mike was offensive-minded. He shot a lot, but that was his job, to get in there and put the ball in the basket. In those days Coach Wierwille wanted us to push it inside.

When I came to Berea the three-point shot was new. That was a shot for me. By going back two steps I could get three points. Some coaches didn't think it would last, but others did. At the time I graduated from high school a lot of guys were getting Division I scholarships who weren't near the athletes that some of the Berea players were. Because they could shoot three-pointers they got scholarships from coaches who said, "That's here to stay, and my team is going to do it."

As a freshman I was a reserve player. Sometimes I played fifteen minutes, sometimes just two or three. If I was in the game I shot the three-pointer whenever I had an opening. That was my mentality. Coach put me into games late if we were behind, to add some offense. My three-point percentage was very good. When the first stats came out, I was leading the entire district in three-point percentage. I had fewer attempts than a lot of the players on the list, but I had just enough to be listed in the category.

While I was stretching one day Coach told me he couldn't believe that he had the leading three-point shooter in the league. He said he hated the three-point rule! He didn't want me to miss them, I know that. Shooting more three-pointers might have helped us, but we still had some size on the team, so Coach's philosophy was unchanged: go inside. Eventually he came around, but we never dared to cut loose like his players do now.

Coach was very controlled. When Antonio Woods joined us he had to change his playing style, because he was used to getting out and going. Antonio was a good enough athlete to do what he needed to do for the team. He was a big-time point guard. At first Antonio's job was to feed the other guys, but later on Coach started letting him loose outside, where he really excelled.

The people Coach Wierwille brought to Berea were not merely good athletes. They finished up their school, and they were good people. That's what you want. I wouldn't have made all the friends I did if they hadn't been such good people. Terry Tapley was a case in point. He was a great individual in a tough situation. He was a point guard who was a good ballhandler and shooter, but we had several point guards. Coach went with whoever was hot at the moment, whether it was Antonio or Terry or Robbie Taylor. Terry, if anything, was too nice. He could have been meaner at times.

Dester Terry was another fine athlete who could have used a little meanness. He could do anything, but he was unselfish to a fault. He would always pass first. At his size he could have taken over a lot of games if he'd wanted to. He could post you up and score or take you outside, either one. Dester's facial expression was always the same whether we were ahead by twenty or losing by twenty. I tried to model my demeanor on his, because anybody could read what I was thinking like a big billboard.

I had some good games. In my freshman year I got to play in a game with Pikeville and scored ten points against Todd May in the first half. I've got a neat picture that shows me shooting over him on a layup. He actually blocked the shot, but it was called goaltending. We led off my sophomore year with a real nice win against Lindsey Wilson at Homecoming. I didn't play a whole lot, but I managed to score fifteen points. I keep talking about the points I scored, but I liked it a lot better when we won, believe me.

Basketball was my main athletic interest when I came to college. I started playing baseball my freshman year, but Berea College didn't put a lot into their baseball program. At Madison Central High School we won the mythical national championship my freshman year and were in the state tournament all three years after that. We never lost more than two or three games a year. Baseball at Berea wasn't very organized, so I stayed with basketball.

In my junior year Coach Ridder took over the baseball program. He knew I was a decent player, and he asked me to play. I told him I'd love to. We had a wonderful season. Coach Ridder fired us up. Shane Lakes hadn't pitched for three years, but he did an unbelievable job for us. I hit over .300 playing first and second base and made all-conference as a utility infielder. We beat a lot of people. Georgetown was nationally ranked, and they defeated us by just one run.

We ended up making it to the conference tournament. We got rained out against Cumberland, who were the studs at the time. We were scheduled to play them at Clinch Valley to go to national tournament but ended up getting rained out four days in a row. We stayed at Clinch Valley in some little podunk hotel and never did get the chance to play Cumberland.

Things were settled with a coin toss, and we lost. That was sad, but our successful baseball season lifted me up after a frustrating year in basketball.

Coach Wierwille wasn't happy with my defense, and he stopped playing me as much as he had been. We talked about it. He thought I couldn't guard some of the smaller guards in the conference, and we had some other guys who were playing good. The minutes I was getting were at the end of games, and I wasn't hitting my shots. It's tough to come in and shoot when you're not loose.

Finally Coach said, "You need to get your shooting eye back. I want you to play a JV game for Coach Ridder. They're going down to London to play Sue Bennett College."

Sue Bennett had a lot of good players, but I was not happy about having to play a JV game as a junior. I kept quiet about it. As a veteran player I tried to be a leader. I went down there with a good attitude, knowing I was going to play a lot of minutes.

While I was warming up I saw Robert Phillips and Carlos Verdecchia come in. Almost every player on the varsity showed up to watch that game. Did they do that to support me? My parents thought so. I never asked them about it, but they'd never done anything like that before. I felt a lot of love for those guys that night, and I shot the ball very well. I think I had twenty points in the first half. I proved to myself and to Coach that I could still shoot if I got the chance to shoot. After that I came back and played with the varsity again.

I started some games in my senior year, but we didn't win too often. We didn't have much success going inside, and we lacked a big defensive standout leader who could play at the point of the one-three-one we used to run. Coach Ridder left before the season started, and we missed him. He was such an important part of our program.

I can't say enough about Coach Ridder. He was a wonderful individual. You'd try to run through a brick wall for him and get mad at yourself if you didn't do it. Coach Ridder was as different from Coach Wierwille as night and day, but he was Coach's right hand man, another good basketball mind.

I majored in business administration. I'm not the smartest guy in the world, but I was always in class, and I tried. Academics for me meant a lot of late nights and a lot of help from tutors and smart guys. But I never doubted that I'd be able to do the work. I knew I'd get it done one way or the other. I got good grades and did well in school.

Ed McCormack taught some of my accounting classes. He was a real person who understood what people go through in college. He was good in accounting and I wasn't, but he helped me by showing me that accounting is something you learn as much of as you can and utilize. If you're not an MBA in accounting, it's not going to kill you.

I battled with Phil Spears in Organizational Behavior. The whole class was love-hate throughout, but he taught me a lot. He told us that participation would be a big percentage of our grade. I counted on that, because

I was a guy who would stand up and talk. Dr Spears said he wanted give-and-take discussions like in the business world. He and I went back and forth, he'd come out with his opinion, and I'd say, "Yes, sir."

At the end of the semester I got my grade in his class, and it was a D. I was expecting a C at the worst, because I'd participated and done fairly well on the papers. I called him at home and said, "This is a mistake, isn't it?"

"It's no mistake, Chad. That was a really tough grade for me. It was hard for me to give it to you."

"Tell me why you gave it. What's the deal? My average on the tests was a definite C, and my participation should have pulled me up to a B."

"I thought about that. But when we got to talking and I pushed you, you backed down."

"Well, Dr Spears, I was raised up by my mom and dad that teachers and coaches are in charge. I'll argue, but if the people in charge tell me how it is, I say 'Yes, sir' and go another route."

"No, Chad. In the real world you can't do that."

I said, "All right, Dr Spears. I've got you this spring for Marketing. I'm going to bust your —-!" And I said what it's called.

In Marketing we did a lot of presentations. This was my junior year, the year I played baseball for Coach Ridder. The team was scheduled to play at Pikeville, and we were going to have to leave at seven o'clock on a morning I had Marketing at nine. I said to Dr Spears, "I've got to leave the campus early on this particular day. Can I do my presentation in an earlier class or set it for a later date?"

"Chad, if you have a business meeting, you can't switch it. You'll have to be here to give your presentation."

I said okay. He was still doing his thing. But then I asked, "Can you at least allow me to go first that day?" He said yes.

When the day came the baseball team left for Pikeville, but my mother took the day off to pick me up after class and drive me over there. I delivered my presentation and did great on it. The class asked questions, as they always did. Then Dr Spears started asking questions, really stupid questions, dragging things out on purpose. Finally I put my foot down. I said, "Dr Spears, it's my time now. I've made my point. I'm finished. I'm leaving, and I'll see you in the next class." As I walked out I could hear him laughing all the way down the hall. He taught me something, and I got an A in the class.

My first labor assignment was janitor in the gym. I also served as Coach Ridder's teaching assistant for some classes. After two years I got a job in the Public Relations Department running the tour center. I loved it. I met some nice people and got to show off a nice college.

When I got out of college I asked myself, "Do I have any skills?" Thinking about my tour job, I realized that it's a skill to be able to communicate. I like to talk and I communicate well, so sales was a good career for me. I work for Sysco Foods, the largest food distributor in the world. My home office is in Louisville, and my territory includes Lexington, Nicholasville, Richmond, and Berea. I deal with restaurants, delis, school cafeterias, daycare centers, anywhere that serves food. I sell as much food and equipment as I can to each customer, help them with whatever they need. If someone opens a restaurant, once they've built the building and put up the wallpaper and the paint, I can sell them everything for that restaurant. It's work I enjoy.

These days I'm a softball fiend. I play a little basketball, and I can still shoot and score, but softball is my love now. In the summer I travel every weekend. I was fortunate enough this past year to travel to China to play softball for two weeks.

December 3, 1998

Robert Phillips   1986-90

I grew up with my grandparents in eastern Kentucky. We had a career fair at Belfry High School when I was a senior, and I believe John Cook was there to represent Berea College. I read Berea's literature and sent them a letter.

That summer I came to the campus for placement testing, and while I was there I introduced myself to Coach Wierwille and asked him about the basketball team. That was the only contact I had with him before I enrolled, and I initiated it.

I went to college strictly for academics. When I came to Berea I thought about going out for the team, but I hadn't decided for sure. Although I loved to play ball, my main focus was school.

Before the season started I played pickup ball with the varsity

Robert Phillips: "A good person through and through"

players every day between four and six-thirty. Steve Ridder, the assistant coach, saw that I could compete with those guys and hold my own. He sent a note to my post office box asking if I'd be interested in coming out for the varsity team. That note definitely changed my mind. When I had talked to Coach Wierwille he mentioned that he had a lot of good ballplayers coming back, so I didn't know if the team needed a player like me. Steve's note was encouraging, indicating that what I could offer would be welcome.

Steve Ridder was the type of coach who could motivate people to do almost anything. We would run through a wall for that man. I liked Coach Wierwille's traditional-style approach to the game. He took it very seriously. He drove and energized us to give everything we had on the floor. And he really cared about his players.

We didn't shoot the three much. We had a conservative game plan. We played solid D and tried to pound the ball inside. If there was nothing there we'd kick it back outside. The three was always a second option. That's the type of offense we ran.

At six-three I played mostly forward. I was a pretty good defender and a really good rebounder, leading the team in rebounding my last couple of years.

Jay Stenzel got hurt my freshman year, and that helped me gain some playing time. When Jay came back the next year our record improved quite a bit. Jay was a leader on the court, a go-to man, a defender, a great all-around great player. He led us to a solid season, but Transylvania was loaded that year and beat us at the end to keep us out of the national tournament.

Losing to Transylvania or Georgetown made me especially unhappy. Because they offered scholarships they tended to attract a different caliber of player than we would end up with. Whenever we could knock off a program like that, I enjoyed it. Beating Georgetown in my junior year was a big accomplishment for us. In my senior year we beat Transy at home by twenty-six points. We simply blew them out of the gym that night. That game stands out in my memory.

My junior year was the first year I actually started. Jay had graduated, but we had another good season. I attribute much of our success to the presence of Willie Hill, who was in his final year. Willie had a happy-go-lucky, fun-loving personality, but on the court he was very, very serious. We could count on him.

Willie was a tenacious defensive player. He earned respect as the best defender we had. I saw him shut down many great ballplayers. Whenever we played a team that had a thirty-point scorer, Willie guarded him. Willie was a natural leader who wouldn't allow any of us to slacken. He wasn't afraid to yell at us if that was what we needed.

Our guards didn't look to shoot much. Terry Tapley was a traditional sort of point guard who could get the ball up the court and distribute it. He was a dedicated team player. Antonio Woods brought us good ballhandling and defense.

A lot of our scoring came from Mike Sams, who was an offensive machine during my junior and senior years. He could put the ball in the hole. He hated to lose, loved to win, and would do anything it took to win. That was Mike Sams in a nutshell.

Chad Tate was another good shooter who loved to win. Chad was a dominating-type player and a good personality on the team. Dester Terry was a go-to guy, a very solid ballplayer. He shot the ball and handled it well, and he showed a lot of intelligence.

Bob Cowie joined us that year. As a high school player he had a reputation as one of the best rebounders in the state. Bob came in with a good attitude and did a fine job for us. He went to the boards strong.

Our record wasn't as good when I was a senior. The main factor was the loss of Willie Hill, who had been the leader on the team ever since Jay Stenzel left. When I look back on it I ask myself how we could have lost so many games with all the seniors we had. Mike and Chad and Dester and I were all good players, but perhaps we played too much as individuals. Willie hadn't done a lot of scoring, but the loss of his leadership made me realize how important one player can be to a team.

When I signed up for my first semester schedule, my first class began at eleven, with my last class finishing up at four o'clock. Basketball practice started at four. My labor assignment was in food service from six-thirty to nine-thirty Monday, Tuesday, and Wednesday. I did a little bit of everything. I helped make the doughnuts, filled the juice and milk machines, gathered up the dishes. My days were tiring, but they were manageable. A freshman doesn't normally get a lot of rest anyway.

I stayed in Berea the following summer and worked as a waiter at Boone Tavern. The next year I became a janitor-supervisor in the Alumni Building. In my senior year I also worked in Accounts Payable.

I was happy to have the opportunity to play an intercollegiate sport, but at Berea academics came first. Although I took school and studying seriously, I could have done better in the classroom as a freshman and sophomore. In my last two years I really buckled down.

I majored in business administration. Most of my economics classes were taught by Cliff Sowell, a very intelligent man and a great source of information. Phil Spears gave us plenty of real-world perspective. He didn't mind putting us on the spot, because that's how the real world works.

When I graduated I already had a job with the Kroger Corporation. Vance Blade, a former Berea College basketball player, was the man who hired me. I started in Lexington as a manager trainee, but I worked at Kroger just three months.

I had interviewed with State Farm Insurance while I was still in school, but I hadn't heard back from them. Then in August they called me for another interview and offered me a position. I was more interested in insurance than I was in retail, so I joined State Farm as a claim representative trainee.

Now I'm a national catastrophe claims superintendent. I've been doing this job for a year. I love it. It's the best job I've had with the company so far. I have a team of nine claim representatives who work for me.

When you see any type of big weather activity, hail, tornado, flood, or whatever, you can bet it's affecting State Farm. My disaster team travels to each site to get the claims process started. I review their work and help organize everything. Last year I worked in Monroe, Louisiana; Louisville, Kentucky; Minneapolis, Minnesota; Greensboro, North Carolina; and Nashville, Gray, Lawrenceburg, and Springfield, Tennessee. That's a lot of traveling.

Next I'd like to become a divisional superintendent. That would mean managing management people. The person who manages me now is a divisional superintendent. If I rise to his level I'll have eight to ten management people under me. That's getting into mid- to upper-level management for claims.

Working through school helped me a lot. I see, and I hire, many people who graduate from college without ever having held down a job. Mom and Dad or their grandparents have provided everything for them. Berea taught me a lot about independence. When I graduated I was ready to hit the ground running.

October 21, 1998

The Nineties

The story of Berea College basketball in the 1990s was one of decline and resurgence. Between 1989-90 and 1993-94 the Mountaineers won just sixty games and lost sixty-nine, winning more than they lost only once, in 1991-92. Though none of these five teams was a bad one, the program now seemed to be embedded firmly in the middle of the pack.

On November 1, 1994, Coach Roland Wierwille was laid low by a stroke that left him partially paralyzed and unable to speak. While Wierwille battled mightily to recover his health, Assistant Coach Craig Jefferson assumed control of the team and struggled through a 10-15 season. Months of excruciating effort by Wierwille, physical therapist Ernestine Brashear, and speech therapist Ivy Shelton enabled the Berea coach to walk and talk again, and in the spring of 1995 he felt well enough to announce that he would guide the Mountaineers once more that fall.

Coach Wierwille's dramatic return coincided with the long-awaited opening of the Seabury Center, the dazzling multipurpose expansion of the venerable Seabury Gymnasium. Charles Ward Seabury II, a Berea College trustee and the grandson of the original benefactor to whom the college owed its wonderful old gym, helped dedicate the facility with several other members of the Seabury family, which has remained steadfast in its commitment to the College. The Seabury Center, the product of a quarter century of planning and fund raising, immediately became the showcase for an exciting and vastly improved edition of the basketball Mountaineers.

Spurred by the inspired play of senior guards Daniel Brown, Tony Goatley, and Otis Diuguid, the team, which had beaten Campbellsville in overtime in the last game played at Old Seabury in February 1995, inaugurated the 1995-96 season in their new facility by defeating Indiana University-Southeast. To that triumph they added seventeen more victories, some of them spectacular, before checkmating IU-Southeast again in the NAIA district playoffs to earn a trip to the national tournament for the first time in a decade. The 1996 NAIA Division II tournament was held in Nampa, Idaho, farther from their central Kentucky stronghold than any Mountaineer team had ever traveled. In the opening round Berea lost to Tabor College by a single point.

In 1992 the NAIA had split into two divisions, with each conducting its own postseason tournament. The chief distinction between the two divisions was the maximum number of athletic scholarships permitted in each by the NAIA. Berea College, as it always had, chose not to give any athletic grants-in-aid, and school officials decided that the basketball Mountaineers would compete among the schools most resembling Berea, those in Division II, the less professional of the two divisions.

This decision led inevitably to the dissolution of certain longstanding rivalries, most prominently between Berea and Georgetown College. There was some grumbling about this, but Berea's stance was the right one.

The Mountaineers had once played the University of Kentucky Wildcats, but no one was advocating that this custom be revived. By the 1990s many of the smaller Kentucky colleges had abandoned even the pretense of amateurism, and it was appropriate for Berea to seek fairer competition. By mid-decade the Berea basketball team was no longer a part of the KIAC.

Berea chose not to schedule the Georgetowns, but shortly after the 1997-98 season began the team dispelled any doubts about its skill and character in convincing fashion by upending its NCAA Division I neighbor Eastern Kentucky University on the Colonels' home floor, 94-88. Eastern may have expected little more than a glorified scrimmage, but the Mountaineers gave them more than they could handle, and the Colonels' best efforts could not vanquish them. The Eastern game was a one-off scheduling anomaly, and no rematch was contemplated. But Berea's startling upset had a magical, stop-the-presses quality unseen in Kentucky since another Wierwille team shocked Campbellsville 8-7 in the 1980 KIAC tournament.

The 1997-98 season, too, ended in a trip to Nampa. Berea qualified by pulling off another spectacular upset, over the nationally ranked Philadelphia College of Pharmacy in the district finals. A season-ending injury to senior guard and scoring leader Donnie Frazier in the Philadelphia Pharmacy game proved too much for the Mountaineers to overcome, however, and once again the team fell in the opening round of the national tournament, by four points to Whitworth College.

The 1998-99 Mountaineers finally fulfilled Coach Roland Wierwille's dream of not just getting to the national tournament, but advancing. The Mountaineers won twelve of their last thirteen games down the stretch and flew to Idaho determined to make some noise. This they did, posting double-digit victories over Briar Cliff, Milligan, and Viterbo to advance to the Final Four. Underrated and ignored all season, the team had now won twenty-four games, a new school record, and the possibility of a national championship no longer seemed far-fetched. The Final Four showdown matched Berea against Cornerstone College of Grand Rapids, Michigan, the top-ranked team in the nation going into the tournament. Berea battled Cornerstone to a standstill for most of the game before the Michiganders pulled away in the final minutes. Cornerstone won the national title a day later.

No Berea College team had ever accomplished more than this one. Amid all the accolades and awards, none was more emotional, or more deserved, than the installation, in a moving pre-tournament ceremony, of strategist, father figure, disciplinarian, teacher, and coach Roland R. Wierwille in the NAIA Hall of Fame.

Mike Berheide has taught political science at Berea since 1981. He also serves as the basketball Mountaineers' public address announcer. "We stress the development of the complete student at Berea," Berheide says. "We believe that physical activity like athletics helps balance out the brainwork."

When we were going through the process of re-accreditation by the Southern Association of Colleges and Schools a few years ago, I co-chaired the self-study team. One of the first things we noticed was that SACS treated athletics as something totally apart from the academic side, an entirely separate section of their criteria. Our response was to petition SACS to allow us to study and report our findings about athletics directly under the academics section, in recognition of our belief in the old "mens sana in corpore sano" approach to the matter. They were at first unwilling to take such an unusual step, but we were eventually able to convince them that we were serious, and they allowed it.

To me the very fact that the standard way of viewing an institution of higher learning these days assumes such a separation speaks volumes about the way things have changed, and not for the better. But it also points out very clearly the unique place athletics has on Berea's campus.

Berea College has attempted to foster "a strong mind in a healthy body" for generations. Although none of the men whose voices speak to us in these pages won national headlines for their feats of athleticism, they were, and are, exemplars of the Berea ideal. They pass now into legend.

Antonio Woods   1987-91

I grew up in Lockland, Ohio, right outside of Cincinnati. In high school I competed in football, basketball, baseball, tennis, and track.

A man named Layne Cheesman told my basketball coach about Berea College. I visited Berea in the spring. Coach Wierwille asked me to give him a call when I decided where I was going to enroll. I didn't call him back, and I let Berea go out of my mind. I ended up going to Central State University in Ohio on an academic scholarship. Later I learned that the Central State coach arranged that scholarship so they'd have more basketball players there.

Antonio Woods: *"A leader and a motivator"*

I didn't much like Central State and didn't play ball there. I told my high school coach that I was looking for somewhere to transfer to, and he contacted Coach Wierwille again. Coach Wierwille gave me a call. He said that if I was serious about coming to Berea, I should get down there as soon as possible. I sent in all the paperwork, and during Christmas break I got a call from John Cook saying I'd been accepted. Then I enrolled at Berea for the short term.

I had a hard time adjusting to Berea. They had me out at Blue Ridge dorm, the farthest from the campus. I walked out of there at six o'clock one morning when the sun was rising, and there was nothing to be seen. I felt homesick. That night I called my mom and said, "Can you send me an application to the University of Cincinnati?"

"What do you want to go to UC for?"

"I want to transfer back home."

I hadn't made many friends. The people at Berea were friendly, but I wasn't used to that. I came from a rough city neighborhood where it wasn't unusual to fight in a minute. Friendly people made me suspicious. There weren't many blacks at Blue Ridge. The first black I met walked right in my door and sat on my roommate's bed. He said to me in a country accent, "Coach told me to come in here and talk to you." I wasn't expecting a black guy to talk like that. He was Robert Phillips from Belfry, Kentucky, and he was trying to be friendly and helpful. I thought everybody talked funny compared to me. I thought, "I can't stay down here!"

When I started meeting more people, however, I got to like Berea and wanted to stay. But things didn't go smoothly. I got off on the wrong foot with Coach. I overslept the basketball meeting for the year coming up. I happened to have Coach for a physical education class, and I overslept the final exam. He called me into his office. I remember his words vividly.

"You've been a big disappointment ever since I met you," he said. "I asked you to let me know whether you were coming to Berea or not, and you didn't do that. I asked you to attend the basketball meeting, and you didn't do that. Then you overslept my final exam. What kind of kid are you?"

I said, "Coach, I apologize."

He looked at me and said, "Do you have problems getting sleep?" He was being funny then. He could see that I was terrified, so he eased down a bit.

During preseason conditioning my mom was having some problems back home that I wanted to help her with. I thought, "I can't go to Coach about this, because he already thinks I'm a disappointment." So without talking to Coach or anybody else, I left school. I spent a week at home, taking care of some things for my mom. No one at Berea knew why I'd left. When things straightened out at home, my mom said, "Don't worry about me. Just go back to school."

I returned to Berea. Soon after I got there I went into the gym and watched them conditioning. Then I went to Willie Hill and said, "Willie, I really want to play basketball."

He said, "Go talk to Coach."

"I don't think he'll let me back on the team."

"Just go talk to him."

So I went in to talk to Coach and told him how much I wanted to play ball. He called Coach Steve Ridder in and said, "Tell Coach Ridder what you just told me." I apologized for all the heartaches I caused them.

Coach Wierwille said, "We're not going to give you a decision today. I'll talk to Coach Ridder, and then we'll decide whether we'll have you back."

The next day I went back to his office. He said, "What are you willing to do to be a part of this team?"

"Coach, whatever it takes."

"You've missed ten days of conditioning. Are you willing to make those days up?"

"Yes."

"Well, not only will you have to make those days up, but you'll still have to participate in the regularly scheduled activities."

So I ended up going to two practices a day. I did conditioning between classes. I didn't dare show that I was tired, either. It was hard, but before long I was in the best shape I was ever in, and they let me back on the team.

Baseball and football were my best sports in high school, but I loved the

game of basketball. I was too little to play college football. I was still growing when I went to college, and I topped out at five-eleven and a half, just
under six feet. As a basketball player my greatest asset was quickness on
the defensive end, although I became more offensive-minded in college.

I accepted being a role player in my first year. I played some quality varsity minutes, but as the year went on my playing time diminished. My
performance was erratic because I tried to do too much.

Transylvania had a senior named Jeff Blandon who was an NAIA All-
American. I played pretty good defense on him in our first two games, and
then we met them again in the district playoffs. The game was televised in
Lexington, Richmond, and Berea. We put two guards on Blandon and
they had trouble with him, so I thought I'd be going in pretty soon. But I
never got into the game, and we lost.

I was so upset after that game that I didn't want to play on the team any
more. I sat down with Coach Wierwille briefly, but I spoke at greater length
with Coach Ridder, as I usually did. I told Coach Ridder I wasn't going to
play next season because I hadn't played a minute in the Transylvania
game. Coach Ridder gave me a reality check. He said, "Maybe it wasn't
Coach Wierwille's decision. Maybe he wanted to put you in the game, but
I told him you were too inconsistent." What a wake-up call that was!

I'd played sports all my life. Now I was a city boy going to college in the
country, and I couldn't see myself just going to school and not doing anything extracurricular. Intramural competition wasn't enough for me. I
knew I was capable of playing varsity basketball, but was that something
I really wanted? I talked to my mom and my brother, who was in the Army
stationed in Germany. They said, "You always dreamed about playing college basketball. Is it still important to you?"

My great-uncle was a preacher who lived in Ann Arbor, Michigan. That
summer I went up to visit him, and I got to go onto the University of Michigan campus and play ball with Glen Rice, Rumeal Robinson, Gary Grant,
and guys like that. Playing with them made me realize how much I loved
basketball. I decided to work on my game and go back to Berea.

The goal I set for myself was more than just being a part of the team. I
was determined to start. When outdoor conditioning started I told the
captain, Willie Hill, of my intention to start. He laughed at me, but I said,
"Willie, I'm telling you now, I'm going to start this year."

I knew when we started scrimmaging it wasn't going to be easy. I had
a lot of work ahead of me. Then Robbie Taylor got hurt, unfortunately for
him, and Coach Wierwille and Coach Ridder ended up going to a three
guard rotation, starting Willie, Terry Tapley, and me. After one scrimmage
game I messed up my left ankle. That scared me. I was out of practice for
about two weeks, doing nothing but going to Lexington for therapy.
Although I didn't get down on myself, I was sure I'd lost my chance to start.
But once the ankle healed I impressed both coaches enough that they went
back to the same rotation.

We had a lot of good players that year, and everyone knew their role.
Willie Hill was the best all-around player in the league. Dester Terry was
a scorer who played excellent defense. Mike Sams was a good scorer. But

it didn't matter who shot the ball. Whoever took the shot, we knew some-body was going to get back on defense. Our good record was a team effort.

Our main rivals were Georgetown and Cumberland. The Georgetown players used to come to Richmond, where the Eastern guys and some of the Berea guys hung out. They talked a lot of junk about what they would do. Georgetown got the transfers from Division I programs, and Cumber-land got the junior college transfers. We always wanted to beat those schools because we were a nonscholarship program.

I'll never forget my first game at Cumberland. When the announcer introduced Jay Stenzel and all the Berea players, the fans held newspapers up to show they weren't interested in anyone who played for Berea. That was funny, but it was also rude, and from then on I had a strong desire to beat Cumberland.

My sophomore season was Willie's senior season. Willie and I talked a lot because he was from Cincinnati like I was. Cumberland beat us twice that year, and in four years Willie had never beaten them. Then Cumber-land was our opponent in the district finals. If we could defeat them, we'd go to the national tournament.

We had plenty of incentive to win, but we especially wanted it for Willie. It was a heated game. Cumberland was the best defensive team I ever played against. They full-court pressured us throughout the whole game. We lost, but we could have won if we'd made a few more of our free throws and avoided a couple of costly mistakes.

We missed Willie the next year. Everybody stepped his game up, but the team didn't do well. A lot of us weren't willing to sacrifice our personal games to win as a team.

By that time I was the starting point guard. I was the primary ballhan-dler. Perhaps I should have become more of a scorer instead of simply play-ing the point guard role. There were times when I'd get the ball to the big men down low, and they'd find themselves triple-teamed and frustrated. Instead of passing the ball back out they'd shoot and miss, or argue with one another. There was a lot of jealousy.

Dester Terry was a hell of a player. He played well on both ends. His first step was incredible. But some of our players wouldn't acknowledge Dester. They'd shoot the ball as soon as they got it. Many times I could have taken an open shot, but Coach Wierwille stressed getting it into the big men who were working underneath for us. Unfortunately, the area underneath the basket was like a vacuum that season. The ball went in, but it never came back out.

When Coach Ridder left, we lost a big motivator. Some of the players stopped working as hard as they normally did. During practice Coach Wierwille liked to walk around on the second level so he could watch from different angles. Anything he might miss while he was walking up the steps, Coach Ridder saw from his position on the court and blew the whis-tle. After Coach Ridder left Coach Wierwille worked hard and made sure that we stayed in line, but he still needed somebody like Coach Ridder to help motivate the team.

As my senior year began, we still hadn't beaten Cumberland. I told the guys my story just like Willie Hill had told me his. Cumberland had a player named Elnardo Givens who had transferred there from the University of Cincinnati. Elnardo was from Lexington, and he was a good friend of my roommate at Berea. Elnardo and I had a rivalry going. We'd say, "We're going to do this to you, we're going to do that to you."

Cumberland beat us on their floor, and a month later we played them at Berea. They used a four-guard rotation on me. One of those guards was Tony Christian, a transfer from Eastern Kentucky University. Every time I went down the court they had a different Division I transfer on me. I couldn't get a break.

With three seconds left on the clock, we trailed by three points. I said to the team, "I'm going to make a hard cut. Throw the ball to me, and I'll take it all the way up the court and see what's there." I got the ball and took off. I stopped behind the three-point line, Cumberland threw a trap, and I stepped out of the trap and threw the ball up. It felt good when I released it and went all the way in. That sent the game into overtime. The crowd was going wild. The players were going wild. I was going wild. I told them, "We're going to win this game!"

We took command in overtime and beat them. Afterwards I got a chance to talk to Willie and say, "Willie, we beat Cumberland." That was fun.

My closest friend on the team was Lawrence Chappell. Lawrence was put together real well physically, and he was hard-working. He could shoot, but he wasn't a good dribbler, so he was mainly a reserve player. When Lawrence sat on the bench he was in the game, observing what was going on. If somebody's game wasn't on, he'd never say anything negative. He'd make helpful suggestions. And if a person was in trouble, Lawrence was a good guy to talk to. He'd always sit down and listen.

That's what stood out about Coach Wierwille, too: a caring attitude and a willingness to listen. His main concern wasn't basketball, but how we were doing as people. When he asked us what was going on in our lives, he wasn't asking just to ask. He was truly interested.

Many coaches only listen to their assistants. Coach Wierwille was willing to listen to his players. Willie Hill or Jay Stenzel might say, "Coach, they're overplaying us on the top side. Maybe we can cut backdoor on them." Coach didn't say, "Well, we'll think about that." He said, "Let's try that one time down the court and go from there." He had been coaching for a long time, but he was willing to listen. I'd never had a coach who did that.

Speaking of Jay, I'll always remember the game in which he broke the all-time Berea College record for points scored. Jay had superior talent, but he wasn't a selfish player crying for the ball and refusing to play defense. If Jay didn't get the ball, he didn't pout, he didn't frown, he didn't shout. He ran back full speed as if he'd just scored two points, and then he concentrated on defending. It was very exciting for me, a freshman, to be part of the team when a guy of that caliber broke the school scoring record.

I majored in physical education and recreation, with a health minor. I knew that I wanted to work with kids after I graduated. When I was growing up I didn't have an older role model to work with me. It was just my mom, me, and my brother, who's only eighteen months older than I am.

The Berea professors were like Coach Wierwille. They cared. They didn't want us to get lost in the system. They wanted us to make our grades and succeed. That's something you don't see at the big universities, the professors taking care of every individual at the College.

My adviser, Mary Lou Pross, made sure I did what I needed to graduate. She was willing to sit down and talk to me, to listen and understand what I was going through. She was never biased about anything. She was a big help. I didn't have any classes with Betty Olinger, who taught in the Nursing Department, but she was another person who was always there to talk to me.

Oddly enough, I made my best grades during the basketball season. That's because I was so focused. Coach told us to bring our books with us on bus trips to away games, and we did. If one of us had a major paper due and needed to miss a practice or even a game, if that's what it took to get that paper done, Coach didn't take an attitude. That rarely happened, but the policy was always there.

When I came to Berea and applied for my labor assignment, I wrote on the application that I wanted to work in an activity center. I was thinking about the tote box in the gym, but they put me in the Alumni Building, where the Campus Activities Board is located. I started out as a janitor, working in the school year and during the summers. When Gus Gerassimides, my supervisor, saw that I knew how to do everything, he made me head janitor.

In my junior and senior years I worked as a certified lifeguard and instructor. I became head lifeguard at Seabury. I loved that job. I got to teach the swim classes to the little kids. They were so excited that Antonio Woods, the Berea College basketball player, was teaching them how to swim!

After I graduated I took a job as a recreational programmer in Coral Springs, Florida. I went around to the various recreational sites in the city, swimming pools, tennis courts, and so on, planning activities. I didn't stay down there long. The prejudice was obvious. I could see it wherever I went. After four years at Berea I wasn't used to that, because at Berea everybody got along regardless of color. So I came back home. Now I'm employed by the Pendleton County, Kentucky, Juvenile Court, working with youth in a detention setting.

In our holding facility we counsel young people who have been accused of a crime. I'm a supervisor now with a staff under me. We set up programs and activities for these kids and encourage them to change their lives. We can't help all of them, of course. I've had the experience of going out to eat and running into a kid who was a knucklehead when he was in detention, always talking about how he didn't care and wouldn't change and wouldn't get a job but would sell drugs to make his money. Now he greets me, "Hey, Mr Woods, how are you doing?" He's off the streets, has a job, and is earning his money in a legitimate way. That kind of thing makes me proud. They make all kinds of threats, "I'm going to see you when I get out, and then I'll do this and that." But when I do see them, they speak to me respectfully. It's amazing.

I'm thinking about moving into the adult probation field, perhaps at the federal level. That would free up more of my time for community service. I can see myself coaching, starting off with the Little League and working my way up to high school and maybe even college someday. Right now I just want to help as many youth as I can. If nobody's there to help them now, we might not have any colleges in the future.

I'm not coaching now, just helping out. I can't be a head coach because of the hours I work. We're a twenty-four-hour facility, and when someone on my staff calls in sick, I have to make sure it's covered. Sometimes I'm the one who has to cover. I don't want to donate my time to young athletes if I'm never there. I turned down three or four high school assistant coaching jobs, mainly because of my schedule. But one day I'm going to be coaching somewhere.

This fall I plan to start classes at UC to get a teaching certificate and a master's degree in education. I never wanted to teach, but the more I talk to the kids in my facility, the more I disagree with the way these kids are handled today. When a kid is struggling, they separate him and just teach the others. That kid needs help too, but instead of talking to him the teacher calls the principal's office, the principal calls the police, and the police bring him to detention. When I was in school, if a kid went to the principal's office, the principal talked to the parents. Now it's straight to detention.

Growing up I had just one parent, my mom. A lot of the people around me were negative, smoking, drinking, and everything else. That wasn't my thing. I made every effort to try to better myself. I made straight A's in school, but people didn't look at my grades. They talked about this football star and that basketball star. Sometimes we'd have no electricity at home, so I'd have to go to the library at night to study. But I was a good athlete, too, and I used sports to help me get into college.

Some people consider a person successful if he lives in a certain kind of home or makes a certain sum of money a year. Success to me is, I played varsity basketball at Berea College, I earned my degree, and I've got a job I like. If you're making millions of dollars that's fine and dandy, but you're not going to be happy unless you do something you enjoy. I enjoy what I'm doing and I'm making decent money, so I consider myself successful.

I've had quite a few job offers. Employers are impressed by the Berea College degree. It certainly means a lot to me. I see many kids who are in the same situation that I was in when I was growing up, but I don't always recommend them to Berea College. I was respectful and knew how to talk to people. Kids with a bad attitude would mess up the Berea program, and I don't want anybody like that down there. I'd only recommend a person who is willing to work hard for the chance at a better life.

July 22, 1998

Shane Lakes   1988-92

Coaches never had to yell at me. I worked hard and tried to do what they said all the time. Coach Wierwille realized that. He would get on me, but he knew what I responded to and what I didn't, and he was very good at getting his point across to me. I got along well with him and respected him very much.

Coach Wierwille told it like it was, and that's one of the things I liked about him. He didn't pull punches. After my freshman season he called me

Shane Lakes: "He got real physical with you"

into his office and said, "Shane, I don't know if you'll be able to play here. You may not be good enough. You're a good kid, and I like you. But I don't know if you'll be a player." He was straightforward. I didn't know if I'd be able to play, either, but what he told me inspired me to work harder.

I came to Berea from Madison Central High School in Richmond, Kentucky, not far away. Berea had a reputation as an excellent academic school, and its close proximity meant my family would be able to come to see me play, so that's where I enrolled.

I'm six-four and a half, but I was by no means a great athlete. Coach Wierwille's words didn't surprise me because I knew I was way behind. I was a late developer in high school. I was still playing on the JV team as a junior. In my senior year, though, I started on the varsity. We had a very good team that went to the Final Four of the state tournament. I thought, "Shoot, this isn't bad at all!" But I had only that one year of playing on the high school varsity level before I came to college.

In high school you may have one or two decent players on the court. In college all five of them can play. In high school you don't have to play defense, but in college I discovered very quickly that you can't loaf on defense. Coming out of high school I was very suspect defensively, and I wasn't very strong. I played pickup games with the Berea College team before my freshman season. Whenever I got a defensive rebound they would take it away from me before I could get it to the guard. Only when I learned to protect the ball did I begin to believe that I could play college basketball. I never became a great defensive player, but I improved considerably.

I played the power forward position. When I came to Berea I wasn't much of a scorer, but Coach Steve Ridder worked with me every day to improve my shot and my moves and my footwork. I got to the free throw line often, and fortunately I was a pretty good free throw shooter.

I enrolled at Berea in the fall of 1987. I did not dress varsity that season. The varsity had an excellent team led by all-American Jay Stenzel. We had thirteen returning varsity players, six freshmen, and a transfer, Antonio Woods. Antonio dressed varsity, but the six freshman played only on the JV team. We played a lot of junior colleges.

The summer after my freshman year I lifted weights pretty heavy and played basketball every day for about three hours. Gradually I became a better scorer. I'd been a garbage man in high school and remained one in college, but I learned how to put the ball in the basket more frequently. I didn't quit, and eventually my game got better.

The varsity had another very good year when I was a sophomore. Only two of the six freshmen returned, myself and Lawrence Chappell. Antonio, who was classified as a sophomore, also returned. All three of us sophomores played varsity minutes. Lawrence and I both played on the JV team and played sparingly on the varsity. If there was an injury or one of the upperclassmen wasn't playing up to par, Coach put me in there. In a few games I played twenty minutes. Although my high game that year was just seven points, I came a long way, and I think I convinced Coach that I had something to contribute.

I remember a funny incident that occurred during halftime of one of our games at Seabury that year. Every halftime Coach Wierwille came into the locker room, pulled the door shut that went to the showers, and turned the fan off so everybody could hear him. Then he sat down on a long bench at one end of the room while the assistant coach went to the board with a marker.

We were playing Georgetown that night. They were tough, the game was tense, and Coach was not in a good mood. As always he came in, pulled the door shut, turned the fan off, and sat down on the end of the bench. Coach Wierwille is a large man, and that night he flopped down on the very end of the bench, which was not nailed down. As soon as he did, the other end flew up into the air. Dester Terry grabbed the bench to stabilize it and keep Coach from hitting the floor. Coach never broke his sentence. He just kept on talking. All of us had to bury our heads in our towels. It was hilarious. Whatever he told us must have sunk in, because we won that game.

Before the next season started I was playing in a pickup game in Seabury. It was a very hot day, and the floor was damp, perhaps with condensation. Mike Sams threw a pass to me, I jumped to catch it, and I landed in the bench area, off the main playing floor. My left foot hit a wet spot. The foot went to the right, the knee to the left. I was in severe pain for about thirty seconds.

I went to see Dr Mary Lloyd Ireland about it. She said I had some cartilage damage and needed a scope. She thought I'd be out two weeks. When she got in there she saw that I had a partially torn anterior cruciate ligament, and she repaired it. When I woke up from surgery she told me I'd be on crutches for six weeks and wouldn't be able to play at all that season.

That was a blow, but Dr Ireland reassured me that I wouldn't have any problems coming back. I'd have to rehab heavily, but in a year I'd be able to play again. The injury occurred around September 20 of that year of 1989. I had surgery on October 4, the day they put Secretariat to sleep. I had a whole year to recover before the 1990-91 season began.

I never considered not playing again. I wanted to get back into it. The college experience wouldn't be the same for me if I didn't play basketball. I wanted to play as soon as possible after I got my knee fixed. That was the entire purpose of the surgery.

I had to wear a large brace with a big cover over it. It extended from about four inches above my ankle to halfway between my knee and my hip. It was uncomfortable. It was very light, but a pain to wear. I had to tug at it constantly to make sure it stayed up. There was a pad that went under the brace, and I had to apply tape every night to hold it on. It was a struggle, but I did it because I wanted to play.

In the long run the injury didn't hurt my game at all. I'd never been able to jump well, and I'd never been very fast. My game did not rely on leaping ability or speed. I needed strength at power forward, so while I rehabbed my knee in the weight room I lifted with other parts of my body and got much stronger. I'm a late summer child, so I was just seventeen when I enrolled at Berea. My redshirt year matured me physically and caught me up with guys my own age. There were a lot of juniors and seniors on the team in 1989-90, so I would have been eighth or ninth man on the totem pole. In 1990-91, though, I was a starter, contributing a lot of minutes. I was looked up to as one of the team leaders. In my final year I was elected captain.

I loved playing in Seabury Gym, where we had a huge homecourt advantage. It wasn't the nicest gym in the world, but Coach made sure it was always clean. He also liked to keep it very warm, and both players and spectators were soon in a sweat. I don't think that other teams liked to come in there to play. We beat a lot of teams at Seabury that we probably shouldn't have beat.

The court was not regulation width. Along the side we barely had room to stand between the three-point line and the out-of-bounds line. When it was very crowded the spectators were practically on the court. They could reach out and grab players as they ran by. We couldn't shoot out of the corners because we were hemmed in by the track that went around overhead. That was the best place for people to sit, because they could look over right on top of the court. We'd hear them yelling at us from above. Despite the fact that we couldn't shoot out of the corners, Seabury was an excellent shooter's gym because everything was so close.

The one shot I remember best in that building was the one Chris Haggard hit to beat Transylvania in 1991. Transy was tough. In those days

Daniel Swintosky was in his heyday. We were back and forth all night. With just three seconds to play the game was tied, and we had the ball. Jermaine Jackson took a shot from about seventeen feet out. Everybody went to the board, but the ball hit the rim pretty hard and nobody caught it underneath. It bounced way out to Chris, who happened to be standing out at the three-point line. He let it fly just before the buzzer went off. Bottom! That was a big win for us.

I had my best game at Seabury. I was a senior then, and our opponent was Lindsey Wilson College. I had thirty-three points and fourteen rebounds. I was eleven of thirteen from the field and eleven of twelve from the line. It was one of those nights when the ball seemed to bounce to me like I was a magnet. Everything I did went right. The guy I was playing against was six-seven or eight and a good athlete. He took a lot of head fakes. Everything fell into place for me. We won the game, but the way I felt, I didn't ever want to quit playing. When it was over I didn't want to leave the gym.

The best player I played with at Berea, although we weren't on the varsity together, was Jay Stenzel. 1987-88 was his senior year. He was coming off an injury. He had torn his Achilles tendon and sat out the previous season. He still had problems with it. He often talked to Coach Ridder about whether it would hold up for him. Luckily, it did. Jay could do it all. He could shoot, he was strong, and he could run like a racehorse. Jay was six-six and weighed about 215, but he could have played guard.

The closest friends I made among the players were Dennis Sargent and Dester Terry. Dennis was from Berea, and he and I knew each other from high school. Dennis was quiet on the court and didn't get frustrated. But you didn't want to make Dennis mad, because he was very competitive and wouldn't let you get the best of him. Dester was the same way. That's why I admired those guys so much. They didn't show much emotion on the court, but they had an inner fire.

Dester was friendly, not a bit arrogant. He never met a stranger. Anybody could talk to him. If you liked sports, if you didn't like sports, Dester was good to everybody. He was an excellent player and a super person.

We had several jokesters. Robbie Taylor was a lot of fun. Every two days we got our towels and practice uniforms washed at the laundry. They were returned to us in a big hamper-like laundry basket. One day Robbie, who was rather small, got into the basket, and a few of us covered him up. One by one the players came through the door, saying, as they always did, "What's Coach going to do to us today?" They were pretty startled when the basket started talking.

The funniest practical joke I remember didn't involve me. It was one that was pulled by Terry Tapley and Dester Terry, and the victim was Willie Hill. Willie does not know to this day what happened.

Terry and Dester were roommates in Danforth dormitory. The dorm has two towers, with the lobby in the middle. From the rooms above you can see down into the lobby. Willie was in the lobby one day watching television by himself, and he was visible to Terry and Dester from the window in their room.

Terry got on the phone and dialed the phone in the lobby. A guy walking through there picked it up. Terry said, "May I speak with Willie Hill, please?" The guy called Willie over. Dester was watching from the window above, and as soon as Willie got to the phone, he signaled Terry to hang up. Willie said hello, but there was no one there, so he put the phone down.

Dester watched Willie walk back to the TV and sit down. As soon as his tail hit the chair, Terry dialed the number again. The phone started ringing. Willie sat there watching TV and let it ring and ring and ring. Finally he got up and went over to the phone. As soon as he put his hand on it, Dester signaled and Terry hung up again. Willie said hello, heard no reply, and once again went back to the TV and sat down.

As soon as Willie was comfortable, Terry dialed again. Willie did a double take and looked over at the phone. He sat there for several minutes. Terry let it ring. Nobody else was in the lobby. Finally Willie got back up and walked over to the phone. The moment he put his hand on it, they hung it up again. This went on two or three times more. Each time Terry hung up an instant before Willie said hello. The last time Willie, after putting down the phone, did not go back to his seat but stood right beside the phone waiting for it to ring again. He stood there for about five minutes. Nothing happened. At last Willie turned around, walked back to his seat, and sat down. At that moment the phone rang again. That was enough for Willie. He got up and left the building. He still doesn't know who did that. I'm sure he thinks it was some unexplainable coincidence.

My first labor position was as custodian at Seabury Gym. After one semester I switched to the tote box, where people checked out basketballs and other sports equipment.

Sandy Bolster, who worked in the computer center, knew I was interested in computers, so when I was a sophomore she got me out of the gym and into the computer lab. I worked as a consultant, which meant that when students came into the lab to type papers and work on various things, I was there to help them if they needed it. I did that for a year and then became a student programmer for the College. I worked on projects for the Development Office. My boss was L.D. Montgomery.

I majored in physical education, but I got a teaching endorsement in computer science. I took my studies seriously after my first semester, when my GPA was a not-so-good 1.66. In high school I coasted my senior year, and I wasn't quite prepared for college. Coach Wierwille had a nice talk with me. He said, "We can't have this." After that I improved. I learned how to use my time, and I got most of my labor hours on Sundays.

After I graduated I was immediately hired at Madison Middle School in Richmond. Coach Wierwille helped me get that job. He knew I wanted to stay in the area. At that time the school was being remodeled. It was a high school that was reopened as a middle school. I was certified five-through-twelve in computer science and phys ed, so I was able to get a job there right off the bat. I teach computer science and coach boys' basketball. I'm also the assistant baseball coach at Madison Central High School.

I felt fortunate to be able to come back to the county where I grew up.

The principal at my school was my middle school principal when I was a kid. I'm working for him now. A lot of the teachers at my school are ones I had for class. I have my master's degree now, and I'm certified as a principal. Some day I'll probably apply for a principalship or a high school coaching job. I don't want to leave this area. I'm content here. I like Richmond and always have. It's the perfect size. It's not too big, not too small. It's the only place I've ever known, and I'll probably die here.

July 23, 1998

Bob Cowie

I live in North Carolina, far away from Berea, but if you mention the name Berea College around here, people recognize it. They say, "Is that the school where everybody has to work?" It's not like some other schools, you say the name and people don't know anything about it.

Bob Cowie: "He was relentless"

Steve Ridder was the assistant basketball coach at Berea when I played high school ball at Fort Thomas Highlands in northern Kentucky. He came to see me play a couple of times, and during my senior year I went down and visited Berea and met some of the players and Coach Wierwille. I decided Berea would be a good place for me to be. It was good academically and had a good basketball program.

When I played high school sports I looked up to my coaches, and when I thought about the influence they had on me, I decided that I wanted to be a teacher and coach, too. My high school basketball coach was Ken Shields, who is now the coach at Northern Kentucky University. I believe Coach Shields is the winningest coach in northern Kentucky basketball history, so he's obviously a very good coach. He was a personable man who would help you. He was easy to talk to, concerned with personal things.

Coach Wierwille was a lot more intense. He was an excellent motivator who could get people to play extremely hard for him. When I got to Berea I noticed how hard the upperclassmen played, both in practice and in games. Coach Wierwille pointed that out: "Look at what these upperclassmen are doing, that's how we do it here." Anybody who didn't catch onto that didn't make it very long at Berea.

Coach Wierwille wouldn't put up with things. If you weren't in school to get a good education, if you were interested in doing detrimental things off the floor, or if you didn't play hard, he didn't want any part of you. He wanted to do things the right way. Our gym, for instance, wasn't the nicest or most modern facility, but it was always the cleanest. We always made sure that other teams were treated properly.

Usually I got along well with Coach Wierwille, but we were both strong-willed people and had our disagreements at times. Nothing really serious, just two people wanting to win and wanting to do the best they could do, with different ideas about how to do that.

Fortunately most of our Saturday night games were home games, and my parents came to the majority of those games. I actually started my first varsity game, the Homecoming game with Carson-Newman in 1988. That was a big thrill. I started off and on throughout my freshman year.

I'm six-five. My game was rebounding, playing physical inside with a lot of intensity. The first couple of years I wasn't a scorer, but we had some other people who could do that. I worked to improve my offensive skills, and in my junior and senior years I scored a little bit more.

On defense we played some man, but in the first two years we were very good at a little three-two matchup zone which we played quite often. One of the keys to its success was Willie Hill. He played in the middle at the top of that zone and made everybody good. Willie was a great defensive player, but he was real good all-around, one of the few people at Berea to have 1000 points and 500 rebounds and 500 assists. He was a superb athlete, and after he graduated the matchup didn't work as well. We ran it and a two-three zone, but we were predominantly a man team when I was an upperclassman.

Mike Sams was the player who showed me around when I came to visit. After I enrolled we became good friends and hung out together a lot in my first two years at Berea. Mike could score both inside and outside, and he was a very good player in big games. If you needed a big point or something good to happen, he was always there in the middle of it.

Another fine player who was ahead of me in school was Dester Terry. He wasn't heralded, didn't get the publicity that some of the other ones did, but most of the players on the team realized how good Dester was. He was certainly one of the best in my eyes. Dester did the little things to make other people better.

We were a very good team in my freshman year. We made the playoffs, beat Alice Lloyd, and then went to Cumberland. At that time Cumberland had their older gym, not the nice new one they have now. They beat us, a real tough loss for us. Going into my sophomore year good things were expected of us, but for whatever reason, I'm not really sure, we just teetered around the .500 mark most of the year.

We simply lacked enough good athletes. When we went up against some of the better teams in the conference like Georgetown and Cumberland and Transylvania, we were less athletic than they were. Their basketball programs gave athletic scholarships, and we never seemed to have the athletes they had. They were spending forty or fifty thousand dollars on each player. Any time we could beat a team like that, it was extra special. Fortunately we were able to do that a few times while I was there.

Although our players were sometimes undersized and overmatched for what we were asked to do, we played very hard and managed to hold our own. Shane Lakes is a good example. Like me, he wasn't a great athlete, but he got more out of what he had than anyone else I played with, and he seemed to come out on top a lot.

I majored in history education. For two years I worked as a janitor at Dana dorm, and after that I worked in intramurals, organizing the different intramural sports, football and basketball and volleyball and softball.

After I graduated I coached the JV boys for a year at Richmond Model High School in Richmond, Kentucky. Then I moved to North Carolina, where my wife is from originally. I'm a teacher at Lincolnton High School , and I'll be the varsity basketball coach this year after serving for four years as JV coach and varsity assistant. I'm looking forward to it. There's a lot of satisfaction in taking someone early in the season and working with him and seeing him improve throughout the season, not only as a player but as a person.

September 2, 1998

Dennis Sargent   1989-93

I played basketball at Berea Community High School. In my senior year I went over to the College with a teammate of mine, Eric Pridemore, and had a conversation with Coach Wierwille. He told us he'd like us both to come. I was happy that he offered me the opportunity to play, because I wanted to stay close to home.

At Berea Community High School there were no walls in the classrooms, and it was always loud. At the College the classrooms were closed-in and quiet, and I actually had a harder time concentrating in a quiet, enclosed room than I'd had in high school, which I was used to. In college I found myself looking around, not paying attention. It took me awhile to adjust, but once I did, I got to like it. I lived at home. After basketball practice I normally went home and ate a home-cooked meal. Most of the other players lived in the dorms and had to go over to the food service.

Eric Pridemore played just one year. He found out that he

Dennis Sargent: "Outstanding athletic ability"

had sugar diabetes, and he started needing shots. After practice his body was physically worn down, and he couldn't study like he wanted to.

I'm six-five. When I graduated from high school I was real skinny. I picked up quite a bit of weight in college, a lot of it from lifting weights in the summer. I played swing man, forward, and, in my senior year, center. My exact role changed from game to game, depending on who we were playing. Coach Wierwille told me to take whatever the game gave me, whether it was getting a rebound or getting open for a shot or setting a pick. I was always supposed to make sure I got offensive and defensive rebounds. In my sophomore and junior years I did a bit of scoring. In my senior year we had some guards who needed to shoot the ball, so I was asked to set a lot more picks.

Coach Wierwille and I never had any bad disagreements. He got on me like any coach would if I was lackadaisical in practice. The only time he got

— 273 —

on me pretty hard was in a practice my sophomore year. To help us prepare for Campbellsville we tried to simulate their style, running the ball
real quick and shooting, threes especially. I came down on a fast break,
and nobody else on my team was back, so I shot a three. Coach jumped up
and stopped practice. He said, "This isn't the University of Kentucky!" I was
little aggravated, thinking, "Coach, all I did was what you said you wanted
us to do!" For practice purposes he wanted us to get into that running
and shooting mentality, but then again he didn't want me to learn that
style of play, because that wasn't what our team was going to play in the
game. I let it go. When Coach told you what to do, that's what you did.
There was no use trying to argue with him.

Coach Wierwille's best attribute is his desire to win. I don't mean that
winning was all he cared about. My point is that by pushing so hard to win
he made us all better players. Knowing how much he wanted to win, we
played harder. We wanted to earn his respect. The first time I met him,
shaking his hand, the first thing he said was, "Look in my eyes when you
talk to me." I'd never had anybody tell me that, and it woke me up. From
Coach Wierwille I learned the value of discipline. I learned to pay attention to what I did and how I presented myself. I learned the meaning of
respect and what to do to gain respect. Those lessons have helped me in
life more than anything.

Craig Jefferson was Coach Wierwille's assistant when I joined the team.
Coach Jefferson was the type of person who wanted everybody to be happy.
Nine of us came in at the same time, and out of that nine probably eight
were good ballplayers. Coach Jefferson did his best to give all of us equal
playing time. He was about my height, and he worked with the forwards
in practice, hacking and beating on us. We had a shooting drill where we
shot from one side and Coach Jefferson pushed us from the other side. In
those ways he helped us improve our skills. Coach Jefferson had an
upbeat personality and tried to motivate us. He was good to have around.

Willie Hill also helped out as an assistant coach. Willie was a senior in
college when I was a senior in high school, but I played some ball with him
during the summers. He was always trying to challenge you to do better. If
he had the ball, he could get it to you. In fact, if you didn't have your head
up and your eyes open, he'd hit you in the back of the head with it.

Dester Terry was a senior that year. He was an exceptionally nice person who was always there to help. When the team went on an overnight
trip Dester and I stayed together, senior and freshman. That's something
you don't usually see. He treated me like he'd known me all his life.

Dester was a bit taller than I was, and he had one of the quickest spin
moves I ever saw a big man make. One night at Pikeville he didn't miss a
shot the whole game. When he took the ball it was, that's two points, everybody, just write it down. If you played one-on-one with him in practice
and he scored, Coach would say, "Do it again." You had to keep going
until you stopped him, and that was very, very difficult. He had an outstanding all-around game.

Bob Cowie kept us entertained and loose, but he was a hard-nosed ballplayer. Bob didn't have the athletic jumping skills that some players had, but he would wear you out on the inside. He would rebound you to death. In practices Bob and Shane Lakes taught me a lot about playing on the inside. They were physically bigger than I was and knocked me down a couple of times. I learned from that.

Shane Lakes was the type of person who would beat you to death with his body. He got real physical with you. He muscled you to get rebounds. Like Bob, Shane lacked the jumping ability to grab rebounds by leaping over you, but he got as many rebounds as anybody else because he knew how to do the fundamental things and get position.

On offense Shane got you so off balance that you never knew what he was going to do. He head-faked you until you got tired of jumping, then shot over you. After Shane hurt his knee, he worked really hard to come back, and that was a big plus for us. We needed him on the inside.

When I think of Shane I remember a game we played at Pikeville. In the first half Pikeville was killing us, and Coach got so mad at us that he got up and went to the end of the bench and stared at the wall. He didn't want anything to do with us. Seeing that, we started pulling together as a team. We gave it our maximum effort and came back. With seconds left on the clock Shane hit a little turnaround jumper and won the game. When Shane turned the ball loose we were all holding our breath. It bounced around a little bit, and I remember looking at the basket and thinking, "Go in, go in!" When it fell through and the buzzer went off, it was a big victory for us even though it didn't mean anything in the standings.

Shane was laid-back and upbeat. He tried to keep us happy and smiling, and he always had some kind of joke to tell us. We hardly ever saw him mad. If Shane was mad, somebody had to have done something really bad to make him mad.

Antonio Woods was another upbeat person. He was a leader and a motivator who was always trying to get us to play harder. Antonio would do whatever it took to win. If the game was on the line, he wanted to take the shot. He wanted to take the risk.

Of the nine freshmen who began the 1989-90 season, Ron Kinmon and I were the only two left when we graduated. Ron became like a brother to me. If I ever needed anything, I could call up Ron and he'd get there as soon as he could. Our personalities were very similar. We both hated to lose in anything. Our senior season was not a good one, and that was hard on both of us beause we wanted to go out winners.

Ron was one of the most hard-nosed people I ever met. Offensively he worked hard, did whatever it took. If Ron had a shot, he'd take it, and he got in there and fought for rebounds. He was a good defensive player with quick hands. Coach often put him on one of the team's better players.

Ron and I are the same size, and we were the biggest players on our team when we were seniors. We couldn't match up with Georgetown or Transylvania at center. They had six-eight, six-nine, six-ten guys who weighed 250, and they could play. Physically we couldn't push that type of guy around. Ron and I did better as swing persons. We had some good guards, but the lack of a big man hurt us.

Jim Conway was the same size and type of player as Ron and myself. Jim was a hard worker. He was excellent at working on the inside, but we had a hard time keeping him inside because he wanted to go out and play on the floor. He had a decent jump shot and could shoot the three if he had to.

Ron and I hated to guard Travis Earlywine in practice because he was nonstop, running, running, running. He was on the go constantly. He never got tired. Travis had a good jump shot, and he would use his quickness to get in and out for rebounds. It was hard to keep a body on him because he moved around so much.

Chris Haggard was a player who kept getting better and better. When he came to Berea he had the skills but hadn't developed. He grew as a player as the years went along. If you left Chris open for a three-pointer, he would knock it down. He would beat you to death with threes if you let him get his feet set and shoot the ball. Chris shot the ball as well as anybody I ever played with.

In my junior year we took a trip to Charlotte, North Carolina, to play in a tournament. We had never traveled that far to play, and we had a great time. We stayed at the Marriott. My parents and Ron's grandparents came to watch us play, and Ron's grandfather treated us to a nice breakfast.

In one of the games I had a real good shooting night and played very well. Afterwards I was sitting in the locker room when the coach of the other team came in and congratulated me personally. I'd never had a coach do that, and it caught me off guard. I didn't know what to say except, "Thank you." After he left I just sat there. For the rest of the night it puzzled me. I asked myself what I should have said back to him. It made me feel good that somebody else, especially a coach, would recognize the good game I'd had.

That year was Tony Goatley's freshman year. Tony was one of the best players I'd seen in a long time. He had a direct impact on the team the first time he walked onto the floor. He could take the ball to the basket or pull up and jump, whatever it took to score, and for a guard he was a fantastic rebounder. He jumped over everybody, just went in there and took the ball away from them.

In my senior year we played our Homecoming game against Embry-Riddle. Their coach was Steve Ridder, the former Berea College player and assistant coach. I had heard many stories about him. We knew it was a big game for Coach Wierwille, and we played very well and beat Embry-Riddle. I think that victory made Coach Wierwille's season although it was just our first game. It certainly started us off on the right foot.

I graduated before the new gym was built. The old gym had its advantages. It was unique, and I liked playing there. We knew where we could shoot from on that court. If we got somebody in the corner we could double-team him, knowing he couldn't throw up over us because of the circular overhang on top. It was so close and compact in there that a crowd of 150 people seemed like 1500. It took hardly anything to get the crowd in an uproar. That atmosphere made me want to play. Later I played in some alumni games in the new gym. There were just as many spectators present, but they were so spread out that the place seemed almost empty. The new gym is a lot nicer, but I would rather play in the old gym, and I'm glad I did.

I had my first labor assignment in the gym. I was a janitor. At the end of my sophomore year I switched jobs and went to Accounts Payable. I was a business administration major, and I wanted to get into a business office so I could learn something. When anything was ordered by the College, we had to post the accounts to the computer and send the checks out.

The teacher who most influenced me was Phil Spears. I waited until my senior year to take his class, Organizational Behavior, which everybody called O.B. It was a class for business majors. We had to dress up in a suit and give presentations. At that time I had a hard time talking to people I didn't know. I had a couple of interviews which didn't go well because I was nervous and didn't present myself effectively. The class made a big difference. It certainly helped me in interviews. I went to work for the Bank of Mount Vernon the day after I graduated, and I had the fresh memory of that class to take with me into my new job.

Berea College opened that door for me. Cleo Routin, the CEO at the bank, called the College and asked them to send him some students to interview. He was looking for an employee he could count on, and he knew Berea College's reputation. So Ron Kinmon and I and Johnny Hopkins, who had played baseball at Berea, went to interview. Mr Routin intended to hire just one of us, but he offered both me and Ron a job. Ron decided that he wanted to go back to where he was from, so Mr Routin hired Johnny, and the two of us started on the same day.

As a senior in college I didn't know exactly what I wanted to do. I didn't know much about banking. My mother worked in a bank when I was very young, and my aunt is a loan officer at a bank. My aunt told me some things about the business, but I still wasn't sure what to expect when I was hired. Now I've seen just about every side of the business. I started out in accounting, then went into compliance, and finally made my way to lending. I'm a loan officer managing a loan production office. All we do here is make loans. We have to analyze potential borrowers' credit history and their ability to pay so the bank won't lose its money if we lend it to them. It's a big responsibility. The next stop for me will probably be commercial lending. Eventually I'd like to become a bank president or CEO.

If I had it to do over, I'd go to Berea College again even if I didn't have the chance to play basketball there. My Berea College education led directly to my present job, which I like very much. A Berea College degree is so well respected that I'd have no trouble getting a good job just about anywhere.

September 4, 1998

Ron Kinmon   1989-93

The opportunity to go to Berea College was the best thing that ever happened to me. I'm proud that I made it through four years of college. I was the first member of my family to earn a degree.

I came to Berea from Dry Ridge, Kentucky, a small community where my entire family history was known by everybody. At Berea I was able to establish my own identity. It was never easy. There were a lot of troubled

Ron Kinmon: "His play was a plus"

times, but the four years I spent at Berea were the best of my life. I learned what I had to do to be a successful student and a successful ballplayer. The people at Berea instilled traits in me that made me a better person.

I wasn't familiar with Berea College when I was growing up. I didn't think I'd have any opportunity to play college basketball. Playing for Grant County High School I hit a shot to beat Scott County, and after that I got a call from Coach Wierwille. Scott County's coach was a Berea graduate, Mutt Varney, and he'd recommended me. Coach Wierwille asked me if I would consider coming to Berea. I told him I'd get back to him. When I asked my guidance counselor for information about Berea College, she told me it was a superb academic institution. I called Coach Wierwille that night and told him I'd be honored to come.

The first time I met Coach he shook my hand, gripped it real tight, and told me to look him in the eye. That grabbed my attention immediately. I thought, "This man's not fooling around. He's going to teach me a lot." I was one of eleven freshmen players who enrolled in the fall of 1989, and I kept hearing that we were a wonderful recruiting class. But injuries and academics took their toll, and only Dennis Sargent and I played for four years. That gives you an idea of what both the College and Coach Wierwille demanded of a student-athlete.

I was six-four when I arrived and grew another inch that year. But Coach thought I was too skinny to play on the inside. He wanted me to work on my ballhandling and shooting so I could play out on the floor. I improved my game in those areas and played good defense. I moved inside later in my career.

I got into a few varsity games as a freshman. One of our players had a relative pass away before our game with Pikeville College early in January. We ran low on guards due to foul trouble, so I got to play the last four or five minutes of regulation plus the overtime. We won the game, and I played okay. I scored three points by hitting three out of six free throws. But a few days later I broke my right wrist in a junior varsity game. That put me out for the season until the last game of the year, which I played with a cast on my arm.

Willie Hill was still at the College then. His playing eligibility had expired, but he stayed an extra year and helped Coach Wierwille. I was very impressed with his leadership abilities. He knew how to inspire players to play hard. I also looked up to Dester Terry, who was a senior. I liked how he went about his business as a basketball player. He didn't believe in showboating or talking trash. He simply tried his best, quietly, to win basketball games and be a good person. I thought that if I could become just like Dester I'd be in good shape.

Dennis Sargent and I became friends. Walking onto the campus as a freshman that fall, I was very unsure of myself. Dennis was a town student who had taken a summer class and knew some of the players. Although he was more outgoing than I was at first, we hit it off well from the very beginning. Dennis had outstanding athletic ability. He was explosive on the court. He could run and jump and had a soft shooting touch.

In my freshman and sophomore years I often guarded outside players. Coach stressed quick feet, and as he taught me to use my quickness I was eventually able to get around guys who were bigger than I was. He believed strongly in denying the post, so I had to do a lot of fronting. He ran a simple three-out, two-in offense with two wing players and a point guard and two inside players. It was pass and pick across, with some options to enable us to get the ball to the inside players. He came to allow the players a lot of creativity to make their own decisions on offense.

I had an excellent relationship with Coach Wierwille. He tried, and succeeded, to make me a better basketball player, but I believe that his ultimate goal was to make me a man. He accomplished that, too.

Near of the end of my sophomore year I suffered a seizure on campus. Nothing like that had ever happened to me before. The previous evening I'd driven home to play softball with my dad's team, but I had an accident. I had planned to type a final exam paper before playing the game, but because I got home late I had to wait until I returned to Berea to do the typing. I didn't get to bed until five or six in the morning.

The seizure occurred as I was walking across campus, exhausted, from my dorm room to lunch. An ambulance came and took me to the hospital. I woke up with grass stains all over me, frightened when I realized where I was. Coach Wierwille was there by my side. He said, "Are you okay?"

"I'm fine."

His next question was, "Were you drinking?"

If I had been drinking, of course, that might have caused my seizure.

Coach was ready to tell me right then and there in the hospital that drinking was the wrong thing for me to be doing. Well, I had not been drinking, and the question offended me a little. I thought, "Is that all he cares about, that one of his players might be drinking?" Later I realized that Coach's question showed that he cared about me as an individual, not just as a basketball player.

I was in the hospital three or four days while they ran tests on me. They never did figure out what caused my seizure, so we assumed it was simply stress and exhaustion. Over the course of four years at Berea with Coach Wierwille I learned to understand him better. We had to earn his respect, but he was trying to teach us what to do to get respect.

Coach Wierwille would not accept defeat. He had a strong will to win and wanted us to play extremely hard at all times. There was no easy day. There was never a day when we could come in and coast. Every day was a challenge. We all had to work as hard as we could. Those who could accept that, and understand that Coach was not picking on them but simply challenging them to improve, had a good relationship with him.

Of all the players I played with at Berea, the closest in personality to Coach Wierwille was Bob Cowie. Bob didn't have a lot of athletic skills. He had bad ankles, and his knees weren't very good either. He couldn't jump at all. But he was relentless in his work ethic, often outmuscling bigger players. Bob hated to lose, and he was headstrong and emotional. He butted heads with Coach Wierwille sometimes because they were so much alike. But in the locker room Bob was able to lighten up.

I always took it as a challenge to try to beat Transylvania. I liked Coach Don Lane and thought he was a good man, but he once told my high school coach that I could not play at the college level. Because of that, beating Coach Lane's team became a bit of a personal vendetta on my part. We won just one of the games against them in which I played, when Chris Haggard hit a last-second heave out of a loose ball pileup when I was a sophomore.

Coach Wierwille got his 300th win when I was a junior. That was something special. I didn't have any remarkable individual accomplishments as a college player, and it felt good to be part of something historic.

We went to Charlotte, North Carolina, in January of that year to play in a tournament called the Marriott Classic. We stayed at the Marriott Hotel. We'd never been on a trip that nice. Transylvania was down there also, and they had plenty of money, so they flew their players down there. We traveled in our bus as we always did.

Going into the tournament we'd won all six of the games we'd played. We were having a pretty good season. We won our first game in Charlotte but lost our second, a game in which we didn't play well at all. Coach Wierwille got very upset and yelled at us. He said, "I try to be nice to you. You have the nicest bus here. I don't understand why you can't play any harder than that for me." As soon as he walked out of the locker room we remembered that we were the only team there that had taken a bus. Everyone else had flown!

My grandfather and grandmother came all the way down to North Carolina to watch us play. Our team was on a budget, and every morning we'd go out to McDonald's to eat breakfast while Transylvania ate in the Marriott breakfast area downstairs. Finally my grandfather offered to buy our team breakfast at the Marriott. Coach Wierwille refused. He didn't like to accept a gift.

Finally my grandfather said, "I'm buying breakfast here. There's no reason for these young boys to go to McDonald's. Transylvania is not going to rub that in our noses." Coach gave his consent, and we ate at the Marriott that morning.

For the next game Coach Wierwille changed the starting lineup. He put Chris Haggard in for Jermaine Jackson, Shane Lakes for Bob Cowie, and me for Dennis Sargent. That put me in a difficult spot. It looked as if I got to start because my grandfather had bought us breakfast! That was not the reason, of course, because Coach Wierwille was not the type of person to do anything like that. It was an odd coincidence. There was no animosity among my teammates, but they made fun of the three new starters and nicknamed us "The Breakfast Club." It was a standing joke for awhile.

We were basically a .500 team during my years at Berea. When we won we did it on hustle, determination, and hard work. We struggled with our inside game. Coach had trouble recruiting good big men, because anybody who was big and talented received scholarship offers from other colleges. When I came to Berea Coach had me playing guard or small forward, and by the time I was a senior I was playing center. We tried to compensate for our lack of height that year by shooting a lot more three-pointers.

Tony Goatley joined the team when I was a junior. He had all the athletic skills in the world. The next year Daniel Brown arrived, the best shooter I've ever been on the court with. At times I questioned their shot selection, and that caused some friction. As an upperclassman I felt I should provide some leadership, but I wasn't entirely secure in that role. I guess I felt a little threatened by Tony and Daniel because they were the wheels that made our engine go. Without them we probably wouldn't have won many games as we did.

Sometimes I didn't feel that every member of the team was willing to go to war for each other, and that was disappointing. We weren't a perfectly knit group who were always together. We didn't even sit together at food service. In my junior year some of the basketball players got into a food fight over there. One of the players tossed a pea at somebody sitting at another table, and it escalated from there. It wasn't a major battle, but it was enough to get noticed, and somebody brought the incident to Coach Wierwille's attention.

The team paid a price. We had to donate some labor to food service and do some extra running in practice. Coach called me in and wanted to know what happened. When some of the guys said they weren't part of it, I stood up and took responsibility for their actions and accepted my punishment. That was part of learning to be a man. I felt closer to Coach Wierwille then, because he thought enough of me to call me in.

One of the people honored with Dennis and me on senior night was a cheerleader named Del Burgess. Del was a roommate of mine for awhile. I had a wonderful relationship with him. Del was an African-American and I was a guy from a small country community that had no African-Americans in it, so I didn't know what to expect at first. But our personalities clicked immediately. Del was the nicest person I ever met.

He was also very instrumental in the dramatic improvement in our cheerleading over the course of the four years. When I arrived the cheerleaders were almost a mockery. People made fun of them. Del was very athletic, and he was also aggressive in trying to get things done. He worked hard to develop the cheerleading abilities of the squad, and largely through his efforts they became a very effective group of individuals.

It amazed me to hear stories of people flunking out of college. Anyone who puts effort into his course work ought to be capable of passing his classes. As a student-athlete I sometimes found myself stretched a bit thin, but I could always find time to get my work finished. Getting to play a varsity sport was such a great opporunity for me that I refused to allow myself to mess up.

I majored in business administration with an emphasis in accounting. A couple of my business teachers were particulary outstanding. Ed McCormack was a country person who never tried to be something that he wasn't. He was a down-to-earth teacher who allowed us to see the personal side of him. I liked his openness with his students. Phil Spears, on the other hand, had an intimidating manner. I waited until the last semester of my senior year to take his Organizational Behavior class. He knew I needed it to graduate, so he challenged me in much the same way that Coach Wierwille often did. I passed the class, and it was a good learning experience for me.

I had one labor assignment my whole time I was there, and I really enjoyed it. I worked in the Testing and Tutorial Department. I started there as just an employee and worked my way all the way up to office manager. I worked there fifteen hours a week as a senior. My supervisor was Linda Avery. Linda and Jackie Betts, who worked out of the same office, were very nice ladies, but they ran a tight ship. They never let you slack off and say you worked two hours when you only worked one hour. Every hour I ever worked was by the minute. If I said I worked two hours, I worked two hours exactly.

The basketball players had to come back early from Christmas break every year. The dorms were closed, so we stayed in local residents' homes. In my freshman year I stayed with three seniors at the home of Joyce Nixon. My relationship with Ms Nixon over the next four years was absolutely marvelous. The seniors all graduated, so the next year I was the veteran of the group that went to Ms. Nixon's house. It was me and freshmen Chris Haggard and Travis Earlywine. Ms Nixon was like a mother to us. She cooked us breakfast and treated us like kings. I got so close to her that I lived at her house during the summer between my junior and senior years when I was doing an internship in Barbourville. She wouldn't accept any rent payment. She was a wonderful lady.

I married a Berea College student named Jamie Abrams. Before we were married Jamie picked me up every Sunday morning to take me to church. She helped me stay on the right path at a time when there was a lot of partying on Friday and Saturday nights.

After I graduated I took a job working for Picway Shoes in Florence, Kentucky, while I waited to hear from State Farm Insurance. I was assistant manager at Picway. Our manager was Steve Lawson, who graduated from Berea the year before I did.

Several months later State Farm contacted me, and I started working as a claims adjuster for them. At Berea I had taken a lot of accounting classes, but by the time I was a senior I knew I didn't want to become a CPA, even though I would have made good money in that profession. I had to make an adjustment, and that affected my marketability. I worked at State Farm for a year and a half. Although I was happy with my job, I wasn't content with what I was doing with my life. Deep down I'd always wanted to become a teacher and coach. I began taking classes at Xavier University and got my teaching certificate.

Now I'm working in the Grant County school system I grew up in. I coach junior varsity basketball and teach the alternative classroom. When I was working for the insurance company I handled automobile accidents claims. If I paid too much money to an injured person my boss was upset with me, and if I didn't pay enough money, the person receiving it was upset with me. I wanted to make a positive difference in people's lives. Working with troubled kids in Grant County, I've had the opportunity to help some individuals. That's more rewarding to me.

August 24, 1998

Travis Earlywine   **1990-94**

I enjoy watching an NAIA basketball game more than I do an NCAA Division I game. I've heard many people say the same thing. I've thought about writing a book about that. If I ever do, I'll call it *One Step Below*. Most of the players on the NAIA level don't have the skills that the Div I guys do, but many of them have bigger hearts.

The University of Kentucky players can't go anywhere without being noticed, but nobody cared about us. One time during the Lions Club Tournament a group of kids asked us for autographs after the game. I was amazed. I thought, "Why in the world are they asking us for autographs?" That was the only time in my career that I signed an autograph. These were seven and eight-year-olds, and I guess they thought they were watching big-time ballplayers. I look at it this way: to a lot of people we were big-time, because many high school players don't get to go to college and play. So we were a step below some and a step above others.

I loved our small gym, and I believe all of my teammates loved it too. No matter how many scholarships our opponents had, when they came to Seabury Gym we had a chance to beat them. We had some wild fans. In my freshman and sophomore years, for instance, there was The Bob Squad,

a bunch of guys who loved Bob Cowie. They cheered with their shirts off and the letters B-O-B painted on their chests. They brought cow bells and stuff, and it got rowdy in there. That helped level the playing field, you might say.

I grew up in Paris, Kentucky. My parents were divorced. I lived with my mother until I was eight or nine years old. Then I went to live with my father, who remarried. My father owns a fencing business.

Paris High School was a very small school. If you could play a sport, they didn't object if you played one day and not the next. They didn't have the luxury of being able to tell people not to do that. I pitched on the baseball team every year,

Travis Earlywine: "He had his head on straight"

but I also had a job, so usually I played only on the days I was scheduled to pitch. I also played tennis and basketball.

Coach Wierwille heard about me through a friend of my father's who was a Berea College alumnus, Parke Carter. Coach Wierwille watched me play in the district tournament in my senior year, 1990, and introduced himself after the game. Before that I didn't know much about Berea. Except for some small schools out of state, no one else was interested in me as a basketball player. When Coach Wierwille told me he thought I could play basketball at Berea College, I got interested in Berea College. I visited the campus, watched a game, and met the President. I liked it, and that's how I ended up there.

Coach Wierwille made a favorable impression on me. He was intimidating, but I got the sense that he cared about me. My father taught me to look a person in the eye when I shook his hand, and that was important to Coach Wierwille too. Coach Wierwille was old school, and I liked old school.

I wasn't a great shooter in high school. I became a better shooter in college because I knew I had to if I wanted to play. In high school I posted up. At six-three I was the tallest guy on the team my senior year. I was the center when Coach Wierwille saw me play. I played with my back to the basket. Coach Wierwille said, "You're not going to be able to do that at Berea. If you want to play, you're going to have to handle the ball." That summer I practiced my ballhandling and my shooting and developed those areas of my game. I could always jump, and I liked to offensive rebound.

I got into very few varsity games as a freshman, although I dressed for every game. Mainly I played JV. Jermaine Jackson and Chris Haggard, who were freshmen like me, played a lot more varsity minutes than I did. I wondered why. I thought I was as good a player as they were. Finally I went to talk to Coach about it. The moment I stepped into his office he said, "If this is about playing time, take your ass right back out of here."

But I didn't leave. I sat right down in front of his desk and said, "Coach, I'm not coming in here to gripe. I'm not going to tell you that you're wrong for not playing me. I just want to ask what I need to do to play more."

He said, "You need to work on your defense." I knew he was right, and I took his advice. By the end of the season I was playing more minutes.

Coach and I had our good times and our bad times. When I look back on those days now, I concentrate on the good times. I talk to him every year at the state tournament. I write to him sometimes, and he writes me back. We had our ups and downs. I was more outgoing than Chris Haggard, my roommate. Chris didn't say a word to Coach, and Coach seldom spoke to him. I was a verbal person, so I talked to Coach about what was on my mind.

Coach could get more out of players like me and Chris and Ron Kinmon, players who didn't have all the ability in the world, than anybody I've ever seen. He could make our team believe that we were capable of beating Georgetown or Transylvania, when on paper there was no way we could compete with teams like that. He certainly knew how to motivate me. Sometimes he did it by intimidation, which challenged me to do better.

Other times he complimented me to boost my confidence. I always went aggressively to the offensive board, and if I couldn't grab the ball I'd hit it as hard as I could to midcourt. Once Coach told me, "You're one of the best I've ever seen at doing that. When you get the ball back out to our guard, that's another possession for us."

I worked as hard as I could work at all times. Ron Kinmon was that way too. Like me, Ron wasn't tremendously talented. He couldn't handle the ball, he couldn't jump, and he wasn't a great shooter. But he gave 100 percent all the time, and his play was a plus for us. If he did something terrible, he always did something good to make up for it. Ron was the kind of player who would dive after balls. He'd go up into the stands for them if he had to.

Jermaine Jackson helped me improve my defensive game. I hated having him guard me in practice. I couldn't stand it because he was always on me. Finally I asked him to teach me some of the things he knew.

Jermaine showed me an effective way to defend against a player dribbling to my right. I'd been stepping toward that man with my left foot, but that gave him an extra step. It's better to step with your right foot first, then come back with your left. That way you get there quicker to cut off the angle. I teach that in camps today.

Jermaine pointed out that anytime I reached with my hands toward a player driving with the ball, the refs called a foul. I'm righthanded, and Jermaine showed me how to keep my left forearm on my stomach and my right hand in the air. As soon as the ballhandler bodied up to me I could push him hard in the belly with the outside of my left forearm, and the refs wouldn't call it. That was good to know.

The senior guard I looked up to was Antonio Woods. I liked the way he handled himself. Antonio was confident and outgoing. He'd get us together and want to lead us. In all my years at Berea we never had another leader like him.

Antonio had a little showboat in him. He was the type of player you love, hate, and then love again. He'd make the most unbelievable move and shot you ever saw, follow that with a terrible shot at a terrible time, then steal the ball or do something else to redeem himself. He was our point guard, and nobody could get the ball away from him.

Bob Cowie gave me a hard time when I first met him. Bob was a junior when I joined the team. When we were at dinner the night before the Lions Club Tournament he said some stuff to me to try to get me mad. He was six-five and outweighed me by at least fifty pounds, but I said, "Bob, I'm tired of this. You may beat the heck out of me, but I'll come across this table with forks and knives and everything else if I have to, to get you to leave me alone." He laughed it off, but right after that we started getting a little closer, and eventually we became very good friends. He just wanted to see what I was made of.

Bob was rough as a cob. He didn't take any crap from anybody. If you came into the lane he wasn't afraid to shove you. He wasn't the best basketball player ever, but he was intimidating, mean on the court. He was red-headed, and when he got a red look on his face to match his hair, we knew he was going to get the next rebound and knock over anybody who tried to stop him. I loved him.

There was a camaraderie among the players, and when we get together now we have a lot of funny stories to tell. In my sophomore year we played Wilberforce in the Lions Club Tournament. They were thirty minutes late for the game. The fans were sitting there waiting. There was another game scheduled after it. Finally Wilberforce showed up.

Coach was hot. He came into our locker room boiling mad and said, "All I've got to say to you is this: don't blow me!" We looked at him and thought, "Don't blow me? What the heck is he talking about? We certainly weren't planning on it!" I think what he meant to say was, "Don't make me blow up." But he actually said, "Don't blow me."

In the first half we absolutely stunk it up. Wilberforce had a terrible team, but we led them by only two points when we should have been up by twenty. Coach left the court before the half was over. When we got down to the locker room, we didn't know where he was. All of a sudden we started hearing boom, bang, crash, smash! There was a lounge right outside our locker room, and Coach was throwing the chairs into the racquetball courts. We sat there listening to all the banging and crashing, mad at ourselves and not saying a word. Finally we looked over at Bob, who was team captain. Bob raised his head and said, "We blew him."

Every one of us busted out laughing. If Coach had heard us, there's no telling what he would have done. We ended up winning the game by thirty points. I told Coach this story at the state tournament this year, and he laughed and laughed.

A month later we played in a tournament in Charlotte, North Carolina. At the time Chris Haggard and I were starting along with Bob and Dennis Sargent and someone else in the frontcourt. Tony Goatley was coming on strong as a freshman. He probably deserved to be starting over Chris or me because he was playing very well at guard. In Charlotte Tony really stepped up. He was taking the ball to the hole and dunking. We were impressed. Chris and I looked over our shoulder every time the horn sounded because we were afraid one of us was coming out. We were roommates and best friends, but we battled to hit the first three-pointer, because whoever hit it might get to stay in when Tony entered the game.

We were undefeated when we got to Charlotte, but after we lost a game Coach changed the starting five completely. Chris and Bob and Dennis and I were out, and Tony and Ron Kinmon and two or three other guys were in. The benched guys made a big to-do about it. Ron's grandfather had bought breakfast for the team that morning, and some of the fans said that was the reason Ron started. We knew that wasn't the reason, but we joked about it.

I don't think I ever laughed so hard as I did on the bus ride back from Charlotte. We called the new starting five "The Breakfast Club." We meant no disrespect to Ron's grandfather. He was a great guy, and we liked him a lot. He didn't try to buy Ron's way onto the starting five in any sense. My family did things like that too. My stepmom used to make cookies for us and bring us drinks. But Chris and Bob and I made a big joke about the breakfast. I laughed so hard that I threw up back in the toilet. Kelly Combs, our assistant coach, was trying to find out what the three of us were laughing about. We wouldn't tell anybody. We didn't mean anything bad, and we let Ron in on the joke later.

Chris Haggard was my roommmate for three and a half years. He and I got together that first December and stayed together until we graduated. We lived in Dana our freshman and sophomore years, then moved to Danforth. Chris was quiet. He didn't say a whole lot, but like most people of that type, he opened up once you got to know him. He had a great sense of humor and was a good, moral person. As a player he was a deadly shooter. Once he got a look at the basket and set his feet, you could write it down.

Transylvania was the team I wanted to beat more than any other, although I don't think I even got into our only victory against them, which occurred when I was a freshman. Chris, however, played a big role. The score was tied in the closing seconds, and we had the ball. Coach called time out and set up a play, but it didn't run as Coach designed it. Jermaine Jackson ended up shooting a fifteen-footer that bounced off the rim. Chris caught the ball twenty-five feet from the basket and launched it at the buzzer, good. That was huge.

My most memorable game was against Brescia College on December 3, 1991. Coach was going for his 300th victory. Shane Lakes had gotten hurt the previous game, so I made my first collegiate start. Owensboro is a long way from Berea, but we had at least three fans at that game: my dad, my stepmom, and my little brother. They made signs that said, "Going For 300."

The game went back and forth. With three seconds to play we trailed by three points. Tony Goatley attempted a three-pointer and was fouled. Obviously we wanted him to hit all three of his free throws, but he missed his first one. Then we figured our only chance was for Tony to make his second shot and miss the third one, which we could try to tip back in. Well, Tony missed his second shot too. We didn't have any timeouts left, but Brescia called one.

In the huddle Coach told Tony to miss the third shot on purpose. He wanted Bob Cowie to go to the center of the lane and the rest of us to flare out to the three-point line. The idea was for Bob to get the ball and throw it to one of us. I was on the top block next to Tony. When he missed his shot, the ball came off the left side, and I ran to the corner and grabbed it. I took one step, turned, and flung it, all in one motion. The ball went way up in the air, came down, and went in. That sent the game into overtime, and we ended up winning it. It was my first start, I scored the most points I'd ever scored, and we got Coach his 300th victory. They said something on the news that night about all the threes: December 3, three seconds to go, down three, three free throws, my three-pointer, and Coach's 300th win.

Later that year we beat one of the top NAIA teams in the nation, Cumberland, at Berea. Cumberland had Elnardo Givens, a transfer from Cincinnati, and Bengi Frazier, who had transferred from another big Division I school. They were so much better than we were that we shouldn't have even been in the gym with them. My family always sat up on the track that overlooked one of the goals. Bengi Frazier dunked the ball so hard that they thought the whole track was going to come right off. I'm surprised it didn't rip the goal off. We had people who could dunk, but not like Bengi Frazier. Nevertheless, we beat Cumberland that night.

We had a decent team, but we lacked height. I don't want to take anything away from our big men, because they worked hard. But our big men were six-five, and often they were trying to play against guys who were six-nine or six-ten. We got outrebounded a lot. Our guards were some of the best in the nation on our level, but our four and five men would probably have been three men on most teams. Dennis Sargent was sometimes in the game as a five, and he was really a three. So we got killed on the blocks at times.

Dennis was a year ahead of me. When I was a freshman I said to myself, "What in the world is this guy doing at Berea College? He's incredible!" As a sophomore Dennis would go down the lane and dunk on people, but he could also shoot threes, and he could handle the ball. At the end of that season he hurt his ankle, and after that he lost a lot of his jumping ability. He went on to have an excellent career, but he was not the player he had been as a sophomore.

I suffered a major injury in my senior year. Six weeks before the season began we had an open gym to show some of the freshmen how we did our drills, and I tore the meniscus in my left knee. I had surgery and rehabbed hard to be ready for our first game.

Eight games into the season, playing at Berea, I dove after a loose ball and reinjured the knee. It seemed okay, so I continued to play, and we won the game in overtime. However, when I got out of bed the next morning I set my leg on the floor and collapsed. I had never been in so much pain in all my life.

All they could find wrong with it was a deep bone bruise, but it kept me out of fourteen games. Every time I walked on that leg it felt like somebody was driving nails into my knee. It was four weeks before I could even consider jogging. Dr Mary Lloyd Ireland in Lexington worked with me. She told me that she'd seen football players who hit their knees on other players' pads and had to miss two seasons. The blood builds up under the kneecap, and there's not a daggone thing you can do until the blood works its way out of there. I went to Lexington three times a week for electrical stimulation and ultrasound.

With just a few games left, I went to Coach and said, "I don't want to sit here and watch the whole year go by, my last year ever. My knee still hurts, but I can play." He didn't have to play me, but he did. I wasn't 100 percent and was ineffective. I was limping at the end of the games.

We went to Louisville Gardens to play Spalding in our last regular season game. I'd been getting ultrasound treatments before playing to loosen up the knee, but Louisville Gardens didn't have an ultrasound machine, and my knee felt tight the whole game. I got the ball on a fast break and shot a layup. When I elevated off my left leg, it collapsed. The ball hit the bottom of the goal and caromed back and hit me in the head. I knew it was over then. I looked over at Coach and raised my hand. When he looked at me I pointed to myself and said, "I've got to come out."

Daniel Brown was a sophomore that year. Daniel was tough to stop in the middle, so Coach put in a spread offense, with two big men and two guards in the corners. Daniel could do what he wanted.

Daniel was another one of those players we loved and then hated. We loved him because he was great, but we also hated him because it seemed as if he shot the ball every time down the floor. His talent was awesome. I would rather have had the ball in his hands than anyone else's, especially after his freshman year. If they threw the ball to me at the end of a close game, I'd probably throw it to Daniel. But we thought he was a hot dog who shot too much.

A Daniel Brown shot was a point of controversy in our game against Georgetown at Berea my senior year, through no fault of his. Georgetown was ranked number one in the nation, but they led us by just three points in the final seconds. Daniel hit a three-pointer that would have tied the game, but the officials counted it as a two. Georgetown inbounded the ball, and because we were still down by a point we had to foul. They made both of their free throws and ended up winning by three points.

Coach had a broken ankle, but he stomped across the floor hollering, "Give me the tape! That better not have been a three!" The players went down to the locker room to shower and change, but I was in street clothes because I was injured, so I went with Coach to his office. The tape showed that Daniel was three feet behind the line when he went into the air. When he came down he ended up at about the free throw line, which was not unusual for him.

Coach hurled his remote and broke something in his office. About 400 people had stayed to find out what the tape would show. Coach walked out and shouted to them, "It was a three!" Everybody cheered as if that changed the outcome of the game, but it didn't, of course. We still lost. Coach sat outside where the refs were getting dressed. Mrs Wierwille called somebody and said, "If you don't get up here, Roland's going to kill them when they come out!" Finally they got him away from that door. To this day I have no idea what he would have done to them.

My first labor assignment was in dorm maintenance. We went around fixing doorknobs and screens and toilets and things like that. Then Chris and I became janitors in Phelps-Stokes, where the chapel is. That was a good job because we could work on our own time.

I was a physical education major. I wanted to earn good grades and strived make the Dean's List. My professors were fair and never overloaded us. Joy Hager was serving as president of the Kentucky Association for Physical Education, and she made sure that nobody made fun of the physical education major. I liked Martha Beagle, who was fun to be around, and Mike Johnson, a nice, down-to-earth guy who really cared about sports.

I graduated in December 1994 after doing my student teaching that fall. I went back to Paris and substitute taught. When the next school year began I got a job teaching physical education and health at Marion County

High School. I was there for three years. Now I'm teaching physical education at Southside Elementary School in Harrison County, which is closer to home. If a secondary teaching job opens up in Harrison or Bourbon County, I'll go after it.

My long-range dream is to be a college professor, but I don't know if it's possible. I could have studied for my master's degree as soon as I left Berea, but I couldn't afford it. I needed to get a job right away. I'd love to teach and coach at the college level. Students are there because they want an education.

An education is what I wanted, but after four years I couldn't wait to get out, just like every other student. Now I'd give anything to be back. Everybody probably goes through that too. But I'm proud to tell people that I graduated from Berea College.

September 1, 1998

Chris Haggard   1990-94

In the fall of 1990 we started out with eight freshmen basketball play-ers. Maybe three of us made it through all four years. I saw them drop out as freshmen, sophomores, juniors, and seniors. Bob Cowie knew how the program worked, and that's why he didn't give any of us freshmen respect at first. It took a very special person to finish basketball and school at Berea College.

What did it take to get through the program? First, you had to come in with a sound grasp of fundamentals. College isn't the place to learn fun-damentals. If you didn't bring them with you, you had no chance to play.

You had to have character, too. You had to be willing to work hard, because nothing was given to you. You had to be dedicated to the program and to Berea Col-lege in general. And you had to be willing to go through the ups and downs. It wasn't all up for a Berea College player. Inevitably you hit a few down spots. That's what made you stronger. If you can't go through life's downs, why live at all?

The people who played four years of basketball at Berea Col-lege and graduated are great peo-ple. They know what it takes to succeed. When I came to Berea I thought everyone would look up to me because I played basket-ball. That didn't happen. A few teachers may have actually looked down on me because I was an athlete. But whether they

Chris Haggard: "A player who kept getting better and better"

liked me or not, none of my teachers gave me anything. I earned everything I got. That gave me the strength and the ability to take on any job. I know I can accomplish anything I put my mind to.

I grew up in Lexington, Kentucky. I didn't play on an organized bas-ketball team until my junior year in high school. I used to work out at the YMCA. Even as a junior I played JV, because at Henry Clay High School we had a lot of talent. A lot of people left after that year, and as a senior I finally got the opportunity to play on the varsity. I played well and started a few games, but then I broke my foot and missed about half the season. That crushed me. But I was well enough to play our last three or four games, and I picked up where I left off. We were one of the top teams in the state, but we got beat on the final shot in the semifinals of the regionals.

I didn't think about playing college ball. It never entered my mind. It was great just to play at the high school level. But some friends of mine at the Y said, "Chris, you need to try college ball. We know you can do it." So I talked to my high school coach, Al Prewitt.

He said, "I want you to know about a school called Berea College. Roland Wierwille, their coach, has a nice program." I had never heard of Berea College. I didn't know it existed. I didn't even know there was a town called Berea.

A friend from the Y took me down to Berea one day. I looked at that little gym and about died. I was used to playing in front of two or three thousand in Lexington. I couldn't believe this was the college level. But Coach Wierwille encouraged me to come to Berea. He loved Al Prewitt's system. He used the same three-two matchup zone and some of the same offense, so he knew I'd fit in well. He told me all about it and said, "If you enroll here, you can come and try out."

I thought about it and talked to my mother, who was ill with cancer. She hadn't been well enough to see me play some of my high school games. She said, "Going to Berea would be a great opportunity for you. You'll be the only kid of mine who goes to school, and I'd love to see you do it." I went to Berea.

Most players go to college recruited. I knew I'd have to try out. Some of my friends who were ex-college players said I'd be all right, and I was. Coach Wierwille was impressed with what I could do in practice. The one thing I lacked was experience. Everybody else had played at least ten years by the time they got to college ball. It was a big step for me, and I was nervous at first. But I fit right in.

Communicating with Coach outside of ball was great. We had some of the deepest conversations I'll ever have with anybody. He was very interested in my personal life. I went through so many personal things, I'm surprised I made it through school. I was glad I could come to Coach and talk about things. He was open-hearted to me.

My mother was very ill when she sent me off to college. I had to fight for an automobile, because Berea College didn't normally allow students to have automobiles. A friend helped me buy an automobile so I could get back to see my mother.

I'd drive up to Lexington and get back at three in the morning. Coach understood. He didn't push me. He said, "Just take your time and get through this." When the basketball season started, I played some varsity minutes off the bench.

One morning early in December Coach called me into his office. The chaplain was there. Coach said, "Chris, I got a call. You need to go home." That was all he wanted to say. He didn't want to go into detail. I knew that something bad had happened. I found out that while I was driving back to Berea that morning my mother had passed away. I regret not being there in her last hours. But I knew she was proud of me for being at Berea College.

I was very down. It happened during finals, and I missed a couple of them. I had to go back to Berea and take them. That was horrible. I ended up with a GPA of one-point something. I almost gave it up. If I hadn't been on the basketball team with the group of guys I was with and the people around me, I couldn't have gone on.

After Christmas I returned to Berea with the rest of the team. The dorms were closed, so we stayed with families in town. I stayed with one of the most fascinating people I met at Berea, Joyce Nixon. She took me, Travis Earlywine, Ron Kinmon, and a fourth person I can't remember. For her to open up her house to four guys she didn't know was amazing to me. She knew I was going through some rough times, and she talked to me. She enjoyed having us there, and being there meant a whole lot to all of us. She took the whole basketball team to Cliff Hagan's restaurant one night. She did that for several years. As it turned out, Travis and I were the last persons she ever took in. To this day we keep in touch with her.

I'm six-two. I could handle the ball and shoot it when I was open. In high school I asked Coach Prewitt, "Do you mind if I shoot the three?"

"Chris, I'd rather you shoot a three than a layup. I have more confidence in your shot than in your ability to go to the basket."

Because I started playing so late, I kept developing each year. I continued to improve even after I graduated from college. My shooting ability was my greatest asset. I must have shot a million threes in practice, and it paid off.

Kids who play at the NAIA level are not the tallest or most athletic players, but they're the best fundamental players I've seen. I was fundamentally sound, and that's why Coach Wierwille played me right away. I could run his offense, but he knew I wouldn't force any of the action. I could pass, I could penetrate when I saw an opening, I could hit an open shot, and I could hit my free throws. I was an all-around player who didn't try to do more than I was capable of. I played three positions, depending on how Coach wanted to use me. I played point guard, two guard, and small forward.

Antonio Woods, who was a senior, guided our way my freshman year. He was a great leader. He knew that we didn't have a very good team, but he gave it everything he had and picked us up when we needed it. He would take the big shots, but he tried to get the rest of us involved too. I respected Antonio tremendously and enjoyed playing with him. He showed me a lot.

When I met Bob Cowie I thought he was a jerk. His attitude was, "I'm the big man here. You'll respect me regardless of what I do." You had to show him respect before he gave it to you. You had to prove to him that you were capable of sticking it out and helping him on the court. Bob came around to me quick because I played a lot of varsity. I enjoyed playing with him. His mastery of fundamentals made him an effective player. He was only six-five, but he got a lot of rebounds because he knew how to use his body. I liked Bob after I got to know him. He was a great guy to talk to.

Shane Lakes wasn't quick and didn't have a lot of athletic ability, but he knew how to score. He could score on the best of them. He found a way to score. He had more moves around the basket than most people I've seen. Unfortunately Shane had a lot of injuries, so he might not have had the career he hoped for.

I loved playing in Seabury Gym. It was old, but we took care of it. We'd walk in there hot and sweaty, feeling loose and enjoying the sound of the people screaming for us. We believed we could beat any team in the NAIA at Seabury Gym, and that was the greatest feeling ever.

I had some of my best games in that gym. A month after my mother passed away we played Transylvania. Our record was mediocre, and Transy was ranked in the Top Twenty. They had big Daniel Swintosky, a dominant player, and some great guards. By that time I was playing again. Coach had enough confidence in me to put me back out there. Coach had enough scorers, so my job was to do the little things as a role player.

The game was a battle to the end. With two or three minutes left we led by six. Travis Earlywine's cousin Brett Eades played for Transy. He did something mean, and I might have bumped or pushed him. He faked and fell down. The refs called me for an intentional foul. I thought Coach was going to scream. That was a big turnover. Brett hit the buckets and Transy went on to tie it up. With thirteen seconds to go we had the ball, and Coach called time out.

Coach wanted Jermaine Jackson to handle the ball and get it to Antonio Woods. Of course everyone, including Transy, knew that Antonio was our best guy. The ticks ran down, but Jermaine couldn't get Antonio the ball. Finally he shot it himself. It was a brick. When it came off the rim I was standing right in front of Transy's bench. I caught the ball and shot it. Nothing but net, and then the horn went off. I don't know how high Coach jumped up. Everybody went crazy. I was mobbed. It was the bomb of the century. That was our biggest win that year.

We were never better than a .500 team. We had the guards, but we didn't have any of the six-eight dominating guys who could clog up the middle and intimidate people. Six foot to six-two guards are easy to find, but players who are six-eight don't go to a school that can't grant them an athletic scholarship. If we'd just had some intimidating big men, we could have gone right to the top.

In my junior year the program was down, down, down. Morale was bad, and Coach was upset with us. It looked like some of us weren't there to win, but were just playing for their own stats. After our season ended, our locker room was full of people saying everything you can imagine about the program and the coach. A lot of those things should not have been said. They were said in anger, but they didn't necessarily express what people felt deep down in their hearts. I said some bad things I didn't mean. To this day I regret that I said them. We had a lot of anger built up, and many of us let it out in the locker room. After that it was over, and everything worked out for the best.

In my freshman and sophomore and junior years I started a few games and came off the bench in others. I began my senior year very confident. I was averaging thirteen or fifteen a game and playing well. Early in January Georgetown came to Seabury, nationally ranked, and I said to myself, "I want to have a good game against a good team for once."

I came out weak in the first half, but the team played well and hung in there, so I didn't worry about myself. In the second half the game caught fire. We were throwing bullets at each other, shooting, bombing, talking smack. I ended up with twenty points, and we almost beat them. Daniel Brown hit a three-pointer that should have tied the game, but the officials wouldn't count it.

During that game I tried to block a Georgetown player who was going in for a layup. He bent down, and I flipped up in the air and landed on my head and my back. I lost consciousness for five or ten seconds, just blacked out. I thought I'd hurt myself seriously. It was one of the scariest moments of my college career. A bunch of people were around me trying to get me up. I finally stood up. I could have kept playing. I wanted to, but that was my fifth foul. I left the game and put ice on my back.

At first I wasn't sure I'd be well enough to play again right away, but it was my senior year and I wasn't really hurting all that bad. A few days later we went to Asbury. Joking around before the game, someone asked me how many points I was going to score. "Thirty," I said.

I played poorly in the first half, scored maybe two points, and Asbury led us by five. Coach had a fit in the locker room. He jumped all over our butts. He said, "Boys, I'm going to tell you right now, if you don't show me anything in the next few minutes, every one of you will be on the bench."

When the second half began we didn't look good the first minute. I missed a shot and thought I might be going out. Then all of a sudden something clicked, and I hit seven three-pointers in a row. I'd never felt that good in my life shooting the ball. Travis, who was injured, was trying to help John Cook keep the stats, but he couldn't do it because he was so happy for me, jumping up and down. I finished with thirty-two points, scoring thirty in the second half, and we beat Asbury by about twenty.

That was a wonderful feeling, and it was extra special because Al Prewitt, my high school coach, was scouting that game for Transylvania, where he'd been hired as an assistant. He came up to me, shook my hand, and told me I'd had a great game.

The following Saturday, one week after the Georgetown game, we played Lindsey Wilson at home. I didn't do anything spectacular, but I played a consistently good game and finished with thirty-one points. Coach Wierwille was happy for me. He was glad to see me finally break out and do what I was capable of doing. He called me into his office a few days later and said, "Chris, I'm proud of you. You've been named NAIA Player of the Week." That's an honor I'll always treasure.

Travis Earlywine gave us 100 percent. I say that because I don't believe in "110 percent." Travis gave us every bit of 100 percent when he was out there. He knew what had to be done and he did it all, ballhandling, shooting, rebounds. Travis and I fought over playing time, but I didn't begrudge him any of the time he got. He was out there for the same reason I was, to win. For a guy six-two he played very strong. He was a guy who could get you five or six rebounds, ten or twelve points, and three or four assists a game if he got to play enough.

Travis and I were roommates for three and a half years. We were very much alike. Often we sat up and talked all night long. He had girl problems, and I had girl problems. He loved to have fun, but he didn't like to drink and party, and neither did I. He had his head on straight. He taught me a lot about the Christian religion. He was very strong in that. Travis knew what he wanted from his education. He could sit there and read a book and memorize it. I had to read it ten times to get that much out of it.

Ron Kinmon was another great guy. I talked to him a few times about my personal problems, and he listened to me. To look at Ron, you didn't think he'd be able to play ball. He didn't look like an athlete. He was six-five but didn't dominate inside. But Ron was a 100-percent type of guy who loved to hustle. He came up big in some games. Dennis Sargent, who like Ron was a year ahead of me, was a great player. He could shoot the shot, go to the hole, and surprise people now and then.

Tony Goatley arrived the year after I did. Tony had a great freshman year. He had some incredible moves to the hole. He was very gifted, and he bonded well with his teammates. When a player with that capability tries to bond with you, you respect him more.

When Daniel Brown came to Berea he didn't bond well, although he tried to. Many of us had a bad impression of him. He got away with a lot of stuff. He was very talented, and no one denied his ability. But if he'd gone to any other school he wouldn't have had the career he had at Berea, because Coach let him let away with so much. In high school he was a person who got the ball a lot, got to shoot a lot, and that carried over in college. Daniel came to the perfect place for him. Coach modified our offense so that Daniel could continue to get the ball and shoot it. There's nothing wrong with a coach setting up plays for his best players.

Corey Craig was a freshman when I was a senior. I could tell that he had his head on straight. I knew he was going to be a finisher. It's an accomplishment to finish school, but someone who finishes both school and basketball has to have his head on straight, and that was Corey. He worked hard. He was certainly a workhorse under the boards, and Corey accepted his role. By that I mean he did not try to do more than he was capable of doing. That's a desirable trait in a player.

Life was a bumpy road for me at Berea. The basketball team lost some games we shouldn't have lost, and there were down times off the court as well. But I'm a very patient person. I don't expect a lot. If you're patient your time will come, and you'll get what you want out of life.

During the basketball season our late-afternoon routine was to practice, take our showers, and go over to the cafeteria and eat. One day a bunch of us were eating when somebody got the bright idea of humping some Tater Tots at Tony Goatley. I said, "Guys, don't be doing all that." But they got silly and threw Tater Tots and milk and everything at Tony. I didn't throw anything. I didn't move. But Tony got mad and threw some stuff that hit me, so I retaliated.

The cafeteria people got very angry at us. They called Coach Wierwille, who had been watching his son play ball. Three or four of us were reffing intramural games when he came steaming in. He told us to come out of there and said, "I want one of you guys to tell me exactly what happened, right now."

Bob Cowie was our leader, and we were all looking at him. As Bob opened his mouth to talk, Coach said, "No, Bob. Chris, I want you to tell me." I almost peed in my pants. I hope I told him the exact truth. There were about ten people involved, and he was thinking about not playing any of us in the next game. But if he did that, we would have had to forfeit. So instead he brought us in one by one the next day and talked to us. Then we all had to do some extra running.

My major was economics. I failed Accounting One, the only class I ever failed in my life. That hurt my grade-point average, believe me. I knew I was failing but couldn't get out of it in time. I didn't like the teacher. I didn't want her to give me anything, but she wasn't about to help me, either. I had to repeat the class, and when I did I got a good grade.

People like Travis could get good grades with a lot less study than I needed to do. I had to study my butt off. Succeeding in one of my toughest courses showed me that I could survive in college. It was a course in linear algebra. I loved math, but I failed the first test. So many of us failed that the teacher gave the test to us again. I swear, I must have studied for a month. I went to the library three or four nights a week because I couldn't study like I wanted to in the dorm. It was study, study, study. I busted my tail for a B or an A on that test, and I ended up getting what I needed. There were times when I got down in college, but I learned how to come back. It was an awesome feeling whenever I could get over the hump and accomplish something like that.

In my sophomore year I tried to sign up for a particular class before the team went to Charlotte, but my adviser was out of town. I was afraid I wouldn't be able to complete my schedule. I talked one of the cheerleaders and asked, "Is there any way I can get this card through so I can be enrolled in this class?"

She said, "Just scribble your adviser's name on it. People do it all the time." She ended up writing his name on it, and then I put my class cards through and didn't think anything more about it. But I got a note in the mail saying I'd been rejected for all my classes. They'd discovered the forged name on the class card.

I went to Coach Wierwille to ask for his advice. He told me to tell him exactly what happened, and I did.

"Chris, you'll have to go and admit it."

"I will, and I'll take the full blame. I don't want to get this girl in trouble. I want to keep her strictly out of it. It was my card, and I was the one who told her to sign it."

Coach told me I needed to go to my adviser and apologize. I did. Then I went before the disciplinary board. I told them what happened and took full responsibility. They put me on probation for a year. I made a big mistake, paid the price, learned from it, and moved forward.

My first labor job was selling Berea College crafts in the Log House sales room. I worked there for two years and enjoyed every minute of it. After that Travis and I got a job cleaning classrooms. It wasn't the best job, but we could schedule it ourselves. We did it from ten to midnight.

While I was looking for a job after graduation, my dad asked me to work with him for awhile. He owned his own painting business in Lexington. We painted some amazing houses. We painted Rick Pitino's house, and we painted one on Winchester Road that was twenty thousand square feet. He was one of the best painters in Lexington and taught me well. I might have gone on to run the company, and he and I talked about that a couple of times, but he just wouldn't pay anything. Finally I took an office job at a big company, Lexmark.

That was my first experience with a big-time job, and at first I was overwhelmed. But I got the hang of it pretty quick, and before long I thought it was too easy and started looking for something else to do. If you want to move at Lexmark, you can move. There are all kinds of opportunities.

I'm a contract administrator now. I'm doing great and I'm proud of everything I've done, but I can always reach out for more. I want to explore. Maybe there's something out there I'm missing.

Sometimes I'm around people who don't want to work, who want only to get by. They want things, but they don't want to work for them. That's not what life is about. They ask me how I'm so organized. I tell them that organization is the key to work. The better you're organized, the more you can accomplish.

I can't begin to tell you how much my Berea College degree means to me. I worked harder for that than I did for anything else in my life, and nobody can take it away from me. At Berea I had some of the most memorable experiences of my life and made friends I'll never forget. Even if I never see them again, they'll always be in my memory.

September 8, 1998

Jim Conway   1992-95

My mother and father were divorced when I was four, and they each remarried. I lived with my mom and stepfather. I went to Dixie Heights High School in Crestview Hills, Kentucky. I loved football and played both defensive and offensive end. I'm six-five, but I never got into the weightlifting thing, so I wasn't big enough to play football at the college level. I hoped to play basketball in college.

Jim Connor is a friend of Coach Wierwille's who watches a lot of high school basketball games in northern Kentucky and calls Coach whenever

Jim Conway: "Coming to Berea was the best thing I ever did"

he sees a player who might fit into the Berea program. Mr Connor saw Dixie Heights play once or twice and gave Coach my name. Coach came up to see me just before my senior season and told me that he'd like to have me come to Berea.

Dixie Heights had a new coach that year. None of the players wanted to see the old coach leave, because he was a real good coach and a father figure to everybody. He was dismissed because of his won-lost record. We didn't like that situation. The coach doesn't get out there and play, so we didn't think he should have to take the blame for what we failed to do.

When the new coach came in, I got along with him at first. But he put a lot of pressure on me because I was a captain and expected to score a lot of points. I had some things going on in my personal life, too. One night, in a game with Covington Holmes that we were losing badly, all the pressure, teenage pressure, got to me. I walked off the court, quitting my

high school team right in the middle of my senior season.

After about a week of watching my teammates play without me, I realized I'd made a big mistake. I still wanted to play. The new coach, who was trying to establish his authority, thought it wasn't appropriate to let me back onto the team.

There was an article about me in the paper, and when the colleges saw it they stopped sending me letters asking how I was doing. I wrote to Coach Wierwille, telling him that I still hoped to play college ball. Coach replied that he was understanding about some situations like the one I was in, and he told me that I could come down to Berea after the season and talk about it with him.

After he and I discussed what happened, he said, "I'm going to give you a chance." So I came to Berea and he gave me a chance, but he didn't make it easy on me. In fact, he tried every way he could to run me off. He needed to see if I was a quitter or not, if I had what it took to be a Berea player.

In that first year there were a few times when I wanted to pack it up. At one point I went into Coach's office and told him I was going home. My mom was having some problems, and I thought I could be the solve-all. Coach said, "It's your life. Think about it. There's the door right there. You need to decide what you're going to do." I decided to stay.

As a freshman I didn't even dress on the varsity. In my sophomore year I started playing a little bit. I was a role player, just doing what was asked of me. Coach told me I didn't have to shoot it. My strengths were setting screens, getting our shooters open, playing defense.

As a freshman I had to go up against seniors Bob Cowie and Shane Lakes every day in practice. Those two used to beat me to death. One of our guards, Jermaine Jackson, took me under his wing. When I had bad days in practice I'd get really discouraged, thinking I'd never make the varsity. Jermaine kept me positive about everything. Even after he left the team, he and I were very close.

At that time we had an abundance of good guards: Jermaine, Chris Haggard, Travis Earlywine, Tony Goatley, and Daniel Brown. Some people had to sit. Jermaine went from starting to coming off the bench. His playing time faded out. He and Coach talked about it. I never asked him what was said. All Jermaine told me was that he wasn't going to play any more. I left it at that. He was my friend, and I wasn't going to poke and prod at him.

Bob Cowie took up a lot of space. He was so big and wide that once he got the ball down low, he could score on anybody who wasn't six-ten or taller. He rebounded real well, too. Bob was a guy everybody respected. What he said, went. He'd tell you honestly how he felt. I was playing against him in a game one day before the season started, and I was gung ho and elbowed him. He turned around and said, "If you ever do that again..."

When I got to know Bob, I found he was just a good old boy who took people as they were. He and I had a lot of good times. He was there my sophomore year, too, because he did his student teaching that fall.

We called Shane Lakes "Old Up and Under." Every time he got the ball he'd give you a pump fake and go up under you. He was a workhorse. He'd hurt his knee earlier in his career, and it still gave him pain when I played with him. We could all see that Shane gave it everything he had, and that inspired us to do the same.

We didn't have many big people. Bob and Shane graduated after my freshman year, which left us with Ron Kinmon, Dennis Sargent, Tino Ballenger, and me. That was it. Then Ron and Dennis graduated, leaving just Tino and me and Corey Craig, a freshman. Tino had real long arms, and he could jump. He rebounded well and could score when he wanted to. But our inside play was our biggest problem. We simply didn't have enough size, and we played a tough schedule.

When Corey Craig came to Berea in the summer before his freshman year, I played with him in our summer recreation league at the College. Our team was Corey, Sean Horne, Jackie Steele, Coach Wierwille's son Roland, and me. I could see right away that Corey was going to make an impact. He was a big boy and a hard worker. He was better than I was, so I knew he would cut into my playing time. I had no problem with that because he worked hard and knew his role on the team. Corey didn't look to shoot the ball all the time. He was very humble. He made a good impression on me.

In my senior year, though, I became a better scorer after Corey, who started, got hurt. My post moves improved as my playing time increased. I was starting every game, and the team began to rely on me to score. Daniel Brown was still our top scorer, but I was asked to contribute some points, and I did.

Daniel was the cockiest player I ever played with, but I was happy he was on my team. He and I argued all the time during games because he was such a competitor. He wasn't mean. He just wanted us to play as hard as we could, and he didn't want us making any mistakes. He got on himself too.

I had to earn Daniel's respect. As I said, I wasn't much of a scorer. I just played my role, but in my senior year my role changed. I was doing more than setting screens or throwing the ball back out. Now I needed to make some moves myself, do whatever I had to do to score. Once Daniel saw me doing that, we didn't argue as much.

I'd always done my best to make sure Daniel got open to shoot the ball. We ran a double-high set with the big men at the top of the three-point line so we could set screens there for Daniel to get open. I loved that offense. Three of my fouls every game were for setting illegal screens, because I did anything and everything I could to get Daniel a little opening he could shoot out of.

I did the same for Tony Goatley, another good shooter. Tony could score whether he was out on the key or down low. Tony had a great personality, and we became good friends. We hung out a lot together. We were all one on the team. Any time something was going on we notified each other and got together. We played a lot of cards and golf. Roland Wierwille, Coach's son, was by far the best golfer.

Having the coach's son on the team didn't bother any of us, because he was a great guy. There might have been some jealousy if Roland had started every game, but he didn't play much. I was glad to have him as a teammate. He's my best friend.

I think I earned Coach Wierwille's respect as time went on. I always stood up to the challenge he gave me, and when he saw that, I got to play more. Then in my senior year he had his stroke, and that brought us a whole lot closer. He was always such a strong man, such a strong presence, but after he got sick I went to see him at his house and he couldn't talk to me. That hurt. Later when he talked to the team in practice, struggling to get the words out to tell us that he wasn't going to be coming back that season, that really hurt. But it drew me closer to him. We became very close when I coached for him for two years after my playing career ended. The first year I watched what I said all the time to make sure I didn't overstep any boundaries. Then I loosened up and joked around with him a little bit. I got to know the human side of him, and now I consider him one of my best friends.

Coach Wierwille's greatest attribute as a coach is that he's not concerned only about basketball. Whoever stays with him for the whole four years can't help but be a quality person by the time he graduates. The first thing Coach says every year is, "We'll get along fine if you keep your nose clean, make sure your grades are good, and be on time every day." Those are things that every person needs to do in his college life and beyond, but many other coaches either overlook them or don't push them as hard as Coach Wierwille does. He hates to lose, but what he wants most is to have good people on his team.

Every year we started out with twenty-three or twenty-four players in practice, and by the end of the year we had fifteen or sixteen. They weeded themselves out. Those who stayed grew up because of Coach. He turned us into men. That's what he did for me, and there's no way I can repay him for it, except to make good at whatever I attempt in life.

It was hard for Coach Craig Jefferson to take over for Coach Wierwille that year. Coach Jefferson was laid back, a true player's coach. When any of us had a personal problem or a problem with Coach Wierwille, we could talk to Coach Jefferson about it. The freshmen and sophomores especially were too afraid of Coach Wierwille to go to him with those kinds of concerns, but they knew they could talk to Coach Jefferson about anything. He was always there with an ear. He had been through it all, and he knew what Coach was like, so he could tell a player what to expect.

We regarded Coach Jefferson as a friend, and when he had to take over the reins after Coach Wierwille went down, it was hard for him to adjust. He had been close to us, but now he had to step away from us to act as the authority the team needed. The transition was difficult for him and for us, but he did a good job. He often asked Tino and me what we thought the team needed to do. He was willing to get some input from the upperclassmen, and we appreciated that.

On a Tuesday night in January we played at Campbellsville, who had some real horses. I was playing defense when one of their guys caught the ball, spun on me, and swung his elbow into my ribs on the left side. I didn't come out of the game, but in practice the next day I went to Sandy Williams, our trainer, and said, "I could hardly sleep last night. I might have cracked a rib." She examined me and said, "We'll get an x-ray and find out." Sure enough, two of the ribs were cracked. She put a little pad there and wound some tape around me, and I played against Transylvania in Seabury that Saturday. I wasn't going to miss the Transy game!

Campbellsville was our opponent in the last game played at Old Seabury, which was also my senior night. That made it doubly emotional for me, because my wife and my parents were there. I remember looking at the clock with about a minute and thirty left, and we were down by eleven or twelve. I thought, "This is not the way for us to go out."

Suddenly everything started happening right for us. Our shots flew into the basket. Officials' calls went our way. There was no way we were going to lose that game. We came back, tied it, and won it in overtime. There were probably more people watching that game than had ever been in that building before. It was unbelievable.

When I first visited Berea I looked at the gym and said, "You've got to be kidding me! This is where they play? This is college?" My high school facility was bigger than Seabury was. It seemed so small and old, and the track hung over part of the playing area. But when I attended a game that night, I was impressed by the atmosphere. As soon as the game started people were going crazy. I said, "This is all right."

The gym grew on me when I started playing there. I liked the cubicles in the locker room. In high school we had the old-style metal lockers. At Seabury the JV locker room was downstairs, and the JV players fought to get upstairs, where the varsity players had their pictures and nameplates over their lockers.

Seabury was old, but it had a lot of character. Teams like Transy made fun of it when they came in, but we defended it. The atmosphere at all of our games was unlike anywhere else. The fans were so close to the court that if a player dived out of bounds trying to save the ball, he landed in somebody's lap. I once I dove into the lap of President John Stephenson!

The circulation desk at the library was my only labor position at Berea College. Mrs Barbara Power, the head of circulation, was one of the people at the College who were instrumental in my life. On my senior night I talked about her for maybe ten minutes.

Mrs Power didn't baby the people who worked for her. Anyone who didn't do the work didn't last long in the library. She was like Coach Wierwille in that regard. She made us work, but she was very fair, and she wouldn't let anything bad happen to us. She was always there for us to talk to. She made time for us, no matter what.

I kept on doing my job for her every day, showing up on time and getting all my hours in. I worked for her for two summers. Eventually I became her student assistant, and I had a say in what the students who worked there did. She put a lot of responsibility on me. She always listened to what I had to say, and she had suggestions if I had trouble with anything. Mrs Power meant a lot to me and still does.

A professor who influenced my life was Eugene Startzman. When I came to Berea I thought college was a big game. There was basketball, and that was it. Dr Startzman woke me up. I had him for Freshman Composition, one of the first classes I had at Berea. My writing skills weren't satisfactory, and a student who couldn't write couldn't get through Berea.

I needed a mature outlook to cope with Dr Startzman. I needed to realize that a college education was not just a ballgame. He and I struggled to get along. I was arrogant. I thought I was the main show. Dr Startzman let me know that the class was his, not mine, but he did it professionally. He didn't play any games. He was straightforward, and gradually he taught me how to write.

Dr Startzman used a red ink pen to correct papers. When I got my papers back they looked like a bloody mess, red everywhere. At first I got mad about it. But I worked at it, and finally I was able to give him what he wanted. Then I made real progress. I started writing like I should. Dr Startzman was always pushing, never satisfied. That's good. I think he pushed me because he wanted me to grow up and become a worthwhile person someday.

I majored in physical education and health. I graduated in December, so it was hard for me to get a teaching position right away. I coached for Coach Wierwille and substitute-taught in the county system and at the community school. The next fall I tried to get into the school system full-time, but that was hard to do without experience. I continued to sub through the next year and assist Coach Wierwille. Finally I got in as a teacher's aide, just to get my foot in the door.

I've just accepted a job in Russell, Kentucky. My old teammate Sean Horne went to high school in Russell. He's been working at the middle school. Sean knows a lot of people, and when they were looking for someone they asked him for some names. He told them I'd be interested. The wheels started turning, and everything went real well for me. I was in the right place at the right time. I'll be teaching physical education at a brand-new elementary school, and I'll be the JV coach at Russell High School.

I haven't thought yet about what's way down the road. I've been too concerned about beginning my career. I think it would be good to be a head coach at a high school, and if there is ever a possibility that I could coach at the college level, I'd like to do that. The experience I had under Coach was very valuable. As his assistant I did a lot of scouting and recruiting. I guess my ultimate goal is to run a program of my own, one where I can use the things I learned from Coach Wierwille.

Looking back on it, I'm glad my high school coach didn't let me come back to the team after I left it. That humbled me. If he had not done that, I would probably have never come to Berea. I'd been getting letters from some bigger colleges. If I'd returned to my high school team and scored a lot of points, I would have remained arrogant, signed with a bigger school, and failed to make it through because of my attitude. Coming to Berea was the best thing I ever did. The education was unbeatable, and having to work at a college job was good for me.

All the people I met at Berea were quality people. They pushed us to do a little bit more, a little bit extra, because they knew that if we approached life that way we'd become better people. That seemed to be everybody's ultimate goal. Our professors taught the subject matter, but they also taught us how to be grown up and do the right things. At some schools nobody notices or cares if students show up just for the tests. At Berea I had to be in class every day. It was the same with my job at the library. If I was scheduled for eight o'clock, that's what time I had to be there, and I was. That got me ready for the real world. Life after college is not a big game or a big party. It's responsibility. That's why we were taught to be punctual and do our best.

Yes, Berea was the best thing that happened to me. Being able to say that helped me recruit when I was Coach Wierwille's assistant. I know and appreciate what Berea did for me. I could tell a kid what Berea could do for him and be truthful about it, because I'd been through it all. Most kids' parents are less interested in the number of basketball minutes their son is going to play than they are in the quality of the education and the value of the entire college experience. I could answer those questions positively and honestly because I knew what Berea was all about. Everybody at Berea is working toward the same goal. They carry on a wonderful tradition.

August 12, 1998

Craig Jefferson (2)

Steve Ridder was Coach Wierwille's assistant for seven or eight years, and he wanted to move on to the head coaching job at Embry-Riddle in Florida. I was mowing my grass when Coach called me one day and said, "Can you come up here?" When Coach calls, you go! So I went up there, and he talked to me about being his assistant. He knew I loved basketball and came to all the games. Obviously I knew basketball a little bit. He gave me the opportunity to be his assistant, and I was excited about it.

The job was part-time, but it was really full-time. I was still in print-ing, and I had to talk to Brenda Bowman, my boss, because of the hours, getting off at four or three-thirty. But she was a good boss. She let me work around it.

Coach Craig Jefferson: "I tried to be a role model, a leader"

During practice I often worked with the big men, the post players. Coach would get intense during the game, and sometimes I had to keep him off the floor. I did a lot of recruiting. I went to all-star games, talked to guys on the phone, talked to parents, showed them around campus, and things like that.

Tony Goatley is a good recruiting story. He was a ballplayer in Louisville. Great guy. He was in an all-star game in Louisville I was watching. All the coaches were watching. A lot of big guys who went to schools like U of L and the University of Tennessee were down there playing. But Tony stood out in my mind. He could play, but for some reason a lot of people didn't recruit him.

I stayed after him. He had made his test scores, he had a 3.0 GPA. He was a good kid. I visited his family and brought them to Berea. They loved the campus, and we got along real well. Tony was a good ballplayer, and after we signed him the other coaches saw him and wondered how I got him at Berea. Well, I think I know ballplayers pretty well.

I tried to be a role model, a leader. Players who had a problem could come talk to me. They could trust me. That was the main thing. They knew I was a friend, and if they ever needed anything, they could come to Coach J. That's what they called me.

I liked the assistant's role, helping Coach out, scouting the ball games and recruiting. He and I would butt heads sometimes, but we had a pretty good relationship. When Coach had his stroke, I filled in for that year.

When they called to tell me about it, I was upset and scared for him. But Coach is a strong man, and he came back from it. He called me when he got home from the hospital. I went over there, and I think Cecilia was there. He couldn't speak that well, but he looked at me straight and said, "You're the man right now." I told him I would take the job. I would do whatever I could. It was a good feeling that he trusted me, that he had faith in me to take over the program for him until he could get back.

That year was a good year, a fun year, a learning experience. For the team it was an adjustment, of course. They'd had an intense guy, and I'm a more laid-back guy. So the players had to get adjusted to that.

I had always been an assistant, a friend. To be the head coach I had to separate myself from being buddy-buddy. I had to be The Man. The players tested me, and I had to pass that test. A couple of stars tested me by coming in late or not telling me beforehand that they were doing something. I had to sit them down. After that, they understood.

We lost some games, and just keeping their head above water, keeping them inspired, was tough. I told them to play like Coach wanted them to play, play hard and play smart. I kept them all together and kept them working hard. At the end of the season, when they put their trust in me, we overcame a lot.

After that season I went back to assistant, and we took a team to the nationals. We had good guard play with Tony Goatley and Daniel Brown, and we had Corey Craig at center. That was our first year in the new Seabury Center. We had to play IU-Southeast to get to the nationals. That was an intense game that came down to the last shot. They had the ball, and we were up by one or two. In our huddle I told Tony, "You go ahead and get this rebound." Because Tony could jump, and Tony had great hands. I told him, and then all I saw was his hand up above the rim getting the rebound. Then we ran out the clock.

So we went out to the NAIA tournament in Idaho, our first time out there. We had a good, talented team, and I think if we had won the first game we would have gone pretty far. We played in a nice stadium that held three or four thousand. You would think that nobody would come to those games at nine o'clock in the morning, but it was packed. It was a well-run tournament. They did a wonderful job. Each team had a sponsor. They did it up right, and I guess that's why the NAIA keeps the tournament out there. I think Berea's in a league now where they have a shot at going to the national tournament every year, and that's a good sales point for young recruits.

High school prospects see that Berea's a winning program, but they see when they come that people are generous. All the ballplayers will talk to them and show them around if they have questions. When they come to a game they perceive how hard Berea plays and how well the team plays together.

It seems like everybody's on scholarship now. Berea players want to play ball, and it's fun to play at Berea. It's a small place. Guys all get along. There might be some wars out there on the practice floor, but you leave it there. You don't have to worry about scholarships. Individual players who have scholarships might say, "I don't have to play hard." But at Berea everyone is equal. Coach emphasizes playing hard, intensely. You practice hard and transfer that over to a game, playing hard. You learn to manage your time, because you have to deal with the work program, the convocations, and your studies as well as basketball.

When you work hard, good things happen. When I was recruiting I had a lot to say about academics. In *U.S. News and World Report* Berea was always ranked in the top two or three. I sold that to parents. I said to parents, "At Berea, academics is first. Coach Wierwille has a 100 percent graduation rate. If you want your son to play ball and to graduate, you want him to come to Berea." I pointed out that Berea College was a well-known school all over the United States, and I showed them what companies Berea graduates were working at.

I place a lot of value on my degree. Whenever I want a job, to sell myself to an employer, I know that the name "Berea College" is behind me. People know they will get a good person.

Right now I'm a loan originator, a broker. I do loans and refinances for people, consolidation, mortgages. It was a big change in career, but I had a good opportunity. I worked in insurance for five years, and I was doing insurance for this mortgage company. They just asked me one day. I could make more money with them, and I jumped at it. I don't have time any more to be an assistant coach, but I still live and work in Berea. It's going real good.

I love basketball. I still play basketball in a thirty-five-and-older league. Arno Norwell plays in that league. We play on the same team. Both of us just love the game.

May 5, 1998

Tony Goatley   **1991-96**

Growing up in Louisville I loved sports, especially basketball. My favorite player was Michael Jordan, but there was no imitating him. I watched James Worthy, Len Bias, Milt Wagner, Lancaster Gordon, and other players, and I tried to incorporate some of their skills into my game.

I went to high school at Louisville Butler. In my junior year the head football coach asked me to come out for the football team. He wanted me to play quarterback and a guy I played basketball with to play tight end. He said he would give us starting positions. But my basketball coach didn't want me to play, and when I told my mother about it she said no, so I didn't play football. I guess my mother thought of me as the baby. I was the youngest of the family, and she didn't want me to get hurt.

After I played in an all-star basketball game in Louisville, Coach Craig

Tony Goatley: "I left the game of basketball on a high note"

Jefferson approached me and gave me information about Berea College. I visited Berea and met Coach Wierwille. He encouraged me to come to Berea, but he told me right off the bat that I wasn't guaranteed a starting position or even playing time. He spoke first about the academics at Berea, and then he talked about the Athletic Department.

My mother made the decision about what school I would go to. I stayed out of it. Central State University had also recruited me. My mother did some research, and she told me that Berea College was the better choice for me because of its academics. I told Coach Jefferson that I would be attending Berea.

I'm six feet tall. I brought competitive fire and athleticism to the team. I was an all-around player, although my ballhandling needed improvement. I worked on it a lot in practice.

When I joined the team I was impressed by Travis Earlywine, a tremendous player who deserved more playing time. Bob Cowie and Shane Lakes also opened my eyes. They weren't nearly as athletic as the players I was accustomed to playing with, but they still got the job done. They went out there and gave it 100 percent every game. I never had to question their heart.

As a freshman I played point guard. I got into the first game, Homecoming against IU-Southeast, with eighteen minutes and forty-eight seconds on the clock. I thought I'd play a lot that night, but I didn't think I'd get in that soon. In pregame warmups I landed on Shane Lakes' foot during layups and turned my ankle. In all the excitement I didn't tape it, and the next day it swelled up on me. But by the fourth game of the season I was starting.

Early in January we took a trip to North Carolina to play in a tournament. We played against some NCAA Division II schools who had some great athletes. I thought we had a shot at winning it, but we didn't. In one of the games I dunked the ball over a guy who was probably six-nine. Afterwards some of my teammates carried on like they'd seen something unbelievable. I said, "What are you talking about?" That was something I was used to doing since I was a sophomore in high school.

We had a decent team, but we lacked a real big man as a defensive presence, somebody who could guard the middle. We didn't have that six-seven big guy who could block shots or score when he wanted to. That's the one thing that kept us from competing with the Georgetowns and Cumberlands.

We had three good coaches who worked well together. Coach Kelly Combs was a strategist. He scouted teams and players and gave us reports. Coach Jefferson brought tangible experience for us to learn from. He'd had a fine playing career and had played with some legendary players. He told us stories of Bill Nichols and Arno Norwell and Ed Flynn and Steve Ridder and explained what it took to play at their level. Coach Jefferson was the players' spokesman. If any of us had something to say or had a suggestion, we went to Coach Jefferson, who would relay it to Coach Wierwille. Coach Wierwille was the organizer. Everything was on a schedule, and he demanded punctuality. If he said something, it was final. We gave him our respect.

When Daniel Brown came to Berea my sophomore year, it was immediately obvious that he could shoot. He was a deep threat to score, but he could also handle the ball. I told Coach Combs, "We've got a nice point guard here." We needed that. A lot of teams had been double-teaming me, and I knew Daniel's presence would open up my game. Coach Wierwille switched me to two guard.

To this day, I've never seen anybody shoot like Daniel. Shooting the ball, he was nasty. His ability to score inside the lane in traffic amazed me. I had always believed that in order to do that you had to have a lot of leaping ability. Daniel wasn't a leaper, but when he ran to the basket he was just as effective as when he was shooting the three. As a junior and senior he worked on his in-between game, his pull-up game. That took him to new heights. Daniel had many skills, and every game he came out ready to play at both ends, offense and defense.

When Daniel was in high school he scored a lot of points, and when he came to Berea he scored a lot of points. Some people thought he did that for selfish reasons, but I told Coach Jefferson that Daniel's style was simply the style he was brought up playing. Daniel was brought up to shoot a lot. In contrast, my style was to get other people involved, and when I was a freshman, Coach Jefferson and Coach Wierwille told me that I needed to shoot more. At any rate, it wasn't true that Daniel didn't pass the ball. Obviously he did, because he's second on the all-time Berea College assists list.

Daniel loved to play just as much as I did, and his attitude and personality meshed with mine the first time we met. The two of us became inseparable. We were always together, and we had a wonderful time. We had some arguments, but that's not unexpected when two people are together all the time, like two brothers. Daniel was a spontaneous person, the type of person I could sit back and have a nice time with.

Daniel was the fieriest player I've ever played with. He wanted so much to happen all the time, even though some of the other players might not have liked him for that. Daniel would get on people in practice. But once the words were said on the court, they were left on the court. Afterwards we'd all shower, and everything was over with.

Both Daniel and I got along very well with Coach Wierwille. One incident in my sophomore year made me feel particularly close to Coach. He asked me to come into his office. He was contemplating retirement, and he asked me if I thought he needed to step down, if the game had passed him by. I told him no. He asked my opinion, and I gave him a straight answer.

Apparently some people were saying that we weren't winning because of our offense. But the offense was not the problem. Whatever your offense, if you execute you should score and you should win. Coach knew that, and I think his real concern was that players weren't playing hard for him. I told him that he couldn't program players like a computer. The desire to play hard comes from within a player, from his will and his heart. All Coach ever asked of us was to play hard for him. Playing hard is what wins games. Not even a Rick Pitino can win many games if his players don't play hard. If some of us were lacking that, it wasn't Coach Wierwille's fault. He did everything he could with the program, and still does. As long as he's capable of coaching and wants to coach, he should do it.

When Coach showed enough confidence in me to ask my opinion about a matter as important as that, I knew there was nothing in the world I wouldn't do for him. He respects his players enough not to be checking up on them every day, but his caring for them is genuine. That's his best attribute.

After growing up in the projects in Louisville, I didn't adjust easily to life at Berea. I was not used to people who didn't know me saying, "Hi, how are you doing?" That didn't happen where I came from.

One night I'd been drinking, and I was walking down the street with Daniel. Some guys from Richmond were talking about beating up some punks from Berea, and I thought they were talking about us because they were looking our way. I didn't know what they were going to do, and I felt threatened. I got into my defensive Louisville mode. I reached into my car, took out a gun, and fired it into the air.

I went on trial for that incident and got a year's probation. The school didn't tell me I had to leave, but I told Coach Wierwille I was leaving anyway. I was homesick, I was having problems with my girlfriend in Louisville, and my grades were not what they should have been. I planned to return to Berea College in a year, and I knew that when I did I'd be on social and academic probation.

Then I got a phone call informing me that I needed to go and see the President. Apparently some faculty and staff members were upset because they believed I got off lightly because I was a basketball player. President Stephenson told me that I was suspended for at least a semester.

That was painful. But I'm glad I left school at that time. That's when I matured the most and put everything in perspective.

I spent the year working at United Parcel Service in Louisville. I broke up with the girlfriend I'd had since the eighth grade. I found myself spending more time with my family, and I began to look at everything differently. My nephews and nieces didn't know what had happened at Berea. When they got old enough to ask me about it, what would they think about me? I had no doubt that I was going to go back to school and earn my degree. I owed it to Berea College, to my coaches and teammates who stood by me, and especially to my family.

Ever since the fourth grade my life had revolved around basketball. Basketball was my world. My first goal at Berea College had been to have my picture on the wall next to the picture of Tommy Owsley and the 1985 team that won the district. But when I returned to Berea after a year away, my goal was to graduate. Whether I was played ball or did anything else, I going to graduate. I didn't set any athletic goals or GPA goals. All I wanted was to graduate.

Coach Jefferson and his family, Coach Wierwille and his family, and the entire basketball team became my Berea family. They took the trouble to get to know me and understand my situation. If I needed someone to talk to, they were there for me. If I needed anything or wanted anything, they were there for me.

Coach Wierwille's stroke was further proof that life is more than just basketball. It was a blow to me and everyone on the team. Coach Wierwille had been unstoppable for us. When we went to war, he led.

When Coach Jefferson took over, many of the players didn't show him the same respect they had showed Coach Wierwille. People were walking out of practice, or wearing shorts under their practice shorts and T-shirts under their practice shirts. Coach Wierwille didn't tolerate those things. One day Coach Jefferson had enough, and he told us we weren't going to disrespect him any more.

That was halfway through the season, and right after that we began to play better. I realized that I needed to support Coach Jefferson. I had probably been guilty of disrespecting him the most, so I apologized to the team. I stepped up, Daniel stepped up, and Tino Ballenger stepped up. We knew it was time for us to show some leadership. Although Coach Wierwille wasn't going to be returning that year, we decided that in practice and in games we would play like he was sitting on the bench.

We upset Pikeville in the opening round of the postseason tournament. The week before we'd hung with them, and we all felt we should have beaten them. When we met them again we stepped on their floor knowing we were going to win, and that's what happened. We had been taking a lot of bad shots. I told Coach Jefferson, "I'll play the point guard. I'll take fewer shots if it will help the team succeed." After that, everybody started wanting to pass the ball around. When we started playing more as a team, our confidence grew.

When we first heard that Berea was going to drop to Division II of the NAIA, no two players were more upset than Daniel and I. We had worked since our freshman year to have a competitive team that could win the KIAC. Now it seemed that we were going to be cheated out of our just.

Not having Georgetown College on our schedule upset us more than anything, because we felt we were finally ready to beat them. Georgetown liked to load up on transfers from NCAA Division I schools, cocky six-seven guys who acted like we were beneath them, that they could half-play against us and win. That fired me up. I knew I could hold my own against Division I players. I had played against Jermaine Brown in middle and high school. I didn't think that he was any better than I was, even though he was named Mr Basketball in 1991 and signed at the University of Tennessee.

By the time Daniel and I were seniors, we couldn't wait to play Georgetown. We had Coach coming back and a strong team. With Georgetown off our schedule, we were frustrated. So we talked about it. There was no point in sulking; we were just going to have to play. That's what we did. From our first practice we were confident that we'd be going to the NAIA Division II national tournament in Idaho.

I'll never forget the first game at Seabury Center, Homecoming against IU-Southeast. It was opening night in our new building, and it was the first time my brother and two sisters ever saw me play at the same time. It was the only time my older sister saw me play. That was special. I didn't have one of my best games, but I hit six free throws in a row to ice the game. For them to see me playing college basketball and doing well meant the world to me.

To have Coach Wierwille back with a new building and a contending team was heaven. It was an enormous relief to get our general back. From the top players on down, everyone always played harder for Coach Wierwille. He didn't have to say anything. Nobody wanted to go over to the bench during a timeout and have Coach look at him.

The trip to the national tournament was a wonderful experience. I'd never been in an airplane before, and it was a thrill simply to touch down in the different cities along the way. In Idaho we welcomed the opportunity to measure ourselves against elite competition. Coach Jefferson had never been to a national tournament, and neither had any of the players. The only one who had been to a national tournament was Coach Wierwille. Many of us were nervous. I didn't get nervous before basketball games because basketball was no longer my whole world, but it still reassured me to look at Coach Wierwille and see that he knew what he was doing. He had plenty of confidence.

I left the game of basketball on a high note. I still play now and then, but I don't have the desire to go out and play five nights a week.

I worked at Seabury the whole time I was at Berea, either as a janitor or issuing equipment in the tote box. At first my major was physical education, but I found that it came too easy. In high school I had taken advanced classes for the simple reason that they pushed me to learn. I was no great scholar, but I needed a challenge, something to keep me focused.

I decided to switch my major to economics or math. I talked to a teammate, Chris Haggard, who was majoring in economics. Chris told me that it was mostly math and theory. So I went to talk to Dr Cliff Sowell, who taught in the Economics Department. He told me what classes to take and when to take them.

Economics was a tough major, and Cliff Sowell helped me stay with it. He knew the capabilities of each and every one of his students. In class he would go over something, then look around. He could tell if somebody didn't understand. Whenever I has having trouble with the material he gave me extra instruction, extra help after class.

After I graduated I worked at Footlocker for a year while taking classes at Eastern Kentucky University. I'm presently working at Mayfield Elementary School in Richmond as an instructional assistant. I help kids who are having trouble in reading or math, and I enjoy it. I wish I'd had someone like that when I was growing up. Lately I've been spending a lot of time with Craig Jefferson, who is now a loan officer for a mortgage company. He's letting me work with him so I can get some experience. I've been learning the system and meeting prospective customers. It's a business I'd like to get into.

Earning a college degree was a goal I wanted to achieve for the sake of my nephews and nieces. They can say, "My uncle went to college. He played basketball, and he earned his degree." So many children in Louisville look up to drug dealers and people who are doing wrong because those people have big homes and nice cars. I want nice things too, because I want my nephews and nieces to see that if you stay on the right path and go to college and get your degree, those things will come sooner or later. I live my life to set an example for them.

November 17, 1998

Daniel Brown   1992-96

I grew up in a rural community, Carlisle, Kentucky, population 1800. My dad was a factory worker. My mom worked for Food Town. We raised a little tobacco.

I played four years of baseball, football, and basketball at Nicholas County High School. Roland Wierwille and Kelly Combs got interested in me halfway through my senior year. I don't think they missed the last ten or twelve basketball games I played. Many schools recruited me, but Berea was the most beautiful college I visited. Its small size appealed to me, and the people made me feel at home.

Daniel Brown: "Nobody could guard him"

Ed Oakley and Bobby Storie, my high school coach and his assistant, had both been college players at Transylvania. That's where they wanted me to go. In high school the only offense we ever ran was Transy's offense. Transy coach Don Lane came to watch me a couple of times, but he told my high school coach that at five-eleven I was too short to play for his club. Coach Wierwille knew about that, and he used that story later to get me motivated. I always played better against Transy.

I could tell right off that Coach Wierwille was very well respected. He demanded the respect of his players. I liked that, because my high school coach had also demanded respect. I knew that Coach Wierwille cared about his players because 100 percent of the people who played under him for four years graduated. That caught my eye right there.

Coach Wierwille put a lot of time into trying to get me to come to Berea, but when I arrived I had to prove myself to the team. I was well known coming in from high school. I had led the state in scoring, and everybody knew who I was. They kind of shied away from me at first.

Personality-wise I think we all got along pretty well in the locker room. But even as a freshman I wasn't shy about shooting. If I had a shot, I'd shoot. I started taking a lot of the minutes of a senior guard who had been playing there for three years, and he ended up quitting. So my teammates and I had to adjust to each other.

Ron Kinmon and Dennis Sargent were seniors that year. It took them awhile to get used to me. As the year went along I think they respected my game, and I respected what they had done. I didn't ever back off them, but they were the captains, and Coach let them decide what was going on. That's the right way to run a team.

Ron didn't have all the talent of the world, but he worked his butt off. That's Berea College basketball, always. Dennis was that way too. While Ron would show his emotion, Dennis was very quiet. Dennis would show up at practice every day and never say much to you. Both of them were excellent players.

We were rebuilding that year, and it was rough. We were overmatched because we lacked size. Ron and Dennis at six-five were the biggest players on our team. Many of the teams we played had guys six-seven or six-eight across the front line.

My specialty was shooting three-pointers. Coach Wierwille built his offense around me from the start. He changed his whole approach by going with his three-point shooters, which Berea had never done. But Coach made it very clear to me that if I didn't play defense, I wasn't going to play. Plus, I needed to change my attitude. I was kind of a hothead coming in, and Coach Wierwille didn't to go for that. We butted heads a couple of times. It didn't take long for me to learn.

We were playing Pikeville College at home. I was having a good game, and we were beating them by fifteen or twenty points. I stole the ball and thought I'd be a hot dog, so I bounced it up and went up to get a lob and didn't make the basket. Coach called time out right there. He got me over to the bench and put his forehead to my forehead and said, "Don't you ever, ever do that again, or you'll never play for me." It was real intense. Right then I knew, it was his way or the highway.

I would never disrespect the coach. When I spoke to him it was yes sir, no sir. I listened to him. But I would also voice my opinion, although that got me chewed up a few times. Eventually my speaking up helped to open my relationship with him.

Some coaches recruit a player, he plays basketball for them, and that's it. Coach Wierwille respects you as both a player and a person. He cares about you. He cares what's going on in your classes and your social life. He's always asking questions: "How are you doing? How is your family doing?" He earns the respect of all his players because he gives respect back.

I was the guard who had the ball ninety-five percent of the time. If I didn't, Tony Goatley ran the guard position. Tony was the complete player. He always came through with the big assist or the big shot or the big rebound. I learned a lot from him. Without Tony I could never have accomplished what I did.

When I came to Berea, Tony was the first guy who met me on campus. He became like a brother to me. Tony grew up in a tough part of Louisville. He was hot-tempered and could get loud, but one-on-one he was soft-spoken. I found him easy to talk to. When I arrived Tony lived in another dorm, but he would come over and stay up with me until two or three o'clock in the morning. Although we weren't allowed to be in the gym, we'd get the janitor to open it up so we could shoot baskets and play H-O-R-S-E.

Tony and I shared a love of basketball. For me it was my first love. If it wasn't for basketball I probably would not have gone to college, and when the basketball team struggled I thought about leaving school. But I made up my mind that I wasn't going to go home. I stayed at Berea because I felt I'd found a home there.

I was a pitcher and shortstop on the baseball team. Playing two sports wore me out. When the basketball season ended the baseball season had already started, and I jumped straight into it. It seemed like I was always doing my studying on the road on buses. But I don't blame sports for my academic problems. I didn't put the effort into my studies that I should have, and my grades suffered for it. Eventually I matured. When you're in high school your mom and dad stay on you. When you leave home to go to college your coaches and teachers stay on you. But you've got to learn to be responsible for yourself.

The team had had a good practice the day Coach Wierwille had his stroke. Coach Craig Jefferson called Tony and me that evening. We couldn't believe it. We were relieved to find out that Coach was going to be all right. But we thought, "Where is this ballclub heading now?"

Tony and I agreed that somebody was going to have to step up to keep the team together. We didn't want the season to be lost because the coach couldn't be there. Sometimes players don't respect an assistant who has to take over. Tony and I thought that might be a problem with our team. If we were leaders, we could help the younger players make the transition. We'd set a good example if we'd work as hard in practice for Coach Jefferson as we had for Coach Wierwille.

Coach Jefferson did an excellent job. He was a player's coach. Although he got mad at us a couple of times, he was usually relaxed, and his relaxed personality helped us. At the end of the year we almost upset number one Georgetown in overtime in their building. We were able to do that because Coach Jefferson didn't put any pressure on us. We just had to perform.

Coach Wierwille told me that I was overweight, so I dedicated the off-season to getting in shape. I'd been playing at 195, 200. That whole summer I just played and played, and I came back at 175. Everybody was excited about Coach Wierwille returning. We were all looking forward to seeing him back on the sidelines. That feeling carried over all year long.

Tony and I were seniors now, and Coach could depend on us to do a lot of coaching on the floor. He would bring us into his office and tell us what he wanted. When he'd get mad in practice he'd criticize Tony and me the most, because he knew we were the ones who should be setting an example for the younger players. We accepted that. It helped him and helped our team.

Within Coach's system he wanted the team to play under control, and he wanted everybody involved. I had a tendency to try to take over a game. I had one of those nights at Thomas More's tournament in January. I hit three or four three-pointers in a row, and Coach told me on the sidelines, "Don't try to take over this game. You've got four other players on this team." Those reminders made me a better player.

We had better team unity that year. Players accepted their roles. Otis Diuguid didn't start, but he helped us a lot. Otis was a great friend, but I hated to have him guard me in practice. He was the best defensive player I've ever been around. Donnie Frazier could shoot the ball. He fed off me and helped take the pressure off. Crawford James didn't have real good hands for the ball, which limited his offensive effectiveness, but C.J. was tenacious on defense.

Corey Craig was a junior that year. Corey was big, and we needed his presence. As a freshman he had come in soft. I got on him and stayed on him. I felt that was my job. I'm sure I got on his nerves, but Corey played better when somebody got under his skin. He knew as a freshman that he had to pick up weight and get stronger. After he started doing that he became a totally different player. He worked very hard.

Having Coach back and playing in a brand new gym in my senior season was just like a fairy story. I had great memories of the old gym, of course. There was a lot of tradition there. It was hard for teams to beat us at Old Seabury. We'd push them into the corner under that overhead track where they couldn't shoot the ball. It was loud. 500 people would feel like 3000, they were so close to us.

It took awhile for me to get used to the new gym. It wasn't a shooter's gym like Old Seabury, and the ball didn't bounce as high off the floor. But Berea really needed the new building, not just for the gym itself but for the spacious weight rooms and everything else. The whole college benefited.

I played for four years to get to the national tournament, and to accomplish that in the year the new gym opened and Coach Wierwille came back was so, so sweet. But I was disappointed with the way I played in Idaho. I hated ending my college career on terrible one-for-eleven shooting. I couldn't hit the shot from three. The one I hit was the one that put us up, with twelve seconds left and Berea down by two. I thought we had it won, but their guy hit two free throws at the end to beat us. Berea had one of the top teams out there, but things didn't work out for us. That happens in basketball sometimes.

I had several labor jobs. I was a janitor at the gym, then worked in the tote box. I was a janitor at the dorm. When the new gym was built, I got back over there.

Physical education was my major. I took three classes under Phil English, who taught communications. I could talk to him like I was talking to a friend. He was down to earth. He let me be myself. He helped me out of some tough situations in college, and he knows I'm forever grateful to him. He's a great man.

I went through a lot of struggles to get my Berea College degree, and there are no words to explain the feeling I have for it. My wife and I are both very proud to be Berea College graduates.

Jorene Wylie, the woman I married, was originally from Lexington. She spent seven years in the Navy before coming to Berea to study nursing. The basketball players used to sit on the wall at the CPO, checking out the incoming freshmen. I saw her walk by wearing all this Kentucky stuff. I got interested and said, "Hey, Miss Kentucky." That same night I had my senior picture taken and walked by her all dressed up, and I must have made a decent impression. I asked her out one night, she said yes, and we've been together ever since.

After I graduated I stayed for a year as Coach Wierwille's student assistant coach while I worked as a teacher's assistant at the Bellevue alternative school in Richmond. All I've ever wanted to do is coach and teach.

Today I run a middle school ISA, In School Alternative, in Winchester. I work with students who have behavioral or learning disorders that make it hard for them to be around other kids. The regular teachers can't teach class with these students in the room, so it's my duty to take them into my classroom and try to get them to do their schoolwork. It's not a job I want to stay in forever, because there's a lot of stress. It's a real challenge to keep these kids going for seven hours. But I think I've earned their respect.

I'm assistant girls' basketball coach at my school and assistant high school baseball coach. In the next five years I can see myself coaching boys' basketball in high school. Eventually, though, I want to get into college coaching.

Coach Wierwille came to my wedding, and Cecilia, his wife, told me that he has never stayed so long at a wedding reception for any of his players. He and I have always been close, but we've become closer over the years. When I played for him we came to understand each other. I didn't like to lose, and that's what he liked in me. He hated to lose worse than I did, and I didn't think anyone could feel that way. My relationship with him is a father and son relationship, and he knows that. I'm not ashamed to say that I love him to death, and I've told him that to his face. I get teary-eyed thinking about him. I owe him for motivating me to get through school.

I'd like to say something about Kelly Combs. He's the one who got me to Berea by staying on me. He called me at high school every day. After I came to Berea, Kelly became someone I could talk to.

Kelly Combs does a great job of recruiting for Berea College. He has a knack for locating players who have the style and personality to fit the program and will stay four years to earn their degrees. Kelly will make an excellent head coach. He'll have to change some to do it, because when you're head man you've got to be the head. He'll be making the decisions, so he'll have to find another assistant to do for him what he's doing for Coach Wierwille. Kelly knows basketball, and he works too hard not to be successful. I think he'll do great, and I wish him the best of luck.

September 21, 1998

Roland C. Wierwille   1992-96

I grew up in Berea, of course. I never wanted to go to college anywhere else. I knew that I could play golf at Berea and get a good education. I was a pretty decent golfer in high school, and that was one thing I knew I wanted to do in college. I probably could have gone to Cumberland or Georgetown and played on a good golf team, but I didn't see any reason to do that.

I played basketball at Madison Southern High School, but I never intended to go out for the Berea College team. My dad and I talked about it. He felt it might damage the relationship we had at home. If I were on the team and he got on me, I might bring some feelings home. So I didn't try out.

The first day they practiced I was in my room, and I got a phone call from my dad. He said, "Do you want to play basketball? We've had a couple of guys quit and a couple guys go home, so we need some more players."

I said, "We talked about it, and it's up to you. I'd love to, and if you think it's all right, it's fine with me."

I was on the team for four years. The only reason I wanted to play in college was to stay in shape for golf.

Roland C. Wierwille: "I never wanted to go to college anywhere else"

I was a starter in high school, but in college I was on the bench. Any time I got into a game was a thrill for me. Generally it happened when my dad was fed up with one of the guys underneath who wasn't getting it done. My only goal was to go in there and bang it up with some people, let them know I was there and that they weren't going to push me around. As a freshman I was six-one and a half, and I grew another couple of inches and gained some weight.

In my freshman year some of the juniors and seniors were hesitant to say things in the locker room, thinking I'd go back and tell my dad. That was a tough situation. After about three weeks I said, "Fellows, listen up. When I'm in here or when I'm out there I'm no different than you are. I play, you play. He's my dad, but here at the gym he's our coach. You don't have to worry about what you say about him. It won't go home with me." Nothing was wrong after that. I probably said things about him too!

Playing college basketball was a great experience for me, not because I played a lot of minutes, but because of the places I went and the people I met. A lot of my teammates will be my friends for life. I was especially close to Daniel Brown and Tony Goatley. What got me attached to them was the fact that when we'd play pickup games they'd always pick me up because they knew I'd play hard for them. That meant a lot to me. They could have picked up somebody six-eight to play with them, but they always picked me up. That started something for me, because they respected me.

Daniel was a good leader, and everybody looked up to him. He saw the floor so well. He really knew what he was doing. Somebody might come in and not know his role, and Daniel would pull him to the side and tell him what was going on. If I were ever playing basketball again, Daniel Brown is the first person I would want on my team. I don't know what it was about him, just something in his blood, but with eight or nine seconds to go you wanted him to have the ball.

Daniel is a good guy all around. He's very cordial and polite. He's shy if he doesn't know you, but if he saw you on campus he'd still say, "Hi." I think that came from where he's from, a small town where everybody knows everybody. That's what I liked about Berea, too. You can walk around any time during the day or night and say hello to everybody, and a lot of people know you by name.

Tony is another great guy. Berea did a lot for him. He came from a tough part of Louisville, and if he'd stayed there there's no telling where he'd be right now. He's a very personable person who'd do anything for you. As a player Tony reminded me of Craig Jefferson, who always read the floor real well. Whenever they were coming down Craig could look and see and know where their guy was going to pass it, and he could get a steal or something. That's how Tony was. He could see what was going to happen before it happened. That's what made him a good player: he could see what was going on and kind of overplay. He was a very hard player. When he first came to Berea he was real skinny. He gained some weight, but he was always physical, always took the ball to the hole strong. You couldn't beat him. If anyone was going to beat him, it would be himself.

It's hard for me to talk about my dad's illness. I sometimes ask myself why it happened to him. You see a person who's ninety years old and has been smoking and drinking all his life, and then you see a guy who doesn't drink or smoke at all, lives clean, works out every day, watches what he eats, and dies of a heart attack at forty-five. It's weird.

For my dad ninety-eight percent of the problem was stress. Getting beat would bother me for a little while, but soon I'd get over it. He'd come home and go back in his bedroom and lay there and read the paper and think about it the rest of the night. He'd fall asleep but wake up in the middle of the night and yell at himself because he thought he'd done something wrong. He put so much stress on himself. After awhile you've got to let it go. It builds up so much that it's not worth it.

It drove me insane to listen to him get on himself. It was never the players' fault, it was his fault. That got on my nerves. If he knew what we needed to do and told us what to do and we didn't execute it, it was our fault, not his. But he put it on himself so much. There are times when he does that now, but as intense as he used to get, he doesn't do that anymore. Nothing like I saw my freshman year. There were times in game situations where I'd see him get frustrated and get real red, and I knew he had so much energy built up in his brain and his whole body that it looked like he was going to explode. Today he still knows what he wants to do and can still get the point across, but he realizes he doesn't have to be as intense as he used to be. That's good for him. He's done so much to come back to where he is today.

He's doing a great job right now. Today all he's scared of is that when he retires, whoever comes in might not run the program the way he does. He's from the old school. He likes to do things the old way. He likes to get kids in as freshmen and work them through the program for four years. Graduating his athletes is a big thing for him. He's afraid of somebody coming in and getting a lot of transfers, running kids in and out, and giving Berea as bad a name as some of the schools have today. A team we played against my senior year had a guy who played seventeen or eighteen games in the second semester, and after the last game they never saw him again. That stuff is ridiculous. At schools like that I wonder if the administration simply doesn't care. It's all right to want to win, but you've got to have standards.

Going to the NAIA tournament in 1996 was an unforgettable experience. We lost our first game, and it was hard for Daniel and Tony and Otis Diuguid and me to think that we'd never play organized basketball for a high school or college ever again. But the number of games we won was not what mattered most to me. I felt happy, not that it was over, but just that I was able to experience it. That was the biggest thing. You've got to go on with the positive things like what you learned and the experiences you had.

When Boise and Nampa come together to host the NAIA tournament, it's almost like the NCAA Final Four for a whole week. They do it up so nice with honorary coaches and sponsors. They just built a new facility for twenty-seven or twenty-eight million dollars, all of it community money. That indicates to me that all the people in the community want you to be there. It's a great atmosphere. If you go somewhere wearing a shirt that says Berea College or some other college, people are always talking to you, asking you where you're from. Businesspeople sit there all day and watch the games. The schools from surrounding communities bring their students. The kids love it. They pick a team and cheer for them.

There are some great teams in the NAIA national tournament. You see the team concept a lot more than you do in the NCAA, where you often have one or two players who light it up while everybody else stands around and watches. In Kentucky ninety-five percent of the people are UK fans, but I don't really root for them, and people ask me why. It's not that I don't like UK, but ever since I was born I grew up around NAIA basketball at Berea College. That's who I support. During the week and on Saturdays when I was a kid I never watched TV, I went to Berea College games. People might say, "Who's Berea College?" They see an NCAA game on TV and are not aware of the competitiveness and excitement of NAIA basketball. Kids can stay at home and watch UK or North Carolina, but if they really like basketball they'll have fun watching a team like Berea College, seeing guys who are out there not because they're getting something but because they love to play.

I grew up around the program, and pretty much everybody who came through it gave me a little bit of something. I've got so many memories that I could talk to you from here until next year.

Sometimes I went on trips with the team. When they traveled to Pikeville or Alice Lloyd they'd stay in a rundown little motel called the Mountaineer. I'd be staying with my dad and say, "Dad, I'm going down to see the guys for a minute." I'd go over there and they'd wear me out for an hour and half, wrestle with me, throw me against the bedpost, or pull my underwear up over the top of my head.

I sat on the bench with the players and gave them water. I remember saying to Coach Steve Ridder when I was little, "Coach, what's the score of the game?" He'd tell me, and I'd say, "Who's winning?" I had no clue! I was just sitting there and loving it.

The player I remember most is Vance Blade. He was always very friendly with me and always did things with me. In the final game of his senior year we went down to Cumberland and got beat. I was only about seven, and I was down in the locker room crying. Vance picked me up and put me on his shoulder and took me out to the bus and sat me down in his lap. He was always great to me.

My first college labor assignment was in Woodcraft. I'd always loved working with my hands around the house, so I started doing that. I spent the first semester making pieces for skittles games. I was making good money because I was turning out sixty-five or seventy of them in an hour, but it got a little monotonous after a while. I like to be around people, and I couldn't handle being at the lathe by myself for three or four hours at a time. So I worked in the finishing room for the next year and a half. That was fun, finishing dressers and beds and stuff like that. There were other people around, and I had the satisfaction of helping to make that furniture look really nice.

Woodcraft was only open from eight to four and was closed on weekends, so it was hard for me to get my hours in with class and basketball practice at three o'clock. So when I was a junior I got a teaching assistant's position over at the gym. I did that and worked in the tote box a little bit.

I decided to major in industrial technology management after taking an Appalachian crafts class under Gary Mahoney. He became my adviser and helped me a great deal. He wasn't like some teachers who talk above your head. He listened when I asked a question and often responded by asking me a question. That's how it was in the Technology Department. You asked a question and instead of an answer you'd get another question. That approach helped you figure a problem out.

I gained a good understanding of woods and metals, and I learned a lot in the management classes that a lot of business majors take. The industrial technology management major is great for people who want to enter middle management in manufacturing situations. Some of the people I graduated with are project engineers or are doing quality control. I had opportunities to do that kind of thing, but I wanted to teach. I'm now enrolled at Eastern to get certified in technology ed for grades six through twelve.

I think I'll be able to get a job just about anywhere I want. There's a great need for industrial technology teachers because industry pays more than teaching and doesn't come with the hassle of having to worry about kids. Those are pluses for some people, but I like to teach. I'd rather help kids than work eight to five in a factory.

August 29, 1998

Corey Craig   1993-97

The first time I met Coach Wierwille, I walked into his office chewing gum and wearing a hat. He looked at me and said, "Don't ever chew gum around me again. And when you walk into a building, take your hat off." Since that day I rarely chew gum anywhere, and I hardly ever wear a hat.

Corey Craig and Coach Roland Wierwille

My first impression of Coach Wierwille was that he was a stern man. If I didn't do as he asked, I wasn't going to be there. I liked that. I was raised to respect my elders and do what they expected of me. If my mother or father or uncle asked me to do something, I did it without question, saying "Yes, ma'am" or "Yes, sir." No back talk! Coach Wierwille gives his players 100 percent of himself, and he expects his players to give him 100 percent of themselves. I wanted to do that, and he recognized that and respected me for it. In turn, I respected him.

His greatest strength as a coach lay in his ability to get the most out of his players. Few of us were among the most talented of athletes. We succeeded because Coach Wierwille motivated us to play at a higher level. He helped me develop the inner strength to push myself beyond what I thought were my limits.

I grew up in the country between Brodhead and Mount Vernon, Kentucky. My whole family has farmed their entire lives: tobacco, corn, hay, beef cattle. My uncle has a lot of pigs.

I played basketball at Rockcastle County High School. At six-seven I was recruited by Morehead State, West Virginia Wesleyan, Lincoln Memorial University, Cumberland College, and Abilene Christian College in Texas. Shelby Reynolds, who lived in Rockcastle County, was a Berea College alumnus who had made friends with Coach Wierwille when he was there. He contacted Coach Wierwille, who contacted my high school coach. As a result I went over to Berea for a couple of visits.

I chose Berea for a couple of reasons. I knew that I'd be able to get a lot of playing time right away, and that was appealing. More important was the knowledge that if something happened to me physically at Berea College, if I could no longer play basketball, I could still remain at Berea and receive the same education at the same price. That was reassuring. I was an okay player, but nowhere near talented enough to play professionally. I didn't want my whole future riding on what I might do on the basketball court.

I started several games my freshman year. I was known as a rebounder. When I was a senior in high school I had led the state in rebounding. At the time I held the Kentucky state record for the most rebounds in a game, thirty-two against North Laurel High School. But a lot of that I attribute simply to me being bigger than everybody else. When I got to college and started to play with people my size who could jump as well or better than I could, I struggled a bit. At Berea rebounding and defense were the keys to being successful, so Coach worked with me individually on footwork in the post, positioning, and proper rebounding techniques.

In high school I had been the go-to guy. I played inside, I played outside, I shot threes. I had to forget about a lot of that stuff when I came to college. It quickly became obvious, too, that I had to improve my post defense. In high school I thought I was a pretty good post defense player, but in college I needed to be a lot quicker and stronger. In my first two years in college I lifted weights to add bulk and strength. I weighed 200 as a freshman and finished my sophomore year at 220. That summer I did even more lifting, ate a lot, and beefed up to 260. That was good for banging, but I lost some of my foot speed and endurance up and down the floor. By the time I ended my junior year I got back down to 240, and my senior year I played at 230.

As a freshman I tore ligaments in my back, which kept me out of the last seven games of the season. The next year I broke my hand in a scrimmage the week before the first game, and I couldn't play the first seven games of that season. After that I missed just one or two games the rest of my career, due to a bad ankle. I'd twist it, but then I'd do a lot of rehabbing and come right back.

I liked being the guy who took the charge, who dove on the floor, who hustled to make a good defensive play, who got the crowd excited. I took pride in leaving everything I had on the floor at the end of every game. I always played 110 percent with my heart.

I wasn't our first option to score. I was a role player who was expected to get my ten points and ten rebounds a game. That was fine with me. In my last two years I probably got a double-double around seventy percent of the time. I wanted to be a team leader, and even as a freshman and sophomore I had the type of attitude a leader should display. I tried to be the guy who kept the team intact, who kept things going.

When I first joined the team the upperclassmen who impressed me most were Travis Earlywine and Chris Haggard. Travis was a leader, and he too was a guy who would take the charge, dive on the floor. Like me, Travis had the ability to score, but he realized that that wasn't always where he was most needed. Chris was a tremendous outside shooter.

Both those guys went through a lot. Travis suffered many injuries, but he never got down or felt sorry for himself. He kept a positive attitude and stayed involved with the team.

The basketball team was like a fraternity, in the best sense. Players would come and go, but the ones who stuck it out and stayed there with you were the ones you formed the strongest bonds with. I made several close friends on the team. Shane Tarvin, my roommate my junior and senior years, became like a brother to me, perhaps because we were together so much. He and I were a lot alike. He took winning and competing very seriously, but when it came time for the other things in life, he wasn't going to be so serious that it dragged him down. Shane was a guy I could talk to about anything, and he with me. As a player Shane was a good jump shooter and rebounder. He was a tremendous leaper.

In my sophomore year Coach Wierwille had his stroke. That was a big blow to me personally, because he was a close friend to me. For the team it caused a lot of turmoil.

It happened so suddenly. We weren't far away from the beginning of the season, and it was extremely traumatic to have our coach laid up, not knowing if he was ever going to talk again, let alone coach. It brought everybody down. Morale deteriorated, and a lot of negativity was tossed around. It seemed like everything that was said in practice and in games was negative. I thought "If this is how it's going to be the rest of my time at Berea, I don't know if I can handle it."

It was a tough for Coach Jefferson to take over the team. Coach Jefferson had been everybody's buddy. If one of us heard a good joke he was the first guy to tell, because he'd get a kick out of it. Whenever a problem came up, academic, personal, or whatever, 100 percent of the players felt 100 percent comfortable talking to Coach Jefferson about it. But now he had to assume a different persona. He had to be more detached, less friendly, to try to get the most out of us. It was an awkward transition.

When I was growing up I was taught that the best way to learn things was to listen to people who had been there and done that before. At Berea College nobody had more knowledge and experience than Wilson Evans. I had a chance to sit and talk with him when he came to practice one day. We were getting ready to wrap up, and I was messing around shooting before going into the locker room. He walked out onto the floor and said hi to me and shook my hand.

I said, "Hello, Dean Evans, how are you?"

"The question, Corey, is how are you? And how is the team?"

"We're struggling right now. Our morale is down. Nobody has a lot of energy."

Dean Evans recalled a similar situation in his life. Then he suggested that instead of playing for individual goals, we should strive to make the College and the community proud of us. He spoke of the privilege of wearing the Berea College jersey, and pointed out that winning or losing matters less in the great scheme of things than playing with pride and honor. That comforted me quite a bit. Whenever I saw Dean Evans I remembered his words and quit feeling sorry for myself.

Our last home game that season was the very last game in Old Seabury. There was a tremendous crowd, including Coach Wierwille. We heard that the fire marshal wanted some of the spectators to leave, and he was told to take a hike.

Our opponent was Campbellsville. We'd had trouble with them in the past. Their coach, Lou Cunningham, knew how much adrenaline we had going, so he had his team up. Visiting teams were always pumped up when they came to Old Seabury anyway. Campbellsville was playing at the top of their game, and they got ahead and forced us to play catch-up.

In the last ten minutes we stopped struggling and began firing. Daniel Brown drove the rest of us. He hit eleven three-pointers. We could see in his eyes that nothing was going to stop him from leading us to victory. At crunch time we were telling ourselves to pick it up more, more, more. We were all just about to die because we were giving so much.

We beat Campbellsville in overtime When the game was over, Daniel ran straight to Coach and hugged him. He told Coach that we had won the game for him. That's the way we all felt, and we signed the game ball and took it directly to him. That night gave us hope for the future of Berea College basketball.

After the regular season ended we went down to Pikeville to play the first game of the postseason. Pikeville had beaten us twice. This game was close. As a competitor and a dedicated member of the team I wanted very much to win. But the year had been so trying, I couldn't help thinking that if we lost I'd feel relieved that our season was over. We won the game, and when all was said and done I was glad of the outcome. But after Georgetown beat us a few days later, I wasn't sorry that this stressful season had come to an end.

I had been asking myself what I would do if Coach Wierwille didn't come back. I decided to wait and see what would happen. If Coach Wierwille didn't come back, would I want to play for the man the College hired to replace him? If not, I should transfer. I couldn't imagine staying at Berea College and not playing basketball. Every time I walked across campus people would look at me as a guy who betrayed them, who let the school down. I couldn't have handled that, so I would have had to get away from it.

I was tempted to make a quick decision, but I didn't. I remembered something that happened when I was a freshman. A student from Laurel County came in with me, Jackie Steele. We were the big arrivals on campus. We had both been successful in high school, all-staters and so forth. Jackie played a lot, more than I did, and had a very good year. Then he transferred to Georgetown, and Coach Wierwille felt betrayed by that. When he found out about it he called me into his office and asked me if I was going to leave, too. I assured him that I wasn't, that I was very happy at Berea and looking forward to my sophomore season. Well, that season came, and Coach had a stroke and we struggled without him. But when I found out Coach was coming back, that was all I needed to know.

I can't describe the way I felt at homecoming my junior year, playing in the new Seabury Center with Coach Wierwille leading us again. The place was packed. Emotions ran high. We believed that nothing could go wrong, and we got off to a good start.

We got good senior leadership from Daniel Brown and Tony Goatley. Both had been around the block a couple of times and knew what was going on. In previous years Daniel's attitude and the way he went about things were criticized by his teammates and people associated with the program. In his senior year, however, he was a completely different person. He was 100 percent dedicated to the program, and that made a huge difference. Tony Goatley was the same way. That meant a lot, because they were both tremendous ballplayers.

Daniel and Tony were fearless competitors. Daniel's style was to make something happen. Nobody could guard him. He claimed to be five-eleven, although I always told him he was five-ten, and nobody looking at him would think he was very strong or quick. But there was no one I ever played with who I'd rather have on my team in the last thirty seconds with the game on the line than Daniel Brown. Daniel truly had ice water in his veins, as the saying goes.

Tony was a very good jump shooter, and he was so strong that it was hard to match up against him. Opposing guards were not usually strong enough to guard Tony, so he would post them up and score on the post. If they tried to put a big guy on Tony, he'd take the guy outside. Tony was a very versatile player, a big threat for our team against anybody.

We had other experienced guys like me and Shane and Otis Diuguid, another player who accepted his role. Otis would enter the game in that lull at the end of the first half when our guards were getting worn down. He'd get a couple of steals and a couple of layups and revive us. We called Otis "The Sparkplug." His hands and feet were so quick that if he didn't get a steal, he would at least cause a deflection. Crawford James was a big rebounder and shot blocking threat. He intimidated a lot of people with his size and demeanor. He could jump really well.

Our first game with Transylvania that year was in their building. Berea hadn't beaten Transy since 1991, a span of eleven games in a row. Transy was the school where Coach Wierwille got his start coaching, and I knew how much he hated to lose to them. Coach's expectations were so high and he drove us so hard that we wanted to live up to his expectations at all costs. We knew that if we made him happy, we'd make ourselves happy. When we beat Transy on their home floor it felt great, and beating them again at Berea gave us the momentum push we needed to get to the national tournament.

To qualify we had to get past IU-Southeast. From six hours before that game started until six hours after it was over, I was on the biggest high of my athletic career. I had been playing well at the end of the season, and I came into that game determined that no one was going to deny us our chance to go to the national tournament when we were so close.

I played a solid game, with seventeen points and nine or ten rebounds. I was in a zone you couldn't have got me out of by hitting me in the face with a baseball bat. I never felt tired, because I had an adrenaline surge that wouldn't stop. I couldn't forget the work and the sweat and the pain and the grief we'd all gone through. We won the game, and when the buzzer went off I fell to the floor and cried with relief. To come this far made all the strife of the previous year worthwhile.

In Idaho we felt festive and happy. Everybody was upbeat. The whole trip was great. We had smooth flights, nobody got lost, nobody got left, nobody lost their luggage. The team we played was tough and beat us, but we all learned a lot from the experience, and it was good to gain some national exposure for our program.

The next year we no longer had Daniel and Tony, who between them had probably accounted for fifty percent of our production. Their skills were unique, and we didn't groom anyone to replace them as individuals. This was something I felt very strongly about and conveyed to the team in every meeting we had. I believed that if we all picked our game up ten percent, we could make up the loss collectively. That approach worked for the most part.

Jeremy Wood was a very good three-point shooter. He was asked to play the point guard position, which was unfamiliar for him. But Jeremy wouldn't accept not being the best he could. Although he had some difficulty, he adapted. Jeremy was a tremendous defensive player who would always guard our opponent's best player.

Donnie Frazier was a hard-nosed player and a tremendous shooter, superb at coming off a screen. At that point he had not yet developed a sure sense of when to shoot and when not to shoot. Donnie had a free hand and could get hot, but he didn't always move the ball around as much as he should have. That came with experience. Another key player that year was David Jackson. David was a talented athlete. He had a great body for the game and he had good skills underneath, but he marched to the tune of his own band. He stuck it out and played that year, but after that he left school.

We traveled down to Florida to play in Embry-Riddle University's tournament. It was a great experience. There's nothing better than being in Daytona Beach in January. Most of us had met Steve Ridder, Embry-Riddle's coach, when he brought his team to the NAIA national tournament the year before. We knew what he had accomplished as a student and assistant coach at Berea. In Idaho the Embry-Riddle players sat behind our bench and supported us, and we did the same for them when they played. When we came to Florida Coach Ridder invited us to his house. He welcomed us with open arms and treated us like we were his children or his brothers.

The first team we played in the tournament was Hope College. We learned a huge lesson that night. It was one of the worst beatings I've ever taken in a basketball game. I don't mean that they beat us up physically, but they outscored us by almost fifty points. They really put it on us.

Although they were a good team with plenty of talent, I know we were capable of beating them. But we couldn't do anything right.

It was very embarrassing for me and for the whole team. We had an opportunity to show a lot of people what Berea College stood for, and we disgraced the name of Berea in front of Coach Ridder and everyone else. I was really upset about it. There wasn't much any of us could say.

Whenever I play poorly, I cannot wait for the next game. I'm eager for the chance to show what I can do at my best. I think a lot of the guys felt that. We didn't want the spectators to base their opinion of Berea College basketball on how they saw us perform against Hope College. I wanted to go back and play again and show those people what we were really made of. The next night we played at the top of our game, and we went on to have a winning season.

My first semester as a college student was tough on me. Berea's academic expectations are high, and I wasn't a good manager of my time. Students are expected to spend two hours out of class for every hour in class. They must work and attend convocations. Athletes have to practice two to three hours a day in addition to games. I had a hard time balancing all that. I had back trouble, too, and spent several weeks in considerable pain. Finally I decided to sit down every week and block my time out, write a written schedule of everything I had to do each day. I had to get used to doing that, but it made things easier for me.

I had several labor assignments in Seabury Gym. I was in the tote box, worked as a janitor, and served as a teacher's assistant. For two years I had a second job cleaning classrooms in Danforth at night so I could make extra money.

My major was business administration, with an emphasis in accounting. One of my professors, Phil Spears, was demanding in a way that reminded me of Coach Wierwille. In his classes you either sank or swam. Dr Spears came from a successful corporate background. He'd seen all the cutthroat moves and knew what could happen in that environment. I learned a lot from him and attribute much of the success I've had after leaving college to him, because I often recall his teachings and adapt them to situations I encounter.

Immediately after I graduated I moved to northern Kentucky to work for Fifth Third Bank. After a little more than a year I moved back home to Mount Vernon. I'm the manager and executive loan officer of a branch of the Bank of Mount Vernon.

My goal ever since day one of college was to give something back to the community that raised me to be the kind of person I am. My family has very strong roots in Rockcastle County. It's a wonderful environment. There is no better place to raise a family. But not many Rockcastle County High School students go to college, and of those who do, few return to the county to live and work.

Banking is appealing to me because it gives me pleasure to help people out. I'm glad that somebody can call me up and say, "We need to put a new roof on our house." It means a lot to me to help a family buy a new home, to go to the closing and see the smile on their faces when they get the keys.

My ultimate ambition is to own my own bank. I have a three-step plan. The first step was to graduate from college and get some banking experience. The second step will be to get into upper management, which my present job is going to lead to. Step three is to become the controlling shareholder of a bank.

If I could go back and do it over, there's not a thing I would change about the four years I spent at Berea. It was a marvelous learning experience. In my senior year I had four or five job interviews, and at every one the first thing they wanted to talk about was Berea College. Employers appreciate Berea because they know the students have to work as well as study. When I told people that I played a varsity sport for four years, they knew that I knew how to manage my time.

I consider Roland Wierwille one of my closest friends. I ask his advice before I make important decisions. I talked to him before I accepted the job with Fifth Third Bank when I was a senior in college. Later three other opportunities came my way, and we both agreed that they weren't right for me. When the opening back home appeared, we talked again and agreed that this one was right. I have the utmost respect for the man. There's nothing I wouldn't do for him. I will be loyal to him and to the program at Berea College until I die.

August 6, 1998

Crawford James II   **1995-98**

I was born and raised in Cincinnati and went to Princeton High School. I learned about Berea College when Coach Craig Jefferson saw me at a shootout in Louisville and asked me my name. My father and I started doing our own personal research about Berea. It seemed to be a good school academically, and geographically it was well-situated. We decided that enrolling at Berea was in my best interest.

Crawford James II: "Tenacious on defense"

I didn't play basketball my freshman year. Berea has academic standards that are higher than those of the average university. I was not aware of that until just before I was ready to enroll. Coach Wierwille suggested that I spend my first year adjusting to the school and building myself up physically. That worked out very well for me. The summer after my freshman year I stayed in Berea, working out daily and playing basketball. I put on ten pounds of muscle, and my endurance improved maybe seventy percent.

I'm six-six. I played either the three and four position. What I brought to the team was rebounding, defense, and motivation. I tried to be a floor general in the post. I was responsible for setting a lot of screens and making sure key players came off certain kinds of screens and went to certain areas. I wanted everybody to play his position right and work as hard as possible.

I started every game my sophomore year. We had a very good team, with veteran leaders where we needed them and young talent coming up. Our point guard was Daniel Brown. I had met Daniel the previous year, although the only time I got to play with him was during some open gyms. When I joined the team as a sophomore I knew that how far we went would depend on how well Daniel played. He had a fine year. D.B. was one of the best shooters I've ever played with, and he was a hard worker and excellent motivator. We became good friends off the court. I'm very glad I had the privilege of playing with him.

Tony Goatley was the two guard. His game was that of a slashing, power guard. Tony was a good rebounder, too. With his experience he gave us leadership at the two position.

Otis Diuguid played behind Daniel and Tony, but he was an important factor. There are many things a player can contribute off the court and in practice that are necessary to make a team go. Otis got along with everyone. As a senior, he made sure everybody knew that his intention was to make each of us work harder and get better. Otis was, hands down, the number one defender on the team. He played the best man-on-man defense. He made Daniel and Donnie Frazier, in particular, a lot better than they would have been had he not been there.

Donnie, like me, had just come off a whole summer working on his game. He came in and shot the lights out. Corey Craig, our center, was big and strong in the blocks. Shane Tarvin, David Jackson, and Jeremy Wood contributed off the bench. We had a lot of good, hungry players giving it their all, and that's why we had the success we did.

It was special for me to begin my career at the new Seabury Center. In my freshman year I watched Old Seabury come down and the new Seabury Center put up. I didn't realize the significance of Berea's athletic tradition until I looked in the trophy case and saw all those old basketballs and bricks. To play in the first game ever played in Seabury Center, and for our team to win the championship and go out west to the national tournament, were very important events in my life.

We qualified to go to Nampa by beating IU-Southeast for the third time that year. It was difficult playing a team for the third time, much less a team we had beaten twice. IU-Southeast had a lot more to play for than just going to the national tournament. It was very tense down the stretch, but we came out on top.

We had a lot of fun in Nampa simply by being there with each other. We would have had fun in the middle of a desert. Twelve guys who go through a long season together can find a way to enjoy themselves. Perhaps we didn't have a lot of freedom, but there was a lot of smiling and laughing in the hotel where we stayed as teammates. There were a couple of other teams there, too, and off the court we were all friends. Everyone wanted to meet everyone else and exchange stories. It was an excellent time, a growing experience.

Our opponent, Tabor College, was a nationally ranked team, but we knew that every team in Nampa was going to be good. We never felt that any of those teams was better than we were. We lost to Tabor by just one point. Daniel didn't shoot very well in that game, and after it was over he blamed himself. Although he told us that he took personal responsibility for what happened, it was a team loss. We gained a lot of respect in that game and earned recognition for Berea College. Even though we lost, we knew after that game that we could play with anybody in the country.

After my sophomore year I planned to transfer to North Carolina A&T University. I was ready to enroll in the school of business there. But that didn't work out for various reasons, and I returned to Berea.

I decided not to play basketball my junior year. I wanted to make the most of what Berea had to offer, and that meant focusing on academics. It was time for me to grow intellectually, to become the great student I wanted to be, to get myself on track for my post-graduation career.

I remembered something Coach Wierwille had told us the previous year. He said, "I've had players leave the team but stay in school." John Henderson had done that. I thought about John when I was making my decision. When I told Coach what I intended to do, he understood. He showed no animosity. He was completely professional about it.

That year was the first since the fifth grade that basketball was not the main focus of my life. In my time away from basketball I began to realize that my reason for playing had been more a liking for the people than a love for the game itself. I missed being in the locker room with the guys. I missed the relationships, the friendships. Moreover, I noticed that when I wasn't playing I had less discipline than when I did play. The time management skills I'd had to use as an athlete had made me a better student.

When I rejoined the team in my senior year, I had matured considerably. I was now a true student-athlete, a young adult. I was also much more aware of the business side of a college athletic program. I was a business major and tended to think along those lines. It made basketball that much more fun for me.

After not playing any basketball at all my entire junior year, I came back in August to start conditioning and get back into the flow of playing. My game was very rusty, and even by the time we started scrimmaging it was bad. When the first game came around I had just reached the point where'd I'd feel comfortable playing in a pickup game. But I knew that it was just a matter of time before my stroke would come back and things would start clicking again. I stayed after practice to shoot free throws and get my form back and my stroke together. Once I started making my free throws I got my confidence back, and soon I was knocking them down again in game situations.

Our team was successful that year because everybody was dedicated. All the guys worked hard and played their roles well. Compared to the previous team I'd played on, there wasn't as much experience in certain positions. Sophomore Jeremy Wood, a converted two guard, was running the one, which was much different than having Daniel Brown, a senior, as our point guard. Donnie Frazier's pure shooting had replaced Tony Goatley's slashing, power game at the two position. It all balanced out, but little things like that change the makeup of a team.

That was my first year playing with Gary Burns, so I wasn't familiar with his game. Gary had some big games, and Gary had some games where he could have played bigger. That happens to everyone, but Gary's coaches and teammates stayed on him hard because we knew he was a big part of the future of the program, and we wanted to get him established. In some games Gary would be dunking on people, but in other games he was tentative and wouldn't go to the boards strong. Sometimes he was a better practice player than he was a game player. But I looked at him as a player who, if he continued to work hard, had an incredible future ahead of him at Berea.

The mental part of the game is the most important part. If you go into a game mentally beaten, you're beaten, period. As we prepared to play Eastern Kentucky University, we knew that the most important thing was not to be intimidated. Our bus ride to Eastern that night was completely silent, because everybody focused on the game. We knew what we had to do. We weren't mentally whipped at all. That was never an issue.

Coach Wierwille had told us about his association with Eastern, and we knew how badly he wanted to win that game. He had us practice for a couple of days in their gym to get ready. It didn't matter to me that Eastern was a quote-unquote bigger team. We always had tough competition to play. Eastern was just the school up the street.

Coach Kelly Combs talked to us about being strong and physical. We needed to play hard. We needed to dive on the floor after every loose ball. If we didn't get the rebound, we had to at least prevent our man from getting it.

It was important to run our offense with precision. We didn't have a true point guard in the backcourt. Our guards, with the possible exception of Tad Brewer, had been two guards in high school. They could bring the ball up the court, but none of them had played the point guard full-time. That created some problems, because it's best to have someone out there who is very confident with the ball.

Eastern figured to press us, so in practice we pressed a lot against each other. We got ourselves ready for them. We knew we could break their press and back them off a bit. Once we got a couple of easy baskets, a couple of quick threes, they got out of it pretty quick.

After the first half I knew we had the game won. There was no way we were going to come out of there with less than a victory. After we won, it was wonderful to see the look on Coach's face. I thought, "This is what you play for." I was very glad I was at Berea to experience that.

To reach the national tournament we had to beat Philadelphia Pharmacy. When we looked at them on videotape, we saw what we had to do. They had some big bruisers, and they set a lot of screens. So in our practice drills we bumped each other more than we usually did. An important part of our plan was to keep Philadelphia Pharmacy off the boards, because they had a good shooter we wanted to key on.

Philadelphia Pharmacy had won a lot of games, and Coach had the idea that they had brought a snobbish Northeast attitude to good old Kentucky. Because our team was a home-grown team, all Kentuckians except me, that got to us. Coach told us that they looked at our gym and said, "There are nothing but tobacco farmers in Kentucky, so how can they afford all this? We live in Philadelphia, and we have this and that." Coach said it really ticked him off. I understood what Coach was doing, feeding that through to us. We definitely didn't want to lose to a team like that! Nobody was going to come into our place thinking of us as just a stepping stone to the national tournament.

The game was close. As time as running out we were down by a couple of points. I've always been one to say the game is never over. I told myself, "That team is not walking out of here a winner."

Philadelphia Pharmacy had the ball. Donnie Frazier and I were both running after the guy who had it, and Donnie dove after him and hurt his hand. He had to leave the game. Tad Brewer replaced him and fouled out immediately, so Donnie came back in. How severely Donnie might be injured never entered my head. If his hand was still attached to his arm, he was going to play. I assumed that since he was coming back in, he was okay.

With one second left Philadelphia Pharmacy led by two. Jeremy Wood was on the line to shoot two free throws. When somebody goes to the free throw line during a game he's usually thinking about practice. Woody always had good form and generally hit nine out of ten in practice, so I was confident he was going to make those baskets. He did.

We knew then that it was going to be our game. Once that overtime started, there wasn't a doubt in anybody's mind that it was going to be all Berea. I'd hadn't had a good game, I'd been playing like a dog, but when the jump ball went up in overtime I told myself, "It's time to play now." I jumped up and got that jump ball, and when my dad saw that, he knew I was ready. With our whole team energized, Philadelphia Pharmacy never stood a chance. Those guys never knew what hit them.

In Idaho we were matched with Whitworth College, who were ranked pretty high in the country. Because we had to play without Donnie, our four-year leader and leading scorer, everyone had to adjust. We didn't change the way we ran our offense, but some of us needed to shoot the ball more frequently than we usually did.

We had some early-game jitters and started horribly, falling behind 26 to 6. But I never got down on us. I knew that things would start to click for us, and sure enough, we finally got going and caught up to them. But Whitworth pulled ahead at the finish and beat us, ending my college basketball career.

When I first knew Coach Wierwille I could see that he loved the game and felt a strong desire to win. Later I came to appreciate his love and admiration for us, his team. All twelve or thirteen of us felt like a second son to Coach. We knew that he put his whole life into the team. That alone guaranteed a 100 percent effort from us. We never thought about giving anything less.

Coach Combs was very important to the success of the Berea program. Coach Combs did the scouting and recruiting, and he ran our practices. He was always there, hustling and working hard. He made sure that we worked hard and ran the plays right, and that we knew who was on the other team and what they were going to do. Like Coach Wierwille, Coach Combs gave his all.

During my freshman year I worked in the mailroom of the Development Office. I worked in the Alumni Office that summer, and when the school year started I became a resident assistant in the dorm while working some hours at the Alumni Building front desk. My junior year I continued working at the front desk and served as a teaching assistant for Dr Warren Lambert. That was my primary position from that time until graduation. I also managed to squeeze in a labor position as a janitor at the museum.

Dr Phil Spears in the Business Department was the best teacher I had at Berea College. I had him my entire senior year, in the fall, in short term, and in the spring. I enjoyed spending my time around him.

Dr Spears set up his classroom in a non-traditional way. He didn't lecture while we listened and took notes. He started class with the phrase, "What do you want to do today?" Then we'd get into the previous night's reading and the case study we were working on. Dr Spears acted as manager while we acted as employees. One thing I learned was that although I was going to have to work with people I might not like, for at least eight hours a day I'd have to get along with them as colleagues if I wanted to be successful.

I've always wanted to pursue a career in business. My specific plans have evolved as I've grown and interacted with various people and taken classes. When I first entered school I wanted to go into the entertainment business as a record company executive. Then I thought about becoming a buyer for a major retailer. Now I'm hoping to land a position as a diplomat or an international consultant.

In my junior year, the year I didn't play basketball, I realized that I ought to go to graduate school. That's my main focus now. I won't be pursuing an MBA. I want an MA in international affairs or international law and diplomacy, and there are only a handful of universities that offer such programs. They are all schools with very high admissions criteria, so I'm going to boost my resume before I apply.

I have some very good recommendations and some solid work experience in accounting for a firm in Mason, Ohio. Right now I have a summer job as a program instructor with the Village of Woodlawn, Ohio, Recreational Department. Soon I'll be starting an internship at the World Affairs Council of Greater Cincinnati. After that I may seek a position in Washington, D.C., en route to graduate school. The schools I'm interested in prefer two years of work experience and some travel.

I'm happy with the quality of my Berea College education, and I'm not referring only to the book work. The Berea experience is the curriculum, the classes, the labor program, the diversity of the campus, and the relationships you form with staff, professors, coaches, and fellow students.

July 7, 1998

Donnie Frazier   1994-98

At the end of my senior year we had to beat Philadelphia Pharmacy to get to the national tournament. When they walked into our building they seemed to be thinking, "How does a weak team like Berea College have a place as nice as this to play in?" Coach Wierwille takes any kind of insult very seriously. He tried to get us fired up about their attitude. It didn't bother us like it bothered him. It irritated us a little bit, but we didn't let it throw us off our game.

Donnie Frazier: "He came in and shot the lights out"

Philadelphia Pharmacy had a smooth little lefthanded point guard, Shannon Overton, who was their only offensive threat. But they were well coached. As a team they did equally well against our man defense or our zone. Their big men found their spots down low, the gray areas. They knew exactly where to go.

Jeremy Wood did a great job on Overton. He got his points, but in the second half Woody started to wear him down. The game was close. With Philadelphia Pharmacy ahead by one in the final minute, Overton got the ball and went flying down the floor. I was chasing him, and if I didn't dive and foul him, he had a layup for sure. So at halfcourt I dove, and that's when I broke the middle metacarpal in my right hand.

I knew something was wrong. My finger felt like it was loose. It was flopping down between the others. I went over to our trainer, Sandy Williams, and shook the finger in front of her. It didn't feel like it was attached. I had to come out of the game while she taped the finger to the one next to it.

Overton missed both free throws, but Philadelphia Pharmacy got the rebound and got the ball to him again. Tad Brewer, my replacement, fouled him. That was Tad's fifth foul. I checked back into the game, taped up.

Overton went back to the line and missed two shots again. Woody had worn him out. They got him the ball back again, we fouled again, and he went to the line again. This time he hit one of the two. With about five seconds left Woody had the ball. I wanted it. I streaked down the left sideline, and Woody was coming my way. Although I knew there was something wrong with my hand, I felt that I could hit the shot, and I wanted to go out trying to win the game myself. But one of their guys reached around Woody's body and fouled him.

There was one-point-one seconds left. To loosen Woody up I said, "Concentrate, Woody. No pressure!" His first shot was a swish. The second one had a little rim to it, but it went in to tie the game. We went into overtime.

By this time my hand was swelling up, I suspected that a bone was broken. In the overtime we didn't give Philadelphia Pharmacy a chance to breathe. We put them away right off the bat. Woody hit a couple of threes, and we had a three-point play down low. I missed a three and missed a short jump shot of about fifteen feet, but I hit a layup. I knew we were going to the tournament again, and this trip would be sweeter than the one in my sophomore year, when I had to look to Daniel Brown and Tony Goatley for leadership. This time all the underclassmen were looking me in the face, and I knew I couldn't let them down.

After the game Sandy iced my hand, and then we went to the hospital and got it x-rayed. When she looked at the x-ray and put her head down, I knew something was seriously wrong. There was a visible crack on the x-ray. Five or six of the players were waiting on me, and I had to tell them that my hand was broken.

It was hard to watch the team practice all week, preparing to go out to Idaho, and it was hard to sit on the bench when we got out there and fell behind Whitworth College 26 to 6. I couldn't help asking myself, "Would this be happening if I was in the game?" Whitworth pressed us, but we'd defeated pressing teams like Virginia Intermont and Eastern Kentucky. We fought back, got the ball where it needed to go, and led by three at the half. But a couple of plays killed us at the end, and we lost.

It hurt me to see them lose. Woody tried so hard. He came up to me and said, "I tried to win it for you." If we had won that game I would have taken the cast off. They told me that if I got hit in the finger hard enough it might drive the bone through the skin, and then I'd have to have it operated on. But if we'd won that game I would have taken the cast off, taped the hand up, and played. A week after we got back the cast was removed, and in two weeks my hand was almost healed. It was amazing. Two weeks was all it took.

I grew up in the country in McCreary County, Kentucky. My parents were divorced, and I lived with my mom. She usually had two jobs. She drove a school bus and was a substitute teacher. Sports was about the only thing I did when I was growing up. We didn't have the money to do anything else.

When I was a senior at McCreary Central High School, my coach, Jerry Stephens, called Coach Wierwille and asked him to come and see me play. Everyone was urging me to go to Berea. I wanted to play baseball as well as basketball, and I knew I could do both at Berea. That's why I enrolled there. I ended up playing two years of baseball and four years of basketball.

I'm six feet tall. Shooting was the strongest part of my game. Shooters are born. You can improve certain things, but either you can shoot or you can't.

I needed to improve my ballhandling. Dribbling drills in practice with Coach Combs helped me do that. I carried a basketball around campus and dribbled all the time. I even dribbled tennis balls.

When I came to Berea I needed to get stronger physically. The only difference between levels is size, strength, and quickness. The players at UK were four or five inches taller than we were, but they didn't shoot any better. To increase my strength I lifted weights. Brandon Wilford, who'd gone to high school with me, lifted with me my freshman year. After that I was on my own. I devised my own workout.

Coach Wierwille had his stroke soon after I arrived. I didn't even know it happened until the next day. I heard rumors about it, but I didn't know if it was for sure or not. When I heard the news I didn't know what to think. People said he might not be back. When we started the season there wasn't a lot of discipline. Some players quit and then came back and played again. It was very frustrating. I wasn't used to anything like that. If you quit at my high school, you were gone. You didn't get a second chance. We finished the season strong, beating Pikeville and almost beating Georgetown, but I didn't know if I would return if Coach Wierwille didn't. There wasn't enough control of the team when he was gone, and I didn't like that.

I worked very hard that summer. I worked two jobs. One was all night long and the second one started as soon as I got off. I just quit sleeping there for a while, because I played ball from five to seven in the afternoons. To strengthen my legs I used a shoe that was supposed to improve your jumping ability. When I came back in the fall I was playing like I'd never played before.

Coach Wierwille came back, and when he saw me working hard he said, "Keep it up and you'll earn yourself some playing time." That was what I wanted to hear. When the season opened we started three guards, Daniel Brown, Tony Goatley, and me.

I started the first game in our new Seabury Center, and I hit the first basket. Of course Daniel and Tony took their shots first, thinking they could get it. I wasn't even thinking about it. But then Tony threw me a lob, and I scored. I didn't play well, although I hit a big shot at the end. But we won that game and were seven and two at the Christmas break. We didn't get too high after a win or too low after a loss. Coach helped keep us on an even keel. We had almost the same team as the year before, but our record improved dramatically. A team is only as good as its coach.

Daniel grew up a lot. The previous year I'd hated him sometimes. Little things he did in practice bothered me. I'd come around a screen and be open, and he'd throw the ball so hard it would implant itself in my chest. If I managed to play good defense on him and stop him from hitting a shot, he'd say it was a foul. That sort of thing drove me nuts. I couldn't do anything about it because he was an upperclassman. I got mad and cussed him a little bit, but he still took the ball.

Daniel could do it all, shoot, pass, dribble, and play defense. He didn't set out to play a lot of defense, but you couldn't get by him off the dribble. He didn't rebound that much, but he was a lot stronger than people thought he was. He could push people out of the way, and he got to a lot of opponents by talking to them. He'd give them fits.

It wasn't smart to underestimate Daniel. We played a game at Morehead State. Morehead didn't recruit Daniel. They told him he was too small. He scored thirty-eight points against them, although we lost. At Georgetown they called him every name in the book, and he stood at the free throw line and winked at them. At Pikeville they called out his name and yelled ugly things at him. That was at the end of the season, and they beat us. Daniel said, "You wait, you sons of bitches. We'll come back next week and kick your asses." Sure enough, we put it on them. There was nothing they could do.

Daniel never let a hostile crowd or another player get in his head. They tried, but they couldn't do it. I saw him mad, but I never saw a player eat him up. He'd talk back to them, saying, "I'm here, I hear you." But they didn't bother him. Daniel taught me that no matter how bad a crowd gets on you, you need to act like they're not even there. That was an important lesson for me.

Daniel might have been the best player ever to play at Berea. He could have played at another level. He didn't have the height, but he had the heart. He had more competitive spirit than anybody I've ever met, and I don't like to admit that, because I'm very competitive myself.

I loved playing with Daniel in my sophomore year. I fed off him and Tony. Everyone keyed on those two. I got a lot of wide-open shots when my man tried to help out on one of them.

I learned a lot about playing offense from Daniel and Tony. I observed the little things Daniel did to get open. He knew where to go and when. Tony was good at that too. In practice once I was guarding Tony on the block. He pump faked. I thought he was going to shoot, so I put my hands up. He didn't just hump me with his arm and go around me. He took his elbow and pushed me right out of the way. He could do that so smoothly that the referee couldn't see it. Later I worked on that with him, trying to add that move to my game. Scott Moore does a good job of it now.

I watched how Daniel and Tony and Otis Diuguid used their body on defense. If a guy started to go by them, they'd give him a little push with their forearm, and it killed the guy's momentum. Then they'd slide back in place. When Tony saw the ball coming from one side of the floor back to the top of the key to his wing, he was ready to jump into that passing lane. Then he'd catch the ball and start running the other way. I learned how to do that by watching Tony from the bench. In my junior and senior years I did it a lot.

Otis hardly ever got to play, and if he did he knew that all he was going to do was handle the ball a little and play defense. He wasn't a great shooter, but he could set in the defensive position for hours at a time. He brought a spark off the bench. If we looked like we were dragging ass, leave it to him. He'd yell at us in the huddle, and then he'd go into the game and get a deflection or a steal.

In practice Otis was one of the hardest workers up and down. One day in my freshman year we were trying to get ready to play Pikeville or Georgetown. Somebody hit a crazy shot and was laughing about it. Otis jumped the guy and said something to him. The guy said, "Stay out of my business, Otis."

That was the maddest I ever saw Otis. He got right in the guy's face and said, "We're trying to get the varsity ready for a damn game. If you can't do that, you can go downstairs and take a shower and leave."

Otis could be a funny guy, but he knew when to cut up and when to be serious. He played an important role for us, especially when we tried to press somebody. We pressed Campbellsville in the last game in Old Seabury. I was in the game with Otis and Daniel and Tony and Tino Ballenger. We put a press on them that was hard for them to get through, and we won the game. Otis knew his role and accepted it. He really helped us.

My sophomore season was a great year for our team. It was the first time I'd ever experienced a winning season in basketball. In my junior year in high school my team went to the regional finals, finishing with a record of fifteen and fifteen. When I went with Berea College as a sophomore to the national tournament in Idaho, I felt that my turn had come at last.

The mountain scenery out there was beautiful. You could look forever in every direction. We enjoyed that, but we played a lot of cards just so we could sit around and talk about the game and this and that. The Kentucky state high school tournament draws crowds of 18,000, and in the NAIA tournament in Idaho we played before 2500. But it was a good feeling to run out there on the floor to compete with one of the best teams in the country.

I had a good game against Tabor College, a double-double with points and rebounds, but we lost at the very end. It was difficult to watch the seniors after that loss, knowing their last game ended in a terrible disappointment. I knew I'd miss them.

Despite all the graduations, we did a pretty good job in my junior year. We won eighteen games, just one fewer than the year before. Corey Craig started picking up his play, and David Jackson came on strong. Shane Tarvin had hardly played at all the previous year, but he came in with a good attitude and started. Scott Moore, a freshman, played well off the bench.

Jeremy Wood was my biggest concern. We thought we'd run three guards again, Woody and me and either Tad Brewer or Casey Lester at the point. It didn't work out that way. Woody took over the point and Tad and Casey came off the bench. People said, "Jeremy Wood's not a true point guard. He doesn't know when to pass and when to shoot." Before we went home for Christmas break I said to Woody, "We're eight and one, and I think you're doing a hell of a job. Evidently we're doing something right."

The end of the season was rough. We beat a good Indiana Tech team to earn the right to play IU-Southeast for a slot in the national tournament. But I hurt my left ankle against Indiana Tech. It was one of the worst sprains I had. I taped it up and tried to play on it at IU-Southeast, but I couldn't go. Scott Moore turned his ankle in the first half, and they beat us. That was the first of two years in a row I didn't get to play in the final game of the season.

Early in my senior year we played at Eastern. Before the game Coach told us to look them right in the eye and go straight at them. We talked about what we wanted to do. Among ourselves we tried to act like it wasn't a big deal, but in the back of our minds we knew how much we wanted to win. I remember Devin Duvall saying, "We can beat those guys. You know we can." Nobody outside the team thought we could defeat a Division I school, but I was sure that if we didn't turn the ball over a lot we could go up there and beat that team.

While we were warming up, three of their players started pointing at us and counting how many white guys we had on our team. I knew exactly what they were doing, and it made me angry. I told Crawford James, "They're counting our white guys." He didn't like it either. They were building it up, and we were building it up. Casey was talking trash to Marty Thomas, who he'd played with in high school.

We knew that if Eastern pressed us we'd have a better chance. Sure enough, they let us throw the ball in on the side every time, and we'd cut a guard right through to make it two on one. They stopped the layup, but they didn't play effective transitional defense. They didn't find the shooters. I hit some threes and so did Woody, Tad, and Kelly Day. They made a run at us at the end, but they couldn't catch us.

After the game everybody went nuts. The videotape shows everybody running and jumping, but I'm nowhere to be seen in the middle of those pictures. During the celebration I was sitting over on the bench, laughing by myself. It was a moral victory for me because I'd been told I couldn't play for Eastern. They were waiting on another guard, Chris Fitzgerald. So I burned them for thirty-four points and eleven rebounds and five assists. I had my turnovers to go with that, but that was one of the better games I played. As a team we beat the snot out of them for at least thirty minutes out of the forty.

Afterwards President Shinn came and talked to us in the locker room. Reporters were throwing questions at me from everywhere. I saw it as a great win, but I didn't want us to get too high on one win. It wasn't as big to me as it was to Coach Wierwille and Coach Combs. Coach Combs would have been happy if we'd ended the season that day. Every time we practiced before the Eastern game he wanted us to go little bit longer. He'd say, "Eastern is in there practicing right now. They're lifting in the morning and practicing twice a day." Finally I said, "That's Eastern. We're our own team." But he kept on it, Eastern this, Eastern that. After we finally played Eastern and beat them, it was such a relief to get him to shut up about Eastern!

Our first game with Transylvania that season was at their place. The day before we played them up there, Scott Moore hyperextended my left elbow in practice. I couldn't dribble the ball after that. I could barely bend my arm. I didn't tape it because I didn't think I'd be able to play, but I told Coach I'd go through warmups and see if it would loosen up any.

The game was televised. Before it started Alan Cutler, the TV announcer, asked me if I was going to play. I explained that I'd hyperextended my elbow the day before and could hardly bend it at all. He kind of called me a sissy right to my face. Then Sean Woods, his partner, came over and talked to me. I didn't know who he was. He said, "I hope to see you in action today. I've heard a lot about you." All I could think of was Cutler's insult. I went over to the bench and said, "Tape it up. I'm playing." We had about four minutes left to warm up.

My shooting had been off for a couple of games, but that afternoon I found a way to shoot and ended up with another double-double. We lost in the second overtime. I think that if I hadn't fouled out in the first overtime, we would have won.

When Transy came down to Berea they beat us by sixteen. I was healthy, but I couldn't find the basket. The only highlight of that game for me was when I hit a full-court shot at the end of the first half. Transy hit a three with about five seconds left. Casey inbounded the ball to me, and as soon as I got it I turned around and fired it. It was a dead bullet, and I thought it had no chance. But it went in, and they counted it. The tape shows that the ball was still in my hand when the clock went double zero, but the horn didn't go off, so the shot actually did count. That was the longest shot I ever hit in a game. I was standing well within the circle of the free throw line, so that shot, with the little bit of arch it had on it, traveled almost ninety feet.

Coach Wierwille and I had a good relationship. I was able to talk to him the whole time I was there. I could tell him about any problems I had or whatever was on my mind. I was the same way with Coach Stephens in high school. I got along with coaches. It wasn't difficult to coach me. Coach said at the senior banquet that I was the hardest working player he'd had at Berea College. He said I made myself. Well, how can a coach not like a player like that? My coach at home told me the same thing. I don't see the point of not working hard in practice. Why do that, when it's going to hurt you in a game? You're out there for a reason, so don't waste your time.

Under Coach Wierwille we were disciplined in practice. He had enough authority to tame a wildcat like Daniel Brown. When Coach Jefferson or Coach Combs yelled something to Daniel in practice, he'd cuss at them. If Coach Wierwille said the same thing, Daniel would reply, "Yes, sir."

"Did you say something?"

"No, sir. I just said yes, sir, I understand."

My closest friend on the team was Devin Duvall. He was my roommate before I started rooming with Scott Moore. Devin was real easygoing. I've got a temper, and little things can get me fired up for an hour. But I never got mad at Devin in the whole time I was there. If I had something to talk about, he'd sit there and listen. He could tell if I was upset as soon as he walked into the room, and he made me feel better by listening to me and giving me good advice.

I admired the things Crawford James did for the team. C.J. was a hard worker. He sprinted every time he came off the floor. If somebody was about to shoot free throws, C.J. took him aside and offered words of advice. I noticed little things like that. C.J. made his presence felt at the defensive end around the basket. He got plenty of defensive rebounds, and that's the most unselfish statistic in basketball.

C.J. got the team excited when we played at Alice Lloyd when we were seniors. The shot clock was winding down, so I motioned to him to come over and set me a screen. He set the screen, I rolled to the right, and his man came up on me. So I hooked the ball and put a little spin on it. C.J. didn't have the greatest hands, but he caught that ball like it was a pick and roll in the NBA. After he caught it he turned and dunked it right in their kid's face. I'll never forget that.

When Jeremy Wood came to Berea I wanted to hang out with him because he was a lot like me. He did the same kind of things I did. We played alike. I picked him on my team in preseason scrimmages. It was me and him and three other freshmen against Daniel and Tony and Otis and Tino and Shane. We beat the crap out of them. I thought, "I like this kid. I like the way he plays."

Woody worked hard to improve his defensive game. He usually guarded the other team's best guard, especially if it was their point guard. If it was the two guard I generally took him, but often Woody and I would switch in and out on a guard. In my junior year Woody held a guy from Milligan who was averaging twenty-seven points a game to a goose egg.

Woody could always tell if I wasn't in a rhythm. When we played Bethany in my senior year we went ahead of them by about twenty, but I had made only two shots in the game and missed five or six. Woody tried to do something about that. He started running plays just for me, to get me into the flow of the game.

At IU-Southeast one night I had the worst shooting game of my life, about one for eleven from the field. They had a pudgy kid of maybe six-five who was tattooing me. Nobody was calling out screens, and I couldn't see him coming from my blind side. Toward the end of the half the guy started talking some trash to me. I was getting upset.

I tried to run off a screen to get a shot. At the moment I came off the screen that big old dude stepped over, intending to hit me. I ducked my shoulder to try to slide by him, but he kept coming, so I raised up and put my shoulder right into his stomach. That forced the breath out of him and knocked him down. Their assistant coach screamed, "Frazier's playing dirty. He's a dirty player."

I said, "Your fat kid is the dirty player. He's been cheap-shotting me all night."

We were ahead at halftime. Both teams exited the court together. They were cussing at us. I didn't say anything, because I didn't want give them the idea that they were in my head. I just kept walking. Somebody yelled out, "We got you, Frazier. We got you on lockdown." All of a sudden Woody turned around and starting cussing them up and down. I never saw him do anything like that before. He said, "You're not in his head! He's in your head! You can't get to him!"

When we went into the locker room, I grabbed Gary Burns by the shirt and said, "Gary, if you don't call out the next screen I get hit on, if you don't let me know it's coming, you're going to regret it." I was shouting at him. Coach opened the door and said, "Donnie, come here. Did you say *** to their coach?"

I didn't, so I said no. Coach said, "Donnie, I'm on your side here."

"But I didn't say it."

"Who did?"

"I don't know," I replied. But I knew exactly who had done it.

In Coach's office the next day he asked, "You know who said that, don't you? If it wasn't you, who was it?"

"It was Woody."

Coach kind of smiled and said, "That little....." Meaning, that feisty, hardheaded little guy. Woody always gave it everything he had. He kept us in a lot of games. Sometimes he alone kept the other team from running us out of the gym. He was a great teammate. Seeing how badly he wanted to win that last game in Idaho when I was injured made me feel especially close to him.

I majored in physical education and health. My first labor assignment was janitor in Dana dorm. I did that my freshman and sophomore years. Then I moved over to intramurals, because it was good experience if I wanted a career in recreation. I organized intramural sports, made schedules, put teams together, kept the stats, and refereed some games.

Judy Davidson, one of my health teachers, did a lot to help students who were planning to teach. She went over the Kentucky guidelines with us as we formulated lesson plans. Then she videotaped us as we taught our lesson plans to students, so we could see what we might be doing wrong. She'd interrupt us or do other things to give us a sense of what an actual classroom would be like.

I went an extra semester so I could student teach at Berea Community School. My labor position was student assistant basketball coach. I've been doing a little scouting and coaching our blue team in practice, incorporating what I know our next opponent will do to help the varsity get ready. I talk trash to the varsity guys from the sidelines, telling them my blue team is whipping them, anything to fire them up and motivate them. I try to show the freshmen the little things I wasn't shown but had to pick up by myself by just watching. They call me "The Old Man."

I'll be substitute teaching this spring. Next fall a new transitional school will open up in Fayette County. All the positions are open, and I've applied for one. I'll probably go to graduate school. I don't see myself coaching. I've always been interested in weightlifting, and ultimately I think I might go into the personal training field. My fiance, Melissa Mullins, is going to be pursing a career in nutrition and dietetics, so I can learn a lot of useful things from her.

Like me, Melissa played varsity basketball at Berea. She didn't like to take any advice from me. When we walked around campus people would say to me, "Good game the other night, Donnie." I think she was a little bit jealous of that, because not a lot of people went to watch the women's games.

We tried to work out together, but it got too competitive. She hated to lose to me in anything. She beat me in a couple of games of H-O-R-S-E. That didn't make me mad, but when I beat her she got upset. But when my shot was off and I didn't have anybody to help me out, she'd come in and rebound for me.

Last summer I went to Germany for a professional tryout. I wanted to see what it was like, whether I could play over there. I didn't want to say later that I had a chance to go overseas and try out but didn't do it.

I went with a team of college players put together by Jeff Lanham, the assistant coach at the University of Rio Grande. Coach Combs knew him. When I gave Coach Combs my videotapes, I was trying to get hooked up with Athletes in Action, who tour the U.S. playing exhibitions with college teams. But I ended up in Germany instead.

I thought Andrei Kholodov and Vince Bingham from Transylvania were going with us. But Andrei ended up taking a job somewhere and Vince signed with a pro team in Austria or Australia, one of those. I was the only senior on the team. We weren't that strong. I was probably the best all-around player on the team. We had a couple of decent big men and a good point guard, plus a guy from Marshall who was one of the better shooters I've seen. If he was open it was a layup for him, but he couldn't play defense on his shadow.

That wasn't the first time I'd been to Europe. In my senior year in high school I played on a Junior Olympic team in Spain, France, and Switzerland. On this trip we played in Luxembourg and several German cities, including Munster, Hannover, and Frankfurt.

I hung out with one particular guy on the team. We went out a little bit, but we didn't stay out as late as the rest of the guys, who did whatever they wanted to. I was over there for one reason, to try to get a job done. My friend and I came in early and got our sleep. You could see the difference when we played.

It was a fantastic trip. Overall the competition wasn't bad. The German professional teams were organized into divisions. We played one Division Three team that our Berea College JV team could have beaten by thirty points. Then we played two Division Two teams and beat them both, one of them very convincingly. Then we played a Division One team who beat us by two in overtime, a Division One team we beat, and another Division One team who beat us by a point.

At Berea I played within a system I knew. I knew when and where I'd get screens. In Germany I was playing with a bunch of guys I'd never played with, and we didn't really have an offense to screen and do the little things. I had to do everything on my own. But all the same, we won.

I wasn't offered a contract, but I wasn't disappointed because I proved I could play over there. I dropped forty points on one of those Division

One teams. The German teams are allowed just two American players, and they usually pick horses of six-ten or six-eleven.

I graduated just last Sunday. It felt good, but my stomach was churning beforehand. I actually had more butterflies getting ready to walk across that stage than I can remember having in any basketball game I ever played in.

Berea College stands for hard work, no doubt about it. I'm proud to say I'm a Berea graduate. I loved being a Berea student. Berea's not for everybody, but it was for me. If I had to do it over again, I would do it in a heartbeat. I wish I was a freshman again. The hardest thing this fall was living off campus and not being around my friends. I missed the dorm life.

I knew just about everybody at Berea. It's small and compact. The first car I've owned is one I got for graduation. I've heard people say, "I don't know how you guys go to school without a car." Well, everything I needed was within walking distance. I liked the small atmosphere. I had a wonderful time. It went by too quick.

December 15, 1998

Jeremy Wood   1995-99

I came to Berea the year the new Seabury Center opened. The four years I played were Seabury Center's first four years. In each of those seasons we left the court as winners. It was tough for us to lose in the semifinals of this year's national tournament, but we had a heck of a ride. It was very satisfying to know that we were one of the best teams in Berea College history.

My dad's a farmer in Scott County, Kentucky. He raises tobacco and some cattle. That's where I grew up, on a farm with tobacco. When I tell people that, some of them don't believe me. I don't know why. Maybe I don't dress like they think a country person does or ought to.

My coach at Scott County High School talked to me about different colleges. I was looking for a place where I could play basketball, and he thought Berea College would be a good fit for me. The assistant principal at my school was Mutt Varney, who mentioned to me that he had attended Berea and played there, but he didn't try to sell me on Berea or any other college. When Coach Wierwille came to my high school to see me, Mr Varney was the one who came to get me out of class. I thought I was in trouble at first!

For Coach Wierwille to come to see me made a big impression on me. His son Roland came with him. I was nervous when I met Coach because he's such a big guy. At

Jeremy Wood: "He wouldn't accept not being the best he could"

the time he couldn't speak real well because he was still recovering from his stroke. I had a hard time understanding him. But everyone told me that he was an excellent coach. Berea was the only place that seemed to want me, so that's where I ended up.

I wondered how much coaching Coach Wierwille would actually be able to do, because he was still struggling to regain his speech. But he stuck it out the whole season, and his presence was one big reason that we made it to the national tournament that year. Coach's return gave the seniors and the rest of us extra incentive.

The four seniors were Daniel Brown, Tony Goatley, Otis Diuguid, and Roland Wierwille. I didn't get to know them well. I didn't spend much time with my teammates my freshman year. I stayed in my room and kept to myself.

Daniel was one of the best players I played with at Berea. He was short, but he could go underneath and bang with the best of them. Daniel was a natural scorer. He knew how to put the ball in the hole. He either got his shot off or got fouled, one or the other. He found ways to get to the line. I learned a lot from Daniel, especially about defense. He knew how to use his body and his arms, how to get away with holding here and there.

Tony was an all-around good player. He knew what he was doing out there. He could rebound, he could shoot inside or outside, and he could stop anybody on defense. It was amazing how well he and Daniel could play defense, and Otis too. Otis didn't get to play a lot, but he kept the team up. He was always cracking jokes. When he did come in, he played exceptionally hard, giving us a defensive spark.

As a freshman I played the two guard position, shooting guard. I'm six foot, six-one, depending on how you measure me. One of the things I brought to the program was my defense. I was a good defensive player coming in, and what I learned from Daniel and Tony and Otis made me better. I hustled on defense to earn a spot on the team.

When I turned my ankle in practice that year, everybody gave me a hard time. Coach got really upset about it, and I didn't understand why. Maybe it was because he thought I was a big part of the team, but I was just a freshman. We got out of practice early that day because of that.

Going to the national tournament at the end of that year was very exciting. No Berea team had been to the tournament for over ten years. Just to be in Idaho was fun, because most of us had never been that far west. The guys on the team bonded out there. Every night we played cards or something. That's when I began to hang out with the guys, in Idaho that March.

After Daniel and Tony graduated, our team's style changed. We were no longer a one or two-man show. Our scoring was more balanced. One thing that drove us was hearing people talk about how we wouldn't do as well that year because we had lost such good players. We wanted to go out and prove that we could play.

Crawford James, who had been an important part of the team the previous season, sat out my sophomore year. He had trouble with his grades and realized that basketball is not everything. After he got his grades back in order, he came back the following year to help us qualify for the national tournament again.

I really admired C.J. He got everything he could out of his ability. He didn't score a lot of points, but at six-six with very long arms, he was such a presence underneath that our opponents would keep the ball outside when he was on the floor. C.J. was one of the most eloquent speakers I've ever heard. He'd talk all the slang in practice, but off the court he became a totally different person. He's extremely intelligent and is going to be very successful.

The teammate I got closest to was Donnie Frazier. Donnie was an outstanding player. He wasn't scared to shoot it, and he could shoot it from anywhere. Donnie hustled, and a lot of his offense stemmed from playing really hard defense. Seeing him working so hard and wanting to win so badly rubbed off on me.

Donnie was a class act. Even after we got beat he was able to talk to people. He hid his emotions well. Sometimes after a loss I came out and saw him talking to the fans. Donnie could get carried away with himself occasionally, talking about old times and stuff he did. He knew it, too, because we always gave him a hard time about telling so many stories from his past. But he's been a really good friend.

With Donnie starting at shooting guard, I got switched over to point guard as a sophomore. That was somewhat difficult, but my ballhandling skills were already decent. I could get it up and down the court. I didn't have much of a left hand at first, but I developed one over the three years I played point guard. I was smart, and I didn't turn the ball over a lot.

In my sophomore year we went to a tournament in Florida right after New Years. We didn't do well down there. In the first game we played Hope College, who whipped us decisively. They had a guard who was unreal. I can't think of his name. He was about six-three and could handle the ball and shoot. He'd come down and pull from thirty feet, easy, and make it. Once he attempted a three from over in the corner, and Devin Duvall yelled at him from our bench, "No way, no way!" The guy shot the ball, turned around, pointed to Devin, said "Good," and ran down the floor before it even went in.

There were three teams I especially liked to play: Asbury, Indiana-Southeast, and Transylvania. Asbury wasn't one of the best teams, but they played hard all forty minutes no matter how badly they were getting beat, and we beat them pretty badly at times. My best friend in high school, Tony Johnson, played for Asbury. I grew up with him playing in the back yard. He never did beat me in college.

IU-Southeast was an opponent in our region, and every year it came down to us and them for a chance to go to the national tournament. In my freshman year we beat them three times. They beat us three times my sophomore year. We split with them my junior year and beat them twice my final year. It was always good to beat IU-Southeast because we knew we had to get past them to make it to Idaho.

It made Coach's year if we could beat Transy. Beating a bigger school that handed out scholarships was always an accomplishment. In my years we were .500 against them.

Soon after my junior season began we played Eastern, and that was a game I won't forget. It was a David and Goliath matchup because Eastern was an NCAA Division I school, while we competed in Division II of the NAIA. 15,000 students at Eastern, 1500 at Berea. Coach told us the story of how he had applied for the coaching job at Eastern and been turned down. That made us want to win it for him.

What I remember most about that game was how quick Eastern's players were. We knew they played at a different level, of course. When we looked down at their end we saw them laughing it up, and it seemed to us like they weren't taking us seriously. They found out we were for real when we jumped out to a big lead.

Donnie was outstanding, and Kelly Day stepped up. That was Kelly's freshman year, and in that game he showed the kind of player he was going to be. I didn't have a great game. It was difficult to excel against a really quick guard who knew all the tricks. Whenever I came down and started to spin, he'd get hold of my shorts and pull me backwards to make me lose my balance.

We had a lot of fans there, probably more than we had at any other game. After we won I ran across the floor to where the Berea fans were. People were jumping up in the crowd and hugging us and saying, "Good job." Coach ran down the floor with his hands raised and blew kisses to the crowd.

To advance to the national tournament we had to beat Philadelphia Pharmacy at Seabury. We were confident, although we knew they would be tough because they were ranked in the Top Twenty. We were going through our warmups when they walked in. That's what they did, walked. They had their heads up high and strutted around like the game was going to be a cakewalk. That got us fired up.

The game was exciting, close most of the way through. Somehow at the end they missed four or five free throws. They'd miss, get the rebound, we'd foul again, they'd miss, get another rebound, and we'd foul again. Finally I got to take the ball down to our basket, and they fouled me.

We were trailing by two with time running out. I wanted to take the shot, but if Donnie was open I was going to look for him. I dribbled the ball down. When I got to halfcourt I crossed over to my left hand, and a Philadelphia Pharmacy guy reached in. He didn't hit me very hard, just hard enough to throw me off balance. I was surprised that the refs called a foul. Usually in situations like that they don't call it if it's not obvious.

There was just a second left. When I got to the line I thought, "This is great. This would be a perfect ending to a messed-up year for me." Earlier in the season I'd pulled some ligaments in my thumb. The thumb was taped for over a month and had a big cast-like thing on it, which kept me from shooting well.

Because I'd struggled with that thumb injury, I could see me missing those free throws. I actually expected to miss one of the two. Scott Moore came up to me and said, "Knock these down, Woodrow." As they left my hand I thought the first one was short and the second one long, but both of them found the middle somehow. We went into overtime and ended up winning by quite a bit. I hit a couple of threes, and Kelly Day came up big.

Although we won that game, we suffered a big loss when Donnie broke his hand. We didn't know how serious it was because he came back into the game and played after it happened. We figured he might have jammed a finger or something. After the game, when we found out that he'd broken a bone, we were somewhat down. But then we thought, "We beat Transy earlier in the year without Donnie. Let's go out to Idaho and win some games for him and ourselves." Unfortunately we lost to Whitworth College in the opening round.

The next year, my senior year, we had no Donnie Frazier, no all-American, but before the season started I thought we had a chance to be an excellent team. We didn't have any established stars, but we had a lot of players who could give us a lift on a given night.

Our season started in the summer, when we got together a few times and played. That helped us to jell. We played Centre College in preseason. They had a pretty good squad, but we went over there and beat them and had a great time doing it. We were laughing and cutting up, but we knew what we had to get done, and we did it. That carried over into the season. We had a good time out on the floor. It wasn't uncommon to see us joking around a little bit.

We started off by beating two good teams in the Lions Club Tournament. We lost just one of nine games before Christmas, to Maryville. After Christmas we hit a little lull, losing four out of five. A lot of that had to do with coming back after a whole week of vacation and playing with just one day of practice. After losing at home to Transy early in January, we won our next six games.

A couple of nagging injuries made the season difficult for me. I had shin splints in both shins. For five or six games they really bothered me and affected the way I played defense. I felt a whole step slower than everybody else. My mental game suffered, because I started thinking that I couldn't do it. I had an ankle injury as well, and that slowed me down even more. I could hardly cut at all. Those injuries kept me out of some practices. When you sit out practices but play in games, people think you're being a baby in practice. Believe me, if I could have been out there, I would have. I wasn't the type of person who sat out, but those shin splints gave me some of the worst pains I've ever felt.

I'd take a couple of days off, then try to go out and shoot a little bit. In games I could tell I hadn't practiced because I'd lose my breath. I have to give credit to the training staff. Sandy Williams, Michelle Anderson, and Brandon Pyles worked with me, trying to get me back. I came in an hour early before practice to have ultrasound and whirlpool. Afterwards I stayed another thirty or forty minutes to ice down.

I tried everything. My parents had heard something about rubbing Listerine on a person's legs and wrapping them with brown paper bags. We tried that. We tried rubbing vinegar on my legs. Any suggestions, we tried. Eventually the shin splints went away. I don't know why, but they did.

The team was playing very well when we went down to Bethel, Tennessee. We had beaten them by sixty points at Seabury, but they defeated us on their floor, and I still can't understand how in the world they did it. Their gym was way out in the country and real small. We felt like we were playing in a barn. We didn't play terribly bad, but everything seemed to go Bethel's way. They had one guy who kept hitting shot after shot.

Something happened in that game between me and Coach. Generally I got along with him pretty well, although he kept his distance from the players off the court. In my sophomore or junior year he was on us pretty hard one day, and I was having a bad day and backtalked. He got mad. That was the last time I said anything until that game at Bethel my senior year.

We were down at the half by about fifteen points. As we were coming in at halftime Coach said something that seemed encouraging to the other team. Maybe he meant it to be reverse psychology, but it didn't sit well with a lot of us. I said something sarcastic like, "Yeah, Coach, that's real good." He happened to hear me, and after the game he brought it up. I could see that I'd hurt him, and I felt terrible about it.

Two or three days after we got back, he called me up to the old gym and sat me down. He told me how much he respected me. He said that he might not be one of the best coaches, but he tried to do the best he could do and run a class program. I realized that, and I tried to express the respect I had for him. That cleared the air between us.

The loss to Bethel may have been the best thing for us. I told Tad Brewer I was getting worried that we were going to think we were too good, and if we did that, something bad would happen to us. That loss made us realize that we couldn't take any games for granted, that we would have to play hard in all of them. We didn't lose again until the Final Four of the national tournament.

Not many teams could score with us that year. We averaged around ninety points a game. There were times, too, when our defense was awesome. Often several minutes would elapse between baskets for our opponents, while we were scoring ten or fifteen points.

Man-to-man was our main defense. Coach threw in a three-two matchup, and we ran that several times. Toward the end of the year we switched up sometimes. We'd go man for one trip down, then Coach would call the zone on them. The zone was helpful. Many teams didn't shoot well from the outside, and the zone threw them off. They didn't know how to get the ball inside. Toward the end of the year we started playing a lot more thirty-two.

We finished the year with another trip to Idaho, and this time we were a lot more confident. The previous year many of us hadn't been out there before and were excited just to be there. My senior team was determined to make some noise. We didn't get any respect in the polls the whole year. We'd advance to number twenty-two or twenty-five, then drop out.

That visit to Idaho was especially meaningful because Coach Wierwille was inducted into the NAIA Hall of Fame. Former Berea player Steve Ridder made a speech introducing him, and then Coach stood up and spoke. Steve Ridder talked about Coach running a classy program with discipline, and graduating 100 percent of his four-year players. He called Coach a legend, and I realized that he was right.

The guys on the team didn't say a lot to each other. We knew it was a special moment, especially when Coach got up and started talking. We hadn't known all of the things he had done. Donnie Frazier was out there with us as student assistant coach, and he and I teared up a little bit to see

Coach finally get his turn. It was very emotional for everyone.

My mom and dad came to the tournament, plus Scott Moore's parents, Gary Burns' parents, and Tad Brewer's grandparents. Our first game was with Briar Cliff College. That was a no-doubter for us. We were certain we'd win, and we did. Beating Briar Cliff got the monkey off our backs. We thought, "That's one down."

Our next opponent was Milligan College, the four seed in the tournament. We should have been worried that they'd beat us, but we had an air of confidence about us that made us think we were going to knock them off. We saw that game as an opportunity to show people who we really were.

Milligan had some really big guys down low, guys who beat and banged and pushed and shoved. They substituted a lot, running guys in and out. One of their guards who'd shot well in their previous game lit up the first half. In the second half another of their players hit five or six threes in a row. We couldn't do anything with him. Yet somehow we won the game by ten points, and it felt like a blowout to us.

Viterbo College got a lot of press as some kind of Cinderella story. We didn't know much about them. Once the tournament began we didn't have time to prepare for every possible opponent, so we just went along. Once again people seemed to write us off. We didn't get a lot of respect out there. All that did was give us an extra spark to knock Viterbo off. They were another big team, but we beat them too.

Cornerstone College, our opponent in the Final Four, was definitely the best team in the tournament. They were solid at every position. All their guys were big, even their guards. We lost to them by fifteen, but the game was not one-sided. With a couple of bounces here and there, we could have won it.

Our three-point shooting touch deserted us. If we'd shot just our normal percentage, we could have won. But I give credit to Cornerstone. Every time we did something, they answered back. Every time we had a lull, they kept going to extend their lead. Every time we made a run to within six or so, they pushed their lead back out. Finally we had to foul, and they made their free throws. I truly believe that if we had found a way to beat that team to get to the finals, we would have won the national championship.

Scott Moore carried us in Idaho. He averaged over twenty

Tad Brewer: "The opposition didn't want to be around him"

Scott Moore: "He carried us in Idaho"

points a game and about ten rebounds. He took it upon himself that we were going to win it all, and we almost did. Scott is six-three and goes inside like a seven-footer. He's amazing. Whenever they shut him down on the inside, which was rare, he moved back out and shot threes. Scott was one of the best players in the NAIA that year.

Gary Burns grew up in that tournament. Coach said he became a man. When Gary first came to Berea I thought he was kind of soft. He didn't like the contact inside. But in Idaho he really turned it on, getting the ball and taking it strong to the hole, and grabbing rebound after rebound.

I think Kelly Day will be one of the best players ever to play at Berea. He was so good that it was hard for me to believe that he was just a sophomore. Kelly didn't like to go inside, and we got on him about that. But he was a great shooter and passer. He tried to do a little too much at times, but that's something that improves with experience.

Tad Brewer was short and stocky, but in practice he'd act like Shaquille O'Neal. Tad was the guy who kept us loose, although sometimes a little too loose. A couple of times we got mad at him for goofing around so much. But Tad knew when it was time to get serious. He could come off the bench and score very quickly. In one game he came in and hit five shots within a minute. And Tad did the little dirty things that need to be done occasionally. If a guard was hurting us, Tad didn't mind holding him a bit or giving him a little shove or elbow every now and again. It was amazing how Tad, at five-ten, could pull down so many rebounds. The way he banged and pushed, the opposition didn't want to be around him. They'd clear out, and Tad would get himself a rebound.

Coach Kelly Combs contributed a lot to our success. He really cared for us players, always asking us how things were going, even inviting us to his house for meals once in awhile. If something difficult came up in our lives, he was there to offer a helping hand. Coach Combs did most of the recruiting and the scouting of other teams. Those things meant a lot to the program.

My senior season was the greatest of my career, and not just on the floor. I got very close with the guys. I remember sitting with Scott and Tad in our hotel in Nashville when we went to play Bethel. We talked about high school and different games in the past. I realized then that my teammates were my best friends. Not just Scott and Tad, but a lot of the guys on the team. I've made friends at Berea who I want to stay in touch with my whole life.

It was wonderful to see the number of Berea fans who came out to the national tournament to watch us. It's an expensive trip from Kentucky to Idaho. Because we played four games we were out there for a whole week, and they stayed the whole week. I was happy that some of the parents could make it out there. After we we were eliminated my father

Gary Burns: "He really turned it on"

came down to the locker room. He walked up to me and gave me a big hug and told me he loved me. That moment capped off my year. Thinking about it still gets me emotional.

As a freshman I struggled with the academic side of college. Basketball was all I wanted to do when I first came to Berea. With practice two or three hours a day, ten hours a week of work, and social time, it was hard for me to find time to study and to make myself study. But I learned from Crawford James' experience to take my classes seriously.

Madeleine Watkins taught my Stories class my first semester. I had a hard time reading all that stuff and trying to figure out what it meant. I felt I couldn't do it and stopped paying attention. She stayed on me all the time. I didn't like that at first, but gradually I understood that she did that because she cared whether I succeeded or failed. After that semester she'd always say hello to me and talk. Dr Watkins was a French teacher and wanted me to go to France, but with basketball I couldn't find the time to do things like that.

I majored in business administration. I'll remember many of my business teachers, but Phil Spears in particular. He had a reputation as a tough teacher. Before I took his Organizational Behavior class, I heard stories about students crying and running out of the room because of things he said to them. We had to give a lot of presentations in that class, and he really got on us. He did that to help us understand what we'd encounter in the world outside college. I liked him once I got to know him. He had tons of fascinating stories.

I worked as a janitor in Dana Hall my first two years. I liked that because I could do it before basketball practice or come in late and do it. My junior year I was monitor in Dana, supervising the janitors and making sure the building was clean. The next year I became a teacher's assistant in accounting and worked in the business lab with the computers. I wasn't real strong in accounting, but I knew enough about it to be able to help people. I knew that becoming familiar with the computer would pay off for me in the future. It was a good experience.

I haven't decided what field I'll get into. Banking is a possibility. I've talked to my old teammate Corey Craig a couple of times about it. He enjoys the banking business, and the things he does sound interesting.

When former players speak at our spring basketball banquet, they usually talk about what Berea College means to them. Most of them say they didn't realize what it meant until they'd been out for a few years. Simply to graduate from Berea means a lot to me right now. Earning that degree took four years of hard work. I've been dedicated to my studies, my job, and basketball. I don't know what the future holds for me, but I believe it's going to be something special.

May 11, 1999

Kelly Combs   **Assistant Coach, 1991-**

I'm the son of a coach, and I wanted to be a coach myself since I was three or four years old. I grew up in Richmond, Kentucky, right here in Madison County. My father was a coach when I was born, at Kit Carson Elementary School. I went to every game and sat right next to him on the medicine chest. I can remember talking basketball strategy before I was ever in school.

I came to know Berea College through Roland Wierwille's basketball camps. Coach Wierwille knew my father and he knew that I could to play a little bit, so he let me in the camp when I was a year too young to get in. It was the first camp I'd ever really been to. I had been to other camps with my dad, but I hadn't been able to participate. So it was a great thing for me to be able to come to Coach's camp. I was just a little old first grader, five or six years old, and he was such a big man, so impressive.

I grew up coming to Coach Wierwille's camps every year all the way up to high school age. His camps were always filled with activities. It was continuous, just like our practices are today. We went right from one drill to the next, bang-bang-bang-bang. We never had a dull moment. There was never a time when we just stood there going "Duh, what are we going to do next?" I learned a great deal from Coach Wierwille's camps, and every year as a kid I thought it was a great experience for me to come. I liked being close to home, and I loved that swimming pool!

Berea's brain trust in the early 90s: Kelly Combs, Roland Wierwille, and Craig Jefferson

Growing up I played a little bit of everything: basketball, football, baseball, tennis, even a little golf. In high school I concentrated on basketball. We had a great year when I was a senior at Madison Central High School in 1987, going to the Final Four in the state tournament. I wanted to come to Berea College really bad, but I didn't qualify financially for admission. My dad was a school principal, and my mom worked in the school system. I was so glad when Coach Wierwille asked me to come back and work camp. It was a big thing to me, growing up in his camp, to be able to come back and work his camp.

I ended up going to Union College in Barbourville, Kentucky, on a basketball scholarship. But the coach I signed for left the summer before I got there, and things didn't work out for me or the new coach. I left, and soon after that he got fired.

I transferred to Kentucky Christian College. They had recruited me out of high school, but I thought I wanted to go to Union because I wasn't thinking about anything but a scholarship. Like every other high school kid, I thought a scholarship was a big thing. I didn't think about going where I would be able to play and have fun and win.

When I got to Kentucky Christian I was known as an offensive player. As a coach's son everything was offensive x's and o's. I knew all that, and I loved it. That was my thing, x's and o's. Then at Kentucky Christian Coach Randy Kirk called me into his office. He said, "Kelly, you're by far the best offensive player I've ever coached, but you don't play a lick of defense. If you don't learn to play defense, you can't play for me. But if you'll learn to play defense and continue to be the offensive player you are, I'll put one of these rings on your finger." And he handed me his national championship ring. They had just won one at Kentucky Christian.

After some hard lessons and a lot of drill work, I finally took defense to heart. I was point guard on a Kentucky Christian team that went thirty and four and won another national championship. Coach Kirk was right: defense wins championships. Ever since then I've prided myself on being a defensive specialist.

Coach Kirk was definitely an open-door coach. He loved to talk with his players. On road trips he played euchre and rook with us on the bus. He wanted to get to know us inside out. He knew everything about our families, every person in each family by name. Coach Kirk was also the Dean of Men, so he was very interested in our academic achievements. Being at a Christian college, he was concerned about our spiritual lives. I'd grown up in a Christian home, and that was very important to me. At Union I'd found an unwholesome atmosphere I was not accustomed to, one which confirmed my desire to transfer to Kentucky Christian.

As a basketball mentor, Randy Kirk was very demanding. He was a Bobby Knight who didn't scream and curse. He spent most of our practice time on defensive drills. We played great defense because he stayed after us relentlessly. It was always positive, constructive criticism. He wasn't demeaning with it. He just was on us to do our best. He pushed us to be the best that we could be at all times and to play as hard as we could at all times.

I was not financially able to stay at Kentucky Christian, so I transferred to Eastern Kentucky University and got my degree there. I intended to play at Eastern, but when it came time to try out I had an opportunity to coach at Madison Southern High School. I decided it would be better for me to end my playing career with a national championship and get started on my coaching career.

During my last two years of college I was an assistant to Tony Cox at Madison Southern. He's another great coach who taught me a lot about the game of basketball. Coach Cox had been my very first coach. He let me play on the White Hall Elementary School team when I was only a first grader. I was too young to be eligible, but he let me on the team.

The second year I was at Madison Southern I coached the freshman team. I had Coach Wierwille's son Roland Cecil on my freshman team. At the end of the season Coach Wierwille asked me to come to his office. I had no idea what he wanted; I thought maybe summer camp or something. Instead he wanted to know if I would be interested in being one of his assistant coaches along with Craig Jefferson. He told me it was a volunteer position and suggested I go home and think about it. Before I left his office I said, "I've always dreamed of being a college coach. If I can get my start as a volunteer at Berea, you bet I want to. No sir, I don't need to think about it. I want to be an assistant for you."

I was the volunteer coach for the first three years I worked at Berea College. The only thing I got paid for was mileage if I went recruiting or scouting. I went right from my undergraduate degree into my master's study, and I had various paying jobs too. I substitute taught in the Madison County school system, then did some sales work, selling cars, motor homes, insurance, a little bit of everything. I tried to do different things that were flexible around my coaching career, because my main desire was to be at Berea College.

My first year at Berea I didn't do much, just kind of learned. Coach Wierwille taught me a lot. He was a great role model at his camps when I knew him as a kid, but that was fun and games. I saw Berea College play a lot of basketball as I was growing up, so I knew the kind of temper he could have. When he talked to me about coming to Berea he said "You may not be able to work for me. I'm a hard guy to work for." He was trying to scare me. That was good for me, because I came in scared to death of him!

From Coach I've learned the importance of discipline and organization and time management. You never waste a moment with Coach Wierwille; every moment of time is used. More than anything he demands that you're always on time and that you always give it your best. If you want to see Coach Wierwille get excited, you be late, or you slack! That's true to this day, even after his stroke. If you want to rile him up and get him hyper, you just come in late, or you get out there and loaf, buddy. You will catch his wrath by doing that.

Coach Wierwille put me in charge of recruiting right after my first year. He knows that's something I enjoy very much. You see, I believe in Berea College. I wanted to come to Berea College, and I tell all the recruits that. I would have given anything. My dad threw the biggest fit in the world

Coach Kelly Combs: "I learned what Berea is really about"

trying to get me into Berea. He had done a lot of things over the years with the College, and when he found out I couldn't get in, he and John Cook went head to head. John Cook stood his ground. He said, "There are no exceptions. Kelly can't get in."

When I starting recruiting kids as an assistant coach, John Cook and I would go head to head on the same things. It's tough when you find a kid who's a great basketball player, a great student, a prime fit for Berea College, and then you find out his parents make too much money. You have to tell that kid, "Sorry, I can't recruit you." I used to have a problem with that, but I learned what Berea College is really about, what the system is, the kind of students who can come to Berea and what happens to them.

I looked at some of the kids who were at Berea when I got there. I got to know them and their family situations. That opened my eyes to what Berea College is here to do. In the years I've been at Berea I've recruited some kids who didn't have anything at home. They had a lot of love, caring parents, but as far as wordly things, financial means, they didn't have anything at all. I've seen those kids come to Berea and get an opportunity for a good education, then graduate and go on and do great things.

A classic example, one I use all the time, is Daniel Brown. Daniel Brown was my first big recruit. He was a little guy who came from Nicholas County and didn't have a lot at home other than a great family who loved him and supported him. I worked my tail off to get Daniel to come to Berea College because I knew what it could do for him. Not just basketball-wise, but to give him an opportunity to get an education and be able to work in the work system and have a little spending money in his pocket. I grew to love Daniel very much and still do. My whole family thinks the world of him, and we were so glad to see that Daniel not only became an all-American who helped take us to the national tournament, but he got a college degree. That's something nobody can take away from him. Daniel really grew up and matured, and he did an awesome job the one year he helped us coach. He's working in the Clark County school system now and is doing a great job, from all the things I've seen and heard about him.

So we look for kids who can qualify not only academically, but financially, to give them the opportunity to come to Berea. When I go and talk to a kid, the first thing I want to know about is his academics. Second, I want to know about his family, his financial situation. Third, I want to know what kind of person he is. And then I also want to know what kind of basketball player he is. They have to fit into all those qualifications to be able to play in Berea's program. They have to be awfully dedicated young people to go through everything they will have to go through. They have to go to class. They have to study. They have to work. And then they have to put the time in for basketball. It is tough, but the kids who want it, they do it.

I tell kids today that if they qualify to come to Berea College and they don't enroll, they're crazy! The quality of the education they can get at Berea College is so strong. When they go to get a job, the reputation of Berea College is unbelievable. I'm amazed every year at how our seniors are landing jobs before they ever graduate. Companies seek them out and want to hire them.

I strongly believe in the labor program. I've recruited some kids who said, "I've heard that if I come there I'll have to clean toilets, and I ain't doing that." I say, "Then you're not made to come to Berea College, probably." I've got to find the kids who say, when I tell them that all Berea students have to work ten hours a week, "That doesn't bother me. I'm used to working." That's the kind of kids I go after.

You see, I always tell them up front, "You're going to work ten hours a week. That's a requirement. There's no guarantee what you're job will be, either. You could be cleaning the bathrooms in the dorm, you could be working in the library, you could be doing a million things on campus." I watch their responses. It's very important to get kids to come to Berea College who aren't bothered by a little work. The work experience definitely builds character, responsibility. It also helps when they go out in the working world. It proves to employers that these guys know how to work already.

Here's another recruiting tool I use. I tell the parents that Coach Wierwille's been at Berea a long time, and of all the players who have played in his program for four years, 100 percent of them have earned a degree. Parents' eyes light up when I tell them that. That's a statistic that tells people that Coach Wierwille really cares about his players academically.

I talk about the strength of our basketball program. It's been up and down over the years, but now it's definitely on the rise. Coach Wierwille did an awesome job building the program, and since I've been at Berea it has continued to grow. When I first came we were right at .500 or a little below, but after my first two years we haven't been below .500, and our record has gotten better and better. The last three out of four years we've been to the national tournament, and we were able to win twenty games in each of our last two seasons. I hope I had something to do with that. I've sure put a lot of blood, sweat, and tears into this program. I love it, and I'm very thankful to be a part of it.

The day Coach had his stroke was just a normal day, nothing out of the ordinary. I didn't know anything about it when I went home. The morning after it had happened Craig Jefferson called me. I could tell something was wrong, because he had a very somber sound to his voice.

I said, "What's up, Craig? What's going on?"

"You haven't heard, then, have you?"

"No. What are you talking about?"

"Coach Wierwille had a stroke last night."

The way he said it, I was afraid Coach was gone. I said, "What do you mean, he had a stroke? What happened?" My grandmother had just had a stroke, and hers was very serious.

Craig told me about Coach leaving the gym, how he couldn't talk when he got home, and how everything went downhill from there, that he was in the hospital paralyzed on one side and unable to speak. Craig didn't know anything else. We didn't know how permanent anything was or how it was going to go from there.

"Where do we need to go? What do we need to do?"

"Coach doesn't want us to go over and see him. You know how Coach is. But we need to decide about having practice today."

"What do you think we ought to do?"

"We'll just go on, the same time as usual. That's what Coach wants."

I figured he'd want it to go on like it was. I spent that day trying to find out what was happening. It was a scary time for all of us because we were used to Coach being there every day, so stable and strong.

Within the first few days things started looking better for Coach, and we knew then that the outcome was going to be positive. First they said, "He'll be okay. He's just going to be out the first semester." We were relieved. Then they decided to name Craig interim coach and me the assistant.

Craig and I got together and said, "We're going to do things just like before. We're going to continue on like it's normal, just like Coach is still here. We'll do practices the same way, everything."

It was a tough time for our players. They were very emotional and uptight. But as things got better for Coach things got better for us, too, because we realized what was going on and understood that he was going to be okay.

After the 1994-95 season Coach Wierwille returned. Once again Craig was going to be the top assistant getting the pay, with me the volunteer. But Craig wanted to pursue other interests and also, though he might not ever admit it, I believe in my heart that he wanted me to get paid. I think he felt bad about how much I was doing although I wasn't getting paid. Craig decided to enter private business, and that opened the door for me to apply for that top position, which Coach Wierwille offered to me. I owe a lot to Craig Jefferson. We're still the best of friends.

I'm very thankful to Coach Wierwille for the opportunity to come to Berea College as a volunteer, then to be the top paid assistant. For two years I was head baseball coach also, and now I'm the college intramurals director as well as basketball assistant. Every year I asked, "What can I do to be involved with the students? Is there a job I can get?" When the intramurals job came open, I knew it would be a great opportunity for me to be involved with more students and with the whole college community. I really enjoy doing it.

The new Seabury Center is fabulous, a tremendous asset to Berea College. I was at Berea when we had the old gym, of course, and I remember the tearing-down of the old building and the construction of the new one.

The old gym had a tremendous atmosphere for basketball games. There was always a full house, great crowd support. Our teams loved to play in it, and visiting teams always seemed to play well because they knew it was going to be a battle.

With the new Seabury Center, there's such a dramatic difference when you walk in. It's such a beautiful facility. Yes, it was hard getting ready for it. In our last year in Old Seabury our space was very limited. There was always jackhammering and beating and banging and construction going on, and dirt flying and dust. But the new building has been such a motivating factor for our kids.

It's also a very impressive place to bring recruits. I tell kids on the phone, "We've got a modern twelve million-dollar facility only a couple of years old. You're really going to like it. It's big, it's beautiful." I've never brought a recruit in and heard him say, "It's not as nice as I thought." I lead them in and stop and look back at them, because I want to see their eyes and their mouths. Their eyes get really big and their mouths drop open. They just stand there and look around like, "Wow! This place is awesome!" And it really is.

It's large, but like the old building it's well-kept and clean. We have a nice locker room and a weight room with all the most up-to-date machines. I tell recruits, "If you can't get big in here, you can't get big anywhere, because we've got everything you need." Other teams are always saying, "Man, how do you guys have such a great place to play?" Believe me, we're glad to have it.

We ended the last season in Old Seabury strong, beating Campbellsville and Pikeville and then taking Georgetown right down to the wire. It carried into the next season. In 1995-96 we had a new gym and a unified team rallying around Coach's comeback. We'd had a solid recruiting year, but a big factor in our success was good senior play. In Daniel Brown, Tony Goatley, Otis Diuguid, and Roland Cecil we had experienced guys who were leaders. Here were players who could take it over when it needed to be done. They led us all the way to the national tournament.

Our opponent there was Tabor College. I wasn't able to scout Tabor in person because the school is so far away. As a rule I try to see every team before we play them. I'm a big believer in scouting, so I travel quite a bit. During the season I see everybody I can possibly see. I try to learn as much as I can about a future opponent's offense and defense, and I also want to spot the tendencies of all their players, the little things they like to do. This guy can't go left, or he always turns right, things like that. I always make sure our kids know that stuff.

All we could get on Tabor was one tape. I called everybody on their schedule. Tabor had one of the most loyal schedules I've ever seen, because nobody would tell me anything about them. They wouldn't give me any detail. They just would say, "Yeah, they're a nice team, they've got a big guy in the middle, dah-dah-dah." But we got a tape right before we went, and I tore that tape all to pieces. I watched it over and over and broke it down on film, made clips of it and showed our kids.

As a rule Coach Wierwille is not a big talker before games. We want our players to arrive for the game prepared. You can't get prepared in the locker room; you prepare yourself to play the day or two before the games by paying attention to and executing the things we ask in practice.

But before the game Coach will let me go over a scouting report. My way of doing it is to go down the opponent's starting lineup and give our matchups, who's going to guard who. I usually give some tips like "C.J., this kid always turns to his right, so if you make him go to his left, you'll be able to shut him down. Tony, if you fake to the right on this guy, you'll always be able to go to the left to get your jumper off. Corey, if you'll box out and get rebounds, we'll be able to run on them." Those are little motivational things to pump our kids up and give them a little extra boost. Then I wrap it up by reminding them: defense, rebounding, and teamwork. After that we give them quiet time. Coach Wierwille lets them sit there and think and get themselves prepared in their minds.

The Tabor game was emotional, full of ups and downs. Berea College hadn't been to the national tournament in many years, and there were a lot of jitters and nerves. I had them myself. I hadn't been to a national tournament since I'd played for our championship team at Kentucky Christian. We got down, got up, got down, got back in the game.

Daniel was not having the typical Daniel Brown game. He was pushing himself, putting so much stress and pressure on himself that it was hurting him. Tony Goatley had a great game, Otis Diuguid gave us good minutes handling the basketball, and we had some other guys who stepped up and did things they hadn't been doing. Corey Craig was on a tear. Shane Tarvin and David Jackson played well, and Donnie Frazier as a young kid was lighting it up. Thank goodness Donnie got hot. He fed off Daniel and Tony. Donnie had a great year that year, and he should have. With two guys like Daniel and Tony to guard, teams usually left somebody open, and Tabor made the mistake of leaving Donnie open. He was filling it up. He had a great game out there.

It was tight at the end. When Tabor went downcourt on the last play, we made a great stand, played defense like we wanted to, made them take the shot we wanted them to take. Two kids went straight up for the ball, and the whistle blew. I still think it was the kind of call you don't decide a game on. You let the kids decide the game, you don't blow the whistle and decide the game for them. But that's what happened. The call was made, and that's the way it goes. The Tabor kid stepped up and hit the free throws. Those were pressure free throws, and the kid did it.

Tabor did have a nice team. They were athletic. They had a seven-footer and a couple of kids who could really shoot. They'd won a lot of games, so they knew what it took to win games. They'd been there before. Their kid stepped up and hit the free throws. For our last shot Daniel got a good shot, well within his range. We always said that if Daniel crossed midcourt he was within his range! So he got a couple steps past midcourt and got off a great shot. It hit the front of the rim and bounced up. We thought it had a chance to go in, but it didn't.

The emotions of losing were very tough, but it was still a big moment for our program. Our kids had a good winning season and won the tournament that qualified them for the national tournament. That senior class set the tone. Their actions showed everybody that Berea College was back. We want to come to the national tournament every year. And we don't want just to come: we want to come and win.

The next year, to be able to get to the championship game to go to the national tournament was a great feat in itself, losing as much as we lost in Daniel and Tony and those guys. That was a lot of production to lose. But we made it that far, and then in 1997-98 we were even stronger.

Early in the season we had an opportunity to play Eastern Kentucky University. I know Coach wanted to play them several times, and there were other times when he didn't want to play them. I have a friend who worked for the *Richmond Register*, and I'd been prodding him for several years to try to get Eastern to play Berea. In 1997 Eastern brought in a new coach, Scott Perry, and I said to my friend, "Tell this new coach that they should play little old non-scholarship Berea for their first game. It would bring a good crowd, and crowd support is a big thing."

I was really excited when we got the call from Eastern. Coach played it out like he always does, playing hard to get. He and I talked about it several times. I was all gung-ho: "Coach, we want to play them!" I thought it was a great opportunity for our kids. Finally Coach had me call Eastern back and say we really weren't sure about doing it, but I had talked him into it. Of course they jumped on that and wanted to play us.

Our kids took it as a challenge. A lot was said about what a great opportunity it was for us to go over there and play a talented, well-conditioned, pressing team in a big gym in front of a good crowd. But those were all things that we believed about our own program. Eastern was NCAA Division I, but we were also a well-conditioned team, able to press and run the floor. And we also had a great gym to play in.

We play one game at a time, and we had some games before we played Eastern. I know they thought we spent our whole year getting ready for them, but we didn't. We had to get ready for some other games first, and we did, but the Eastern game was definitely a big thing to our kids. Coach Wierwille had played at Eastern, and all our kids knew that. They also knew that I'm from Richmond and had graduated from Eastern, and for me it was also a big deal to play them. Eastern gets all the publicity in the local paper. The paper comes out in their town, but a lot of times we felt we should have had better coverage because we were winning. Our kids took it as a personal challenge to go up there and show the people of Madison County that we have a good program at Berea too.

On the first play of the game Eastern went with an isolation play, isolating one of our smaller guys and scoring in the paint. My first thoughts were, "That's kind of shoddy that they would isolate our littlest guy and try to abuse him." Then we went on a six or eight-point run without them scoring. I looked at Coach and said, "We're going to be all right." As Coach is, he just said, "Not yet, not yet." He didn't want to talk about it yet, but all I meant was that we were going to hold our own.

That was what I'd been saying all along, that we could hold our own with them. If we could stay close to the end, we would have a chance to win. As it worked out, we were very fortunate to build a big lead. A big lead was what we needed, because we had to hold on at the end.

It was a great game for us. All our kids played well. We had great contributions from everybody who played, and our bench was extremely into the game. Everybody knew their roles so well, and they played their roles. Guys who knew they were going to be role players on the bench did it, and they cheerleaded and did a great job. The kids who had to play, they did what they had to do that night. They shot the ball well, played good defense, and then hung on at the end to pull the win out. It was a great emotional, spiritual victory for our kids to be able to hold their heads high and say, "We may be a non-scholarship school, but we can play with the Division I schools, and not just play with them, but beat them."

That victory probably cost us a few games later in the year. Before every game from then on, we heard it in the locker rooms and everywhere else: "Let's beat Berea, because they beat a Division I team!" Everybody pumped for us more than they did for their other opponents. But hey, that's what it's all about. That's why we played Eastern, for a chance to beat them even if it meant that everyone else would play us that much harder. We'd rise to that challenge every night.

To get back to the national tournament we had to beat Philadelphia Pharmacy. We knew nothing about them except that they had a great record and were nationally ranked. It wasn't possible for me to see them in person, but I was able to get a couple of game films on them, one the day before we played them and the other on the day of the game itself. One tape was from a small Bible college, and all it showed me was what Philadelphia Pharmacy's kids liked to do when they were blowing people out. But then I got some film from a more competitive game, and we were able to learn a lot about their kids and the system they ran. We didn't have a lot of time to watch it. I cut it up and put it together as fast as I could to show it to our kids right before we played. I think we were very fortunate to play Philadelphia Pharmacy at our place.

At first our kids seemed a little too at ease, being at home, and Philadelphia Pharmacy was very poised. We could tell that they had a good senior leader. They jumped out on us early. But I knew that with the kind of season we had had, the fire in our kids would come back. Remembering when we beat Eastern Kentucky University would still be in our kids' heads, and they weren't going to lay down any. Roland Wierwille's never had a team that lay down. I knew our kids were going to fight and get back in the game.

I kept pushing our kids. "Keep working hard. Play defense. If we can stop them on defense, we'll be okay. Things are going to start falling. Eventually we'll score."

We were able to make some big stops down the stretch, and we started to hit the basket. We fouled them, and they missed the free throws. Those were big helps. Then Jeremy Wood hit two tremendous pressure free throws with very little time on the clock.

We had great play from our underclassmen, but once again the seniors showed the way. Crawford James showed plenty of senior leadership in that game with great defensive plays and awesome rebounds. Donnie Frazier played like a true leader as a senior. He was willing us to win, and he broke his hand doing it.

We were fortunate to beat Philadelphia Pharmacy in overtime. It really hurt to lose an experienced guy like Donnie Frazier who got us so many points and rebounds. But all year long we never knew who was going to be our hero on any given night. Sure, on the statistical end Donnie was the leading scorer. But as the season progressed, each night we had somebody different step up and be the clutch man who hit the big baskets.

Our kids had a good attitude, a mentality that said, "We don't care who does the scoring as long as we play team basketball and we win." With Coach Wierwille and the system we have, we always persist. We go and play the next game, because the next game is the most important game we play. It doesn't matter who plays for us or who plays for them. We're going to go out and do what we've got to do to win the basketball game.

So we tried to de-emphasize the importance of not having Donnie and emphasize the importance of playing a great team basketball game, playing great defense, and doing the little things we had to do to win. We knew we had some guys who were capable of stepping up. C.J. had some big games down the stretch as a senior. Our junior, Jeremy Wood, was a good shooter and could be a leader. Scott Moore was our second-leading scorer, Gary Burns a very capable post player, Kelly Day a strong freshman who could do it. We had guys like Casey Lester and Tad Brewer who could come off the bench and shoot the lights out. Greg Laws was a freshman who had some great shooting nights on the junior varsity level and a time or two on the varsity. We didn't have one person who could do everything Donnie could do, but we had several guys who could play and help make up for the loss of Donnie. Had we had Donnie, had we been full strength, there's no telling how far we'd have gone. But I really felt good about the chances we had with the team we had, all things considered.

We played Whitworth College. That team had tremendous confidence because they knew we were missing a guy who'd hit twenty-two points a game for us. They'd seen game film on us, and it was an obvious boost for them to look down there and see Donnie Frazier with a cast on his arm. And we were real young without Donnie. He was an emotional leader and a vocal leader, and without him on the court our kids had some jitters. We were a young squad out there, with just one senior and one junior, and it was the first time for most of our guys in a national tournament atmosphere. We had some kids who'd played in important high school games, but this was a big-time college tournament.

So Whitworth's confidence and our jitters and unsureness at the start of the game got us into a big hole. We got down significantly, twenty or so points. Once again we told our kids, "We're going to be all right if we just play defense, just play defense, just play defense!" If we could make some stops, we'd start scoring. And that's how things progressed. We'd make a stop and we'd score, make a stop and score. Momentum began to build for us. Our kids began to realize, "We can do this. Let's play that defense, and we'll score one bucket at a time."

So we fought and we scratched and we got back into it. Roland Wierwille's teams are not going to lay down. As bad as it looked, we were not going to get trashed. We were going to claw and fight and make it a game if at all possible. We pulled even, but Whitworth beat us when we ran out of gas. We'd dug ourselves such a deep hole and spent so much energy fighting to get out of that hole that at the end Whitworth was able to capitalize. They were an awfully good team, ranked high in the country with a lot of wins and national tournament experience. They too knew how to battle and how to hold on.

I was very proud of our kids for their fight and determination. I have some friends, coaches in other parts of the country, who came to me after the game and said, "The fight in your kids is unbelievable. They never gave up. They just kept fighting." I smiled and said, "Yeah, and we're young." I looked forward to the future.

I've been very fortunate to be a part of Berea College and to work with Coach Wierwille. I give my wife credit for making it possible. Jody is so very supportive of me. It was our second year of marriage when I came to Berea. She had just graduated from college and got a job as a teacher. She was willing to go to work every day and let me continue to go to college and coach at Berea as a volunteer. At that time I know she thought, "He'll go over there and volunteer for a couple of years, and then he'll go on and get a job and everything will be fine." But my volunteering carried on for several years, and later I was still only a part-timer. It was a part-time job financially, but more than a full-time job time-wise.

During the basketball season, between us playing and me scouting and recruiting, I'm on the road five or six nights a week. For what I get financially out of this job, I'm very lucky to have a wife who's so supportive and willing to get up and go to work every day. I used to worry that Jody was unhappy with me because I wasn't earning any money. I was spending all my time doing this. But we've always said it's going to pay off some day. The big payoff is in being a part of these young people's lives, but we hope that someday all this time I've put in will also pay off with me becoming a head coach. At Berea, I hope. If not at Berea, somewhere else.

Yes, I very much aspire to be a head coach. It's been my lifelong dream. Coach Wierwille knows that. I've made it very clear to him, and he knows that when he's ready to retire, I'm hoping and praying that I have the opportunity to become the next head coach at Berea College. It may be possible or it may not be, but it is a personal goal and a goal of my family.

I've been fortunate to coach under great coaches like Tony Cox and Roland Wierwille. They already had systems in place, and I fit myself into those systems. When I am a head coach there might be things I'll try that won't work, but I pride myself on being the kind of guy who can adapt and change and make things work with what I have.

Any teacher or coach in today's society has to be able to relate to his students. I know Coach Wierwille's from the old school and I'm from the new school, but I hope I can take a lot of things from the old school and adapt them into the new school-type atmosphere. I've been out of high school just a little over ten years, but I can see differences between the kids today and the kids of my time. I want to be able to relate to my players, to understand where they're coming from and what's going on with them.

In my heart I have a burning desire to work with young people and make a difference in their lives. I truly believe that coaching is a wonderful way of helping young people. Winning is important, and if I didn't love to win I wouldn't be in coaching. But you have to learn from all aspects of the game of basketball. It's very similar to life. There are a lot of things you can learn from basketball that you can carry over into life.

To be a successful college basketball coach you have to have some x and o knowledge, sure. And you have to be a great motivator to be able to get your kids to do the things you want done, as hard as they can do it. However, I'm convinced that if you don't have quality students in the classroom, they're not going to be able to come through for you on the basketball court. It's important that you care as much about your players as people and as students as you care that they become the best they can be on the court. You have to be truly concerned about your students academically, make sure they have a good, strong academic background and that they stay on top of their academics.

I have to give my wife and my children a lot of credit for putting up with me and the hours I spend at Berea College. I think I give a lot to this program, but I have to say too that the kids in this program give a lot to my family. The ballplayers mean so much to us. We open our home to them at any time. Our family goal is to make a difference in young people's lives. That's the big reason I want to be part of this basketball program and my wife wants to be part of it. We've all have grown from it tremendously.

May 27, 1998

Roland R. Wierwille (3)   Coach, 1972-

Our sports programs at Berea College are unique. We do not give athletic scholarships, but we can compete against schools that give athletic scholarships. Nobody pays tuition, true, but nobody gets anything to play basketball, either. Berea College players are student athletes who have to work and keep up their studies like everyone else if they want to come into the gym.

Let's say a player finds out that with financial aid and no tuition, it

Coach Roland Wierwille: "Put it all on the line!"

will cost him 1000 dollars to spend a year at Berea College. He comes to school and decides a week later that he doesn't want to play basketball. Well, he's still going to pay 1000 dollars. He's not going to have to pay more. If he doesn't want to play, he doesn't have to play. It's voluntary.

There is pressure on these kids. Getting a 2.5 at Berea College is almost like a 3.5 at some of the schools we play. But the ones who play four years for me have all graduated. Every one. Only one didn't graduate from Berea College. He completed his degree at Eastern about five years after he finished playing. He knew he had to do it, and he did.

We bring kids in, and some of them will stay on campus and graduate. Others can't do it. They get stars in their eyes, but they cannot organize their time, and they get behind. But if they make it through the first couple of years they learn what it takes to work and study and play basketball, and they just do it.

Two hours out of the day doesn't sound like much. At a lot of places the players might spend those two hours taking a nap, but ours have to be working. And then they average three hours a day with practice. Get to the gym, dress, practice, shower, it's about three hours. So there's five. Then they have three or four hours of class. Now it's up to eight or nine hours a day. And they've got to eat, they've got to study. So it's not easy. Berea is unique.

But we can sell Berea College because of its academic reputation. We sell the campus itself. And we sell our facility. Old Seabury was old, but we kept it clean and painted, with nice locker rooms. I prided myself on that. Now we have one of the finest facilities in the United States. So we've got academics, a beautiful campus, and a facility. We also have the reputation of a pretty good basketball program.

I sell myself. I tell the kids and their parents that I can only do so much, but if they need something they can come to me, and if I don't have an answer, I'm going to get somebody who has an answer. I'm from the old school. I'm here to help these kids if they want to help themselves.

They have to make an effort. I'm not going to knock on their door at eight o'clock in the morning and say, "You've got to go to class." Some places do that. They have tutors who get them out of bed and take them to their classes, to make sure they go there. I'm not going to do that. Some places have a study hall, but I don't. They have to be grown up enough to study on their own. They have to get it done.

But I am interested in their academic progress, and I ask about it. Some weeks I might ask them every day about their grades. Other weeks I might not ask them for a while. But if it's getting close to the end of the semester or if I know there's a paper due or something like that, two days do not go by when I don't say something to them. I'll ask and they'll say, "Fine," but if there's a problem I can usually tell, and then I check it out a little bit.

For example, I had a young man who was way behind in his basic math. If he didn't get it finished by the end of the semester, he was gone! I found out he was behind, so I called him in. I felt him out about whether he really wanted to be back here next year. He was one of our top players. He said, "Coach, I want to be here next year. I don't want to go."

I said, "Let me get on the phone. We're going to call the professor, and then we're going to go see her."

She just happened to be in her office, and we went right over there. We closed the door and talked, and he acted in that meeting just like he acted with me, like he wanted to be here. Then he got to work. But if I hadn't taken him to that professor, I don't know if he would have made it.

The kids who want to play here accept the discipline that comes with the program. They shave. They don't look shaggy. And they're on time for practices, meetings, road trips. Often I don't even have to tell them now. The upperclassmen will tell the freshmen, and it filters down.

The players know that when we're going to take a trip on the bus, if I say we're going to roll at ten o'clock, we're going to roll, and they'd better be there. None of them has ever missed a bus. Once I had one who was within thirty seconds. He made it, but I was watching. And he was a starter.

A couple of years ago some players served on a committee over in Student Life. Gus Gerassimides, the Associate Dean, came to me and said, "Your players were the first ones to every meeting. They were never late. They were there. I attribute that to you."

I said, "Thank you."

I tell my players, "If you don't like the way the program is run, or if you don't feel you're being treated right, get out of here." They're not going to lose a scholarship. There are no scholarships. That's one advantage I have: I don't have a lot of money wrapped up in that kid. A coach at another school may give a 12,000 dollar athletic grant to a person, and maybe that person doesn't do what he wants.

A college coach ought to be judged, number one, by the academic accomplishments of his players. You read in the paper nowadays about players in Division I or other schools who come in for a couple years, and they're not there to go to school. They're there to get ready for the NBA, although less than two percent of college players make it in the NBA. Then you read stories about people who have played for four years and do not graduate.

You also have to look at what these players do with their lives after they leave school. We've had so many success stories from former Berea College players. That really makes me proud.

At some schools players use up their eligibility and are never seen again. But at every Berea College game I see several former players who played under me or played before I arrived at Berea. That means a lot to me.

And yes, winning is important too, because the American way is winning. At Berea College winning shows that we can succeed with hard-working young people who want to be part of a good program, even if they don't have the raw talent of some of the players we play against. And when we win games we didn't think we had a chance to win, that really gives me a high.

A graduate assistant at Eastern Kentucky University called me late in the spring of 1997. He asked, "Do you want to play us?"

"Why do you want to play us?"

"We have a new coach, and we want a good crowd."

I said, "Yes, and you want to win, too, don't you? What would the guarantee be?"

"2500 dollars."

I said, "I have to think about this."

"We need to know, because if you don't take it we need to get somebody else."

I said, "Don't pressure me! If you can't wait till tomorrow, you get somebody else."

He said, "We'll wait till tomorrow."

I wouldn't call him back. I told him to call me at ten o'clock the next morning. Then I thought about it. After talking to John Cook and a couple of other people, I thought I'd try it.

When the phone rang I said, "We played Morehead two years ago, and they gave us 3000 dollars. Surely you're not going to let Morehead outdo you with a guarantee if we come."

He said, "I'll have to talk to the assistant AD." Then he called back and said, "We can only go 2500."

I said, "I'm sorry."

"Maybe we can get together some other time."

I said, "Okay. Good luck."

I went to class and started thinking, "Why not? What's the difference? I don't know how long I'm going to coach, and this may be the last opportunity." So I called my assistant Kelly Combs and said, "I can't call them back and tell them we'll do it. You call them and tell them we talked it over and you talked me into playing them!" He did, and then he called me back to tell me it was on. I had turned it down, and then I rethought it. That's how it came about.

After we beat Eastern their coach, Scott Perry, said in the paper that we had been getting ready for our game with them for two months. Not many people know this, but I never mentioned the Eastern game until the Sunday before we played them on Tuesday. I never said "Boy, this is what we've got to shoot for! This is the season!" If I had raved and ranted, we would have been so tight we'd have thrown the ball all over the place. We didn't even have a scouting report. We saw them play in a scrimmage, and we could see they were going to press. But the first time I said anything was when we went over to the Eastern gym to practice that Sunday night.

I told our players, "I'm going to say one thing to you people. When that young coach comes up to me and sticks out his hand, I'm going to squeeze his hand and look him right in the eye. And I want you to do that with them. You're not going to back up one bit from those people. They want you to back up, but I'm not going to back up, and you're not going to back up."

That was about the only thing I said to inspire them. We had a good workout, we had supper, we practiced here Monday, and then we went over there Tuesday night and beat them. I'll tell you what got us going with that game. Saturday night in our tournament we played Virginia Intermont, a very quick, pressing team, and we handled their press pretty well. That's what helped us. It was almost like a practice game to prepare for Eastern. If Eastern had not pressed or if we had played a slower team on Saturday that didn't press, we might not have beaten Eastern. But that was just the way it came about. Eastern had good quickness, and they pressed us. We lost the ball some, but not much. They kept pressing us, and that was to our advantage. We got some baskets out of it.

Eastern never adapted to our thirty-two matchup zone defense, three out, two under. After about ten minutes I looked at my assistant and said, "We've got a chance, because they don't know what to do against our zone." And when we were up 51 to 33 at halftime I thought we had a pretty good chance. Somebody walked in at halftime and saw the score and said, "Well, Eastern's in good shape." Then he said, "Hey! That's Berea College winning!" But I didn't know we were going to win it until it was zero-zero on the clock and 94 to 88 in our favor.

Something like that doesn't happen often in a person's life. It was not only that we beat an NCAA Division I team. We beat a team I once played for, a team whose floor was named for my coach, Paul McBrayer. And we beat a team that didn't want me as a head coach.

You see, I had applied twice for the coaching job at Eastern Kentucky University. Both times I thought I had a good chance at getting the job. I had a lot of people behind me, a lot of townspeople and people on campus, but it didn't work out. It disappointed me to think I earned the chance to coach at my alma mater but didn't get that chance.

But after that 1997 game, with President Larry Shinn sitting right there, I said to our team, "Ten years ago they didn't want me as the head coach at Eastern. And I'm sure the hell glad they didn't!" And they just went wild.

So it was an extreme high for me and our players and our students and townspeople who were there from this whole side of the county. Because some people were picking us to get beat by fifty points. This wasn't the best team Eastern ever had, but if you compare the money they put in their program with the money we put in ours, maybe we should have been beaten by fifty points! When you can overcome those odds, it is truly a once-in-a-lifetime thing.

Everywhere I went, people congratulated us. They couldn't believe it. People I thought didn't even know we played basketball at Berea came up and congratulated me. That's the way it was. And people still comment on it.

After that game I had to bring our players down. We were three and zero after beating two pretty good teams in our tournament and then an NCAA Division I school. But for a while every team we faced played over their heads, because if they could beat Berea College, that would mean that they could probably beat a Division I school! My assistant heard one team going into the locker room saying, "This is our Eastern game."

My son Roland enrolled at Berea College, and he wanted to play basketball. Coaching him was not a problem. He was a hard worker, but he was not a very talented basketball player. If he had been an average basketball player, he might have had some playing time or he might not, but it could have been a problem if he had played in front of someone else. He never played much on the varsity level. I liked him to be around because he worked hard, he was strong underneath, and he helped us in practice, helped make the other guys better. He might have thought he should be playing. But I never had a concern about him hurting us in any way as far as attitude, and he really liked being on the team.

My older sister, Laura, died at age fifty-seven with a stroke. I had my stroke at fifty-five. It happened on November 1, 1994. I wasn't sick, but I wasn't right. We had a practice. I wasn't myself. I didn't have any energy.

After we finished practice I went downstairs and changed shoes. As I was leaving I passed a young man sitting outside the weight room. I started to say something to him, but I couldn't talk. I walked up the steps to my car. Somehow I got the key in. I couldn't use my right hand, and I'm righthanded.

I shouldn't have driven, because I could have wrecked. I should have asked Roland to drive me home, because he was still at the gym. I had an idea about what was going on, but I thought if I could just get home and lie down. So I drove home and went in. I couldn't speak, and Cecilia thought I was playing around. Then I just flopped on the bed, and she knew.

She called 911. They came and took me up to Berea Hospital, then transferred me to UK. I can still hear the sirens in the ambulance. Any time I hear one now, it reminds me of them picking me up. I did not know if I would ever make it back to Berea on I-75.

I couldn't talk. I had lost the use of my right arm and right leg. It was a long, long night.

Then my leg started coming back just a little bit. They started to run tests, and they put me in that thing that x-rays your whole body. That's scary, like putting you in a casket. I was forty-five minutes in that thing. But while I was in there, my arm started to come back, I don't know why. But I could feel it.

Four days passed. A lot of people came to visit me, and many people called. Cecilia took a call from one of my former players, and after she hung up I said in broken speech, "Who was that?" Those were the first words I spoke. Then I couldn't say anything more.

But the next day I was able to count from one to twenty. I had a beautiful nurse. She was not only a pretty girl, but she was a beautiful person. We got her in there, and when I started to count one, two, real broken, she started to cry! Because nobody knew if I would ever speak again.

From there it started coming back a little bit. I left the hospital after four or five days. Then I started my speech therapy and my physical therapy. I had to learn to use my tongue all over again, and I had to work my arm and leg. It was three months of pretty intense training.

That was a tough time. But there is no telling how many cards and phone calls I got from coaches, from guys I played with, from people I didn't even know who had read about it in the paper. That really helped me. I didn't think people would respond that much. I was very fortunate to have that many people hoping and praying that I'd get well.

I didn't think I could coach again because I'd lost my speech. Without that it would be impossible. But whenever I said, "If I coach again," Ivy Shelton, my speech therapist, wouldn't let me say "if." She said, "When you coach again." She just kept going and kept going. I think she took a special interest in me because she knew I was trying so hard.

Ivy Shelton knew that I wanted to coach in the new building. That gave me an incentive to try harder, because for twenty-three years I coached in the old place, and now we were going to have a beautiful new place and I might not be able to coach. That really motivated me. Ivy helped me, and my wife and my kids helped me. I learned to talk again.

I had my stroke just before the season started. Craig Jefferson, my assistant, took over the team. Under the circumstances he did very well. They won some good games.

I came back and watched a game, maybe the second game of the season. I knew then that I couldn't come to the gym and watch the team play. I got too emotional, and I knew it was better for me to stay away.

I wasn't going to come to the last game, either, the last game played in Seabury Gym. My wife and Beverly Harkleroad, my departmental secretary, talked me into it. They said I should be there. So I went. There was a nice ceremony. They honored me and some of the people who were involved with Seabury Gym through the years. And then we won the game! That really helped me.

After that the team went to Pikeville and upset their team in the tournament, then went to Georgetown and lost in overtime. I was so proud of them. Coach Jefferson did a good job. The record doesn't indicate the job that the coaches and the team did that season.

The next year I started coaching again. I still get excited, but I stay under control. I haven't had a technical since my stroke. I think the referees are afraid to give me a technical. They don't want me to go down!

Seriously, though, I can get away with a lot more than a young coach can because I know when to stop. I can get on a referee, but I know when to back off, when to sit down. If the referees respect you, they're going to let you do a little bit more. I don't get personal with them. I'll joke with them on the sidelines a little bit, but then when they know I'm excited, they say, "Okay, Coach. Easy now!" And then I'll be easy.

When I was younger I did not back off, and we probably lost some games because I got too emotional. Still, I was never kicked out of a game because of technicals. If I got one I sat down. If you get too emotional you lose perspective. You forget what you're trying to do out there.

In the fall of 1997 I went to Washington to receive a Communication Award from the National Council on Communication Disorders. C.M. Newton, athletic director at the University of Kentucky, presented the award to me. I met Senator John Glenn, whose wife had received that award because she was once a stutterer. James Earl Jones, the actor, was there. He was a stutterer at one time, and he had received the award. A young man who received the award when I did was in a wheelchair. He communicated through a computer. I felt very fortunate to be in that group of people.

It was such a beautiful thing. My sister Carolyn and my brothers George and Walter were there. Dr Shinn went with his wife Nancy. Ivy Shelton was right there too. She had recommended me for the award. She felt very proud because they recognized her as the one who worked with me.

When I came to Berea I wanted to bring teams in here once a year for a good small-college tournament that our basketball program could be identified with. A friend of mine was a Lion, so we started a December weekend tournament in 1975 with the Lions Club as sponsor. That's how it's been ever since.

The key to a successful tournament is to create a tournament atmosphere. The number one thing is the welcome dinner. We have a dinner at four o'clock on Friday. All the teams are together. We have a member of the Lions Club to welcome them, and sometimes we've had the President of Berea College come in and say, "Welcome to our tournament." Each coach gets up and talks about his team for five minutes, maybe introducing the seniors or captains or assistant coaches.

Everything is organized. Everything is ready for them. It's like clockwork, and they know that. They don't have to ask where to go. Somebody is right there to show them what to do. The teams have their locker rooms assigned. They have something to eat after the games Friday night. We have a nice brunch for all the teams on Saturday morning, a pregame meal on Saturday afternoon. Afterwards we have an all-tournament team and give out trophies. We have had great responses from people who have played, even people who lost two games here, writing notes, thanking us, saying they were treated right. It's really been a good thing.

Speaking of tournaments, going to the NAIA Division II tournament in Idaho in 1996 was a great experience for me and for our players. It's a very well-organized tournament. In 1985 we went to the NAIA tournament in Kansas City, before the NAIA was divided into two divisions. I think the current Division II tournament is better organized than the one in 1985.

You're treated very nice. There's a great banquet to start the tournament. And their new Idaho Center is a beautiful place. They have a CBA team that plays there. When you walk in, it's just like a picture. It's a thrill to play on a floor like that.

Just to see the snow-covered mountains out there is wonderful. I had never seen anything like that. To be associated with all the other teams that have won a championship, that means something. The only thing I don't like about the tournament in Idaho is the distance from Berea, which has kept our fans from going there. If we were playing six, eight, even ten hours away, we would have a good following. But to drive out there, it's three days! President Shinn was committed to something else in 1996, so vice president Leigh Jones went out there to represent Berea College. In 1998 and 1999 Dr Shinn made a special effort and was able to attend in person.

We came so close to winning that first game against Tabor College in 1996. After being ten down late in the game, we came back and went one up. We did exactly what we wanted to do. Their guy took a bad shot. One of our players went up to get the rebound, but they called him over the back, a terrible call at that time of the game. Then Daniel Brown brought it down to midcourt, and when he shot I thought the ball was in the hole. It was maybe a fourth of an inch short or it wouldn't have hit anything but the bottom. I thought it was in from my angle. But it wasn't, and we lost.

To get back to Idaho in 1998 we had to beat nationally ranked Philadelphia Pharmacy at our place. They were a good basketball team with an excellent point guard, Shannon Overton. He made second team all-American, and he deserved that. They had strong six-six people underneath.

They were well-coached by Bob Morgan, who has been around many years.

They jumped out on us in the first half. I think it was 32 to 17, but we scored fifteen straight points to tie it up. At halftime we were four down. In the second half they got another ten-point lead on us, but we came back. Our zone hurt them. They didn't know what to do.

Donnie Frazier hurt his right hand with just a few seconds left. I replaced him with Tad Brewer. We were a couple of points behind and had to foul them. Tad made the play, but that was his fifth foul. We needed Donnie back in there.

I talked to the trainer, Sandy Williams. I have a lot of respect for her, and if she had said, "I don't want him to play any more," I would have said, "He can't play."

I said, "Sandy, are you sure that he can play?" I knew that something was wrong, that something was probably broken in there.

Sandy said, "I don't think he can hurt it any more. He's a senior. This is the last game. Let's let him play."

Donnie went back in and held his own. Their all-American guard missed his free throws, and Jeremy Wood ended up with the ball. We were down by two with one-point-nine seconds left when Jeremy got fouled.

I had a great feeling that Jeremy was going to make those two free throws. I just had that feeling. When I was playing, sometimes I just knew I was going to make them. Well, Jeremy made both of them, and Philadelphia Pharmacy threw up a long shot that didn't go in. We were going into overtime.

When I saw those white shirts coming off the floor toward me, I knew we were going to get that game. I could just see it. Sometimes you start overtime and you're exhausted. But our players, their eyes were wide and they were not even walking, they were bouncing as they come over. And sure enough, when we started the overtime Jeremy hit a three-pointer, Kelly Day put one in from underneath, Jeremy hit another three-pointer, and it was 8 to 0 in fifty-five seconds. And we just stayed right there. Donnie Frazier responded. I don't think he scored in overtime, but just to have him out there, his desire, his hustle, meant so much. I know he went up and got a big rebound for us. He wanted to be there because he was such a big factor in us getting that far. We were in the final game, in overtime, and the trainer said okay, so we stayed with him.

That was one of the bigger games I've coached in. It was a great win for us, a great comeback. And with the emotion that was displayed by our bench, our student body, our season ticket holders, everybody, it was one of the best atmospheres we'd had at Berea in a long time.

Donnie called me after they x-rayed his hand. A bone was broken. He was crying. I said, "Son, things will work out. We'll do the best we can. I want you right there. You are part of this. You're going with us to Idaho."

I asked the orthopedic surgeon, "Is there any way?" She told me that if there was any way that they could do something without hurting him, they would do it. But there was no way, even for him to play in the national tournament in his senior year. So they put his hand in a big cast.

When he called and said it was broken, it really bothered me too. Donnie Frazier was one of the hardest workers that I've ever had at Berea College. He went from being a JV player to a third team all-American. You don't do that without working.

Donnie went with us, and it was emotional for him. I told him I wanted him with us in practice, and he was right there. Without Donnie we fell way behind in the game against Whitworth College, 26 to 6. But then we rallied, went up by two at halftime, and actually led by ten at one point in the second half. Then a Whitworth guy who had made four three-pointers out of seventeen the whole year came in and hit three straight. It was something you couldn't explain. They were terrible-looking shots. If I were there today I'd say, "Let him shoot the ball!" He was not a shooter, but sometimes it happens. He made three straight, and that got them going. We still had a chance, but we ended up losing.

It's good to compete in the national tournament, but we wanted to succeed out there too. We played a good basketball team, and without a full team we were still right there. I was very proud of that, but I wanted to win a national tournament game before my career ended.

I've had a lot of good years and a few down years, but the year of 1998-99 was an outstanding one for me and my family.

We had a good shooting team in 1998-99. We were an excellent three-point shooting team, and everybody knew it. Our opponents had to guard the perimeter, but we also had people like Gary Burns who could post up, and that made us pretty good. We had the same starting lineup all year. I had to change one position for one game. Other than that, it was the same group for thirty games. They got to know each other. They were unselfish. They played well together.

About halfway through the season I was concerned that we were letting the other teams have too many offensive rebounds. After we got back from our Florida tournament I decided to do something about it. Every day in practice we worked on boxing out. That was one of our weak spots, but once we started working on it, our team started coming on.

We had five guys who scored in double figures. Most of the time we were an unselfish team, and we played some pretty good defense. We peaked at the right time. We won twelve of the thirteen games ending in the regional tournament, and then we went to the national tournament and beat three very good teams.

I felt as much pressure in that first 1999 game in Idaho as in any of the games I'd coached at Berea. We'd been to the national tournament three times and lost the first game each time. We were in each of those games, losing them only by three, one, and four points. But I didn't want to hear anyone say, "Berea's going to the national tournament, but they'll be home right after the first round."

But in 1999 we knew our way around. Eight of our twelve players had been there before and played in that facility. I was concerned about our long layoff at the end of the season. We won the region on a Saturday and didn't play in Idaho until a week from the following Wednesday, an interval of eleven days. We wanted to play, but we had to practice. I used different methods, getting on them, being nice to them, to get them ready to play. I guess we did something right, because when they threw that ball up in the national tournament, we were ready to play.

Cornerstone College, who beat us in the semifinals, was the number one team in the nation going into the tournament, and that's out of 179 teams nationwide. They were a good team and well-coached, but we could have beaten them if we'd hit the baskets. I guess you can say that any time you lose, but the fact is, we hit just seven of thirty-four three-point attempts. They didn't shut us down. We moved the ball. We had good looks, good shots. All we needed was our normal shooting game, not an exceptional one, but the ball would not go in.

President Larry Shinn was out there once again. His backing, his interest, had a tremendous effect on the kids. Dr Shinn was present for our first two victories. He didn't want to leave then, but he was obligated to be somewhere else.

Dr Shinn attended the tournament banquet. Over 1000 people were there, including all thirty-two teams. At the banquet I was inducted into the NAIA Hall of Fame. I knew I'd have to speak, and I was concerned about that. Since my stroke I sometimes have a rough time speaking, especially in the evenings when I'm a little tired, but things worked out. Steve Ridder introduced me, my son Roland did the presenting, and then I spoke. Steve did a wonderful job of introducing me and Berea College. I looked at that ceremony not as an individual honor, but as a Berea College honor. It was a very proud moment, especially with my team out there to play in the tournament. To win three straight games on top of all that was almost like a dream.

I'm the Berea College athletic director now. I took over the men's program as athletic director in the early eighties. When the men and women came together in the new building, I became the athletic director for both men and women. We used to have a dual association with the NAIA and the NCAA Division III. After many meetings we decided that the men and women would go together in the NAIA because most of the small colleges in Kentucky are NAIA. If we went NCAA Division III only, we would have to travel long distances to fill our schedules in all sports. We stayed with the NAIA, and it's worked out pretty good for us.

I'm very active in men's basketball, of course, not only in coaching but in recruiting and scheduling and all phases of the sport. I'm also the golf coach. We were fortunate enough to go to the national tournament in golf in 1981, 1984, and 1987. I am also an associate professor of physical education, teaching approximately four classes a semester. I also advise about fifteen advisees a year. So I stay busy. And I want to.

I tell my players to concentrate, and I try to set an example there. When we practice or prepare for a game I want my players to be focused. But sometimes I see myself not completely focused, and I've got to work on that myself. With all the responsibilities I have, my mind might wander. I get excited at my players if they're not focused, but I've got to make sure I'm focused for them to be focused.

I would rather have the other responsibilities. Some of the coaches I coach against, all they do is coach basketball. Or some of these schools' athletic directors do that and nothing else. I enjoy coaching, teaching, and directing the athletic programs. But I've got to be very careful not to neglect one area by giving too much time to another area.

My assistant coaches help me a lot. I set up our practice plan myself, but my assistants participate in practice. They don't sit over on the sideline. I want them involved, and they are involved. Since my stroke it's hard for me to communicate on the floor if I get a little excited. It's easier for me to communicate to the assistants what I want, and they communicate it to the players. But I'm right in the middle, so whether I like or don't like what we're doing I'm right there. During a game I might miss some things, but the assistant can see them and tell me. I did that when I was an assistant.

For the last few years my assistant coach Kelly Combs has done a great job of recruiting. I have to give him credit. Recruiting is harder on me since my stroke because I sometimes have a hard time talking when I'm tired. Kelly has been doing most of the work of contacting prospective players. He brings them on campus, and then I talk to them.

If Beverly Harkleroad were to leave, I'd probably have to leave too. She's been an assistant in the Athletic Department for twenty years. She knows what needs to be done, and she reminds me if I don't think about it. She's the glue that holds our department together. I don't think I've ever asked her to do anything in the line of work that she has not tried to do. You've got to have people like that if you're going to be successful and your program's going to be successful.

John Cook is our statistician. In all the years I've been head coach, you can count on one hand the number of games he's missed. He is a very good friend of mine, and he is so reliable, I don't think he's ever made a mistake in the statistics. John is really a conscientious person, and he's so dedicated to Berea College. As Director of Admissions he helped us with recruiting, talking with prospects. If we got a name, he would check to see if that person was eligible to come to Berea College. Once again, John is the type of person you've got to have on your side to have a good program.

People have asked me whether I would do it over. Yes, I would. To succeed at an institution like Berea College is worth all the time and effort. With all the recruiting restrictions we have in terms of academics, territory, family income, and financial aid, I've been very fortunate to come across young people who have contributed to making our program successful.

Most people see you only when you run out on that floor. They don't realize what it takes to get those twelve guys out there, the time and sweat and heartache and everything else. The crowd is cheering and the music is playing and they think, "Boy, that looks great, I'd like to be a part of that." They have no idea what it takes to be a part of that.

They see me over there sitting down, but they have no idea what it takes for me to be on that bench in control of that team, being part of a program I'm proud of and a lot of people are proud of, representing Berea College. Some people think that successful Division I coaches are the only

Coach Roland Wierwille: "You don't live in the past, you keep going"

people who can coach. That's wrong. I have coached against some outstanding coaches since I've been here.

I can't say those coaches are my friends, because we're rivals, after all. But I would call them good associates. I've said to some of them, "It's a shame, but if I'm up, you're going to be down. For you to be happy, I've got to be disappointed." That's the nature of our profession. But we respect each other.

Some people don't realize the difference between what a Georgetown College or Cumberland College does with its sports teams and what Berea College does. They put a lot more money into their programs. Those schools give twelve full athletic grants. There are now two divisions in the NAIA, and right now we're more competitive scheduling games with the Division II teams. They can give scholarships, but they can't give as many. Many of our traditional rivals are Division I teams now, and they've really changed. When Georgetown won the national championship they had about ten NCAA Division I transfers. Their philosophy of small college basketball is completely different than Berea College's. I don't want to put our team up against odds like that. That would be crazy.

I brought the idea of a summer camp from Transylvania. Lee Rose and I started the Transylvania camp in about 1968. He set it up because he'd been at another camp and got ideas there. We were kind of like partners in getting started. I helped him for four years. When I came to Berea and got the facility decent, I started my own camp. I've been doing it ever since, and I'm very proud of it.

It's a good fundamental camp and a wholesome camp. The kids have a good time, but at the same time they learn things. We average 100-plus kids. Even if they're six or seven years old, they're on a college campus, and they walk around and have little groups. It's organized like clockwork. If it wasn't, we'd have chaos. And we discipline the kids. I don't mean by yelling at them, but we let them know that if they don't behave they cannot stay. I have never had to send somebody home, but I've had to take a few into my office to talk to them a little bit. I'm getting kids now whose fathers were in my camp. That tells you I've been around a long time.

All the members of the physical education and athletic staff had a part in the planning of the new Seabury Center. It was ongoing for a couple of years. We met with the architects and the builders, giving them ideas about what we needed. President John Stephenson wanted two things in the new arena. He wanted all chair-backed seats, and he wanted the seats to come to the edge of the floor. He didn't want the seats away. He wanted them close, to get that atmosphere Old Seabury had.

They let me design the floor itself, and I told them what we needed as far as locker rooms, training rooms, and storage. They put the old building together with the new, renovating Old Seabury to make it more functional. Old Seabury is used now for intramurals, classes, and practices. The new Seabury Center is one of the finest facilities in the United States at any level. It's a magnificent structure, one of a kind.

But there's a difference between just a building and a tradition. We had great tradition in the old place. Everything was painted blue and white, and we had pictures and plaques and records all over the place. I miss that in the new building. The trophy cases in here sat vacant for two years. Somebody else was supposed to put together those displays, but they never did it. Finally Cecilia took the bull by the horns and got that done. She did the research in the library, and now we have pictures and trophies and records down in that one area. We need to spread that out through the whole building so all our student athletes, not just basketball players, will feel more a part of the new building, so it won't feel so empty.

When I think about tradition, I think about people like Wilson and Ellen Evans, two of the most beautiful people in this world, completely dedicated to Berea College, to Union Church, and to the city of Berea. Dean Evans was Dean of Labor and the Dean of Financial Aid for years here. The beautiful Berea College tennis complex is named after Dean Evans and his wife Ellen, who passed away in 1999. We present the Wilson Evans Award to the outstanding tennis player each year.

The College dedicated the tennis courts soon after my stroke. I was asked to speak on behalf of the faculty. I didn't want to do it. I had a hard time speaking at that time. For me to attempt to speak in front of a group was very difficult for me. Therefore it had to be a very special occasion , and I was very honored to be a part of the dedication.

Wilson Evans played in the first basketball game in Seabury Gym, and I wanted him to be a part of the first game played in Seabury Center. I asked him to throw up the first ball. He was so tickled about that. He wanted to do it right, so he started coming in a month before the game was scheduled so he could practice throwing it up. That's the kind of man he is.

I tell my players that they can't live in the past. The victory over Eastern is a great memory. Competing in the national Final Four is a great memory. Those are memories we'll never forget. But that's what they are, memories. Yesterday is gone. You don't live in the past, you keep going. I preach that. But you can't forget the past, either. Great programs are built on tradition.

May 21, 1998/July 9, 1999

The eternal spirit of Berea: 1957 cheerleader Marguerite Dyer

Berea Beloved

Every Berea College graduate has an interesting story to tell. This book focuses on the men whose efforts on the basketball court, highly visible in an area of our country which exalts this sport above all others, brought honor and recognition to the school. They are just a few of the thousands of individuals, past and present, who have done their best to personify the high ideals of Berea College.

Raymond Cable and Wilfred Johnston were Berea College seniors in 1928-29, the year the Seabury Gymnasium was dedicated. Shortly after leaving Berea these two friends decided that the school needed an alma mater. Together they composed "Berea Beloved." For many decades this song has been sung by graduating seniors at their commencement ceremonies. May this tradition continue into the next century and beyond!

Berea, Berea, beloved,
Where friendships are formed fast and true,
And all shall stand shoulder to shoulder
In kinship beneath White and Blue.

When storms raged and danger was threatening,
And stout-hearted trembled with fear,
The spirit of heroes implanted
Their roots in the wilderness drear.

Thy mem'ry be enshrined in ev'ry heart;
Thy spirit be of us a part;
And though we wander far away,
Thy chimes will ring for us each day.
A flower nurtured by a plain
And watered by the mountain rain,
May you ever flourish there,
O Berea, the beautiful, the fair.

Art and Photo Credits

I am grateful to the following for providing photographs for B For Berea.

Berea College Archives 14, 16, 17, 18, 19, 21, 29, 30, 35, 39, 48, 51, 55, 56, 61, 64, 67, 71, 75, 77, 81, 84, 87, 89, 92, 95, 102, 106, 108, 110, 114, 120, 121, 143, 374, 386, 388

Berea College Public Relations/News Services. . . . 12, 44, 122, 139, 153, 157, 163, 166, 170, 172, 174, 176, 180, 186, 189, 192, 194, 196, 199, 202, 206, 214, 217, 219, 225, 226, 235, 243, 245, 251, 257, 264, 270, 273, 278, 284, 292, 300, 307, 310, 316, 321, 334, 340, 351, 357, 358, 359, 361, 364, 374

Corey Craig. 326

Vastervik Tourist Bureau 178

Acknowledgments

I am deeply grateful for the cooperation and hospitality of the former players and coaches who agreed to be interviewed for this book. They were a pleasure to talk to. I found each one of them to be a man I'd be proud to have as a father, a brother, a son, or a neighbor.

This book could neither have been researched nor written without the assistance and encouragement of many individuals who presently work at Berea College. I wish to extend special thanks to Roland R. Wierwille, Martha Beagle, Beverly Harkleroad, and Mary Beth Bevins (Physical Education and Athletics); Jackie Ballinger, Melanie Turner, and Amy Adams (Alumni Association); Ed Ford and Linda Reynolds (Public Relations); Sidney Farr, Steve Gowler, Edith Hansen, Eileen Hart, Susan Henthorn, Judy Kallam, Carolyn Nicely, Barbara Power, Harry Rice, Marsha Segedy, Kit Roberts, Patty Tarter, Pat Taylor, Kathryn Turnbull, and Jane Wilson (Hutchins Library); Mike Berheide, Steve Boyce, Jeanne Hoch, Warren Lambert, and David Nelson (Faculty); Janet Tronc and David Trammell (Bookstore); Linda Kuhlmann (Printing Services); John Cook (Student Administrative Services); Larry Shinn (President); Rod Bussey (Development); and a host of Berea College students, too numerous, alas, for me to remember them all by name. I owe an enormous debt to Gerald Roberts (Head, Special Collections) and Shannon Wilson (College Archivist) for their endless patience in helping me to locate essential facts, documents, and photographs.

I thank the librarians, archivists, and sports information directors at many of the institutions mentioned in this book who answered my inquiries.

I am grateful for the technical assistance provided by Glenn Wenz, which was essential to the successful completion of this project. Thanks also to Harald Aardman, Andy Balterman, Robert Clinton, Arnold "Tex" Davis, Dr Ignacio De Areta, Enrico Edagiata, Evan Farber, Major Gardner, Joseph H. Gluck, J.B. Hoover, Paul Jenkins, Maud Ray Kent, Rick Lundin, Gorm Munksgaard, Joyce Nixon, Don Terman, Ross Thrasher, and Cecilia Wierwille for their kindness and aid.

I dedicate this book to my wife, Anne Wenz Chase, Berea College's Director of Information Resources and Services. Thank you, Anne, for everything.

BEREA COLLEGE YEAR-BY-YEAR

SEASON	WON	LOST	COACH
1923-24	12	1	John Miller
1924-25	9	1	Waldemar Noll
1925-26	7	6	Waldemar Noll
1926-27	7	4	Waldemar Noll
1927-28	8	6	Waldemar Noll
1928-29	6	8	Waldemar Noll
1929-30	5	9	Wilford Fritz
1930-31	10	9	Oscar Gunkler
1931-32	7	7	Oscar Gunkler
1932-33	9	6	Oscar Gunkler
1933-34	14	3	Oscar Gunkler
1934-35	8	6	Oscar Gunkler
1935-36	7	8	Oscar Gunkler
1936-37	5	8	Oscar Gunkler
1937-38	1	13	Oscar Gunkler
1938-39	3	9	Oscar Gunkler
1939-40	3	12	Roger Clark
1940-41	6	8	Roger Clark
1941-42	3	10	Roger Clark
1942-43	9	7	C.H. Wyatt
1943-44	10	3	Ed Petro/Sam Fox
1944-45	1	11	Alvin Sutton
1945-46	3	9	Waldemar Noll
1946-47	4	10	C.H. Wyatt
1947-48	11	10	C.H. Wyatt
1948-49	10	9	C.H. Wyatt
1949-50	6	13	C.H. Wyatt
1950-51	10	10	C.H. Wyatt
1951-52	9	10	C.H. Wyatt
1952-53	14	6	C.H. Wyatt
1953-54	12	7	C.H. Wyatt
1954-55	17	6	C.H. Wyatt
1955-56	12	9	C.H. Wyatt
1956-57	4	16	C.H. Wyatt
1957-58	3	17	C.H. Wyatt
1958-59	10	13	C.H. Wyatt
1959-60	7	13	C.H. Wyatt

1960-61	4	16	C.H. Wyatt
1961-62	0	20	Darrell Crase/C.H. Wyatt
1962-63	2	18	C.H. Wyatt
1963-64	7	14	C.H. Wyatt
1964-65	7	17	C.H. Wyatt
1965-66	3	18	C.H. Wyatt
1966-67	7	17	C.H. Wyatt
1967-68	9	13	C.H. Wyatt
1968-69	10	14	C.H. Wyatt
1969-70	6	15	W.C. Sergeant
1970-71	14	12	W.C. Sergeant
1971-72	9	16	W.C. Sergeant
1972-73	8	16	Roland Wierwille
1973-74	12	16	Roland Wierwille
1974-75	12	13	Roland Wierwille
1975-76	19	9	Roland Wierwille
1976-77	19	8	Roland Wierwille
1977-78	21	7	Roland Wierwille
1978-79	20	9	Roland Wierwille
1979-80	14	13	Roland Wierwille
1980-81	10	16	Roland Wierwille
1981-82	10	16	Roland Wierwille
1982-83	16	11	Roland Wierwille
1983-84	23	5	Roland Wierwille
1984-85	20	10	Roland Wierwille
1985-86	19	9	Roland Wierwille
1986-87	12	15	Roland Wierwille
1987-88	20	8	Roland Wierwille
1988-89	19	9	Roland Wierwille
1989-90	11	13	Roland Wierwille
1990-91	13	14	Roland Wierwille
1991-92	14	13	Roland Wierwille
1992-93	11	14	Roland Wierwille
1993-94	11	15	Roland Wierwille
1994-95	10	15	Craig Jefferson
1995-96	19	9	Roland Wierwille
1996-97	18	10	Roland Wierwille
1997-98	20	10	Roland Wierwille
1998-99	24	7	Roland Wierwille
1999-00	18	12	Roland Wierwille

This game-by-game log shows the date, opponent, result, score, and site of each of Berea College's games, beginning with the 1969-70 season. "T" designates a tournament game. A tournament game played on the home court of one of the teams is designated "home" or "away". Kentucky sites are identified by city, non-Kentucky sites by city and state.

I have not included the results of varsity-alumni games, nor of the pre-season scrimmages against college teams that were played during the Roland Wierwille era. I have not included in Berea's won-lost record its victory over Roane State Junior College in the 1977 Homecoming game. Roane State was a last-minute substitute for Berea's scheduled opponent, who backed out.

1970-71	W.C. Sergeant		14-12		
Nov 21	Wright State	Won	96	79	Home
Nov 24	Campbellsville	Lost	81	91	Home
Dec 1	Eastern Kentucky	Lost	77	111	Away
Dec 2	Morehead State	Lost	90	99	Away
Dec 10	Pikeville	Lost	72	79	Away
Dec 12	Cumberland	Won	88	76	Away
Dec 13	Transylvania	Lost	78	98	Home
Dec 19	Hanover	Won	72	65	Home
Dec 28	Washington U	Won	88	70	T-Danville
Dec 29	Ohio Wesleyan	Won	73	65	T-Danville
Jan 4	Mars Hill	Won (2OT)	108	101	Home
Jan 7	Union	Lost	69	79	Away
Jan 9	Rio Grande	Lost	95	106	Home
Jan 11	Oakland City	Won	105	103	Away
Jan 16	Cumberland	Won	120	109	Home
Jan 19	Centre	Won	90	74	Away
Jan 23	Oakland City	Won	119	110	Home
Jan 25	Campbellsville	Lost	74	88	Away
Jan 30	Union	Lost	85	90	Home
Feb 2	Rio Grande	Won	92	70	Away
Feb 4	Wilmington	Lost	81	114	Away
Feb 6	Pikeville	Won		Forfeit	Home
Feb 11	Transylvania	Lost	81	99	Away
Feb 16	Centre	Won	94	71	Home
Feb 18	Calvary	Won	114	74	Home
Feb 20	Campbellsville	Lost	70	87	T-Away

1971-72	W.C. Sergeant	9-16			
Nov 20	Georgetown	Won	119	100	Home
Nov 23	Campbellsville	Won	106	93	Home
Nov 30	Wright State	Lost	87	88	Away
Dec 4	Wilmington	Won	107	88	Home
Dec 7	Cumberland	Lost	100	102	Away
Dec 11	Transylvania	Won	102	93	Home
Dec 18	Hanover	Lost	79	89	Away
Dec 29	Marietta	Won	101	100	T-Danville
Dec 30	Tennessee Wesleyan	Lost	67	70	T-Danville
Jan 4	Centre	Lost	72	80	Away
Jan 6	Union	Lost	78	87	Away
Jan 8	Rio Grande	Won	104	92	Home
Jan 10	Oakland City	Lost	78	85	Away
Jan 15	Cumberland	Lost	93	103	Home
Jan 18	Pikeville	Lost	50	81	Away
Jan 22	Oakland City	Won	103	91	Home
Jan 24	Campbellsville	Lost	65	67	Away
Jan 29	Union	Won	85	83	Home
Feb 1	Rio Grande	Lost	80	81	Away
Feb 5	Pikeville	Lost	66	77	Home
Feb 12	Centre	Lost	89	97	Home
Feb 14	Georgetown	Lost	84	105	Away
Feb 16	Transylvania	Lost	85	90	Away
Feb 24	Pikeville	Won	71	60	T-Away
Feb 26	Cumberland	Lost (OT)	83	93	T-Away

1972-73	Roland Wierwille	8-16			
Nov 18	Northern Kentucky	Lost	67	93	Home
Nov 21	Campbellsville	Lost	55	68	Home
Nov 28	Georgetown	Lost	61	81	Away
Dec 2	Tennessee Temple	Won	83	82	Home
Dec 5	Cumberland	Lost	45	81	Away
Dec 9	Transylvania	Lost	60	80	Home
Dec 14	Oakland City	Won	65	60	Home
Dec 16	Union	Lost	61	69	Away
Dec 28	Tennessee Wesleyan	Lost	63	66	T-Danville
Dec 29	Centre	Lost	66	71	T-Danville
Jan 8	Oakland City	Won	68	60	Away
Jan 13	Cumberland	Won	87	82	Home
Jan 15	Centre	Won	78	73	Away
Jan 20	Pikeville	Lost	71	73	Home
Jan 22	Campbellsville	Lost	60	68	Away
Jan 27	Union	Lost	61	62	Home
Jan 29	Georgetown	Lost	67	80	Home
Feb 1	Rio Grande	Lost	71	74	Away
Feb 3	Centre	Won	76	74	Home
Feb 5	Pikeville	Lost	61	77	Away
Feb 10	Wright State	Won	80	74	Home
Feb 13	Transylvania	Lost	79	94	Away
Feb 15	Rio Grande	Won	100	85	Home
Feb 22	Georgetown	Lost	61	81	T-Away

1973-74	Roland Wierwille		12-16			
Nov 17	Lee	Won	88	68	Home
Nov 23	Daniel Payne	Lost	63	66	T-Cleveland TN
Nov 24	Alabama-Huntsville	Lost	77	80	T-Cleveland TN
Nov 28	Northern Kentucky	Lost	80	85	Away
Nov 30	IU-Southeast	Lost	71	87	T-Lexington
Dec 1	Lincoln Memorial	Won	95	84	T-Lexington
Dec 4	Cumberland	Lost	72	95	Away
Dec 8	Wilmington	Lost	66	67	Home
Dec 13	Oakland City	Lost	76	86	Home
Dec 15	Union	Won	85	81	Home
Dec 22	Wright State	Lost	56	87	Away
Dec 28	King	Lost	74	81	T-Danville
Dec 29	Emory & Henry	Won	90	69	T-Danville
Jan 7	Oakland City	Won	78	74	Away
Jan 12	Cumberland	Lost	82	91	Home
Jan 14	Centre	Won	80	78	Away
Jan 17	Transylvania	Won	76	74	Home
Jan 19	Pikeville	Won	90	89	Home
Jan 21	Campbellsville	Lost	76	84	Away
Jan 26	Georgetown	Lost	73	76	Home
Jan 29	Transylvania	Lost	61	75	Away
Feb 2	Union	Won	82	72	Away
Feb 4	Pikeville	Lost	87	105	Away
Feb 9	Centre	Lost	82	83	Home
Feb 14	Georgetown	Won	74	69	Away
Feb 16	Campbellsville	Won	86	69	Home
Feb 21	Campbellsville	Won	82	70	T-Home
Feb 23	Cumberland	Lost	78	80	T-Away

1974-75	Roland Wierwille		12-13			
Nov 16	Covenant	Won	71	70	Home
Nov 23	David Lipscomb	Lost	81	82	Home
Nov 26	Wilmington	Lost	64	76	Away
Nov 30	Xavier	Lost	57	77	Away
Dec 2	Centre	Won	94	90	Home
Dec 7	Clinch Valley	Won	98	62	Home
Dec 10	Transylvania	Lost	79	84	Home
Dec 14	Union	Won	107	82	Home
Dec 20	Clinch Valley	Won	100	72	Away
Jan 3	Eureka	Won	100	85	Home
Jan 6	Oakland City	Won	76	68	Away
Jan 8	Transylvania	Lost	60	69	Away
Jan 11	Cumberland	Lost	87	93	Home
Jan 14	Mount Marty	Won	100	94	Home
Jan 16	Centre	Won	74	67	Away
Jan 18	Pikeville	Lost	97	108	Home
Jan 21	Campbellsville	Lost	56	69	Away
Jan 25	Georgetown	Lost	76	84	Home
Jan 29	Cumberland	Won	66	65	Away
Feb 1	Union	Won	81	78	Away
Feb 4	Pikeville	Lost	83	96	Away
Feb 8	Oakland City	Won	102	98	Home
Feb 11	Georgetown	Lost	92	111	Away
Feb 15	Campbellsville	Lost	60	72	Home
Feb 20	Cumberland	Lost	74	93	T-Away

1975-76	Roland Wierwille		19-9		
Nov 14	Tennessee Temple	Lost	64	85	Away
Nov 15	Covenant	Won	98	73	Away
Nov 22	Tennessee Temple	Won	77	64	Home
Nov 25	Wilmington	Won	83	71	Home
Dec 1	Centre	Won	85	57	Away
Dec 5	Warren Wilson	Won	120	74	T-Home
Dec 6	Lee	Won	82	76	T-Home
Dec 9	Kentucky Christian	Won	110	75	Away
Dec 13	Transylvania	Won	84	80	Home
Dec 19	IU-Southeast	Lost	70	77	T-Danville
Dec 20	Kentucky Christian	Won	112	68	T-Danville
Jan 6	Transylvania	Won	82	80	Away
Jan 10	Kentucky Christian	Won	99	46	Home
Jan 13	Campbellsville	Lost	55	58	Away
Jan 15	Union	Won	87	76	Home
Jan 17	Pikeville	Lost	91	100	Home
Jan 21	Campbellsville	Won	94	84	Home
Jan 24	Georgetown	Won	84	81	Home
Jan 27	Cumberland	Lost	96	103	Away
Jan 31	Union	Won	85	84	Away
Feb 3	Pikeville	Lost	85	87	Away
Feb 5	Cumberland	Won	88	79	Home
Feb 10	Georgetown	Lost	80	94	Away
Feb 14	Centre	Won	85	76	Home
Feb 19	Campbellsville	Won	83	79	T-Home
Feb 21	Georgetown	Won	96	91	T-Home
Feb 26	Pikeville	Lost	76	82	T-Away
Mar 1	Kentucky State	Lost	76	97	T-Away

1976-77	Roland Wierwille		19-8		
Nov 20	Lee	Won	65	64	Home
Nov 23	Wilmington	Won	68	65	Away
Nov 26	Olivet Nazarene	Won	80	69	T-Cleveland TN
Nov 27	Lee	Lost	57	61	T-Cleveland TN
Dec 3	Ohio Wesleyan	Won	92	88	T-Home
Dec 4	Thomas More	Won	90	80	T-Home
Dec 8	Centre	Won	94	57	Away
Dec 1	Union	Won	96	79	Home
Dec 18	Carson-Newman	Won	86	85	Away
Jan 3	Transylvania	Lost	68	88	Away
Jan 7	Barrington	Won	102	76	T-Lookout Mtn GA
Jan 8	Covenant	Lost	105	106	T-Lookout Mtn GA
Jan 11	Campbellsville	Won	94	68	Away
Jan 15	Pikeville	Lost	84	100	Home
Jan 18	Cumberland	Won	74	71	Away
Jan 22	Georgetown	Won	89	85	Home
Jan 25	Centre	Won	117	98	Home
Jan 29	Union	Won	96	72	Away
Jan 31	Pikeville	Lost	83	95	Away
Feb 2	Cumberland	Won	81	78	Home
Feb 5	Transylvania	Lost	84	94	Home
Feb 8	Georgetown	Won	110	105	Away
Feb 12	Campbellsville	Won	119	87	Home
Feb 17	Georgetown	Won	122	89	T-Home
Feb 19	Cumberland	Won	90	81	T-Home
Feb 24	Pikeville	Lost	75	79	T-Away
Feb 28	Pikeville	Lost	86	115	T-Away

1977-78	Roland Wierwille		21-7			
Nov 19	Roane State	Won	104	83	Home
Nov 25	Central Wesleyan	Won	102	83	T-Cleveland TN
Nov 26	Lee	Lost	70	86	T-Cleveland TN
Nov 30	Berry	Won	99	68	Home
Dec 2	Shorter	Lost	79	83	T-Home
Dec 3	Thomas More	Won	95	81	T-Home
Dec 6	Centre	Won	100	96	Home
Dec 8	Union	Won	105	85	Away
Dec 10	Carson-Newman	Won	81	78	Home
Dec 17	Pikeville	Won	101	89	Away
Dec 31	Wilmington	Won	89	81	Home
Jan 2	Berry	Lost	80	81	Away
Jan 4	Transylvania	Lost	80	84	Home
Jan 7	Centre	Lost	68	74	Away
Jan 14	Pikeville	Won	52	49	Home
Jan 19	IU-Southeast	Won	93	65	Home
Jan 21	Georgetown	Lost (OT)	83	85	Home
Jan 23	Cumberland	Won (OT)	86	80	Away
Jan 25	Transylvania	Won	79	75	Away
Jan 28	Union	Won	116	93	Home
Feb 2	IU-Southeast	Won	71	58	Away
Feb 7	Georgetown	Won	84	78	Away
Feb 11	Campbellsville	Won	87	71	Away
Feb 15	Campbellsville	Won	116	91	Home
Feb 18	Cumberland	Won	101	78	Home
Feb 25	Georgetown	Won	109	88	T-Home
Mar 2	Cumberland	Won (OT)	86	78	T-Home
Mar 6	Union	Won	87	77	T-Lexington
Mar 8	Cumberland	Lost	74	75	T-Lexington

1978-79	Roland Wierwille		20-9			
Nov 13	Union	Won	94	85	T-Athens TN
Nov 14	Southern Benedictine	Won	84	61	T-Athens TN
Nov 18	Clinch Valley	Won	97	84	Home
Nov 25	Augusta	Lost	76	93	T-Louisville
Nov 26	Lincoln Memorial	Won	92	63	T-Louisville
Nov 28	Transylvania	Won	77	75	Home
Dec 1	Warren Wilson	Won	105	49	T-Home
Dec 2	Tennessee Wesleyan	Lost	79	84	T-Home
Dec 6	Clinch Valley	Won	106	89	Away
Dec 9	Union	Won	84	74	Away
Dec 16	Pikeville	Won	95	76	Away
Jan 2	Urbana	Won	83	71	Away
Jan 3	Wilmington	Won	104	100	Away
Jan 6	Centre	Won	82	80	Home
Jan 8	Campbellsville	Lost	92	100	Away
Jan 13	Pikeville	Won	101	77	Home
Jan 16	Cumberland	Won	95	81	Home
Jan 20	Georgetown	Won	89	80	Home
Jan 27	Union	Won	95	82	Home
Jan 31	Centre	Lost	60	62	Away
Feb 3	Covenant	Won	96	81	Home
Feb 6	Georgetown	Lost	95	99	Away
Feb 10	Campbellsville	Won	111	84	Home
Feb 14	Transylvania	Lost	60	64	Away
Feb 17	Cumberland	Lost	60	65	Away
Feb 22	Union	Won	115	80	T-Home
Feb 24	Cumberland	Lost	80	83	T-Home
Mar 5	Campbellsville	Won	69	67	T-Lexington
Mar 7	Kentucky State	Lost	67	71	T-Lexington

1979-80	Roland Wierwille	14-13			
Nov 12	Tennessee Wesleyan	Lost	63	70	Away
Nov 17	Urbana	Lost (2OT)	62	63	Home
Nov 27	Tennessee Wesleyan	Lost	63	68	Home
Nov 30	Bluefield	Lost	96	102	T-Home
Dec 1	Berry	Won	87	78	T-Home
Dec 5	Centre	Won	64	60	Away
Dec 8	Union	Won	73	62	Home
Dec 11	Clinch Valley	Won	88	61	Home
Dec 14	Pikeville	Lost	70	89	Away
Dec 21	Thomas More	Lost	59	68	Away
Jan 3	Wilmington	Won	94	55	Home
Jan 5	Campbellsville	Lost	74	87	Home
Jan 9	Transylvania	Lost	58	65	Home
Jan 12	Pikeville	Won	91	73	Home
Jan 15	Cumberland	Won	65	60	Away
Jan 19	Georgetown	Lost (OT)	86	88	Home
Jan 23	Thomas More	Lost	74	77	Home
Jan 26	Union	Won (OT)	63	61	Away
Jan 28	Centre	Won	66	65	Home
Feb 1	Clinch Valley	Won	78	69	Away
Feb 5	Georgetown	Won	73	72	Away
Feb 14	Campbellsville	Lost	86	96	Away
Feb 16	Cumberland	Won	64	60	Home
Feb 18	Transylvania	Lost	64	76	Away
Feb 21	Campbellsville	Won	8	7	T-Away
Feb 23	Thomas More	Won	34	33	T-Away
Feb 26	Pikeville	Lost	59	87	T-Away

1980-81	Roland Wierwille	10-16			
Nov 14	Lincoln Memorial	Lost	60	68	T-Lafollette TN
Nov 15	Alderson-Broaddus	Won	85	84	T-Lafollette TN
Nov 22	Lincoln Memorial	Lost	56	58	Home
Nov 25	Clinch Valley	Lost	57	78	Away
Nov 28	Ohio Northern	Lost	53	74	T-Urbana OH
Nov 29	Detroit Bible	Won	114	56	T-Urbana OH
Dec 2	Thomas More	Lost	67	68	Home
Dec 5	IU-Southeast	Won	83	81	T-Home
Dec 6	Tennessee Wesleyan	Lost	75	78	T-Home
Dec 9	Centre	Won	63	56	Home
Dec 11	Campbellsville	Lost	65	71	Away
Jan 5	Thomas More	Lost	68	69	Away
Jan 8	Union	Won	71	63	Away
Jan 10	Pikeville	Lost	71	79	Home
Jan 13	Cumberland	Won	81	76	Home
Jan 15	Transylvania	Won	59	54	Away
Jan 17	Georgetown	Lost	81	87	Home
Jan 22	Pikeville	Lost	65	76	Away
Jan 24	Union	Won (OT)	84	82	Home
Jan 27	Centre	Lost	51	63	Away
Jan 31	Clinch Valley	Won	forf		Home
Feb 3	Georgetown	Lost	54	56	Away
Feb 7	Campbellsville	Won	106	101	Home
Feb 11	Transylvania	Lost	57	58	Home
Feb 14	Cumberland	Lost	49	68	Away
Feb 19	Thomas More	Lost	79	82	T-Away

1981-82	Roland Wierwille		10-16		
Nov 14	Rio Grande	Lost	70	72	Home
Nov 18	Rio Grande	Lost	71	87	Away
Nov 21	Alice Lloyd	Won	68	61	Home
Nov 27	Lincoln Memorial	Lost	76	89	T-Cleveland TN
Nov 28	Alabama Christian	Won (OT)	106	104	T-Cleveland TN
Dec 1	Centre	Won	67	65	Home
Dec 4	Urbana	Lost	70	72	T-Home
Dec 5	Lee	Lost (OT)	83	84	T-Home
Dec 10	Campbellsville	Lost	77	85	Away
Dec 12	Union	Won	92	85	Home
Jan 4	Thomas More	Lost	77	78	Away
Jan 7	Transylvania	Lost	54	61	Away
Jan 9	Pikeville	Lost	89	98	Home
Jan 12	Cumberland	Lost	53	57	Away
Jan 16	Georgetown	Lost	62	72	Home
Jan 18	Centre	Won (OT)	64	62	Away
Jan 21	Union	Won	98	83	Away
Jan 23	Thomas More	Won (OT)	75	73	Home
Jan 26	Pikeville	Lost	73	81	Away
Jan 30	Clinch Valley	Won	86	82	Home
Feb 2	Georgetown	Lost (OT)	59	61	Away
Feb 6	Campbellsville	Lost (OT)	94	102	Home
Feb 9	Clinch Valley	Lost	68	70	Away
Feb 13	Cumberland	Won	88	81	Home
Feb 18	Pikeville	Won	104	81	T-Away
Feb 20	Cumberland	Lost	63	69	T-Away

1982-83	Roland Wierwille		16-11		
Nov 16	Brescia	Won	118	51	Home
Nov 20	Transylvania	Lost	68	69	Home
Nov 26	Trinity	Won	79	64	T-New Albany IN
Nov 27	IU-Southeast	Won	90	78	T-New Albany IN
Nov 30	Centre	Lost	50	53	Away
Dec 3	Ohio Dominican	Won	92	79	T-Home
Dec 4	IU-Southeast	Won	78	59	T-Home
Dec 7	Alice Lloyd	Won	85	78	Away
Dec 11	Union	Won	73	71	Home
Jan 4	Centre	Won	78	63	Home
Jan 6	Thomas More	Won	83	76	Away
Jan 8	Pikeville	Won	59	49	Home
Jan 11	Cumberland	Lost	72	75	Home
Jan 15	Georgetown	Lost	76	92	Home
Jan 17	Clinch Valley	Won	82	64	Away
Jan 20	Union	Lost	75	76	Away
Jan 22	Thomas More	Won	100	73	Home
Jan 25	Pikeville	Lost (OT)	71	73	Away
Jan 29	Clinch Valley	Won	82	79	Home
Feb 1	Georgetown	Lost	56	70	Away
Feb 5	Campbellsville	Won	91	75	Home
Feb 8	Alice Lloyd	Won	105	59	Home
Feb 12	Cumberland	Lost	74	85	Away
Feb 17	Campbellsville	Lost	83	94	Away
Feb 24	Union	Won	86	61	T-Home
Feb 26	Cumberland	Lost	63	75	T-Away
Mar 5	Northern Kentucky	Lost (OT)	81	87	T-Away

1983-84	Roland Wierwille		23-5			

Nov	19	Transylvania	Lost	71	83	Home
Nov	25	Taylor	Won	71	57	T-New Albany IN
Nov	26	Blackburn	Won	82	62	T-New Albany IN
Dec	2	Urbana	Won	90	64	T-Home
Dec	3	Alice Lloyd	Won	84	67	T-Home
Dec	6	Centre	Won	80	74	Home
Dec	10	Alice Lloyd	Won	94	79	Home
Jan	5	Thomas More	Won	86	73	Away
Jan	7	Pikeville	Won	104	56	Home
Jan	9	Centre	Won	70	62	Away
Jan	12	Cumberland	Lost	72	81	Away
Jan	14	Georgetown	Won	105	87	Home
Jan	19	Union	Lost	56	57	Away
Jan	21	Thomas More	Won	86	68	Home
Jan	23	Clinch Valley	Won	74	52	Away
Jan	24	Pikeville	Won	84	70	Away
Jan	28	Clinch Valley	Won	98	55	Home
Jan	31	Georgetown	Won	57	56	Away
Feb	4	Campbellsville	Won	99	94	Home
Feb	7	Alice Lloyd	Won	73	63	Away
Feb	9	Transylvania	Won	69	63	Away
Feb	11	Cumberland	Won	67	56	Home
Feb	16	Campbellsville	Won	87	81	Away
Feb	18	Union	Won	97	92	Home
Feb	23	Alice Lloyd	Won	97	76	T-Home
Feb	25	Union	Won	118	88	T-Home
Feb	28	Cumberland	Lost	51	59	T-Home
Mar	5	Transylvania	Lost	62	63	T-Richmond

1984-85	Roland Wierwille		20-10			

Nov	17	Milligan	Won	82	74	Home
Nov	23	Northeastern Illinois	Won	93	84	Home
Nov	27	Kentucky State	Lost	66	82	Home
Nov	30	Oakland City	Won	85	66	T-Home
Dec	1	Berry	Won	84	75	T-Home
Dec	4	Centre	Won (OT)	80	76	Away
Dec	8	Alice Lloyd	Won	79	67	Home
Dec	15	Campbellsville	Won	81	69	Home
Jan	3	Thomas More	Won	99	83	Away
Jan	5	Pikeville	Won	99	76	Home
Jan	8	Cumberland	Lost	71	75	Home
Jan	12	Georgetown	Lost	73	79	Home
Jan	14	Clinch Valley	Won	77	69	Away
Jan	16	Transylvania	Won	84	82	Away
Jan	23	Pikeville	Lost (4OT)	94	96	Away
Jan	26	Clinch Valley	Won	78	64	Home
Jan	29	Georgetown	Lost	70	71	Away
Jan	31	Union	Won	71	68	Home
Feb	5	Alice Lloyd	Won	97	90	Away
Feb	7	Thomas More	Won	107	89	Home
Feb	9	Cumberland	Lost	64	70	Away
Feb	14	Campbellsville	Won	93	87	Away
Feb	16	Union	Lost (OT)	82	85	Away
Feb	19	Centre	Won	100	85	Home
Feb	22	Transylvania	Lost	88	103	Home
Feb	23	Clinch Valley	Won	65	60	T-Home
Feb	26	Georgetown	Lost	72	87	T-Away
Mar	4	Cumberland	Won	75	64	T-Away
Mar	6	Georgetown	Won	64	48	T-Away
Mar	13	Rio Grande	Lost	86	89	T-Kansas City MO

1985-86	Roland Wierwille		19-9			
Nov 23	Milligan	Won	83	73	Home
Nov 26	Kentucky State	Won	70	65	Away
Nov 29	Hanover	Won (2OT)	96	89	Home
Nov 30	Centre	Won (OT)	78	74	Home
Dec 6	Brescia	Won	86	73	T-Home
Dec 7	Taylor	Lost (OT)	88	89	T-Home
Dec 10	Alice Lloyd	Won	81	68	Home
Dec 14	Campbellsville	Won	77	75	Home
Jan 2	Thomas More	Won	102	88	Away
Jan 4	Pikeville	Won	97	79	Home
Jan 9	Cumberland	Lost	56	92	Away
Jan 14	Georgetown	Lost	64	68	Home
Jan 14	Transylvania	Won	68	67	Home
Jan 16	Union	Lost	68	85	Away
Jan 18	Thomas More	Won	92	72	Home
Jan 20	Clinch Valley	Won	105	96	Away
Jan 21	Pikeville	Lost	83	87	Away
Jan 25	Clinch Valley	Won	86	77	Home
Jan 28	Georgetown	Won	60	53	Away
Feb 1	Campbellsville	Won	86	77	Away
Feb 4	Alice Lloyd	Won	95	84	Away
Feb 8	Cumberland	Lost	66	91	Home
Feb 11	Centre	Won	77	72	Away
Feb 15	Union	Lost	81	83	Home
Feb 18	Transylvania	Won	59	56	Away
Feb 22	Pikeville	Won	120	96	T-Home
Feb 25	Cumberland	Lost	59	69	T-Away
Mar 3	Georgetown	Lost	74	76	T-Away

1986-87	Roland Wierwille		12-15			
Nov 22	Knoxville	Lost	84	92	Home
Nov 28	Bellarmine	Lost	75	82	New Albany IN
Nov 29	IU-Southeast	Won (OT)	78	77	Louisville
Dec 3	Centre	Lost	68	75	Away
Dec 5	Urbana	Lost	78	87	T-Home
Dec 6	Thomas More	Lost	80	95	T-Home
Dec 9	Alice Lloyd	Won	97	73	Home
Dec 13	Campbellsville	Won	97	73	Home
Jan 1	Thomas More	Won	78	75	Away
Jan 3	Pikeville	Lost	82	90	Home
Jan 6	Cumberland	Lost	54	74	Home
Jan 10	Georgetown	Lost	68	72	Home
Jan 12	Transylvania	Won	71	68	Away
Jan 15	Union	Lost	58	62	Away
Jan 17	Thomas More	Won	97	88	Home
Jan 19	Clinch Valley	Lost	83	85	Away
Jan 20	Pikeville	Lost	73	82	Away
Jan 24	Clinch Valley	Won	107	79	Home
Jan 27	Georgetown	Won	70	67	Away
Jan 31	Campbellsville	Won	71	70	Away
Feb 3	Alice Lloyd	Won	102	97	Away
Feb 7	Cumberland	Lost	60	76	Away
Feb 10	Transylvania	Lost	78	87	Home
Feb 14	Union	Won	101	80	Home
Feb 17	Centre	Lost	83	84	Home
Feb 21	Union	Won	88	74	T-Home
Feb 24	Cumberland	Lost	64	78	T-Away

1987-88	Roland Wierwille		20-8			

Nov	21	Lindsey Wilson	Won	98	69	Home
Nov	27	Rio Grande	Won	90	77	T-New Concord OH
Nov	28	Muskingum	Lost	65	74	T-New Concord OH
Dec	4	Lee	Won	118	106	T-Home
Dec	5	Hanover	Won	89	77	T-Home
Dec	8	Alice Lloyd	Won	102	86	Home
Dec	12	Campbellsville	Won	92	84	Home
Jan	2	Transylvania	Won	107	90	Home
Jan	4	Thomas More	Won	74	69	Away
Jan	9	Pikeville	Won	103	73	Home
Jan	11	IU-Southeast	Won	87	75	Away
Jan	14	Cumberland	Lost (OT)	62	65	Away
Jan	16	Georgetown	Lost	67	71	Home
Jan	21	Union	Won	87	63	Away
Jan	23	Thomas More	Won	85	76	Home
Jan	25	Pikeville	Won	97	81	Away
Jan	26	Alice Lloyd	Won	105	93	Away
Jan	30	IU-Southeast	Won	99	91	Home
Feb	2	Georgetown	Lost	61	82	Away
Feb	6	Campbellsville	Won	106	69	Away
Feb	8	Lindsey Wilson	Won	74	63	Away
Feb	13	Cumberland	Lost	62	67	Home
Feb	17	Transylvania	Lost	85	88	Away
Feb	20	Union	Won	84	65	Home
Feb	27	Alice Lloyd	Won	100	65	T-Home
Mar	1	Georgetown	Lost	66	77	T-Away
Mar	5	Alice Lloyd	Won	107	97	T-London
Mar	8	Transylvania	Lost	70	76	T-Away

1988-89	Roland Wierwille		19-9			

Nov	19	Carson-Newman	Won	83	50	Home
Nov	22	IU-Southeast	Won	64	91	Away
Dec	2	Brescia	Won	80	66	T-Home
Dec	3	Tennessee Wesleyan	Won	97	80	T-Home
Dec	6	Alice Lloyd	Won (OT)	79	74	Home
Dec	10	Campbellsville	Won	85	80	Home
Jan	3	Carson-Newman	Won	51	42	Away
Jan	5	Thomas More	Won	79	74	Away
Jan	7	Pikeville	Won	79	71	Home
Jan	9	Lindsey Wilson	Won	100	76	Away
Jan	12	Cumberland	Lost	58	61	Away
Jan	14	Georgetown	Won	82	81	Home
Jan	19	Union	Lost	51	71	Away
Jan	21	Thomas More	Won	92	76	Home
Jan	23	Pikeville	Won	64	59	Away
Jan	24	Alice Lloyd	Won	68	57	Away
Jan	28	Transylvania	Lost	73	84	Home
Jan	31	Georgetown	Lost	69	82	Away
Feb	4	IU-Southeast	Won	73	54	Home
Feb	7	Lindsey Wilson	Won	90	65	Home
Feb	11	Cumberland	Lost	63	70	Home
Feb	16	Campbellsville	Won	82	66	Away
Feb	18	Union	Lost	87	88	Home
Feb	21	Transylvania	Lost	84	86	Away
Feb	25	Campbellsville	Won	98	88	T-Home
Feb	28	Georgetown	Lost	71	72	T-Away
Mar	4	Alice Lloyd	Won	63	62	T-Richmond
Mar	6	Cumberland	Lost	55	62	T-Away

1989-90	Roland Wierwille		11-13		
Nov 18	Tennessee Wesleyan	Won	91	83	Home
Nov 25	Thomas More	Won	85	77	Away
Nov 28	Tennessee Wesleyan	Lost	77	78	Away
Dec 1	Fisk	Won	99	66	T-Home
Dec 2	Union	Lost	56	70	T-Home
Dec 5	Alice Lloyd	Lost	78	90	Home
Dec 9	Campbellsville	Won	86	83	Home
Jan 6	Pikeville	Won (2OT)	108	105	Home
Jan 9	Cumberland	Lost	65	72	Away
Jan 13	Georgetown	Lost	66	93	Home
Jan 15	Lindsey Wilson	Lost	84	86	Away
Jan 18	Union	Won	64	60	Away
Jan 20	Thomas More	Won	100	76	Home
Jan 22	Pikeville	Lost	68	76	Away
Jan 23	Alice Lloyd	Won	101	98	Away
Jan 27	Transylvania	Won	106	80	Home
Jan 30	Georgetown	Lost	54	82	Away
Feb 3	Brescia	Won	93	88	Away
Feb 6	Lindsey Wilson	Won	87	75	Home
Feb 10	Cumberland	Lost	79	84	Home
Feb 12	IU-Southeast	Lost (2OT)	80	81	Away
Feb 17	Union	Lost	48	56	Home
Feb 20	Transylvania	Lost	62	76	Away
Feb 24	Campbellsville	Lost	62	81	Away

1990-91	Roland Wierwille		13-14		
Nov 17	Thomas More	Won	110	93	Home
Nov 23	Taylor	Lost	66	89	T-Danville
Nov 24	Anderson	Won	108	87	T-Danville
Nov 27	Alice Lloyd	Won	85	76	Home
Nov 30	Warren Wilson	Won	100	59	T-Home
Dec 1	Hanover	Lost	63	82	T-Home
Dec 8	Campbellsville	Lost	107	126	Away
Dec 14	Wilberforce	Won	101	83	Away
Jan 3	IU-Southeast	Lost	79	80	Home
Jan 5	Thomas More	Lost	78	83	Away
Jan 8	Cumberland	Lost	56	58	Away
Jan 12	Georgetown	Lost	69	81	Home
Jan 15	IU-Southeast	Lost	63	73	Away
Jan 17	Union	Lost	64	65	Away
Jan 19	Lindsey Wilson	Won	92	83	Home
Jan 22	Pikeville	Won	87	82	Home
Jan 26	Transylvania	Won	78	75	Home
Jan 29	Georgetown	Lost	68	84	Away
Feb 2	Brescia	Won	97	81	Home
Feb 5	Lindsey Wilson	Won	88	78	Away
Feb 9	Cumberland	Won (OT)	90	85	Home
Feb 12	Wilberforce	Won	100	69	Home
Feb 16	Union	Lost	68	69	Home
Feb 19	Transylvania	Lost	71	87	Away
Feb 23	Campbellsville	Lost	93	110	Home
Feb 25	Pikeville	Won	84	83	Away
Feb 28	Transylvania	Lost	75	80	T-Away

1991-92	Roland Wierwille	14-13			
Nov 23	IU-Southeast	Won	85	81	Home
Dec 3	Brescia	Won (OT)	97	93	Away
Dec 6	Virginia Intermont	Won	96	84	T-Home
Dec 7	Wilberforce	Won	99	72	T-Home
Dec 14	Thomas More	Won	80	78	Home
Dec 19	Savannah	Won	116	52	Home
Jan 2	Saint Andrews	Won	83	78	T-Charlotte NC
Jan 3	Queens	Lost	68	76	T-Charlotte NC
Jan 4	Erskine	Lost	75	77	T-Charlotte NC
Jan 7	Cumberland	Lost	70	79	Away
Jan 11	Georgetown	Lost	65	83	Home
Jan 14	IU-Southeast	Lost	65	67	Away
Jan 18	Lindsey Wilson	Won	113	85	Home
Jan 23	Campbellsville	Lost	83	109	Away
Jan 25	Transylvania	Lost	81	88	Home
Jan 28	Georgetown	Lost	38	51	Away
Feb 1	Brescia	Won	85	74	Home
Feb 4	Lindsey Wilson	Won	90	84	Away
Feb 8	Cumberland	Won	68	63	Home
Feb 11	Pikeville	Won	76	64	Home
Feb 13	Thomas More	Won	96	83	Away
Feb 15	Union	Won	89	79	Home
Feb 18	Transylvania	Lost	87	95	Away
Feb 22	Campbellsville	Lost	88	100	Home
Feb 26	Pikeville	Lost	74	93	Away
Feb 29	Union	Lost	71	76	Away
Mar 5	Transylvania	Lost	63	83	T-Away

1992-93	Roland Wierwille	11-14			
Nov 21	Embry-Riddle	Won	100	93	Home
Dec 1	Brescia	Won	112	75	Away
Dec 4	Asbury	Won	96	57	T-Home
Dec 5	Blackburn	Won	98	42	T-Home
Dec 12	IU-Southeast	Won	80	66	Home
Dec 19	Randolph-Macon	Lost	80	82	T-Ham-Syd VA
Dec 20	Hampden-Sydney	Won	68	66	T-Ham-Syd VA
Jan 2	IU-Southeast	Lost	90	101	Away
Jan 5	Cumberland	Lost	75	84	Away
Jan 9	Georgetown	Lost	82	86	Home
Jan 16	Lindsey Wilson	Lost	73	80	Home
Jan 18	Union	Lost	85	96	Away
Jan 21	Campbellsville	Won	101	98	Away
Jan 23	Transylvania	Lost	83	92	Home
Jan 26	Georgetown	Lost	81	89	Away
Jan 30	Brescia	Won	93	87	Home
Feb 4	Lindsey Wilson	Lost	88	97	Away
Feb 6	Cumberland	Won	85	78	Home
Feb 9	Pikeville	Won	115	101	Away
Feb 11	Thomas More	Lost	88	107	Away
Feb 13	Union	Lost	75	83	Home
Feb 16	Transylvania	Lost	84	88	Away
Feb 20	Campbellsville	Lost	81	101	Home
Feb 23	Thomas More	Lost	91	97	Home
Feb 27	Pikeville	Won	115	98	Home

1993-94	Roland Wierwille		11-15		
Nov 20	Asbury	Won	98	83	Home
Nov 26	Olivet Nazarene	Lost	76	86	T-Anderson IN
Nov 27	Anderson	Won	83	71	T-Anderson IN
Nov 30	Brescia	Won	88	77	Home
Dec 3	Spalding	Won	94	84	T-Home
Dec 4	Mars Hill	Won	92	82	T-Home
Dec 7	Union	Lost	79	81	Away
Dec 11	Sue Bennett	Won (OT)	117	113	Home
Jan 4	Cumberland	Lost	68	87	Away
Jan 8	Georgetown	Lost	103	106	Home
Jan 13	Asbury	Won	109	92	Away
Jan 15	Lindsey Wilson	Won	105	98	Home
Jan 22	Transylvania	Lost	88	92	Home
Jan 25	Georgetown	Lost	89	105	Away
Jan 29	Brescia	Lost	75	86	Away
Feb 1	Campbellsville	Won	106	91	Home
Feb 3	Lindsey Wilson	Won	89	85	Away
Feb 5	Cumberland	Lost	74	87	Home
Feb 8	Pikeville	Lost	99	102	Away
Feb 12	Union	Won	79	75	Home
Feb 19	Campbellsville	Lost	97	116	Away
Feb 21	Sue Bennett	Lost	89	117	Away
Feb 24	Transylvania	Lost	104	128	Away
Feb 26	Pikeville	Lost (OT)	111	112	Home
Feb 28	Spalding	Lost	95	104	Away
Mar 3	Cumberland	Lost	71	84	T-Home

1994-95	Craig Jefferson		10-15		
Nov 19	Asbury	Won	115	78	Home
Nov 25	C.W. Post	Won	75	74	T-Newport News VA
Nov 26	Christopher Newport	Lost (OT)	100	112	T-Newport News VA
Dec 2	Warren Wilson	Won	117	52	T-Home
Dec 3	Cumberland (TN)	Won	94	84	T-Home
Dec 6	Union	Lost	92	100	Home
Dec 10	Sue Bennett	Won	99	88	Home
Jan 5	Cumberland	Lost	69	89	Away
Jan 7	Georgetown	Lost	88	111	Home
Jan 9	Wilberforce	Won	98	71	Home
Jan 10	Asbury	Won	119	103	Away
Jan 14	Lindsey Wilson	Lost	91	102	Home
Jan 17	Campbellsville	Lost	110	121	Away
Jan 21	Transylvania	Lost	93	104	Home
Jan 24	Georgetown	Lost	86	113	Away
Feb 1	Lindsey Wilson	Won	92	90	Away
Feb 4	Cumberland	Lost	75	97	Home
Feb 7	Pikeville	Lost	84	96	Home
Feb 11	Union	Lost	81	103	Away
Feb 15	Transylvania	Lost	70	100	Away
Feb 18	Campbellsville	Won (OT)	120	115	Home
Feb 21	Sue Bennett	Lost	71	90	Away
Feb 25	Pikeville	Lost	78	83	Away
Mar 2	Pikeville	Won	72	70	T-Away
Mar 4	Georgetown	Lost (OT)	90	95	T-Away

1995-96	Roland Wierwille		19-9		
Nov 18	IU-Southeast	Won	93	90	Home
Nov 21	Asbury	Won	86	68	Away
Nov 24	Morehead State	Lost	92	113	Away
Nov 28	Cumberland	Lost	46	68	Away
Dec 1	Warren Wilson	Won	83	49	T-Home
Dec 2	Berry	Won	98	72	T-Home
Dec 5	Sue Bennett	Won	93	86	Away
Dec 7	Transylvania	Won	76	73	Away
Dec 9	Asbury	Won	95	86	Home
Jan 2	Saint Ambrose	Won	107	95	T-Crestview Hills
Jan 3	Thomas More	Won	83	77	T-Crestview Hills
Jan 6	Wilberforce	Won	107	89	Home
Jan 13	Lindsey Wilson	Won	93	82	Home
Jan 16	Campbellsville	Lost	71	96	Home
Jan 18	Pikeville	Lost	83	87	Away
Jan 20	Transylvania	Won	92	86	Home
Jan 24	Union	Lost	71	72	Away
Jan 27	IU-Southeast	Won	83	76	Away
Jan 31	Lindsey Wilson	Won	92	80	Away
Feb 3	Cumberland	Lost	76	82	Home
Feb 6	Pikeville	Lost	79	83	Home
Feb 10	Union	Won	85	72	Home
Feb 15	Wilberforce	Won	111	98	Away
Feb 17	Campbellsville	Lost	97	114	Away
Feb 20	Sue Bennett	Won	104	84	Home
Feb 24	Madonna	Won	80	64	T-Home
Feb 28	IU-Southeast	Won	75	73	T-Home
Mar 7	Tabor	Lost	91	92	T-Nampa ID

1996-97	Roland Wierwille		18-10		
Nov 15	Tennessee Wesleyan	Won (OT)	97	90	T-Home
Nov 16	Union	Won	96	86	T-Home
Nov 19	Pikeville	Lost	77	82	Away
Nov 23	Milligan	Won	97	81	Home
Dec 3	Sue Bennett	Won	85	74	Home
Dec 6	Trevecca Nazarene	Won	85	79	T-Wilmington OH
Dec 7	Adrian	Won	89	66	T-Wilmington OH
Dec 10	Wilberforce	Won	95	84	Home
Dec 14	Asbury	Won	118	91	Home
Jan 3	Hope	Lost	82	130	T-Daytona Beach FL
Jan 4	Dana	Won	94	85	T-Daytona Beach FL
Jan 7	Brescia	Lost (OT)	77	90	Home
Jan 11	Lindsey Wilson	Lost	67	87	Home
Jan 14	Wilberforce	Won	104	89	Away
Jan 18	Transylvania	Won	70	60	Home
Jan 21	Asbury	Won	110	83	Away
Jan 23	Spalding	Won	83	81	Home
Jan 25	IU-Southeast	Lost	89	95	Home
Jan 28	Lindsey Wilson	Won	94	81	Away
Feb 1	Transylvania	Lost	69	81	Away
Feb 4	IU-Southeast	Lost	82	102	Away
Feb 8	Pikeville	Won	86	67	Home
Feb 11	Brescia	Lost	66	86	Away
Feb 18	Spalding	Lost	85	87	Away
Feb 22	Alice Lloyd	Won	109	84	Home
Feb 25	Thomas More	Won	94	78	Home
Mar 1	Indiana Tech	Won	98	88	T-Home
Mar 4	IU-Southeast	Lost	64	81	T-Away

1997-98	Roland Wierwille		20-10		
Nov 14	Ohio Dominican	Won	91	77	T-Home
Nov 15	Virginia Intermont	Won (OT)	116	114	T-Home
Nov 18	Eastern Kentucky	Won	94	88	Away
Nov 22	Earlham	Won	97	74	Home
Nov 25	Spalding	Won	86	83	Home
Dec 5	King	Lost	87	89	T-Rome GA
Dec 6	Emmanuel	Won	98	64	T-Rome GA
Dec 13	Asbury	Won	116	97	Home
Dec 29	Shawnee State	Won	87	70	T-Marietta OH
Dec 30	Marietta	Lost (OT)	98	101	T-Marietta OH
Jan 3	Alderson-Broaddus	Lost	75	83	T-Montgomery WV
Jan 4	Bethany	Won	89	68	T-Montgomery WV
Jan 8	Union	Lost	75	87	Away
Jan 14	Thomas More	Lost	86	103	Away
Jan 17	Transylvania	Lost (2OT)	107	112	Away
Jan 20	Asbury	Won	92	79	Away
Jan 22	Alice Lloyd	Won	112	103	Away
Jan 24	IU-Southeast	Lost	79	84	Home
Jan 28	Spalding	Won	85	83	Away
Jan 31	Transylvania	Lost	71	87	Home
Feb 3	IU-Southeast	Won	75	62	Away
Feb 7	Pikeville	Won	96	83	Home
Feb 10	Union	Lost	65	87	Home
Feb 14	Thomas More	Won	87	84	Home
Feb 19	Wilmington	Won	93	83	Home
Feb 21	Alice Lloyd	Won	83	80	Home
Feb 24	Pikeville	Won	83	55	Away
Feb 28	Asbury	Won	79	76	T-Home
Mar 2	Philadelphia Pharmacy	Won (OT)	100	94	T-Home
Mar 11	Whitworth	Lost	78	82	T-Nampa ID

1998-99	Roland Wierwille		24-7		
Nov 13	Tennessee Wesleyan	Won	93	82	T-Home
Nov 14	King	Won	74	66	T-Home
Nov 21	Goshen	Won	82	70	Home
Nov 28	Maryville	Lost	74	88	T-Maryville TN
Nov 29	Webber	Won	98	68	T-Maryville TN
Dec 5	Ferrum	Won	93	83	T-Ferrum VA
Dec 6	Caldwell	Won	88	74	T-Ferrum VA
Dec 8	Spalding	Won	108	95	Home
Dec 12	Indiana Wesleyan	Won	108	91	Home
Dec 28	Defiance	Lost	90	106	T-Defiance OH
Dec 29	Mount Union	Lost	83	89	T-Defiance OH
Jan 1	Lake Erie	Won	94	55	T-Daytona Beach FL
Jan 2	Northwestern College	Lost	80	90	T-Daytona Beach FL
Jan 9	Transylvania	Lost	75	86	Home
Jan 16	Asbury	Won	91	58	Home
Jan 19	Bethel (TN)	Won	108	47	Home
Jan 23	IU-Southeast	Won	90	50	Home
Jan 25	Spalding	Won	104	78	Away
Jan 30	Transylvania	Won	88	80	Away
Feb 2	IU-Southeast	Won	81	71	Away
Feb 6	Bethel (TN)	Lost	81	84	Away
Feb 9	Pikeville	Won	85	70	Away
Feb 13	Union	Won	87	81	Home
Feb 18	Asbury	Won	104	74	Away
Feb 20	Pikeville	Won	110	84	Home
Feb 26	Asbury	Won	94	71	T-Home
Feb 27	Bethel (TN)	Won	93	66	T-Home
Mar 10	Briar Cliff	Won	86	76	T-Nampa ID
Mar 12	Milligan	Won	94	84	T-Nampa ID
Mar 13	Viterbo	Won	85	74	T-Nampa ID
Mar 15	Cornerstone	Lost	85	100	T-Nampa ID

1999-00	Roland Wierwille	18-12				
Nov 12	Goshen	Won	109	43	T-Home
Nov 13	Huntington	Won	91	81	T-Home
Nov 17	Tennessee Wesleyan	Lost	74	87	Away
Nov 20	Union	Won	73	62	Home
Nov 22	Lee	Won	120	86	Home
Nov 26	Missouri Baptist	Lost	80	84	T-St Louis MO
Nov 27	Harris-Stowe State	Won	106	91	T-St Louis MO
Dec 3	Madonna	Won	104	81	T-Mt Vernon OH
Dec 4	Mount Vernon Nazarene	Lost	87	135	T-Mt Vernon OH
Dec 11	Tennessee Wesleyan	Lost	79	83	Home
Dec 28	Centre	Lost	85	91	T-Danville
Dec 30	Millikin	Lost	82	85	T-Danville
Jan 3	Berry	Lost	80	82	Home
Jan 8	Transylvania	Lost	72	79	Home
Jan 11	Spalding	Lost	64	67	Home
Jan 13	Union	Lost	67	70	Away
Jan 15	Missouri Baptist	Won	102	95	Home
Jan 18	Asbury	Won	104	92	Home
Jan 22	IU-Southeast	Won	116	94	Home
Jan 26	Spalding	Won	86	80	Away
Jan 29	Bethel (TN)	Won	86	78	Away
Feb 1	IU-Southeast	Won	88	77	Away
Feb 5	Bethel (TN)	Won	121	73	Home
Feb 8	Pikeville	Won	85	82	Away
Feb 12	Transylvania	Lost	83	90	Away
Feb 15	Asbury	Won	104	91	Away
Feb 19	Pikeville	Won	82	69	Home
Feb 25	Bethel (TN)	Won	104	65	T-Wilmore
Feb 26	Asbury	Won	104	81	T-Home
Mar 8	Grand View	Lost	71	84	T-Point Lookout MO

INDEX